30°   0°   60°

Bermuda is located at 64° 22'
West and 32° 25' North in the
North Atlantic Ocean, some
3,000 miles from Great Britain,
1,000 miles from the West
Indies, and 635 miles due east
of Cape Hatteras, North
Carolina, the nearest landfall.

Home Ports →

Europe

Azores

Gibraltar →

NTIC

Madeira

30°

Canary Is.

CEAN

Africa

Cape Verde Is

E H

This book is dedicated to

THE ACE GROUP OF COMPANIES IN BERMUDA

and

THE ACE FOUNDATION

In appreciation of the outstanding support
they have given to the Bermuda Maritime Museum
and many other charitable organisations in Bermuda

BERMUDA FORTS

1612–1957

My paternal grandparents, Agnes Matilda Whitecross, Bermudian, and Sgt. William Sydney Harris, Bandmaster, 3RD Royal Fusiliers, Prospect Camp 1903–5.

And to the Corps of Royal Engineers, the Royal Regiment of Artillery and the men of the Royal Regiments, the Bermuda Militia Artillery, the Bermuda Militia Infantry, the Bermuda Volunteer Rifles and the Bermuda Volunteer Engineers—who served at the fortifications of Bermuda from 1701 to 1957.

Sgt. and Mrs. William S. Harris on their wedding day in Bermuda in 1905.

Officers of the 39th Regiment of Foot in Bermuda in 1859 (BMM Archives).

Bermuda Forts

1612–1957

Edward Cecil Harris, M.B.E., F.S.A.

*With drawings and photographs by
the author, unless stated otherwise*

First Edition April, 1997
Second printing June, 2001

Bermuda Maritime Museum Press

Bermuda Forts, 1612–1957, by Edward Cecil Harris, M.B.E., F.S.A., Ph.D., Executive Director, Bermuda Maritime Museum; Visiting Professor of Anthropology, The College of William and Mary, Virginia; Adjunct Professor of History, East Carolina University. ■ Book and jacket designed by Paul Shapiro, Brimstone Media, Bermuda. ■ Copyright © 1997 Dr. Edward Cecil Harris, M.B.E., F.S.A. ■ Published by the Bermuda Maritime Museum Press, The Keep, The Old Royal Naval Dockyard, Bermuda. ■ No part of this book may be reproduced in any form without the publisher's written permission. ■ Printed in Hong Kong. ■ ISBN 0-921560-11-7

Contents

Preface

ON BEING TOLD OF THE PRESENCE OF ENGLISH SETTLERS IN THE BERMUDAS, Philip III claimed the Islands for Spain. Meanwhile, the settlers had already begun to build fortifications and when in March 1614 two Spanish ships entered Castle Roads, they were greeted with a couple of shots from King's Castle. The Spanish left, never to return. By the beginning of the 1620s, eleven forts had been completed and the foundations of what was to become Britain's oldest colony had been well and truly laid.

In this excellent book, Edward Harris goes on to describe and illustrate how throughout the seventeenth and into the middle of the eighteenth centuries, more forts were completed to keep Bermuda safe from Spanish and, later, French attacks and from piratical raids: but until 1684 Bermuda remained very much a 'company town' with the Crown taking little interest in this private venture of London businessmen. With the demise of the Bermuda Company in that year, things began to change. There was now to be a Governor appointed by the English government, Sir Robert Robinson, and in 1701 there was clear evidence of rising interest in Bermuda with the dispatch of fifty men of the Independent Company of Foot to the Island.

But the dramatic change came in 1783 with the end of the American War of Independence. The former Colonies now posed a potential threat to Britain and there was a need to create new bases in the West to replace those recently lost. Bermuda, lying halfway between Canada and the West Indies, was an obvious choice. Captain Andrew Durnford of the Corps of Royal Engineers was ordered to Bermuda to refortify the Island and the book explains how by 1809 the total number of forts had been increased to sixty-two. Meanwhile the Royal Navy had arrived and although it was many years before the new Dockyard on Ireland Island was completed, Bermuda had become an important naval base from which in the War of 1812, forty-two ships sailed to attack Washington and Baltimore.

It was in the latter part of the nineteenth century that Bermuda was finally transformed into one great Imperial Fortress, and the Governors of Bermuda played a considerable role in this development. From the days of Sir Robert

Robinson in the seventeenth century, the Governor of the day had been Commander-in-Chief of any troops on the Island. In the nineteenth century most of the Governors were soldiers and from the 1860s, when yet another round of work on Bermuda's fortifications began, they were soldiers with specific expertise in the building of fortifications and defence. Governor Ord (1861–67) prompted the Bermuda Parliament to take an interest in plans to build a causeway linking St. George's with the mainland via Longbird Island and this, when built, along with the South, or Military Road, from Tucker's Town to Church Bay, greatly facilitated the movement of troops from one part of the Colony to another. Governor Chapman (1867–70) was an engineer and an expert in the design, construction and armament of permanent fortifications. Governor Lefroy (1871–77), remembered now for his *Memorials of the Bermudas,* was first and foremost an expert in ordnance and gun design. Governor Laffan (1877–82), who died in office, was a former Deputy Inspector General of Fortifications and before his arrival in Bermuda had served as the Senior Engineer Officer at Malta and Gibraltar. Governor Gallwey (1882–88) was also a Royal Engineer and had supervised the construction of the forts at Lévis opposite Quebec.

By the end of the nineteenth century, the days of vast expenditure on land fortifications appeared to be over, and the author tells us that in 1939 the only guns in operation in Bermuda were those at St. David's Battery. How that was all to change with the arrival of the American Forces in 1941 and their assumption of Bermuda's defence during the Second World War, and how soon great guns were again to cover every approach to the Island, is a story again well told and illustrated in this volume.

There is a photograph of the St. David's Battery (p. 240) which reminds us of another important strand in this extraordinarily interesting history. The photograph is of a gun drill by the Bermuda Militia Artillery sometime between the two world wars, and it reminds us of a step taken at the end of the nineteenth century of great significance in the story of Bermuda. The Bermuda Militia Artillery and the Bermuda Volunteer Rifle Corps (later the Bermuda Rifles) were formed at that time and thenceforth Bermudians were themselves to play a part in the defence of their own homeland. Much later, and after both units had seen service in both wars, they were amalgamated to form the Bermuda Regiment; and today, when there are no longer any British Forces on the Island, Governors, still bearing the title Commander-in-Chief, have ultimate responsibility for the Bermuda Regiment. It is a Force in which Bermudians take great pride, and rightly so.

Dr. Harris' book will be of great interest to archaeologists, but it will also fascinate the general reader because so much of the history of Bermuda can be traced through, and is preserved for posterity in, the fortifications and guns we can still see today. The author points out that it is because so little remains of the first English forts in the New World at Puerto Rico, Roanoke, Jamestown and Fort St. George, Maine, that the early Bermuda fortifications have a very special importance. Every other period during which work on the Island's defences took place has also left its legacy in stone and mortar. It is now up to

Bermudians to protect these wonderful structures, which are such an important part of Bermuda's heritage. I commend the book to the public and congratulate Edward Harris and the Trustees of the Bermuda Maritime Museum on its timely publication.

GOVERNOR AND COMMANDER-IN-CHIEF

BERMUDA

Foreword

BERMUDA, A SPECK IN THE VAST OCEAN, WAS A WELCOME LANDFALL FOR those storm-tossed ships that finally made the refuge of its harbour. Its unique situation was sufficient to fire the imagination of England's greatest playwright, William Shakespeare, when he set a scene of *The Tempest* in that distant post almost as soon as his country had begun to plant there its most remote settlement. Only about sixteen years later, Captain John Smith was to describe the place aptly as *in forme not much unlike a reaper's sickle,* although in plan it looks more like the twisted vertebrae of some ancient carcass. The land had one feature of paramount importance to a rising colonial naval power—an excellent harbour in which to seek haven from the tumultuous gales that swept across the North Atlantic.

Things went fairly well from the start. To find such lush and well-protected islands was propitious; a safe place free from any potentially embarrassing incumbents was an almost miraculous gift, but a gift safeguarded by the perspicacious attitude of the early governors, Richard Moore and Nathaniel Butler, who laid down the ground rules for a well thought out defence policy. They made it clear to the settlers that, despite the truth of Andrew Marvell's words that they were not easy to find for *the remote Bermudas ride in the ocean's bosom unespied,* they should not rely for their safety on remoteness and the task of building fortifications must take precedence over any other job. The early forts they built adopted principles of design ahead of their time and, indeed, ahead of general practice at home.

Although little now remains of the earliest colonial forts built by the English on the mainland of the Americas, there can be no doubt that, in design, they were naive when compared to current practice in Europe, but whoever did design the earliest coastal forts on Bermuda, depicted in John Smith's drawings of 1624 (Fig. 3.2), was certainly no novice. Although their design is somewhat remotely derived from one or two of Henry VIII's coastal forts built nearly a century earlier, they show a plan form of a semicircular multi-gun platform supported by a tower of refuge behind, acting to some extent as a keep, and this was to become the standard solution for coast defence batteries up to the early years of the nineteenth century, particularly those built by French engineers. The semicircular form is, of course, the best shape for a coast defence battery. It allows the guns to engage a ship as it approaches and, if not sunk, as it passes.

The hexagonal towers, acting either as keeps for coast defence batteries, or as free-standing watch towers, are of unusual shape. Most European proto-types were round or square, although a very few were octagonal. The shape chosen on Bermuda may have something to do with the available building stone, but it was a well-chosen shape. Another interesting feature is what looks like a tenaille trace on the early drawing, placed in front of two of the semi-circular gun platforms. However, this may have been no more than triangular fascines added to protect the guns. John Smith shows the guns mounted *en barbette* which, although a simple expedient and easy to build, was unusual at the time. It had the advantage that the guns could be moved around a semi-circular platform with ease, and, maybe, the triangular projections would have provided sufficient protection. Embrasures, though providing additional protection, tended to help enemy gunners on ships identify the exact positions of the defending artillery.

By the end of the eighteenth century the whole coastline was stiffened with coast defence forts and batteries, as fear of a Spanish invasion or of piratical raids gave way to an apprehension of a French attack. By the end of the American Revolutionary War there were some fifty fortified positions, many of them occupied by small coastal defence batteries. But the breakaway of the American colonies changed the whole strategic role of Bermuda. Fate decreed that it would become a British fortress to make up for the loss of valuable naval bases on the mainland of America. This role was reinforced by the construction of the naval dockyard in 1809.

It is surprising that the British built only one Martello tower on Bermuda for, at that time, they had become a panacea for solving most small problems in fortification. A string of them was threaded across the high ground behind Quebec and they can be found scattered as far afield as the Adriatic, South Africa and Mauritius. The United States of America even adopted them in a somewhat modified form.

As a result of influence from the Netherlands, British engineers, at the beginning of the nineteenth century, began to favour the idea of defending the ditch of a fort from galleries dug into the counterscarp. They had built them in 1812 in their forts on Anholt Island recently taken from the Danes and were already using them in Newfoundland. Now they brought the device to Bermuda, where it is well illustrated, and incorporated it into positions like Fort George and the Western Redoubt. Other ideas were being passed from Europe to distant Bermuda and the prototypes for these last designs can be found in Belgium, in particular on the redoubt at Binche, built or com-pleted by the British in 1816. It was designed by French engineers, members of that new breed of imaginative designers breaking out, after the French Revolution, of the straitjacket inherited from Vauban and his followers. These plans were modified and completed by the British as part of Wellington's £5 million project for the refortifying of the Low Countries to counter any possible threat from France after the victory at Waterloo.

The Bermuda forts of the late 1820s are interesting because they show the powerful influence of the Duke of Wellington, whose experience of fortifications had been steeled in the bloody sieges of the Peninsular War and brought up to date during the rebuilding by his British and Dutch engineers of the Belgian fortifications.

The other feature found in these forts on Bermuda was the central keep of last resort, an idea vigorously revived from medieval practice by engineers of that time. For a few years it became an essential British ingredient in the design of free-standing forts.

The detached forts of this period, no longer being capable of being defended from bastions, introduced the counterscarp gallery for close defence. This method of defence had become popular to British engineers after a reappraisal of the writings of Menno van Coohorn.

With the growth in the number of steam-powered vessels, the need for conveniently-spaced coaling stations became essential, and Bermuda was ideally placed as a supply base for the Royal Navy, supported by Halifax to the north and Antigua in the Caribbean, so that the whole length of the North American seaboard was under British surveillance. But steam power was just one of the industrial developments that were to affect the cohesion of the British Empire. The introduction of new, more powerful, guns and the use of a thick cladding of iron-armoured plates on the ships of foreign navies, meant that this vital refuelling station had to be protected by the latest and the most advanced guns available. And so, the building and modification of the coast defence installations continued to be expanded throughout the nineteenth century.

As the Mediterranean was serviced from British bases in Gibraltar and Malta, so the Atlantic was covered from Halifax and Bermuda. Lord Castlereagh summed up the situation clearly: 'Our policy has been to secure the Empire against further attack. In order to do this we have acquired what, in former times, would have been thought romance—the keys of every great military position.' The conveniently-sited islands or defensible peninsulas in the Atlantic, the Indian Ocean and the Mediterranean were to prove vital for the maintenance of British naval supremacy.

Although there was some reluctance on the part of some taxpayers to meet the ever-spiralling cost of defence, Captain T. S. Jackson pointed out that coast fortifications 'should be regarded as a necessary evil so far as our arsenals at home and abroad must be secured against naval attack, and our coaling stations and great mercantile ports must be protected against raids.'

By the 1860s Colonel Wm. F. Drummond Jervois was the acknowledged expert on British coast defence architecture. He visited, reported on and recommended modifications to the defences of nearly all of the naval stations of the British Empire. The subsequent updating of the works, an expensive undertaking that had to be carried out across the Empire, has resulted, partly because of Bermuda's remoteness, in the preservation of a variety of heavy guns which are now pieces of great historical value, and Bermuda possesses the richest collection in the world. Many have been re-sited behind their embrasures and shields, others remain awaiting new carriages which must be made, even though this is an expensive undertaking.

By one of the strange quirks of history, this naval station, designed to counter any threat from the United States from the 1790s, was, during the Second World War, handed over to them so that they might protect it against German raiders.

Dr. Harris' book is a marvel of industrious investigation as he has picked through the threads of Bermuda's military history and the steps taken to safeguard the islands against invasion or bombardment. No story has been left untold, no important episode unrecorded, which would throw light on the evolution of the defences of this fortified island. It is a wonderful record of what has been and what still remains. Its material has been lovingly and painstakingly gathered together and is now presented in this splendid volume. Rich in photographs, some very old, and full of clear drawings, it will provide a permanent record of the defences of Bermuda and will be the standard work on that important subject. Bermuda should be proud of both its glorious military history and this fine achievement in presenting that history to the world.

PROFESSOR QUENTIN HUGHES

LIVERPOOL

Acknowledgements

THIS BOOK MAY BE SAID TO HAVE ITS ORIGINS IN THE ATTEMPT, IN THE LATE 1960s, made by my former teacher of Bermudian history, the late Sister Jean de Chantal Kennedy, S.C. and me to carry out an archaeological investigation of Sears Fort in Smith's Parish. The project would have been the first archaeological work to be done in Bermuda and the first time that one of its coastal batteries had been so examined. Archaeology was a distant land to the other local historians of the day and the project turned not a sod of ground. Since my Bermudian friend and colleague, Dr. David Fleming, did the first excavation at the Tucker House in the 1970s, archaeology has slowly come to assume its proper role in the understanding and preservation of Bermuda's cultural heritage. Work in St. George's and elsewhere by Dr. Marley Brown III, Director of Archaeological Research at Colonial Williamsburg, underwater studies by Professor Gordon Watts, East Carolina University, and coastal defence investigations by Professor Richard Gould, Brown University, and Professor Norman Barka, the College of William and Mary, have added much to Bermuda's history through the archaeological process: to all of these scholars I extend my thanks for their contributions over many years.

This study is an archaeological work and based upon research from 1980, when it was my privilege to join the Bermuda Maritime Museum as its first Director. Over fifteen years, the research has had the support of the Board of Trustees and Staff of the Museum, to whom I express my thanks. In particular, Dr. J. C. 'Jack' Arnell, C. N. A. 'Than' Butterfield Jr., and Paul A. Leseur, M.B.E., as Chairmen of the Board, were of great support, as were Trustees Cyril Packwood, John McCulloch, Robert Steinhoff, Andrew Trimingham, Edwin Mortimer, Sanders Frith Brown and Trevor G. Moniz, M.P., the last providing much encouragement towards its completion. Of the staff, I would especially like to thank the former Curator, Jane Patterson Downing, and the present incumbent, Nan Godet for their assistance over such a long project. The Archaeological Research Committee of the Bermuda National Trust, under the leadership of Susan Kessaram and Stephen Copeland, took part in a number of the projects and I thank them and all their volunteers for their help.

The Museum enjoyed a most cordial relationship with HMS *Malabar* (closed 1995) and the Royal Navy: most of the aerial photographs taken for this study were obtained by helicopters of HM Ships, with help also from the Canadian Forces during their tenure at Daniel's Head Station (closed 1994). To Cmdr. Robin Bawtree, O.B.E., R.N., the last Resident Naval Officer, and the previous Commanders of HMS *Malabar,* the most heartfelt thanks are in order and are here given.

The study of Bermuda fortifications began in the early 1930s when a young American paid a chance visit to the island and saw many of the sites. The trip began an interest of several decades, resulting in the publication of Roger Willock's *Bulwark of Empire* (1962), the foundation of all later studies of the subject. I acknowledge a great debt to Colonel Willock for that work and for his friendship over many years. Other fundamental inspiration came from Austin Collin and Jenny Carpenter for their unrivalled knowledge of historic artillery, exhibited in their survey of Bermuda guns, partly published in their classic book, *Cannon,* in 1993.

My interest in the American defence of Bermuda in World War Two was instigated by Cmdr. Charles Robbins, U.S.N. (ret.) and Capt. David Woods, U.S.N.R. (ret.). Edward Tomasiewicz, Technical Sergeant, 693rd Signal Aircraft Warning Company (1942), added greatly to the cause with his generous gift of documents and photographs on this era to the Bermuda Maritime Museum. Others who provided support on this front were: Col. Charles Beaudry, U.S.A. (ret.), Capt. Frederick W. Clipper, U.S.A. (ret.), Col. Arthur H. Jemmott, U.S.A. (ret.), Cmdr. David Kirchner, (ret.), Jerome Levine, T/5 U.S.A. (ret.), Col. John Stewart Morton, Jr., U.S.A. (ret.), Capt. William W. Swayze, U.S.A. (ret.), Sgt. Michael Q. Wagner, U.S.A. (ret.), Capt. Nathan A. Zelikow, U.S.A. (ret.), and Messrs. C. Spanton Ashdown and Robert Ingalls. Successive Commanding Officers of the United States Naval Air Station, Bermuda (1941–95), and personnel under their command gave assistance in many ways to the project. To all of these military people, I extend my thanks and trust the present volume will somewhat reward their efforts.

A number of institutional bodies were of great assistance to the project down the years. The National Parks Commission and the Department of Parks, particularly under the leadership of its Director, Col. William Cook, U.S.M.C. (ret.) were instrumental in advancing the archaeological study and preservation of some of the sites. John Adams, Archivist, and Karla Hayward and Sandra Rouja of the Bermuda Archives were unstinting in their help and advice. Grace Rawlins, Head Librarian of the Bermuda Library was most helpful with World War Two material. The Department of Marine and Ports Services assisted in the retrival of several large gun barrels. The staff of the libraries of the Corps of Royal Engineers, the British Library, the John Carter Brown Library, the National Army Museum, the British Museum and the Public Record Office, London, were most generous with their assistance with military sources. From Parks Canada, I thank Joe Last, R. H. McDonald and Suzanne Plousos for their help over the years. To Valerie Roberts of the Island Press Ltd., I extend my thanks for many years of photographic work on the plans.

Many volunteers helped in some way or another with the compilation of the data for the study of Bermuda's fortifications. In recognition of the public spirit of the enterprise, my military library and archives will be given in due course to the Bermuda Maritime Museum and I thank them all for each building block contributed to the project: Chris and Betty Bäng, Ron and Pamela Biggs, Jonathan Coad, James Delgado, Robert Dodson, Michael Dolding, Wendi and Reimar Fiedler, Lance Furbert, Thomas Godet, Joyce D. Hall, M.B.E., the late Douglas and Helen Little, Edward Manuel, Terrence McGovern, Jean Trapido-Rosenthal, Professor Emeritus David and the late Alison Quinn, Victor Smith, Capt. Sir David Tibbits, D.S.C., R.N. and John Triggs.

Fay and Geoffrey Elliott kindly gave permission for the reproduction of illustrations of fortifications in their collection and I am especially grateful to them for the use of the watercolours by the hand of Gaspard Le Marchant Tupper found in the colour plates.

Professor Quentin Hughes kindly provided the Foreword and I am grateful to him and to members of the Fortress Study Group for their advice on fortifications over many years. Jean and Bill Pimm, Linda Abend, William Cooke, M.D., Kevin Bartoy and Dr. A. C. H. Hallett willingly performed the onerous task of proofreading the final drafts, and I thank them for their corrections and suggestions. The book was designed by Paul Shapiro, whom I thank for all his work, including many editorial improvements.

Lastly, but in so many ways first, I record my gratitude to the late Rohan and Margaret Sturdy, who visited most of the sites with me and funded some of the projects. To their children, Gay Corran, and Robin, Christopher and Dr. Derek Sturdy, and their good friends, Owen and Ruth Rogers, who were all drawn into the vortex created by more guns and yet another fort to be investigated, I extend my warmest thanks for all that they did for the military sector of Bermuda's heritage.

Any book which attempts to cover as much territory as this does will not be without its shell-holes and minefields: the omissions on this military exercise are mine alone, but one trusts the strategic and tactical errors will be pointed out and corrected in the fullness of the time.

EDWARD CECIL HARRIS

"THE PARSONAGE"

H.M. DOCKYARD, BERMUDA

Introduction

FROM THE TIME OF SETTLEMENT IN 1612 UNTIL THE WITHDRAWAL OF THE British garrison in 1957, some ninety forts were built at Bermuda. They were first studied in detail in Roger Willock's *Bulwark of Empire*, printed privately in 1962 and republished by the Bermuda Maritime Museum Press in 1988. Colonel Willock's work deals primarily with the forts of the later nineteenth century and concentrates on political and strategic considerations for their coming into being. Emphasis is given to the garrison at Bermuda and the costs of building the forts and maintaining the military establishment on the island. His was not an archaeological study and in consequence the development outlined for some of the forts and their armament is not entirely accurate. These minor deficiencies, in an otherwise classic volume, may perhaps be rectified in the present book. The two should be seen as complementary and the reader will see that reference must be made to Willock for details of the nature first mentioned, as they are not to be found in this volume.

For the present study, the forts were looked at from an archaeological perspective, given the primary goal of the project. This was to determine, through archival, historical and archaeological methods, the evolution of each fort as an architectural and military monument. Excepting those sites lost or known to have been destroyed, all of the sites discussed in this book were visited and recorded by photography and survey. The aim included the determination of the number and calibre of the guns employed at each site during a particular period.

As outlined in the ten chapters of this work, the project covered the range of fortifications and artillery at Bermuda from 1612–1957. Again, it deals primarily with the fixed works and takes little account of mobile guns or infantry works and weapons: that is another major story in itself. Nor does it discuss the major deployments of the Royal Navy at Bermuda from the 1780s onwards, part of which is covered in Andrew Stranack's book on the history of the Dockyard, *The Andrew and the Onions*. The present work does not consider the development of the local militias, which again is a major subject partly taken up with the study of the *Bermuda Volunteer Rifle Corps* by Jennifer M. Ingham.

This book begins by setting out the background for the planting of English forts in the New World before the settlement of Bermuda and then discussing the island itself before colonisation. The third chapter accounts for the important, and partly still standing, first eleven forts built in the first decade of settlement of Bermuda, followed by a chapter on the other coastal batteries erected in the decades before the American War of Independence. Chapter Five looks at the works of the first resident officer of the Corps of Royal Engineers in Bermuda, Andrew Durnford, leading into the establishment of the Dockyard in 1809.

Col. Roger Willock, U.S.M.C. (ret.) in 1992 with the RML guns of Fort Cunningham, which he predicted in 1962 would be found in its ditch.

The sixth chapter covers the period from 1809–65, when the Dockyard defences and the forts at St. George's for the defence of the Narrows Channel came into being. Major changes in armaments in the 1860s and 1890s caused the rebuilding of some of the earlier works and the construction of new ones, discussed in Chapters Seven and Eight. Chapter Nine concludes the story of the forts into the Second World War and outlines the coastal defence of Bermuda by the American Forces during that conflict. The final chapter of the book looks briefly at the military camps, additional magazines and some of the surviving historic artillery.

Drawings and Sources

The art of fortification lies in the art and science of land surveying. As we shall see, Andrew Durnford, for example, brought out with him all the necessary tools and measuring instruments for surveying Bermuda and laying out fortifications with military, that is to say scientific, precision. There is no doubt that many of the engineers made preliminary or design drawings of the works to be erected, but few such plans survive for the early Bermuda works. Later on, some works were recorded, prior to, or after, remodelling for new weaponry. For many of the Bermuda forts, there were no known plans, though enticing events, such as the sale by Durnford's former maid of forty of his drawings to the Americans, are recorded.

A survey without a resulting chart, or a fort without its map, is, as Captain John Smith, the publisher of Bermuda's first defence report in 1624, did otherwise say, 'History without Geography, [it] wandreth as a Vagrant without a certaine habitation.' As with my work in archaeology, now used around the world for its efficacy in *showing* stratigraphic sequences, it was my view that one had to *see* a fort in plan drawings, in order to understand its evolution.

Thus for my voyage of research on the Bermuda forts, I set out, with the help of many friends and colleagues, to put the buildings themselves back onto

Fort Cunningham of the 1870s coming to life on the drawing board at the author's home in the 1980s.

paper. The aim was to recreate in drawings the image of the work finally brought into being by the military surveyors and engineers. To that end, I obtained all of the record drawings which could be located in Bermuda and overseas. Locally, all the sites were visited and surveys made if no plans were in existence. In some cases, such as Fort Cunningham, archaeological excavations amplified the records and allowed new surveys to be made. The archival drawings and new site maps were combined as necessary and new ink drawings were penned by the author over many a long night and holiday: much to the distress of those whose time it impinged upon, no doubt.

The result was the corpus of more than one hundred drawings presented in this book, so as to elucidate, by survey plans, the evolution of Bermuda's fortifications. Many helicopter flights were taken to gather photographic material from the air, often the best way to look at a fort, that is, in plane view. At the same time, written reports on the forts were obtained from wherever they could be found. These were amalgamated with the drawings and photographs to fill out this story of the ninety-odd Bermuda forts.

The written sources have been used extensively throughout the present volume. Where the man on the spot said it so well, it seemed better to let him speak in his own words, hopefully imparting more of the flavour of the times, rather than giving a modern gloss. To that end, the spelling has not been modernised and it is hoped that the effort expended on reading the early texts will be rewarded equally by an increased appreciation of those times.

One of the more difficult aspects of Bermuda research is dealing with authors without footnotes or adequate references. In this book, detailed references by way of footnotes have been included, since part of the purpose of scholarship should be to lay foundations which obviate the need to reinvent the wheel at every turn. After the first full citation, references have been abbreviated to save space. A glossary is not included, as most of the terms can be worked out from the context and the illustrations.

This is very much a work of local definition: it is a determination of what forts and armaments existed at Bermuda at certain periods. A work comparing the Bermuda forts with their counterparts in the United Kingdom, the Americas including the West Indies, or latterly the world-wide British Empire, would consume another decade, or perhaps a book for retirement. The Bermuda forts, however, may stand on their own. They exhibit, more or less, almost the entire range of English coastal defence history. The surviving guns display many of the major developments in the history of British artillery from the early 1600s to 1957. All of this may be viewed within the mere twenty square miles of Willock's *Bulwark of Empire*. This was not the 'Gibraltar of the West,' as some like to say: it was Bermuda, an Imperial Fortress in its own right, a record supported by this history of its many works of war.

The late Thomas Martin du Brois Godet surveying in the late 1920s with the King's Castle in the background (courtesy of Thomas Godet and Molly Godet).

Aside from the interests of scholarship and archaeology, my purpose, as a Bermudian, in expending fifteen years for this study, was to bring to the notice of the authorities the nature and wealth of the fortifications of Bermuda. It can no longer be said that we stand in ignorance. These wonderful works must be preserved as a part of Bermuda's heritage and as a potentially vibrant cog in the machinery of cultural and ecological tourism, now the lifeblood of this most isolated of island communities.

With perhaps a destructive inevitability, the European cannon and its gun platforms, the sailing ship and artillery fortification, launched themselves on the outside world in the late Renaissance. The process of conquering and colonisation was accelerated by the Spanish after Columbus came to the Americas in 1492. Bermuda was the second overseas possession of the English and has, in St. George's, its first New World town. The defence of the coming British Empire outside Europe began in Virginia and Bermuda, and continued here until 1957, when the garrison was withdrawn. For a tiny place, Bermuda has figured large on the seascape of history in the Western North Atlantic: the surviving forts and guns depicted in these pages are a significant reminder of the past of all Bermudians. Let them protect us yet, as moorings for our identity as an historic island people, so that we do not, in an increasingly internationalised world, 'wandreth as a Vagrant without a certaine habitation.'

—EDWARD HARRIS

28

1

First English Fortifications in the New World

1 5 8 4 – 1 6 1 1

It [Bermuda] has nothing that anyone wants thus all should stay away from that latitude and place, always giving it a wide berth.

—Mendoza, 1575

THE ISLANDS OF BERMUDA LIE SOME SIX HUNDRED MILES EAST OF CONTI-nental North America, far beyond the reach of the boats of native Americans of prehistoric times. Unlike the eastern coast of what is now Canada, there is no evidence that the Vikings, intrepid travellers though they were, or any other peoples, ever reached Bermuda before Christopher Columbus set in train the European expansion into the 'New World.'

As the Canaries off the African coast slipped astern of Columbus' ships on September 9, 1492, few could have foretold the consequences of his epic voyage. A month later, the 'night of October 11–12 was one big with destiny for the human race, the most momentous ever experienced aboard any ship in any sea.'[1] That destiny spelled disaster for the native American cultures as the new technology, represented foremost by the ships and artillery cannon of late Renaissance Europe, descended on the New World with the landfall of the *Santa María* in the Bahamas chain of the West Indies, a thousand miles south of Bermuda. The cannon, with its attendant ships and forts—both but platforms for its authority[2]—laid the foundation for the European domination of the Americas.

Genocide, epidemic illnesses and cultural emasculation followed in the wake of the European *conquistador,* explorer and colonist. Settling first in the West Indies, the Spanish spread throughout the Caribbean region and into Mexico and Peru, driven by the greed that gold and silver engendered in the European breast.[3] Fortifications accompanied colonisation, of which some remarkable examples survive, though not necessarily of the earliest periods of occupation.[4]

1 Samuel Eliot Morison, *Admiral of the Ocean Sea, a Life of Christopher Columbus* (1942), 223.

2 Adrian Caruana, *The History of English Sea Ordnance 1523-1875* (1994), I, xi.

3 A tradition of colonial exploitation which continues yet through the activities of treasure hunters, particularly on shipwreck sites in the Americas.

4 Comisión de Estudios Históricos de Obras Públicas y Urbanismo, *Puertos y Fortificaciones en América y Filipinas* (1985).

In the colonisation of the New World, the English were relative latecomers, although David Beers Quinn has argued that they had made 'an early and brilliant start' before 1510 under the leadership of the Cabots, when much of the North American coastline was found.[5] It was not until the 1580s, however, that sustained efforts at colonisation took place with the backing of Sir Walter Raleigh in the expeditions known as the 'Roanoke Voyages' between 1584 and 1590. These ill-fated journeys have passed into American legend, with the unsolved mysteries surrounding the 'Lost Colony' on Roanoke Island, North Carolina, but they were the first expeditions which saw the erection of English fortifications in the New World, a little over a quarter of a century before Bermuda was settled and fortified.

After a reconnaissance voyage in 1584, an expedition of settlement comprising seven ships and six hundred men set out from Plymouth in the late spring of 1585. Separated by adverse weather, the *Tiger,* with Sir Richard Grenville, spent several weeks in Puerto Rico in May. It was fortunate that one of the passengers was the artist, John White, who recorded two forts hastily erected on that island.[6]

The first work was a large encampment, near what is now Guayanilla Bay, which was fortified by bastioned earthworks to the north and south. A fortified line, coupled with a swamp, formed the eastern perimeter, and on the west, a river was a natural defence (Pl. 1).[7] The site appears to have been chosen as a rendezvous in 1584 for such later expeditions.[8] Its purpose was to provide defences against the Spanish, who in the intervening year had settled the nearby town of San German and did not react kindly to English incursions of the territory. The fort was built between May 13–15, and was abandoned on the 23rd for the roadstead off San German.

On May 26, Ralph Lane was sent to nearby Cape Rojo at the south-west end of Puerto Rico to gather salt for the ensuing voyage. At that place, he erected a small fort, which enclosed a mound of salt within its north bastion (Pl. 2).[9] The fort held an enquiring group of Spaniards at bay, allowing Lane to load the salt onto his ship and on May 29, he rejoined the expedition off San German from whence they departed for Hispaniola and the North American mainland.[10]

FORT RALEIGH
ROANOKE ISLAND

By the middle of August 1585, the colony was established on Roanoke Island and a fort had been constructed, later called 'Fort Raleigh.' Very little was known of the true shape of this fort (for which unfortunately no John White drawings exist) until scientific excavations were undertaken in the late 1940s by J. C. Harrington.

> The plan of the fortification which emerges is that of a modified star-shaped fort, based on a square laid out on the ground and embellished with bastions. It should be compared with the plans given by Paul Ive in *The practise of fortification* (1589) and with those used by Lane in Puerto Rico. The angles point approximately north, south, east and west.

5 David Beers Quinn, 'The argument for the English discovery of America between 1480 and 1494,' *Geographical Journal* 127 (1961), 277-85.

6 Paul Hulton, *America 1585: the Complete Drawings of John White* (1984), Pls. 3 and 4.

7 Reproduced with permission of the Trustees of the British Museum: P. & D. 1906-5-9-1 (4).

8 David Beers Quinn, *The Roanoke Voyages 1584-1590* (1955), 181.

9 Reproduced with permission of the Trustees of the British Museum: P. & D. 1906-5-9-1 (5).

10 Quinn, *Roanoke Voyages,* 163.

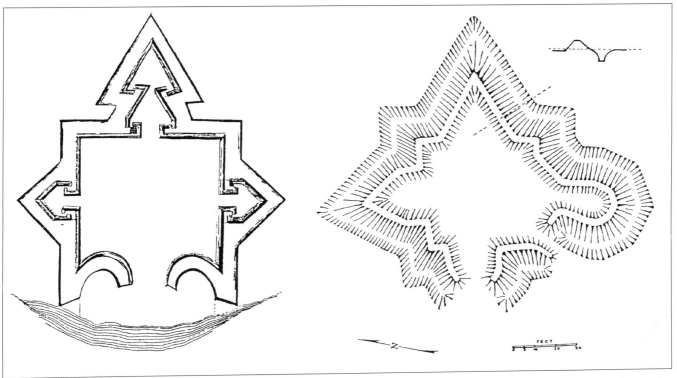

FIGURE 1.1: *The third English fort in the northern New World was built on Roanoke Island (right) and is similar to the second fort in Puerto Rico on the left (courtesy of J. C. Harrington).*

[11] Ibid., 905.

[12] Ibid., Pl. II.

[13] One of the last bastioned defences ever built was begun about 1820 at the Bermuda Dockyard.

[14] Emanuel Raymond Lewis, *Seacoast Fortifications of the United States: An Introductory History* (1970), 15. One is reminded of the very European formalism of fortifications in Hispanic America, but it should be remembered that most of these are late seventeenth- or eighteenth-century structures, e.g., the works at Cartegena. Lewis' comments, however, are very apt with regard to the early Bermuda forts.

Those at the north and east have been modified to about 70° to turn them into simple bastions ('trenailles') and each are likely to have had a gun platform and two embrasures in the parapet wall.

Accompanying the above description,[11] Quinn gives a comparative illustration of the Cape Rojo and Roanoke forts (Fig. 1.1), which underscores their similarity.[12] Within the European tradition of a 'bastioned' work,[13] these two forts and the encampment at Guayanilla Bay were earth and timber structures, unlike the masonry edifices of the Old World upon the plan of which they were based. The forts were surrounded by a ditch, the excavation of which provided the fill of the ramparts. While Fort Raleigh would have had to contend with hostile native Americans, all three of these forts were designed to counter Spanish attacks, with European weaponry at their disposal.

Emanuel Raymond Lewis, in his seminal work, *Seacoast Fortifications of the United States*, has observed that this period saw great changes in fortification in Europe, where the art was becoming a science based upon enormous defensive works on inland sites: [14]

...their elaborate formalism offered little of practical value for the construction of tiny forts across the Atlantic to guard a sparse population against raids from the sea. Nevertheless, certain basic features were carried to America, though in a most rudimentary fashion. Thus while seventeenth- and eighteenth-century works along the coast of the New World were often bastioned...their plans were as a rule products of gross trial and error that rarely exhibited any of the geometric intricacy so typical of contemporary European forts.

It is therefore of interest that further excavations at Roanoke Island suggested a change in the nature of later fortified works, possibly as a reaction against native American attackers with their stone-age technology. In 1965, Harrington found a small rectangular structure, thought to have been built in the log-cabin style, which later came to typify some early American colonial buildings. He considered it as an isolated emplacement,

> …but it now appears more probable that it was the base of a flanker, a projection from a different type of fortification than the star fort, one distinguished by rectangular projections, made of timbers laid horizontally rather than vertically and depending on the stoutness of the timbers rather than on the ditch and parapet of the star fort. Such fortifications have been identified in Virginia for the early seventeenth century, though constructed with planked fences rather than logs.[15]

In the summer of 1586, some 15 men were left at Roanoke, while the other colonists returned to England. Quinn has suggested that they may have been in the course of constructing this smaller work of defence, when they were attacked by the Indians:[16] none had survived upon the arrival of other colonists the following year. Those hapless settlers in their turn were not reinforced until 1590, by which time they had also disappeared, becoming the legendary 'Lost Colony.' Due to the war with Spain, which through its Armada in 1588 threatened England itself,[17] almost two decades were to pass before colonisation was attempted again on the North American mainland, but the second of two efforts in 1607 failed within a year.

FORT ST. GEORGE
KENNEBEC RIVER, MAINE

In August 1607 under the banner of the 'Northern Colony of Virginia,' a group of settlers from England landed on a peninsula on the Sagadahoc, now Kennebec, River, near the town of Phippsburg in the State of Maine. The colonists immediately began work on Fort St. George, which was 'trenched & fortified, with twelve pieces of ordinance [sic] and fifty houses built therein,'[18] making this a form of defended village, not unlike one of the fortifications at Puerto Rico.

A plan of the fort (Fig. 1.2)[19] was sent to Philip III in September 1608 by Don Pedro de Zuñiga, the Spanish Ambassador at London. Allowing for the lack of perspective, Fort St. George appears to be a work in the bastion-trace tradition, as were the Puerto Rico structures. Also depicted on the plan is a small boat, which may represent the pinnace, *Virginia,* built at the fort and part of the 1609 fleet to Jamestown,[20] of which the *Sea Venture,* carrying Sir George Somers, Sir Thomas Gates, and other notables, was wrecked at Bermuda that July. The Kennebec, or Popham, colony was abandoned in 1608 and a visitor in 1624 from a new settlement in Massachusetts Bay found but 'roots & garden hearbs & some old walls.'[21]

Archaeological excavations were carried out in the summer of 1994 to confirm the location of Fort St. George. The work is thought to have been positioned on a small peninsular called 'Sabino Head' on the Kennebec River, but later military and civilian works have obscured the site. Some structural

15 David Beers Quinn, *Set Fair for Roanoke* (1985), 396.
16 Ibid., 394.
17 Samuel Eliot Morison, *The European Discovery of America: the Northern Voyages A.D. 500–1600* (1971), 631, suggests that 'If Spain had defeated England in 1588–90, she would certainly have planted a chain of garrisoned forts along the North American coast, and it is doubtful whether a humbled and subjected England could have fought her way in.'
18 Alexander Brown, *The Genesis of the United States* (1964), 192. Brown suggests that the number of houses was probably five, not fifty.
19 Ibid., Pl. LVIII.
20 Ibid., 193.
21 Ibid., 194.

FIGURE 1.2: Fort St. George, from a plan by John Hunt in 1607, the sixth fort to be built in the northern Americas by the English was at the Popham Colony in what is now Maine (Archivo general de Simancas, Secretaria de Estrado, Legato 2586, f. 147).

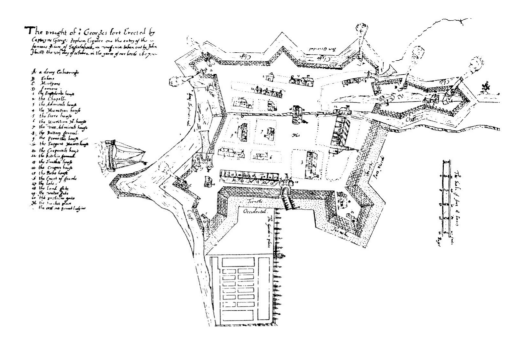

evidence was found which may represent the ditch of the fort. The artefacts discovered were dated to the period of the settlement.[22] As at Puerto Rico, Roanoke and Jamestown, the paucity of structural remains of the first English forts in the New World underlines the importance of the standing Bermuda forts of the period 1612–22.

THE FORTS AT JAMESTOWN, VIRGINIA

The 'southern colony' had been established also in 1607 on James Island, in Virginia, the State which now bears the name once given to much of North America in honour of Queen Elizabeth I. Upon landing on May 14, the colonists' first act was to break ground for James Fort (named for the King), which was completed a month later: for 'the first few years this fort was Jamestown,'[23] and became the origin of the first permanent English settlement in the Americas.

> It was triangular in shape, with a 'bulwarke' at each corner which was shaped like a 'halfe moone.' Within the 'bulwarkes' were mounted four or five pieces of artillery...The fort enclosed about one acre with its river side extending 420 feet and its other sides measuring about 300 feet. The principal gate faced the river and was in the south side (curtain) of the fort, although there were other openings, one at each 'bulwarke,' and each was protected by a piece of ordnance. The church, storehouse, and living quarters were flimsily built of perishable materials, within the walls of the palisaded fort...[24]

James Fort thus had the elements of a fortified camp, similar to Grenville's station at Puerto Rico, but the design of a triangular enclosure, palisaded in timber, perhaps marks the change to a style of fortification adapted for the American wilderness (Fig. 1.3).[25] It is unlikely that much more will ever be known about this fort as it is thought to be partly under the James River.[26] However, archaeological excavations in the 1970s at nearby Martin's Hundred revealed the possible site of Wolstenhome Towne (settled in 1619) fort.

22 Jeffrey P. Brain, 'Fort St. George' (Peabody Essex Museum, 1995).

23 Charles E. Hatch, *The First Seventeen Years: Virginia, 1607-1624* (1957), 4.

24 Ibid.

25 Yet the modified star fort long persisted in American works, e.g., Fort Powhatan at Hampton Roads in 1819, in David A. Clary, *Fortress America* (1990), 74.

26 Philip L. Barbour, *The Jamestown Voyages under the First Charter, 1606-1609* (1969), 465.

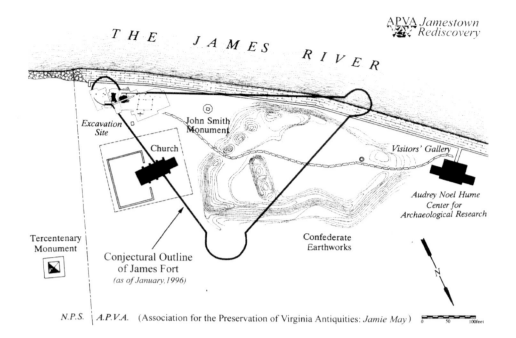

THE JAMES RIVER

APVA *Jamestown Rediscovery*

Excavation Site

John Smith Monument

Church

Visitors' Gallery

Audrey Noel Hume Center for Archaeological Research

Tercentenary Monument

Conjectural Outline of James Fort *(as of January, 1996)*

Confederate Earthworks

N

N.P.S. | *A.P.V.A.* (Association for the Preservation of Virginia Antiquities: *Jamie May*) 0 50 100feet

FIGURE 1.3: *James Fort in 1607, the fifth fortification to be erected by the English in America, marked the beginnings of Jamestown, Virginia, the first permanent English settlement in the New World (by Jamie May, courtesy of Dr. William Kelso and the Association for the Preservation of Virginia Antiquities).*

Although it was a trapezoidal, rather than triangular, structure,[27] it may give some idea of the construction of James Fort.

In 1610, William Strachey described James Fort as built of 'Plankes and strong Posts, foure foote deep in the ground, of Yong Oakes, Walnuts...at every Angle or corner, where the lines meete [there was] a Bulwarke or Watchtower.'[28] This palisaded work of three or more sides is the type which may have been used for the first time at Roanoke Island, as an adaptation to warfare with native Americans. Archaeological work in the mid-1990s has found some structural evidence which may pertain to James Fort, but the remains unfortunately may not prove to be very substantial.

There were several other forts built in the early years of the Jamestown settlement, recorded through Spanish espionage and intelligence gathering.

> At the mouth of this said Bay [in June 1611] there are four earthworks towards the northern side, all on one bank; and the first fort [Fort Algernon] is at the mouth of that river, which consists of stockades and posts without stone or brick and contains 7 pieces of artillery...The second fort stands at two-thirds of a league from the first, and the third at a musket shot, and both of them with their supply of pieces of artillery for defense against the Indians. The principal settlement is the fourth fort, which is 20 leagues up the river from the first fort, and in it there are 16 pieces of artillery...and [it] is surrounded with palisades like the others.[29]

> I have examined several persons of those who have come from Virginia in the last ship [September 1613], and they all agree upon this...that upon the river they have erected five fortifications: the first Gomes [James Fort] which is the name of this King here in English; the second is called 'Henrique' after the Prince who died; the third is Charles [after the present Prince]; Point Comfort [Fort Algernon] the fourth, and Fort Henry the fifth; and these forts are surrounded with earthworks, on which they plant their artillery.[30]

Fort Algernon was built in October 1609 on Point Comfort on the north

27 Ivor Noël Hume, *Discoveries in Martin's Hundred* (1987), Figs. 21 and 26.
28 Samuel Purchas, *Hakluytus Posthumus Or Purchas His Pilgrimes* (1906), XIX, 56.
29 Brown, *Genesis,* 519.
30 Ibid., 660.

side of Hampton Roads and the James River and commanded the entrance to the new settlement against a Spanish attack, its position now occupied by Fortress Monroe. It was destroyed by fire in 1612 and was not rebuilt until 1632, as the possibility of a Spanish offensive receded. Fort Algernon was supported on the opposite shore by Forts Henerique and Charles (known as the Princes Forts) at the mouth of the Hampton River, which were erected by Lord De La Ware shortly after his arrival in June 1610.[31]

Thus by the establishment of the colony at Bermuda in the late summer of 1612, there were six or seven forts of English origin on the North American mainland and two at Puerto Rico. Except as archaeological traces, very little survives of these first English forts in America, largely due to their construction of timber and earth.[32] Perhaps more than half fall into the tradition of European bastioned works, whereas the others represent structures adapted to the local circumstances. The Bermuda forts, 1612–1622, are in neither category but appear to hark back to the coastal defence works of Henry VIII.

Hampton Roads, Virginia, has been claimed to be 'the birthplace and schoolyard of American defense policy.'[33] Its first forts certainly mark the beginning of the coastal defence of the later United States of America. Along with food supplies brought from Bermuda by Sir George Somers, and the timely arrival of Lord De La Ware after James Fort had been abandoned temporarily, these forts ensured the survival of the first permanent English settlement in the New World, though nothing stands of the buildings themselves. As David Quinn wrote: 'The crucial turning point had come and been passed. The road to Jamestown was not to be a mere track into a wilderness but a main road into colonial empire.'[34] The second road into that empire in the New World (and one of its last surviving edifices) was Bermuda, settled in 1612.

■ ■ ■

31 Lyon Gardiner Tyler, *England in America 1580-1652* (1904), 69.
32 By contrast, three of the Bermuda forts erected before 1621 still stand to full height, being erected in stone.
33 Clary, *Fortress*, 5.
34 David Beers Quinn, *England and the Discovery of America 1481-1620* (1974), 488.

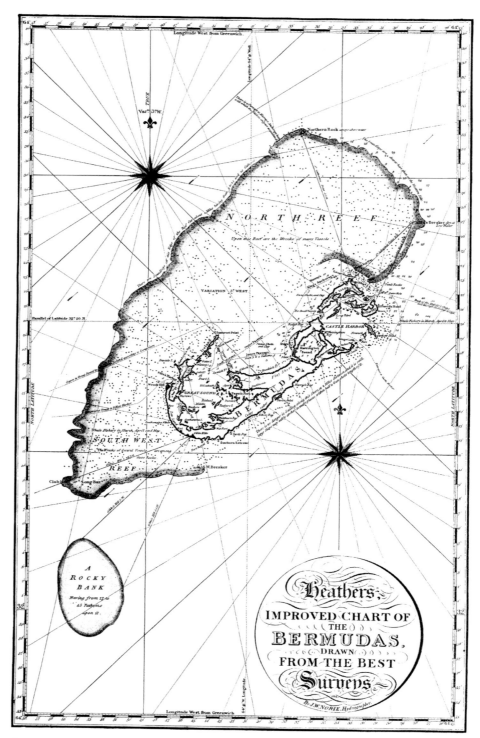

FIGURE 2.1: *The first sea chart of Bermuda was published by J. W. Norie, Hydrographer in 1814 and shows the extensive reefs which protected the island to the north, east and west.*

2

Bermuda Before Settlement

Pre – 1 6 1 2

I was sailing near the island of Bermuda, which is also called La Garza
and which is the most distant island known in the world today...
—Oviedo, 1547

THE ISLANDS OF BERMUDA WERE DISCOVERED BY JUAN BERMUDÉZ, WHO made over a dozen Atlantic crossings, the first possibly with Christopher Columbus in 1492. A man of that name has been listed as being aboard the *Pinta,* with Martín Alonso Pinzón as captain, both men being from the Spanish town of Palos.[1] Research in the Archives of the Indies at Seville in the early 1990s by a scholar from the Bermuda Maritime Museum has indicated that 1505 is the most likely date of the discovery of Bermuda. It was during a return voyage to Spain in the early autumn of that year that Bermudéz was in command of the *Santa Maria de la Antigua,* also thought to be known as *La Garza* (The Heron).[2] The historian Oviedo, who may have known Bermudéz personally, published his version of the event in 1547.

> I have seen the island [in 1515] that is called Bermuda or La Garza from a lombard shot distance away. The ship was sailing near the island until it was in eight fathoms of water. The island is small and believed to be unpopulated. I was determined to go ashore with ten or twelve boys and their firearms to put ashore half a dozen hogs of those that were on board as provisions. They would breed and provide meat when needed. Ready to launch a boat from the nao, a contrary storm befell us. We could not get ashore and had to continue our voyage. It is land, not very high, even though it has a ridge, higher than the other land. There are many seagulls, other water fowl, and many flying fish. It has two names because the nao that discovered it was named La Garza and the captain of the nao was called Juan Bermudéz, who was a native of Palos.[3]

It was not until 1612, one hundred and twenty years after Columbus' first voyage to the New World, that the islands of Bermuda were settled.

During the fifteenth century, the island became a temporary refuge to a

[1] Robert H. Fuson (ed.), *The Log of Christopher Columbus* (1987), 224.

[2] Jonathan W. Bream, 'The Spanish Influence on Bermuda,' *Bermuda Journal of Archaeology and Maritime History* 2 (1990), 15-24.

[3] Gonzalo Fernández de Oviedo y Valdés. *Historía General y Natural de las Indias* (1959), I, 38. I am indebted to Jonathan Bream for the information relating to Bermudéz and his voyages to America and other Spanish sources.

number of shipwrecked mariners, a recently published account being described by David Beers Quinn as 'a particularly interesting story of human frailty and treachery in the face of adversity.'[4] Most mariners built ships on the island and sailed away, or were rescued by passing vessels. No archaeological evidence has been found of any long stays or deaths of such hapless seamen. Its isolated position, treacherous winds and waters, and the lack of any natural mineral resources militated against the settlement of Bermuda by commerce-hungry Europeans.

As they have had such an influence on its history, particularly military, the geological and geographical settings of the islands thus merit mention (Pl. 3). Bermuda is said to be the second most isolated island in the world, possibly only less remote than Ascension Island or St. Helena, two later oceanic outposts of the British Empire. The islands are some 635 miles (1,022 km) due east of Cape Hatteras, North Carolina. Located at 64° 45' West and 32° 20' North, a thousand miles from the northern reaches of the Bahamas and the West Indies, they are the most northerly place on Earth where coral can be found.[5] Bermuda covers less than 20 square miles (52 square km), lying on a north-east to south-west line along 'the southern edge of an oval submarine platform of over 250 square miles' (650 square km).[6]

The only channel for ships into the harbours and inner anchorages is at the eastern end of the island. The 'Narrows Channel' (originally, 'Hurd's Channel') was discovered in the 1790s by an hydrographer of the Royal Navy and since that time its presence has dictated the military development of Bermuda. To the north, east and west, the shallow reefs extend up to eight miles offshore, forming a natural defence, which has ever served the island well. Until the beginning of the nineteenth century, the principal harbours were at the Town of St. George and the nearby Castle Harbour. After the incorporation of the City of Hamilton and the establishment of the westerly Dockyard, other anchorages at Hamilton Harbour, the Great Sound, and Grassy Bay at Ireland Island took precedence.

The unusual form of Bermuda, unlike many volcanic islands, took the eye of early map makers. Although it became one of the most published maps of the seventeenth century, but it was not until 1814 that the first sea chart for the islands was produced (Fig. 2.1). The shape of the Island is due to the fact that the submarine volcano upon which it perches may not have emerged above sea-level to a height sufficient to withstand later weathering and erosion.

'Mount Bermuda' rises about 13,000 feet (4,000 metres) from the Atlantic seabed, with its last eruptions ceasing some 30 million years ago.[7] While the top of this seamount would have been exposed during the Ice Ages, when the sea level dropped more than 600 feet (200 metres), at present volcanic rock has not been found any higher than 100 feet below sea-level. The limestone cap on that volcanic base rises no more than 270 feet above the sea.[8] Unlike Hawaii, for example, which rises some 13,500 feet above sea-level and continues to pour out lava,[9] the hot spot which created Mount Bermuda between 30 and 110 million years ago moved on, with fortuitous consequences for a coral archipelago then formed upon its dormant top.

[4] Lois de La Blochière, 'A Journey to Pérou, Filled with Incredible Events and Dangers,' *BJAMH* 2 (1990), 1-14.

[5] William Livingston, *A Million Years on Mount Bermuda* (1947), 2.

[6] Ibid., 3.

[7] Mark P. Rowe, *An Explanation of The Geology of Bermuda* (1990), 1.

[8] Ibid.

[9] Gordon A. Macdonald, Agatin T. Abbott and Frank L. Peterson, *Volcanoes in the Sea, the Geology of Hawaii* (1983).

All of the rock above sea level at Bermuda is aeolian limestone (calcium carbonate) of varying age and hardness. It was brought into being by the creation of sand dunes, the constituents being derived from the coral and shell life of the reefs, and was formed during the Pleistocene epoch, about 1.6 million to 10,000 years before the present era. During that time, there were major changes in sea level due to the waxing and waning of the Ice Ages. In periods of continental glaciation, the sea level would have fallen, thus exposing the reef life, much of which would have been killed off.

Bermuda at those times would have been about ten times its present size, forming a platform of several hundred square miles upon which sand dunes could be formed. The sand which the wind whipped into dunes was the remains of the dead sea life of the exposed reefs.[10] Over a period of time, the dunes solidified by the action of rainwater on the calcium in the sand, creating the fine aeolian limestone which has been such a blessing to Bermudians since the settlement of the island in 1612. We are presently in an interglacial period with a high sea level, so that little dune formation is taking place, except on a few of the South Shore beaches.

The limestone cap which came to form the summit of Mount Bermuda was a strategic blessing as well, for it gave the Island a number of protected harbours and anchorages. A comparison with other volcanic islands points up this major geographical difference, which is based on the geological composition of the land. Most islands in the Atlantic of volcanic origin lack decent

10 Rowe, *Geology*, 18-21.

harbours, the Azores and Ascension Islands being two examples. Nearer to Bermuda, many of the West Indies are volcanic islands without limestone caps. If the volcano breached the sea-level and continued to erupt, circular islands tended to be formed. Nevis and St. Eustatius are such volcanic outcrops, forming a small mountain around which the life of the island must circulate. The rounded shape of these volcano-islands means that few have any harbours of economic or strategic value.

Bermuda falls into a different geological category, being a coral and limestone archipelago which sits on the top of a submerged volcano. Limestone is subject to forms of weathering and alteration, which generally do not affect the harder volcanic rocks. As rainwater percolates through the porous upper layers of limestone, calcium carbonate precipitates out and is carried into the lower rocks. This material fills up the pores of the lower rocks and ultimately forms a hard, indurated limestone. In the process, caves are formed by the leeching of the upper strata, the roofs of which may collapse, bringing into being sinkholes or tidal basins. Through this process and the erosion of the soft upper rocks by wind, rain and sea, a mass of limestone may take on an extremely variegated shape. At the same time, being a coral atoll, there is a geological tendency to have lagoons (harbours) created behind the protection of the line of reef fronting the open sea.

FIGURE 2.3: *Bermuda hardstone was burnt in kilns such as this one at Ferry Reach to provide the lime for the mortar, plaster, and waterproofing lime-wash.*

These geological factors have given Bermuda its unique and eccentric shape—which has lent it a strategic importance out of all proportion to its size. Without the commodious harbours formed by the presence of atoll and surface limestone, Bermuda could have been a circular volcano in an often turbulent sea, without any safe roadstead except that formed by the lee of the land.

Geology thus provided the island with the blessings of a dormant volcanic platform upon which formed coral atolls and sand dunes that became Bermuda. Geography provided another vital ingredient to the strategic equation by the location of the islands, almost halfway between the British military posts in the West Indies to the south, and those of Canada at Halifax in the north. Thus Bermuda was seen after 1783, according to one British officer, as 'the bit in the mouth' of the horse that was the United States of America. This strategic geographical position was continued, but reversed, in the Second World War when a U.S. base at Bermuda made it possible by air cover to extend the defensive border of the United States up to a thousand miles off its eastern seaboard.

Figure 2.4: A substantial Bermuda home, with out-buildings, which was built of the soft local limestone in Warwick Parish and white-washed (Humphreys Bermuda Houses, 1923).

Figure 2.5: A roadside scene near Bailey's Bay Battery shows a cutting and wall of soft Bermuda stone; the boundary marker W[ar] D[epartment] 68 is a piece of the local hard-stone.

Another asset was the composition of the Bermuda limestone. Most of the surface rock, known as 'Bermuda stone,' is soft and can be cut into blocks with a hand-saw, yet hardens upon exposure to the air (Fig. 2.2). The largely underlying formations are indurated rocks, known to Bermudians as 'limestone' or 'hard-stone.' These strata must be blasted from the ground and shaped into blocks using the hammer and chisel methods of monumental stoneworking, usually associated with granites and other hard rocks. The hard-stone, when burnt, provided the lime needed to make the building mortars (Fig. 2.3). Both these stones are superior in building to the erratic volcanic rocks which make up some West Indies islands, and they played major roles in the construction of the ninety-odd forts at Bermuda.

It may be said that the limestone was the foundation upon which the economy of Bermuda was underpinned from settlement. Used by the first fort-builders, and later for house-building,[11] the use of the soft limestone instead of timber represented a major capital investment, but its durability over the centuries repaid manifold the initial outlay. After a time, nearly all Bermuda homes were made of this stone, with 'slate' roofs of the same, cemented and washed with lime, which bonded the roof into a very heavy unitary structure. By contrast, most houses in the West Indies were of wood and subject to periodic devastation by hurricanes.[12] It could therefore be argued that such substantial buildings—

11 Since little archaeology of the domestic architecture of Bermuda has been done, this point cannot be substantiated; it is possible that stone houses are much earlier features than suggested by art historians.

12 Montserrat, for example, in Hurricane Hugo of 1989, lost upwards of 80 percent of its buildings, mostly in wood and some of historical importance.

FIGURE 2.6: *The stonework of the great Commissioner's House and the fortifications at the Bermuda Dockyard are composed of the older local limestone, or 'hard-stone' (BMM Archives).*

which even today weather hurricanes with ease—allowed Bermudians from the early decades of settlement to begin the accumulation of capital wealth (and its retention by such architectural protection against natural destruction) denied by geological circumstance to other islands (Fig. 2.4).

The hard-stone was little used by early Bermudians, except for 'wharf block,' taken from the shoreline for stone docks and wharves. This indurated limestone came into its own in the nineteenth century for the construction of the Royal Naval Dockyard and forts associated with its defence (Fig. 2.5). It is a pleasant irony of fate that the site chosen for the dockyard was the only place in Bermuda where the hard-stone existed on the surface in quantities which could be quarried, resulting in the magnificent buildings of that naval base (Fig. 2.6).[13]

A final gift of Nature was good building timber, a tree which had been in Bermuda long enough to have developed into the species, *Juniperus Bermudiana*: 'The "divers other plants unknown by name and nature," referred to by Captain John Smith, undoubtably were the endemic and other native plants with which...early visitors would not be familiar.'[14] Known as 'Bermuda cedar,' this timber was used for the roof and floors and other details of early buildings.

> It is a good wood to work with to make boxes, door and window frames and other workings. It is timber that the shipworm and gnawing creature do no damage. For this reason some say that this wood is so free of disease and that the shipworm does not penetrate it...It is true that a few months ago the pilot Bartolomé Carreño brought from the island of Bermuda to the city of Santo Domingo some beautiful pieces or logs of this wood called cedar.[15]

It proved a fine wood for local cabinet makers and provided the timber for the famous Bermuda Sloop of the eighteenth century (Fig. 2.7), which was the fastest ship afloat and much desired by West Indian and American mainland

[13] Edward Harris, 'Bermuda Hard-stone,' *The Bermudian* 53/8 (1982), 24-5.

[14] Louisa Hutchings Smith, *Bermuda's "Oldest Inhabitants"* (1969), 13.

[15] Oviedo, *Historia*, IX, 286.

FIGURE 2.7: *The Bermuda sloop of the eighteenth century, with its distinctive rigging, was built of the local cedar and was the fastest ship afloat (courtesy of Horst Augustinovic).*

traders. Used little in the local forts, Bermuda cedar is said to be found, oddly enough, in the lintels of gunports at Brimstone Hill Fort in St. Kitts.

This, then, was the setting which would have caught the eyes of the London adventurers of the Virginia Company had they set foot in Bermuda with their first group of colonists in late July 1612. A semi-tropical coral atoll fringed with reefs on all sides, but containing several commodious harbours. An abundance of sea life, timber, and stone which could be readily quarried, was married with a mild climate and a position on the sea lanes which was the envy of many, especially the Spanish, a traditional enemy of the English realm. The absence of a native population obviated many of the physical dangers as well as political and moral issues faced in the fledging colonies on the American mainland. The seeds of settlement were planted and nurtured, protected by the early fortifications of the islands. In 1612, Bermuda became the second permanent English settlement in the New World and, in 1995, was one of the last colonies of the greatest empire the world has ever known.

■ ■ ■

Archaeological excavations have revealed much about Bermuda forts: Patricia Samford, Richard Fraser, Amy Kowalski, Helen Fraser and Mike Phillips at Bailey's Bay Battery in 1991.

3

The First Decade
of Settlement

1 6 1 2 – 1 6 2 2

*...the gouernour, who had remoued his seate from Smith's Iland to St.
Georges, for the commoditie and nerenesse of the fresh water; after he
had fitted up some smale cabbins of Palmitoe leaues for himselfe, his
wife, and some fewe others, in that vally wher nowe standes the prime
towne of the ilands, he began to applye himselfe to performe some what
of fortification at the harbours mouthes...*

—Nathaniel Butler, 1622

ON MAY 15, 1609, A FLEET OF SEVEN SHIPS LEFT WOOLWICH, ENGLAND AND
by way of Plymouth and Falmouth on June 8 set sail for the colony at
James Fort, Virginia, which had been established two years previous. The fleet
included the *Virginia,* which had been built at Fort St. George in the
'Northern Colony' (now Maine) in 1607, and the *Sea Adventure, 'Admirall',*
wherein was Sir Thomas Gates, Sir George Somers, and Captaine Newport.'[1]
The vessels were separated after meeting with a hurricane, all but the *Sea
Venture* making James Fort by mid-August.

The *Sea Venture,* leaking badly, had been diverted by the storm and was
within cannon-shot of a sandy beach at the eastern end of Bermuda, when she
foundered on a reef on July 28 (Fig. 3.1). Everyone was saved and the next ten
months were spent building two boats of Bermuda cedar, the *Patience* and the
Deliverance, in which they departed for Virginia on May 10, 1610. Contrary to
its legend as the 'Isle of Devils,' Somers found that 'Bermooda is the most
plentifull place, that ever I came to, for fishe, Hogges and fowle,' and he took
some of the pigs to James Fort.[2] Arriving there on May 23, the fledgling colony
was in such a sorry state that it was abandoned and had not Somers' boats with
the surviving colonists met the incoming Lord De La Ware, it is likely that it
would have died in the bud. De La Ware reoccupied James Fort and Somers
offered to return to Bermuda for more food, which he did on June 19. The gathering

[1] Alexander Brown, *The Genesis
of the United States* (1964),
329.

[2] Ibid., 401.

FIGURE 3.1: *A view of eastern Bermuda in the 1980s; St. Catherine's Point is in the lower right, next to the beach where the Sea Venture passengers landed.*

of supplies seems to have been a protracted affair and Sir George was still at Bermuda on November 9, 1610, when he died. The *Patience*, under his nephew, Matthew Somers, went on to England, bearing his body and news of the Bermudas, later synonymously called the Somers, or Summer, Islands.[3]

No defences were erected at Bermuda between the wreck of the *Sea Venture* and its permanent colonisation three years later, although three men had been left in residence, two after Somers left for Virginia in May and a third after the *Patience* departed for England. Its value as an outpost to succour the James Fort colony had not been lost on either the English or the Spanish. Writing to the King of Spain from London on August 22, 1611, Don Alonso de Velasco noted that Lord De La Ware, Governor of Virginia, had lately returned to England to advocate the reinforcement of the colony, regardless of the great difficulties they had had at James Fort.

> Notwithstanding all this, if it were not that they sadly want some outlet for all the idle and wicked people such as this kingdom has, they will for that purpose even preserve that post [James Fort]. For this purpose they now propose to erect a fort on the island of Vermuda, which, tho' it is two hundred leagues from Virginia, still has been able to succour them very effectually—especially with herds of swine, which are innumerable there and altho' the Coast of Bermuda is dangerous, having no considerable port at all, still they will find shelter there for small vessels.[4]

In June 1612, Velasco again advised the King of Spain that plans were underway in London for the larger scheme to colonise the Bermudas, and that a 'ship will also take out whatever is necessary to erect a fort.'[5] No action was taken by Spain and on July 11, 1612, upon the arrival of the *Plough* with some fifty-odd settlers and the first governor, Richard Moore, the settlement of Bermuda began. The establishment of a second English colony in the Americas must have greatly dismayed Don Pedro de Zuñiga, who for several years from London had been urging Philip III to '*give orders to have these insolent people* [at James Fort] *quickly annihilated.*'[6]

The settlers stayed for a day or two on Smith's Island,[7] where the three men who remained after the departure of Matthew Somers had made their camp. They soon moved to St. George's Island and the first English town in the New World was established.[8] A sketch of it is given in Captain John Smith's map of Bermuda (Fig. 3.2) in which several elements are discernible.

St. George's, or 'New London,'[9] was built around a market square open to

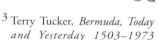

[3] Terry Tucker, *Bermuda, Today and Yesterday 1503–1973* (1975), 37–8.

[4] Brown, *Genesis*, 495.

[5] Ibid., 560.

[6] Ibid., 259.

[7] Which would not have been so called at the time: the date of the naming of the Bermuda lands is unclear, although it may be assumed that this took place before or during Norwood's survey of 1616–17.

[8] Since the original Jamestown on James Island was ultimately abandoned, St. George's lays fair claim as the oldest continually-settled town of English origin in the New World. As James Fort did not develop into a town until about 1619, St. George's is the first English town in the Americas.

[9] So described as late as 1620 by two Flemish men jailed by the Spanish at Santiago de Guatemala, who, in hope of release, provided Philip IV with intelligence and a plan to remove the English from Bermuda. Letter from Diego de Mercado and Simon Zacharias to the Crown, Santiago de Guatemala, January 7, 1620, Archivo General de Indias, Indiferente General 1528. The earliest mention of 'St. George' as the town name may be around 1619.

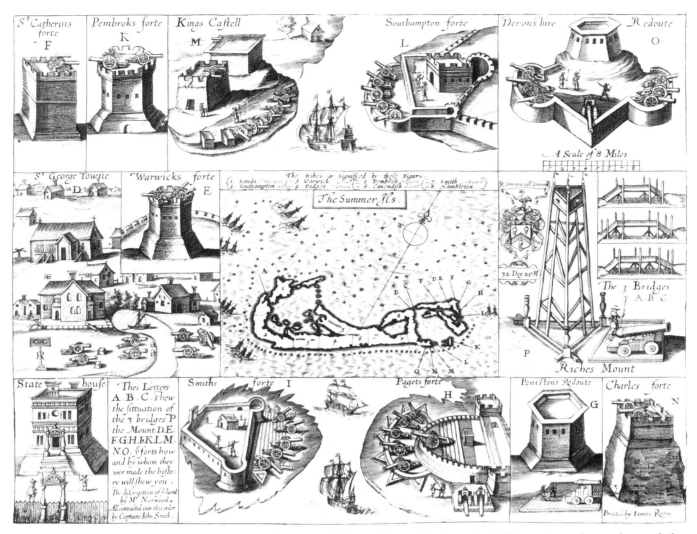

FIGURE 3.2: *Captain John Smith published this map of Bermuda and its forts in 1624 and may have obtained the illustration from Governor Nathaniel Butler.*

10 Because most of the records of the Bermuda Company have been lost, we are reliant upon the accounts of Captain John Smith and Captain Nathaniel Butler, Governor of Bermuda 1619–22. Scholars agree that much of Smith's account of early Bermuda was taken from Butler, who is used here as the primary source for the early forts.

the harbour on the south, with a small inlet next to what may be the town hall, replete with flags as roof finials. The inlet was probably part of a small stream which drained a swamp just to the north-east of the town, on the southern edge of which stands the 1911 memorial to Sir George Somers. The presence of the stream is the presumed derivation of 'Bridge Street,' which forms the eastern boundary of the Town Square. The stream and inlet have been filled up (and the bridge is a thing of the past), making the area of the Town Square one of the earliest archaeological sites of the English settlement of the New World.

On the Square in front of the 'Town House' (Fig. 3.2) stood several cannon and a set of stocks for the public punishment of miscreants. To the rear of the town hall, according to the Smith drawing,[10] was a church, with crucifix finials. Beyond the church are the houses of the town, with chimneys central to the building—not a typical feature of later architecture in Bermuda. In another inset (Fig. 3.2) is the 'State House,' where the first assembly, or parliament was held on August 1, 1620. Since that time, Bermuda has been self-governing, making it the second oldest parliament in the British

Commonwealth and the third oldest in the world, after England and Iceland.[11]

The town and forts in John Smith's drawing evolved over a decade, so that these views represent the situation around 1622. Smith never came to Bermuda and his illustrations of the first Bermuda forts have been described as 'hackneyed,'[12] that is to say commonplace, even fanciful views. Since 1980, however, a comparison of the drawings with the remains of the forts has demonstrated that Smith's views were reasonably accurate.[13]

Given the concordance between his drawings and the archaeological remains, Smith must have obtained his information from Butler or from Richard Norwood, but while the latter had the draughting abilities to produce such illustrations, he had left Bermuda in 1617 before several of the forts were erected.[14] Given Butler's attention to detail, as shown in his *Historye*, it is tempting to see the Smith illustrations as his, Butler's, work. In that context, it is important to remember that the drawings represent the forts in the forms they had acquired by the time Butler left Bermuda in 1622.

The discussion of each site will therefore, where necessary, be carried through from 1612 until the end of Butler's governorship.[15]

• • •

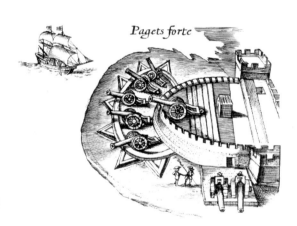

Pagets forte

FIGURE 3.3

PAGET FORT (QUEEN'S FORT)
THE FIRST FORT AT BERMUDA

The town established, Governor Moore began the defence of the eastern coast (which in comparison to the other shores was largely unprotected by reefs and lay exposed to the open sea) choosing (Fig. 3.3)

> to settle his first worck vpon the point of a smale iland lieing on the north-side of that channel that leadeth into St. Georges harbour, wher he cuts out a plattforme, and plant-ed some ordinance [sic][16] to good purpose. This iland was since tearmed Penistons Island, and the fort, which bin also altered (as we shall heare) by Captaine Tucker, is now called Pagetts Fort, in honor of the Lord Pagett, whoe is one of the company.[17]

A few years later under Governor Daniel Tucker (1616–1619),

> some 8 or 10 men are appointed to cutt out a plattforme at Pagett's Fort, the which (as the

[11] The administrative organisation of the Bermuda Company is discussed in Wesley Frank Craven, *An Introduction to the History of Bermuda* (1990), Jean Kennedy, *Isle of Devils: Bermuda under the Somers Island Company 1609–1685* (1971) and Henry Wilkinson, *The Adventurers of Bermuda* (1938).

[12] Philip L. Barbour, *The Complete Works of Captain John Smith (1580–1631)* (1986), II, 335.

[13] The first results of the research on the first forts appeared in Edward Harris, 'American Spies at Bermuda's Forts, 1842–52,' *Post-Medieval Archaeology* 20 (1986), 311–331.

[14] Richard Norwood had been employed by Governor Moore possibly for surveying and setting out some of the forts. That he was interested in the subject was demonstrated by the later publication of *Fortification or Architecture Military* (1639), but the book unfortunately has no references to work at Bermuda. Until the publication of his book, 'we have had nothing original written in English on fortification as a science': Maurice Cockle, *A Bibliography of Military Books up to 1642* (1978).

[15] Richard Norwood in his 'Insularum de la Bermuda Detectio' mentions only that Governor Moore 'built some nine or tenne forts, placing ordnance and munitions in them,' Champlin Burrage, ed., *John Pory's Lost Description of Plymouth* (1918), 6.

[16] The spelling is that of General Sir J. Henry Lefroy's on Nathaniel Butler's papers (British Library, Sloane MS 750) which he edited for the Hakluyt Society as *Historye of the Bermudaes or Summer Islands* (1882), hereafter cited as Butler, *Historye*.

[17] Butler, *Historye*, 23–4.

FIGURE 3.4: *Governor's Island with Smith's Fort is on the left; to the north of the channel to St. George's is Paget Island with Paget Fort on the point and Fort Cunningham behind.*

worck itselfe sheweth to this daye, and euer will doe in despight of all amends) proued so vnfashionable, vncapable and vnsightlest peece in that kind of the whole ilands; and yet by situation and for vse, requireinge as much or more protection than any other whatsoeuer.[18]

It was during Tucker's third Assize (March 1617), 'the first order was sett downe for a presse and leuye of men out of the tribes, for the mountinge of the ordinance in Pagetts Fort.'[19]

After a short deputy-governorship by Captain Miles Kendall in 1618–19, the energetic Butler arrived in October 1619 to begin his term as governor. After settling administrative duties and work on other forts left unfinished since 1615,

he went to Pagetts Fort, where he layd a newe plattforme vpon the topp of the redoubt, and beatinge out a large and hansome porthole he mounted a good peece of ordinance vpon a newe carriage in the same place; and this was done by reason of the vnseruiseable-nesse of the old plattforme lieing vnder it; the which, by being ouer-streight, afforded not any due mannagement of the ordinance, and by its lieinge ouer lowe, and too nere the sea, was so annoyed with the billowe, that euery fresh gale at east and northeast (which are the only proper windes to bring in shyps into the harbour, and so most require the vse of it), it fills it halfe full of water, and so altogether disableth the ordinance from working any good effect.[20]

Some time later, 'Towards the end of this moneth of August [1621] the Gouernour began to sinck two newe plattformes in Penistones Iland; one of them vnder the redoubt of Pagetts Fort…vpon which he mounted two sakers.'[21] Herein end the references to Paget Fort in Butler's manuscript, which are little

18 Ibid., 88.
19 Ibid., 90.
20 Ibid., 231.
21 Ibid., 241.

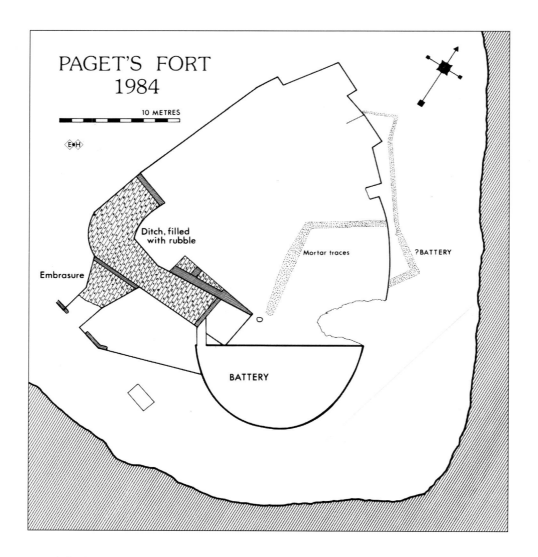

**PAGET'S FORT
1984**

10 METRES

Ditch, filled
with rubble

Mortar traces

?BATTERY

Embrasure

BATTERY

FIGURE 3.5: *In the 1980s, archaeologists recorded the plan of the surface features of Paget Fort, the first in Bermuda.*

amplified by John Smith, except that he wrote that by the end of Butler's governorship, eleven pieces of ordnance were emplaced at Paget and Smith's Forts at the entrance to the channel of St. George's Harbour.[22]

In John Smith's illustration (Fig. 3.3), facing the channel was a D-shaped bastion mounting five guns, which fired through embrasures. To the rear was a higher, semi-circular work with one cannon firing *en barbette* over a curtain pierced with a number of embrasures for muskets: this work may be that built by Butler in his first months.[23] On the seaward side of the bastion was a platform with two guns, possibly those mounted by Butler in August 1621. At the rear of the semi-circular bastion, and forming salients thereof, were two square towers connected by a rear curtain wall with musketry embrasures.

The interpretation of Paget Fort (Fig. 3.4) is aided by a comparison of Butler and Smith with the archaeological remains of the site and a military survey of 1811. In 1984, an archaeological survey revealed the outline of the fort, the remains of walls and mortar traces on the bedrock, probably from other masonry structures (Fig. 3.5). The D-shaped lower bastion is cut into the rock and in bad weather usually contained a foot of water from breaking seas, confirming Butler's opinion (Fig. 3.6). A shallow ditch to the west of this

[22] John Smith, *The Generall Historie of the Bermudas* (1624), 199.

[23] Butler, *Historye*, 18.

FIGURE 3.6: *An aerial view of the 1940s showing the surface evidence for Paget Fort (author's collection).*

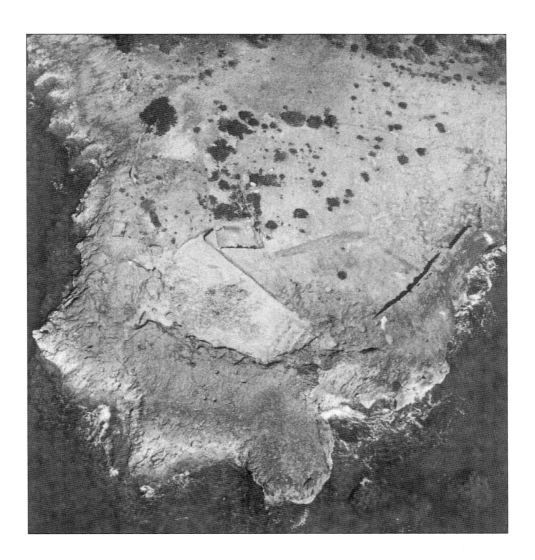

FIGURE 3.6: *An aerial view of the 1940s showing the surface evidence for Paget Fort (author's collection).*

bastion had been infilled, probably in the 1810s, during the construction of Fort Cunningham on the high ground to the rear.

It is to the namesake of the last structure that we owe the important survey of fortifications at Bermuda, which Thomas Cunningham, R.E., submitted on November 25, 1811, including scale drawings of many of the forts. While it is possible that additions may be reflected in his drawing of Paget Fort (Fig. 3.7), a comparison between it, the archaeological plan, the Smith illustration and Butler's text can be made, aided by Cunningham's description.

> The works on Paget Island consist of a lower Battery of a most irregular form, situated on a point of the North side of the entrance of the Harbour, and is closed in the rear by a ditch the counterscarp of which is however but 6 feet high. This work may be said to consist of an upper and lower Battery, if guns placed in the ditch be so considered. There is one French 8 p^r. unserviceable in the lower and three 12 p^{rs}. nearly so in the upper battery.[24]

The archaeological evidence supports Cunningham's report, with the exception of what seems to be an embrasure in the ditch, later blocked, but possibly the position of the French gun. The sea battery was not in use in 1811, but the main building would qualify as the upper work of the Smith drawing, with the Guard House possibly being one of his square towers.

[24] PRO WO 55/1551/2. Thomas Cunningham, Report on the Defences of Bermuda, 1811.

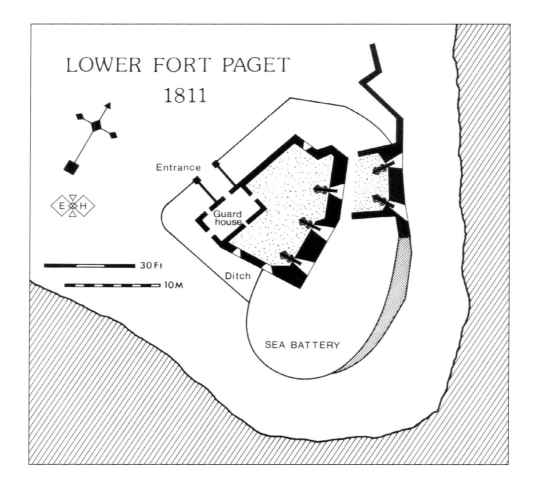

FIGURE 3.7: *In 1811 a Royal Engineer, Thomas Cunningham, made this survey of Fort Paget (redrawn by the author).*

Agreement may be assumed between the two-gun emplacement in the north-east corner of the site in Cunningham's diagram and that on the Smith map, with mortar traces found in 1984 supporting its existence. According to Cunningham, two embrasures flanked the channel from the body of the fort, but its main armament faced the open sea, as noted in an earlier report.[25]

> This lower Battery at Fort Pagett has Platforms made (but God knows when) of pieces of the Wrecke of Vessels they are all consumed and quite decaeed. The Higher Battery has three Embarsures & but two Platforms, the Embarsures are made of fashines [fascines], fill'd up with earth, but are all in ruins, this Battery points to Five fathom hole, formerly mentioned, where ships Come to an Anchor, when the wind is not fair to carry them into the Harbour.[26]

Assuming that the site was little altered from Butler's day, the first Bermuda fort would have given a good account of itself, disregarding Tucker's lower battery. Flanking the sea and firing through embrasures were two guns of the lower platform located in the north-east section of its enceinte. The main body of the fort was an irregular rectangle, 'with a Parapet 8 feet thick and 7 feet high closed in the rear by a Narrow Ditch,'[27] elevated at least by that height above the two-gun platform. From the upper level, one embrasure faced north, two south, and three covered the mouth of the channel to the east. The work was 'closed in the rear by a Narrow Ditch, mounting four 6 Poun^{ds}, it is in tolerable good Repair excepting the Guard House which requires to be new Roofed.'[28] A hundred feet to the west, an entrenchment (now partly buried) may be the 'line for Musketrey' noted by De Butts in 1798.

[25] Scottish Record Office, GD-50/185/267/12/7. Simon Fraser, Report on the Defences of Bermuda, 1783. Reproduced in Edward Harris, 'Bermuda Defences at the end of the American Revolutionary War,' *Bermuda Journal of Archaeology and Maritime History* 1 (1989), 81–107.

[26] Ibid., 91.

[27] PRO WO 55/1551/1. Augustus De Butts, Report on the Defences of Bermuda, 1798.

[28] Ibid.

The design of the main body of Fort Paget is similar to the upper work at the King's Castle, but there the lay of the land allowed for a much larger lower battery. The seven guns at Fort Paget were also only about half the number found at the King's Castle, a few miles along the coast to the south. It would seem that the guns for Fort Paget were among those brought out from England, perhaps as armament on the *Plough.* Governor Moore clearly had no additional weapons, so

> hauinge made the plattforme at Pagetts Fort somewhat seruiceable for matter of offence, weighinge two pieces of artillerye, with much adoe, out of the ruines of the *Sea-venture*, he planted one of them vpon a little iland [Governor's Island[opposite to Pagetts Fort, and the other he mounted upon a rock which commanded the mouth of the west harbour, called the Gurnetts Head [Castle Island], ther to make a shewe for the time, and to serue in some smale steed, vntill he could prouide better.[29]

This activity appears to have taken place before the end of 1612, but before the arrival of the second supply ship. Moore had also been busy on St. George's Island, erecting a church, and overlooking the town, a monument to himself.[30]

• • •

MOORE'S MOUNT

THE 'EYE OF THE ILANDS'

The Company in London sent out the second supply ship, *Elizabeth,* which arrived at the new colony in March 1613, with thirty passengers.

> At her comeinge in, she found the gouernour busied about the rayseinge of a foure-square frame of timber vpon a high hill ouertoppeinge the towne of St. Georges to the westwards, to serue for the discouery of shippinge vpon the coast; the which worcke the gouernour accounted for his masterpeece, and was earnestly affected to haue it carry his owne name, and to be called Moores mount, although (as we shall see hereafter) it proued not long-liued being turned vp by the rootes with a huricanoe, or whirlwinde.[31]

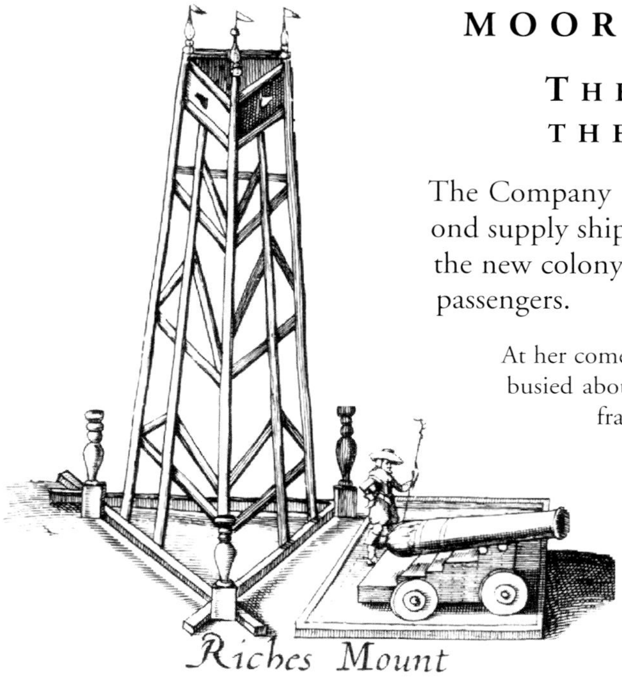

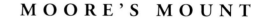

Riches Mount

FIGURE 3.8

[29] Butler, *Historye,* 26.

[30] Paget Fort may be the first English masonry fort in the New World. In 1612 an English fort was built several hundred miles up the Amazon: 'Thomas King's Fort,' at Monte Alegre, was, however, probably timber. Joyce Lorimer, (ed.), *English and Irish Settlement on the River Amazon 1550–1646* (1989).

[31] Butler, *Historye,* 28.

[32] To the left of the tower is Smith's Coat of Arms with the motto, 'Vincere est Viuere' and a north latitude of '32 Deg[ees]. 25 M[inutes].'

According to Smith (Fig. 3.8), this look-out had a triangular base, with a small balustraded platform on its top. To the right was a small timber platform mounting a gun (described by Butler as a 'smale faulcon') for signalling, which faced east towards the town. By the time Smith was writing his history, the reference to Moore had been lost, for the site was re-named by Butler 'Riches Mount,' in honour perhaps of Sir Nathaniel Rich, one of the leading figures of the Bermuda Company.[32] During the first months of Butler's administration (late 1619) several disasters occurred including the destruction of Moore's

Mount, which occupied the site of the later Fort George: 'At the same time also (for one mischeife neuer goes alone) a foure square frame of timber, called the Mount, and built vpon a high hill nere the towne by Mr. Moore (and by him much gloried in), serueing to good vse for the discouery of shyps at sea, and so the Eye of the Ilands, was blown up by the rootes.'[33]

Smith's drawing of the Mount was based upon the form in which it was rebuilt the following year.

> Presently after this Feast of Easter, 1620, the Gouernour, haueing made and launced a newe cœdar bote, to rowe with foure oares only, and built of purpose to goe well vpon the oares, the nimbler vpon all occasions to serue for a boate of aduise, he began to thinck of preparation towards the erecting of a newe mount, in lieu of that formerly blowne downe, and to be raysed in the same place. He sent away, therfore, the lieutenant of his company, Captaine Felgate, into Harrington tribe, and gaue him a commission to fell cœdar ther for the same end, the which wer conuayed to the towne in flotes. He made also a presse of carpenters, the best he could heare of, and commanded them vp to St. Georges, wher he conferred with them about the sayd worck, and propounded diuers fashions and formes to be considered, which of them was the fittest and most sightly, both in respect of strength and hansomenesse. At last, the trianguler forme, being most generally approued, the bussinesse is sett on foote on all hands, the timber squared on the warfe, and from thence, with great toyle and labour, haled and drawne up the hill wheron it was to stand; from which time forward it was so continually and closely followed as that, within one moneth after, this frame is once againe accomplished, and becomes seuen foote higher than it was before; and (to preserue it from the like fortune) is stroungly keyed at the three corners belowe, with very substantiall posts; and playsted and whited at the top, for the better discerneinge of it out to sea; at the foote thereof, also, vpon a cœdar platforme, is mounted a peece of ordinance, taken out of treasorour [*Treasurer*], to serue as a warneinge peece to all the fortes, vpon the discouery of shypps from thence, and the which, by being so loftely placed, is the better to be heard on all sides; and so this worck, being absolutely finished and perfected, is named by the Gouernour Riche[s]-Mount, which hath already stoode stiffly in many a terrible storme, without the least dammage that can be discerned, and may be hoped to doe so in many more.[34]

The solid balustrade at the top of the tower (seen in Smith's drawing), being painted white, thus served as the first lighthouse in Bermuda, or at least as a beacon during daylight. The origin of the gun is found in the fact that early in 1620 Butler found 'the ship called the *Treasurer* starke rotten and unserviceable, hee tooke nine pieces of Ordinance from her to serve other uses.'[35] A keeper was appointed for an 'entertainement' of a hundred pounds of tobacco a year and 'hath an oath giuen him to keepe his due houres of lookeinge out to sea from the mount.'[36]

Butler's workmanship notwithstanding, the structure survived his governorship by only seven years, being 'Blowne downe by the storme that happened on the 16th day of August 1629.'[37] The then Governor, Roger Wood, and the Council agreed that it should be 'reedified' and have the following proportions: 'vizt to be 30 foote square below and 48 foote high and 8 foote square at the topp.' A William Welch was promised a payment of 1,400 lb. of tobacco provided that the job was completed;[38] it is not known whether this work was carried out. By the end of the American Revolutionary War, the site had several guns and later became Fort George, erected by Captain Andrew Durnford, R.E., in the 1790s.

• • •

33 Butler, *Historye,* 161.

34 Ibid., 173-4.

35 Barbour, *Works,* II, 376.

36 Butler, *Historye,* 236.

37 J. H. Lefroy, *Memorials of the Discovery and Early Settlement of the Bermudas or Somers Islands 1515–1685* I (1981), 523–4.

38 Ibid., 524.

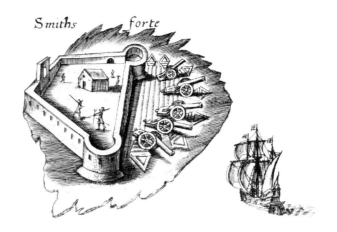

Smiths forte

FIGURE 3.9

SMITH'S FORT

The early summer of 1613 found Governor Moore active at Castle Island, but after the departure of the supply ship, *Martha,* in July

> he remoues the most of his men from thence and begins to fall to worck, in a smale iland lieing on the south-side of the harbours mouth of St. Georges, where, with much adoe, he makes a kind of platforme, planteth some ordinance upon it, and erecteth a redoubt; the which, how it was altered and perfected, we shall see when we come to that time.[39]

The work on Governor's Island became known as 'Smith's Fort,' represented by Captain John Smith in its 1622 'altered and perfected' form.[40] It was the site in late 1612 of a gun raised from the wreck of the *Sea Venture* by Moore, but of his later 'platforme' nothing much can be said. It seems that further work was carried out by Governor Daniel Tucker, but he departed for England in June 1619, leaving Captain Kendall as interim governor.

> Herevpon, the people of the Maine being called to the execution, the perfection of Smithes Forte is first attempted, the which, being begun by Mr. Moore, then proceeded on by Captaine Tucker, is nowe lastly sett vpon to be accomplished by this man [Kendall]; but the rock wheron they wer to worck proueinge exceedingly hard, and the layers out of the plott and ouerseers of it haueing but small experience in such affayres, after a great deale of labour, and many monethes expence, a fayre plattforme and a hansome redoubt is spoyled, and in a manner left vnseruiceable, by being slubbred up with dangerous and vnsure vpperworcks of brittle stone and rubbish, to the extreme hazard and perill, vpon the least occasion and great shott of an enemy, of all such as therin are to mannage and plie those ordinance.[41]

Butler makes no further reference to the structure on Governor's Island, except to note that early in 1621, he made five new carriages for the guns, the existing ones of English elm being rotten.[42] Given his penchant for praising his perfecting of the works of the previous governors, any major alterations by Butler to the fort built by Kendall would have been undoubtedly recorded.

Governor's Island lies on the south side of the channel, which was the only passage for ships to the Town of St. George until the 1920s when Town Cut was excavated. Smith's Fort was the southern flank of the channel, facing Paget Fort on Paget Island to the north. The main armament of the fort was housed in a D-shaped battery containing embrasures for six cannon. This feature was found in the 1980s, yet there was evidence for eight embrasures. It was presumably here that Butler placed new carriages in 1621.

[39] Butler, *Historye,* 29.

[40] Smith's Fort has been mistakenly placed by some scholars on Smith's Island, but there is no evidence that any defence works were ever built there.

[41] Butler, *Historye,* 132-7.

[42] Ibid., 231.

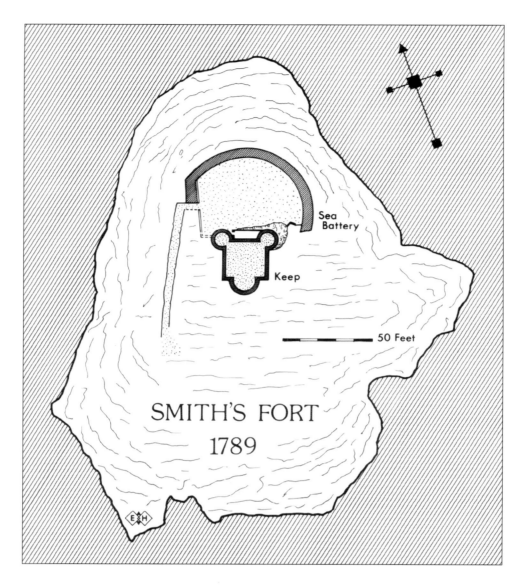

FIGURE 3.10: *A record drawing of Smith's Fort was made in 1789 by the Royal Engineers and gives the true shape of the 'Keep' (redrawn by the author).*

To the rear of the Battery, according to Smith (Fig. 3.9), stood a trapezoidal redoubt, the curtains of which were pierced with gun-loops for muskets. Two round bastions were placed on the corners of the north curtain, with a gate at the gorge, or rear, in the south wall. A small wooden building, possibly the magazine, stood within the courtyard of this little fort. Due to a cover of poison ivy and the later rampart built by Andrew Durnford in the 1790s, this structure was not found in investigations of the island in the 1980s.

Fortunately, a watercolour plan by Henry Lauzan, surveyor assistant to Durnford, survives in the holdings of the St. George's Historical Society, one of the few such drawings of the Durnford period in existence (Fig. 3.10).[43] Lauzan shows the D-shaped battery, but the rear of the fort has a more sensible form, about 20 feet square. The two towers are shown on the north curtain, and the position of the gate (not recorded) at the gorge would have been covered by a semi-circular bastion. The fort has little in common with the other forts, with the exception of the use of gunports for muskets and the rounded bastions, which appear on the landward defences at Southampton Fort erected by Butler. Archaeological excavations may later reveal more details of this

[43] Henry Wilkinson, *Bermuda from Sail to Steam* II (1973), 551, gives a hint of where the other plans could be: 'Meanwhile the Governor [Reid, 1843] learned to his distress that "a mulatto woman," formerly the Durnfords' cook, had recently sold forty plans of forts and defences to the Colonel of Engineers' in the U.S.A.'

interesting structure, but the Lauzan plan would seem to confirm again the general accuracy of John Smith's depiction of the first forts at Bermuda.

By 1619, the entry to St. George's Harbour had been covered effectively by Paget and Smith's Forts. Governor Moore, however, was also intent upon the protection of the channel into what was originally called Southampton (later Castle) Harbour, a few miles to the south. The channels for both harbours led directly to the open sea, for the reefs on this part of the coast extend but a few hundred yards from shore. That is why he placed a gun on Gurnetts Head[44] (Castle Island) in the first months of settlement and looked at other sites.

• • •

GOVERNOR MOORE'S TOWER FORTS

Several other positions needed protection and during his first year, Moore began work on a series of small towers, four along the coast (Charles, Pembroke, Peniston's and St. Catherine's Forts) and a fifth (Warwick Castle), inland and just to the north of the town. Nothing is known to have survived of these structures, and documentary reference to them is scant. Charles Fort, the last survivor of the group, fell into the sea in the early 1960s, with but a few photographs recording its design.

• • •

FIGURE 3.11

WARWICK CASTLE

This small building, apparently an hexagonal tower mounting several guns on its roof, or first-storey platform, was begun in the late summer of 1613 by Governor Moore.

> The *Martha* thus gone…He also layeth the foundation of a large redoubt vpon a hill to the east of St. George's towne, the which he afterwards brought to good perfection, beinge at the present called Warwick Fort, and hauing three pieces of ordinance mounted upon it, serveth both to play out towards the harbour, and to garde the fresh water belouginge to the towne.[45]

Warwick Castle may have been located on the hill now occupied by the Western Redoubt (see Chap. 6). This hill commands all the ground to the east

44 The term Gurnet Rock is applied to a tiny island fronting the sea on the north side of Castle Roads: due to the ocean swell, it is inaccessible except to sea birds. There is no evidence that Moore placed his guns there, rather than on Castle Island, or 'Gurnett's Head.'

45 Butler, *Historye,* 29.

and south (including the town) and westwards towards the rise on which Moore's Mount stood, but is itself commanded by another to the north, where Fort Victoria was eventually built. Given the distance from the Fort Victoria position to the town, a location at the Western Redoubt site is the most likely choice for Warwick Castle. Butler set about improving the fort shortly after his third assize early in 1620.

> Great store of lime was also commanded to be burnt, and the fort commanding the towne, called Warwick Castle, began to be repayred and perfected, the which being left vnfinished by Mr. Moore, and neglected by Captaine Tucker, was conceiued by this Gouernour as a necessary accomplishment, both in regard to its being a sea marck as also that therin the women and children might be bestowed, and preserued from any soudaine fury of an enemye (it being a strength not hastely to be surmounted, but will require the mountance of some ordinance, and with all that it might appeare, so much the more worthy of the noble appellation it was distinguished by).[46]

Nonetheless by the time of Moore's departure around July of 1615, the fort was considered good enough to be a stronghold for some of the townsfolk, who resolved that 'they should retire theither, and from thence playe vpon them with the ordinance,'[47] due to upheavals and factionalism caused by the 'mis-rule of the six governors' left in charge by Moore. According to Smith (Fig. 3.11), it was partly enclosed by a curtain wall with embrasures suitable, no doubt, for the playing of muskets or cannon upon the population without. With its tower and the parapet at ground level, it is similar to Devonshire Redoubt, as built by Butler in 1621.

• • •

ST. CATHERINE'S FORT
(SANDYS FORT)

Over the rise to the north and a short distance from Warwick Castle stood the only work in Bermuda dedicated to a saint. This little work was founded on the northernmost tip of Bermuda, by the beach where the shipwrecked mariners from the *Sea Venture* landed in July 1609, for '...on the north side of St. Georges island, is erected vpon a rock the smale fort of St. Katherines, in garde of a certaine sandy baye; being the same wheron the first that euer landed in thoes partes, first set their feete, and in it are mounted two peeces of ordinance.'[48]

Governor Moore may have begun the construction of this fort in 1613, for by about March 1614, after the arrival of the *Blessinge* and the *Starre*, with 280 passengers, he was intent upon its completion.

All thes people, with their necessaryes, were speedely landed and vewed by the gouernour, who haueinge taken their names, and considered of their condition, distributed and fitted euery one to his employement and labour; for some of them he sent to the Gurnetts head,

FIGURE 3.12

[46] Ibid., 231–3. The 'noble appellation,' in honour of the Earl of Warwick, one of the leading adventurers of the Bermuda Company, thus elevated a mere fort to a 'castle,' but it appears in John Smith's drawing as 'Warwicks forte.'

[47] Ibid., 62.

[48] Ibid., 107. This was 'the first identification of the precise spot where the unfortunate party landed.'

to make that plattforme and rayse thoes battlements, that to this daye lie out vpon the mouth of the harbour; the which, haueinge finished in some reasonable manner, was called the Kings-Castle; others wer employed about the mountinge of such ordinance as wer sent ouer by the newe come shyps; the most of the rest were disposed of to the finishinge of St. Katheraines Fort…[49]

The diversion of the settlers to the works of defence was ultimately held against Moore, amid claims that the planting was neglected in order that the forts might be advanced. The fort which the complaining colonists erected is depicted by Smith (Fig. 3.12) as a small rectangular building of two storeys, with two guns at roof level firing over a crenellated wall. The design is nearly matched at Charles Fort, but there the lower storey is bedrock, while at St. Catherine's it is shown as masonry. No indication is given of any windows or gun-loops in either fort, unlike the presence of the same in Smith's views of the hexagonal towers, such as Warwick Castle.

All traces of the first St. Catherine's Fort have been removed or buried by the construction of a series of later works from the eighteenth century onwards.

• • •

PENISTON'S REDOUBT
(CAVENDISH FORT)

Between St. Catherine's Fort to the north and Paget Fort to the south, the coastline is broken by a little island with two small channels separating it from St. George's and Paget Islands. To cover these channels against boat traffic, Moore erected a tower, later called 'Peniston's Redoubt,' towards the northern end of Paget Island. No description survives of its first days, but Butler recorded his alterations.

> Towards the end of this moneth of August [1621] the Gouernour began to sinck two newe plattformes in Penistones Iland; one of them vnder the redoubt of Pagetts Fort…: the other was layed out vpon a point of that Iland lieinge out to the northwards; and vnder a smale redoubt called the pigeon-house, which being erected by Mr. Moore and left forsaken and in ruins by Capt. Tucker who robbed it also of a peece of ordinance to bestowe it elsewher, was at this time renewed and the peece restored, as findinge it of good and requisite vse for the command of shalopes, which by a smale and narrow chanell might otherwise passe up vntouched into the towne harbour, and very towne itselfe.[50]

The single gun was mounted on a new carriage of Bermuda cedar by Butler, as shown by John Smith (Fig. 3.13).[51] An hexagonal tower comprises the fort itself, with no indication of artillery at roof level. All four of the early forts which have hexagonal towers (Warwick Castle, Peniston's and Pembroke Forts, and Devonshire Redoubt) are shown by Smith as having windows or gun-loops at first-floor level. At Devonshire Redoubt, still standing, the tower is a solid block with only a platform

Penistons Redoute

FIGURE 3.13

49 Ibid., 35.
50 Ibid., 241.
51 There were three states of the Smith map, one being identified by the inclusion of the caption 'Penistons Redoubte' above the fort in vignette 'G' (Fig. 3.2).

and cannon embrasures at 'roof' level. Given the description of Warwick Castle as being a good 'sea mark,' it is possible that some of the towers were simply observation posts, into which category Peniston's Redoubt perhaps falls. In 1985, an archaeological team from the Bermuda Maritime Museum found evidence of a building near the presumed site of the fort.[52] If the foundations of Peniston's Redoubt do exist as archaeological remains, they are of first importance since none of the other individual tower forts are extant and therefore little is known of their dimensions. There are no later references to Peniston's Redoubt, which perhaps fell into disrepair in the mid-seventeenth century.

• • •

Pembroks forte

FIGURE 3.14

PEMBROKE FORT

Serving a function similar to that of Peniston's Redoubt but a mile or so to the south, Pembroke Fort was built by Governor Moore on the seaward promontory of Cooper's Island. It covered a boat channel into Castle Harbour between Cooper's and Nonsuch Islands and flanked the rear of the later Southampton Fort on the island just south of Nonsuch. The following report is all that exists in seventeenth-century writing of this little tower which bestrode one of the most beautiful parts of the Bermuda coastline.

> The harbours being thus cleared of all shyps [April 1614], saue the two pinnaces, the gouernour being well stored with people, falls againe to his fortinge: and hauinge done with Pagetts Fort, he rayseth a fashionable redoubt in Coopers Iland, and calls it Pembroke Fort...[53] From hence (the coast trending to the north-easte) is Coopers island, wher standeth Pembroke Fort, and vpon it three peeces of ordinance...[54]

John Smith (Fig. 3.14) shows a tower very similar to Warwick Castle, but there appears to be a door in the battered foundations of the structure. Such battered footings are a feature of the four hexagonal towers in Smith's drawings. They are exhibited at Devonshire Redoubt on Castle Island, although the splay is not as pronounced as in the Smith drawing. Along with Warwick Castle, Pembroke Fort was severely damaged in a hurricane in August 1629 and its demise may date from that time.[55]

52 Jack Arnell and Edward Harris, 'A History of Some of the Islands in St. George's Harbour,' *Bermuda Journal of Archaeology and Maritime History* 3 (1991), 37–63.

53 Butler, *Historye,* 39.

54 Ibid., 107.

55 Lefroy, *Memorials,* I, 504.

Pembroke Fort was apparently obliterated during the occupation of Cooper's Island in the Second World War by the United States military; and much of the area lay under a NASA tracking station in the 1980s. An archaeological investigation of the area might reveal something of this little work, as there is some evidence on the surface of earlier structures.

• • •

'CHARLES, HIS FORT'

Pembroke and Charles Forts were separated by the major works on Southampton and Castle Island; they were in effect the outworks of the fortifications on those islands which flanked the channel into Castle Harbour. Charles Fort[56] was probably erected by Governor Moore before 1615, as Butler, who much remarked on his own edifices, made but passing reference to this work.

Charles forte

> ...on the west-end [of the main island] is Tuckers Towne, betweene which and St. Georges are erected thes peeces of fortification followeinge: first, the kings castle, wherin on three plattformes are mounted sixteene peeces of ordinance: nere vpon which vpon a high rock to the southwarde stands Charles his fort, wher are two peeces of ordinance; one of them commandeinge the landinge place vpon the castle, the other playeing of to sea...[57]

John Smith's illustration (Fig. 3.15) is the only early evidence we have for the design of Charles Fort. It shows a small rectangular, single-storey work, mounting two guns, which fire through embrasures. It sits, somewhat fanciful perhaps, on an angular mound of bedrock. However, a photograph taken about 1910 from Castle Island verifies the embrasures and unusual hill upon which Charles Fort sat (Fig. 3.16). The fort happens to be one of the few recorded in the 1899 Ordnance Survey of Bermuda, which shows a rectangular building, about twenty feet by forty feet, with its long side on a north-south axis.

FIGURE 3.15

The purpose of this fort was to cover the boat passage between Charles Island and the mainland, which led to the sheltered bay between Charles and Castle Islands. The guns from Charles Fort could also be brought to bear on the landing place at Castle Island which fronts the bay and faces Charles Island. Other than the fact

FIGURE 3.16: In this view from Castle Island about 1910, part of Charles Fort still stood on a small outcrop of rock (Bermuda Archives, Marriott C. Morris Collection).

56 The fort was presumably named for the third son of James I, who was created Prince of Wales in 1616 and acceded to the throne as Charles I in 1625.

57 Butler, *Historye*, 107.

that in July 1621, Governor Butler 'caused likewise a corne house, for the receipt of the prouision for the garrison, to be sett up vpon that smale iland, wherin standeth Charles his Fort,'[58] little else is known of this fortification, which fell into the sea in the 1960s.

• • •

Kings Castell

FIGURE 3.17

THE KING'S CASTLE

By the 1680s, there were three forts on Castle Island, which lies north of Charles Island and is separated from the mainland at Tucker's Town by a channel but a few yards wide.[59] The island forms part of the eastern perimeter of Castle Harbour and flanks the channel into it from the open sea. This channel, Castle Roads, has direct access to the ocean, unlike the more tortuous St. George's Channel, where ships often had to be warped through, due to its change of direction and shallowness. Castle Harbour was commodious and provided good anchorage, except for the occasional gale from the north-west. It was the premier harbour in the early days of settlement.

It was for those reasons that Governor Moore saw fit to cover Castle Roads in his second act in the fortification of Bermuda. Shortly after making a platform at Paget Fort, he salvaged two cannon from the wreck of the *Sea Venture*, placing one of them on Smith's Island and 'the other he mounted upon a rock which commanded the mouth of the west harbour, called the Gurnetts Head, ther to make a shewe for the time, and to serue in some smale steed, vntill he could prouide better.'[60] Some months later, Moore returned to this task.

> …the company at home, resolueinge vpon a thorough plantation, had rigged up and sent out the *Martha,* with about sixty passengers more, who, in June, an. 1613, came to an anchor in the harbour of St. Georges: the gouernour, at her comeinge, being in employment with his best men in rayseinge some fortifications at the Gurnetts Head…The *Martha* thus gone, the gouernour haueinge made up a certaine fashion of fortification, and planted some ordinance at the Gurnetts Head, to serue for the present, he remoues the most of his men from thence.[61]

It has been assumed that 'Gurnetts Head' was the original name for what became Castle Island, although it could have referred to nearby Charles Island.

58 Ibid., 238.

59 A line of rocks joins the channel to the mainland and it is often said that a causeway was erected on them to Castle Island. There is no documentary or archaeological evidence for this claim. Access to the island seems always to have been by boat, and in the first decades the traffic would have been coming from St. George's, not the mainland.

60 Butler, *Historye,* 26.

61 Ibid., 28–9.

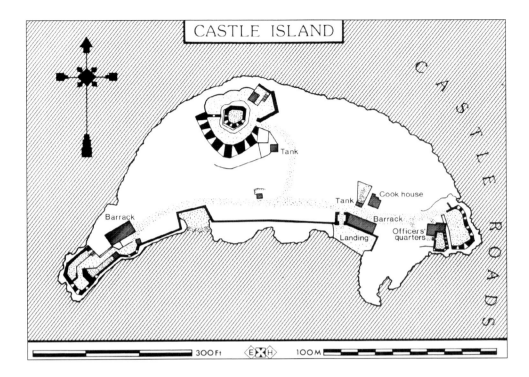

CASTLE ISLAND

Butler, however, confirms the relationship between Gurnetts Head and Castle Island.

> In March 1614, the supply ships, the *Blessing* and the *Star*, arrived in Bermuda. Governor Moore, after taking the names of the immigrants, put them all to work on his projects. Some he sent to 'Gurnetts head' to make a gun platform and build a battlement, which when finished he called the 'Kings Castle.'[62]

The term 'King's Castle' later became a generic phrase for the forts on Castle Island (Fig. 3.18) of which Butler refers to only two: the one fronting the sea was the 'King's Castle' and the second facing the harbour he named 'Devonshire Redoubt.' Opposite the mainland, the third work, which is presumed to have been erected after Butler's departure in 1622, was in place by the 1680s. On the eminence of the island on the site of the later Devonshire Redoubt stood a timber work of unknown dimensions, here called 'Moore's Fort,' which was burnt to the ground just after 'Captaine' Butler's arrival in the *Warwick* in October 1619.

Except through archaeological examination, we may never know the true configuration of Governor Moore's two forts on Castle Island, though it was from one of them, probably the King's Castle, that one of the few hostile acts ever occurring at a Bermuda fort took place.

According to Butler, it was shortly after the departure of the *Elizabeth* in March 1614 that two ships were sighted off Castle Roads, one being towed by its 'skiff,' while sounding the channel with a lead. Only one person on the ships spoke English and Governor Moore therefore concluded them to be an enemy:

> so that the formost shyp being gott up somewhat nere, the gouernour himselfe (who was a very good gunner) makes a shott at randome, and finding that he could reach her, he makes a second shott at her, the which (as it is sayd to haue bin confessed by some that

62 Ibid., 35.

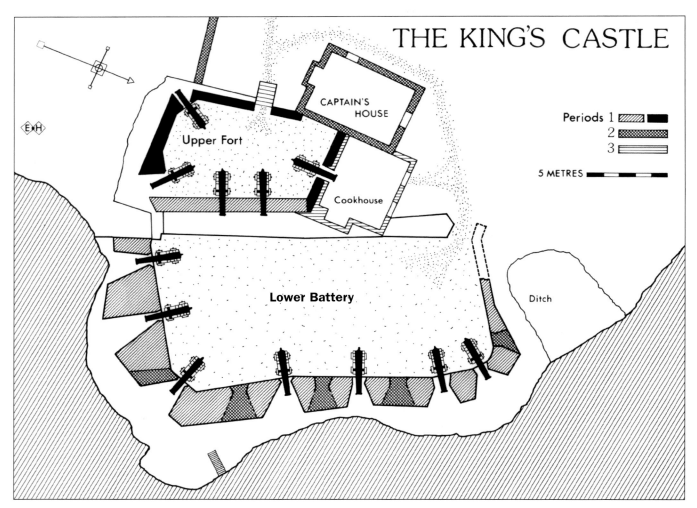

THE KING'S CASTLE

CAPTAIN'S
HOUSE

Upper Fort

Cookhouse

Lower Battery

Ditch

Periods 1
2
3

5 METRES

FIGURE 3.19: The King's Castle was recorded by archaeologists in 1984 to show the arrangement of the major elements of the site.

were in her) passed through and through her. Howsoeuer, certaine it is that vpon that shott, both the shyps, cuttinge their maine-syales, cast about and made quite awaye, and thus ended the fraye.[63]

This was perhaps best for the fledgling colony, for 'military preparedness' at Castle Island amounted to four guns mounted and charged; in addition, 'yet was ther not aboue three quarters of a barrell of powder besides, and one only shott.'[64] Furthermore, in the excitement of battle, it seems that the barrel was spilled under the muzzle of one of the guns which was fired, but by good fortune the gunpowder was not ignited. The Spanish view on the encounter is of interest for its description of the forts on Castle Island.

Captain Domingo de Ulivarri left Santo Domingo for Spain with three naos on 9 February 1614. The naos were loaded with merchandise from Santo Domingo. At the 23° latitude, water was discovered in one of the naos such that it could not be overcome. The people boarded the other two and continued the voyage. On 14 March at the 33° latitude, they woke and found their ships three leagues south of the islands of Bermuda. The captain, knowing that His Majesty desired to know about the English colony, was determined to reconnoitre it. He approached the island from the south until he was in eight fathoms of water. Smoke was spotted on the island and immediately turning towards it, it was found to be emanating from two forts about 100 paces apart. One

[63] Ibid., 31.
[64] Ibid., 32.

FIGURE 3.20: *From the air in 1993, the King's Castle, with its Lower and Upper Batteries and Captain's House, lies to seaward of a barracks and water catchment.*

65 Declaration of Captain Domingo de Ulivarri, Archives of the Indies, Seville, Santo Domingo 272. These accounts are at variance with a report of July 1614 in London, which notes that 'the Governor of the island sent forth a small vessel towards them, to learn what they were, who, perceiving them to be Spaniards, presently returned and advised the Governor thereof, who presently saluting them with a friendly shot of artillery, they rendered him his salute, and instantly retired.' Brown, *Genesis*, 734.

appeared to be built of mortar and stone and the other of wood. They saw people going from one to the other wielding artillery. There were ten to twelve pieces in both forts. One of the ships sailed into the harbour. Thinking the visitors English, the colonists put out in a small boat, stopped a musket shot away, and refused to board. When they recognised the ship to be Spanish, the forts fired. The Spanish left and continued their voyage. The harbour [Castle] on the northern part of the island appeared to divide the island. They sounded the bar and entrance to that harbour which they found to be eight fathoms and a clean bottom. They saw a forested island and lush vegetation. The launches that put out to them were newly built and, they judged, of native wood, because it had very red oars of cedar which is plentiful on that island.[65]

From Butler's account, it seems clear that the wooden fort was the one at the centre of the north side of Castle Island, which later burnt down. The Spanish story may confirm the King's Castle as masonry, making it the second such fort to be erected by the English in the New World. This structure may therefore be the oldest standing English masonry fort in the New World—the 'King's Castle' indeed.

Early in Governor Tucker's administration in the summer of 1616, 'he visited the King's castle at the Gurnetts Head, and appointed one Mr. Stoke, that came ouer with him (being his ancient acquaintance in Virginia, as was

FIGURE 3.21: *An aerial view of the King's Castle from the rear shows the defensive ditch found in archaeological excavations in 1993–6.*

also his wife), to be the prime commander ther, and the title of Lieutenant of the Castle, being the same man, who at this day, by a speciall commission from the Company, holdeth the same command as captaine, which certainely is a charge and place that requireth a very able, sufficient, sober, and trustie person.'[66] Tucker also attended to 'the repayreinge of the decayed platformes in the Kings-castle; whose labour and sweat was for the most part lost and mispent through want of knowledge, good direction, and judgement in matters of that nature.'[67] Very little else seems to have been done during his governorship, or that of his deputy, Captain Kendall, who was in power between June and October 1619, prior to the arrival of Butler, destined to be the third and probably the most active—from a military stance—of the early governors of Bermuda. It is probably largely the later work of Butler which appears in the John Smith view of Castle Island, which earlier buildings 'wer to his smale satisfaction when they wer seene' on the morning of his second day in Bermuda.[68] It was not until late the following year that Butler began to work on the renovation of the King's Castle.

> He at the same time [late October 1620] made three newe carriages for the ordinance in the lower plattforme of the Kings Castle, and spent two dayes ther in cleareing of one of the best peeces which had layne cloyed ouer euer since Captaine Tuckers time, the which, with much difficultie and after many trialls, was at last effected, the shott being much rusted in the concauitie of the peece, and her touch-hole fouly cloyed with peeces of yron.[69] In the beginninge of July [1621], he caused the port-holes of the ordinance in the lower plattforme in the Kings Castle to be repayred and enlarged, that thoes great peeces might the better and with more facilitie be trauersed, and the battlements lesse damnified, which had formerly bin much shaken by being ouer streight. Then and ther also he began to rayse and contriue a stroung and conuenient house of hewen stone for the receipt of the Captaine of the castle and his famely, who formerly had been very meanely lodged and pestred in a poore smale frame, which was nowe turned and fitted to serue for a Corps du Garde.[70]

By mid-1621, the King's Castle had probably assumed the shape illustrated by Smith, recorded by Cunningham in 1811 and, quite remarkably, yet standing

[66] Butler, *Historye*, 77–8.

[67] Ibid., 90.

[68] Ibid., 150.

[69] Ibid., 230.

[70] Ibid., 238. This confirms the date of construction of the 'Captain's House' and its claim to be the oldest standing English house in the Americas.

FIGURE 3.22: *The ruins of the King's Castle overlook a late nineteenth century encampment around the old barracks on the south side of Castle Island.*

in large measure in the mid-1990s. In Smith's drawing (Fig. 3.17), the elements of the fort may be surmised. It had a lower platform for at least seven guns, which was overlooked by artillery on the roof of a small rectangular tower in the rear. To the right of the tower stood a square building with a flat roof, which is assumed to be the house for the Captain of the Castle. Further afield is a small hut, which may have been a stores, magazine or house for the 'Corps du Garde.' This view of 1624 may be measured against a plan of the 1980s (Fig. 3.19), which is in accord with Thomas Cunningham's record drawing of 1811.[71]

The Lower Battery was constructed by the excavation of a platform in the bedrock, with the stone obtained probably being used for the parapet of the work. There is evidence for an earlier arrangement of embrasures, five of which had been blocked up by 1811, at which time there were emplacements for seven cannon. This lower work was entered at its north-west corner. The Upper Battery was not a separate building, as shown by Smith, but was itself hewn out of the rock and surmounted by masonry parapets. There was one embrasure to the north and two facing south on the channel and bay between Castle and Charles Islands, the battery being entered from the west, or landward. Missing in the 1980s, the front, or eastern wall of this redoubt (Fig. 3.20) originally contained four embrasures, giving a total of some fourteen gun positions. The Captain's House, if it is that erected by Butler, was appended to the north-west corner of the Upper Battery and did not interfere with the field of fire from its northern embrasure. By 1811, a cookhouse had been added to the north face of the Upper Battery, and the embrasure became a doorway into its upper floor, the whole being described by Cunningham.

The next points of defence in the district of St. Georges, are the Kings Castle and Fort Southampton commanding the entrance into Castle Harbour. Castle Island on the west side of the entrance is about 270 yards long and 90 yards broad, accessible only on a small part of south side. On the southeast point, two batteries are built one directly above the other. The lower one is well situated and commands the entrance of the harbour; it is in

71 PRO, Cunningham, Defence Report.

a very bad state of repair, the merlons almost in ruins, and only one pine platform remaining in a similar state. There are three 12 and one 18 p^r. mounted. The upper Battery appears to have been formed on the solid rock and is in a very good repair, with a parapet 5 feet high and 3 feet thick. There are three 4 p^{rs}. mounted, but no Platforms.[72]

It is presumed that the hostile action against the two ships of de Ulivarri in mid-March 1614 took place from one or the other of these batteries, since as Captain De Butts, R.E., pointed out in his report of 1798, it would have been very difficult to work both of them to seaward at once.[73]

During archaeological excavations by the Bermuda Maritime Museum and the College of William & Mary in 1993–6, a completely unknown defensive ditch was discovered at the rear of the King's Castle (Fig. 3.21). The ditch runs parallel to the Upper Battery and the Captain's House and thence north to a gap cut in the cliff face next to the entrance to the Lower Battery. Extraordinary deposits of artifacts and faunal material from the second quarter of the seventeenth century have been recovered from the ditch, which is assumed to have been cut before the end of Butler's term of office in 1622.[74]

The batteries are in remarkably good condition, since the island remained military property into this century (Fig. 3.22) and became a National Park in the 1980s. Their significance was recognised as early as 1911, when an Act of Parliament was passed for the preservation of all the forts on Castle Island, although little was done until the 1990s.[75]

· · ·

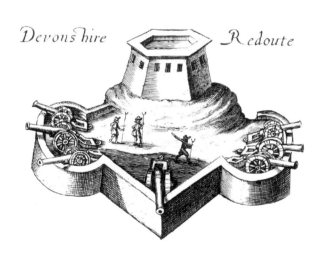

FIGURE 3.23

MOORE'S FORT & DEVONSHIRE REDOUBT

A few hundred feet to the rear of the King's Castle, the ground rises slightly to the highest point on Castle Island. It was here that Governor Moore erected a redoubt in timber, here designated 'Moore's Fort,' mentioned in the de Ulivarri report of March 1614. Of its design nothing is presently known, except that it was still standing when Governor Butler came to Bermuda. Arriving in the 'Earle of Warwicks shyp, called also the *Warwick*,' on October 20, 1619, to undertake the most energetic of the early administrations of

[72] Ibid., 4.

[73] PRO, De Butts, Defence Report.

[74] Norman Barka and Edward Harris, 'The 1993 Archaeological Investigations at Castle Island, Bermuda,' *BJAMH* 6 (1994), 1–80.

[75] *The Historic Buildings Act, 1911.*

Bermuda 'the first act he did as Gouernour was to let them at the towne vunderstande that he was so.'[76] The following afternoon, he invited various dignitaries, including Captain Kendall, who had served as deputy for Governor Tucker in his absence, to the *Warwick*. During these discussions, under the lee of Castle Island, disaster struck Moore's Fort.

> For haueinge bin that morneinge [October 21, 1619] at the Kings-Castle to vewe condition of thoes fortes, which wer to his [Butler's] smale satisfaction when they wer seene, the gunner (with the Gouernours meaneinge, for otherwise it is not likely he would haue suffered it, because he came then but in private) had made ready a peece of ordinance for his farewell, the which at his departure [from Castle Island] he gaue fire vnto; this haueinge done, and being ouer hastie to make after the Gouernour to the shyp, he carelessly left his lintstock with a cole of a match in it vpon the plattforme, the which fallinge downe vpon the plancks, which wer of ceder (and so apt to take fire), it began by litle and litle to kindle, and was not heeded vntill being all on a flameinge fire, word was thus brought to the Gouernour, who instantly, vpon the newes, caused all the botes about the shyp to be manned, and made thether himselfe also in his shalope; but, before he could gett to it, he found that the fire had so generall preuayled on all partes (most of the ordinance being also laden), as noe hope remained of saueinge any thinge, nor of doeing the least good: so that after an houres staye, he returned to the shyp from whence he came; the platforme and carriages of the great peeces being within a while after consumed to ashes: neither did this accident pass without secrett wisperings, and censures of prognostication, the time and place concurringe to augment the credulite.[77]

Moore's Fort must have been a large work, with timbered ramparts or palisades connecting the gun emplacements, otherwise it is difficult to imagine how the burning of a single platform could have affected the others. Archaeological investigations in the 1980s did not reveal any evidence of the design of the structure, Bermuda's only timber fortification.

The loss of Moore's Fort was followed within a month by the loss of the *Warwick* in a hurricane which sent the ship onto the rocks on the south side of Castle Harbour. Undeterred by these adversities, Butler set to work on two new forts, eventually taking guns out of the *Warwick* for their armament, the second work being a replacement for Moore's Fort.

> But in the interim, the Gouernour ther, being cleared from the distractions and impediments of shypinge, goes liuely on with his worcks of fortification; and haueinge fully finished Southampton Fort, he remoues the people to the Kings Castle for the restoreinge of the burnt redoubt and the makeing of a large plattforme vnder it, the which, after eight weekes of hard labour by thirtie men, he absolutely perfecteth; and then planteinge vpon it seuen peeces of excellent ordinance vpon newe cædar carriages, wherwith to playe and commande into all nookes of the harbour to which the aduantage of the site serued very opportunely; he causeth it to be called Deuonshyres redoubt.[78]

This entirely new work appears in John Smith (Fig. 3.23) as a small defensive tower on a pillar of bedrock, overlooking a three-part platform mounting seven guns, as described by Butler.[79] The central salient of the platform is shown as an angular, rather than circular, bastion as were those to its left and right. The central salient is the main difference between the 1624 illustration and the monument itself, which stands (Fig. 3.24) almost as built in late 1620 or early 1621.

The platform, which plays into the harbour, is of three parts, each a curved

[76] Butler, *Historye,* 148.

[77] Ibid., 150–1.

[78] Ibid., 167.

[79] The concordance between the descriptions of the forts in Butler's *Historye* and the illustrations published by John Smith may indicate that it was Butler who drew the diagrams. These detailed drawings would have made splendid illustrations for Butler's text, had it been published at the time: it is tempting to suggest that is exactly what they were for.

FIGURE 3.24: *In this aerial view of Devonshire Redoubt in 1994, Andrew Durnford's work of the 1790s is on the left; the tower of 1621 is in the centre, flanked to the right by its rampart at ground level.*

parapet with embrasures cut out of the bedrock (Fig. 3.25). To its rear, the outcrop of rising land shown in Smith is yet evident, surmounted by a remarkable little tower, partly hewn from the rock and otherwise erected in masonry. The tower had no interior rooms, as suggested by the windows in the Smith diagram, but was a solid block supporting a gun floor at the first storey. It had several embrasures, one of which to the east had a floor of steps, indicating it as the entry, possibly by a wooden ladder. Evidence exists of four other embrasures, but to the north, the parapet has been reduced to a level about one foot above the flagstone floor. Seen in 1811, it was thus described.

> On the North or highest point of the Island, the Castle is situated—an irregular hexagonal Tower from 20 to 25 each side founded on a rough mass of rocks and executed in the rudest and worst manner—'tis about 20 feet high to the top of the Parapet, solid, and the interior of the Parapet (which is *en barbette* towards the harbour) forms an irregular heptagon. There are three 4 p$^{rs.}$ mounted on cedar carriages, and the platform of pine is in ruins.[80]

It is possible that the area *en barbette* was originally an embrasured parapet, giving, upon reconstruction, about eight original gunports. If so, the slighting of the parapet may have taken place in the 1790s, when Andrew Durnford added a considerable work on the south side of Devonshire Redoubt (see Chap. 5).

80 PRO, Cunningham, Defence Report, 4.

70

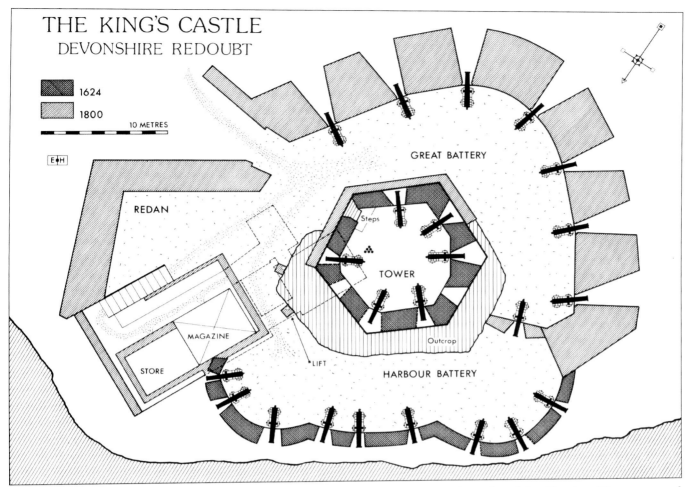

FIGURE 3.25: *Devonshire Redoubt is on the site of Moore's Fort, Bermuda's only timbered fortification. The tower and harbour battery of 1624 were recorded in 1984.*

The importance of the King's Castle, however, was underlined in the first Acts of the General Assembly, or 'Parliament,' which Butler convened on August 1, 1620.[81]

> The third Act was for the necessary mainteninge of the Kings-Castle. The importance of the preseruation and makeinge good of which place, being duely weighed, it was found altogether vnfitt, and a straunge improuidence, to leaue the gard therof, and of three [and] twentye peeces of good ordinance, vnto the care and management of one poore half-blind gunner and his wife, as in former times it had bin; wherupon it was ennacted that twelue able and sufficient men should be continually resident ther, in the nature of a garrison; and that for their foode and entertainement thirtie thousand eares of corne should yearely be raysed, and one thousand waight of tobacco, the which is at the present executed; and the captaine of the castle, together with his famely, commanded by the Gouernour, to be continually in person ther, over and aboue the said number.[82]

From this date, the construction of the existing barracks for such a garrison may be dated and by Butler's account, a house for the Captain was built next to the seaward fort. After 1811, there is scant mention of the three forts on Castle Island, which have survived largely unaltered into present times, representing to a large degree, the works erected by Nathaniel Butler.

• • •

81 'To appreciate the judgement, firmness, and caution evinced by Captain Butler in the conduct of this General Assembly, the reader must remember the entire novelty of Colonial legislation at this time. With exception of the Virginia Assembly of 1619, the proceedings of which had probably not reached Bermuda, as they were only ratified in London in April, this Assembly at St. George's is the first in our Colonial history.' Butler, *Historye*, 203.

82 Ibid., 200.

Southampton forte

FIGURE 3.26

SOUTHAMPTON FORT

The channel of Castle Roads leading from the open sea into Castle Harbour is flanked by Castle and Charles Islands on the south and by Southampton Island a few hundred yards to the north. For that reason, the Bermuda Company had asked early on that the northern island be fortified, so as to defend the channel in concert with the forts on Castle and Charles Islands. Nothing happened until after Governor Tucker held his second Assize in October 1616, but his effort came to nought.

> The Gouernour went, presently after this, to take a vewe of a certain rock lieing in flauncker with the Kings-castle, the which, by an order of court from England, was appointed to be fortified; but findinge a great difficultie in the attempt, both by reason of the badd landinge vpon the place for ordinance, and his owne pouertie of knowledge in thoes affayres, it was quite giuen ouer, and not meddled with [at] all, all his time...[83]

The effecting of the 'Order of Court' thus awaited the arrival of Butler in 1619 and the resulting edifice became, in his eyes at least, his masterpiece, built in the face of several catastrophes, including the burning of the Moore's Fort, the wreck of the *Warwick* and the destruction in a hurricane of Riches Mount on St. George's Island.

> But it seemed that thes straunge and vnauoideable mishaps serued rather to quicken the Gouernours industry than to dull it, so that (haueinge finished the new framed churche, which is a large and hansome one) with the very first of the newe yeare [1620] he begins a newe peece of fortification vpon a rock lieing in flauncker to the king's castle, and excellently commandinge the chanell that leades into that harbour, being a place that at the very first of the plantation, by an Order of Court, was enjoyned to be fortified, yet not ventured vpon vntill nowe, by reason of the great dainger of landeinge of ordinance vpon it, and feare of splittinge the botes. But which (in despight of all difficulties) he found most necessary to be performed, by reason that otherwise, shyps at their entraunce vpon the chanell might shroude themselues so nere and close vnder the high rock of the castle as that they could not be touched with thoes ordinance, which nowe they cannot doe without being played vpon by thes. And to the onsett of this worck, and for the first fourteene dayes, he called all such passengers as wer to passe in that shyp for England, tellinge them that it was fitt and equal that they should doe some publick good ere they went, for he knew not whether euer they ment to doe it hereafter; to the ouersight of which worck (haueing layd it out first with his owne hands) he sent his Lieutenant Captaine Felgate,

83 Ibid., 87-88.

FIGURE 3.27: A plan and elevation of Southampton Fort were drawn by Thomas Driver in 1816. Charles Fort is in the middle distance and King's Castle and Devonshire Redoubt are to the right (Fay and Geoffrey Elliott Collection).

being himselfe constrained to keepe at the towne for the dispatch of the shyp for England...about the 23rd of January, an. 1620, cleares herselfe [the *Garland*] of the harbour, and makes for England: and was saluted at her goeing out with a great peece of ordinance from the newe worck (wher the Gouernour was also in person), that so she might carry the report of it to the aduenturers...[84]

By the *Garland,* Butler also sent his first letters to the Company, in which he pointed out the sorry state of the forts and the lack of munitions. Two further excerpts from his story round out the construction of his new work.

The magazin shyp, the *Garland*, being thus gone, the Gouernour falls closely to his worcks, so that within some fewe weeks the newe platforme is fully finished, and hath fiue good peeces of ordinance mounted vpon it, three wherof wer with infinite toyle, much danger, and some perticuler charge and expence to the Gouernours purse, waighed out of the wrackt *Warwick*. He built for it, also, a smale powder-house of cedar, muskett profe, and in nature of a redoubt, to secure the ordinance; and then honnored the whole peece by callinge it South Hampton Fort.[85] ...The Gouernour is noe soner returned out of the maine to St. Georges, butt he setts twenty men of his owne people on worck at Southampton Forte, the which after six weekes of hard labour is absolutely perfected, and the whole worck shutt in, and ordinance secured, by three smale bullwarcks, two curtaines, and two ravelins: the which not only (being thus putt together) maketh a very fayre shewe out to sea, but is, with all (the naturall site of rock exceedinglie well concurringe) very strong and defensible: being (to saye the truth) the only true peece of fortification in the whole Ilands.[86]

This fort seems to have been completed finally just before Christmas 1621[87] and by good fortune the 'only true peece of fortification' from the first decade of the colony survived into the 1990s much as Butler built it. A comparison of his description with the Smith illustration (Fig. 3.26), a survey made by Thomas Driver in 1816 (Fig. 3.27)[88] and archaeological investigations in the 1980s fill out the picture—'to saye the truth'—of this magnificent work.

Smith's drawing shows a semi-circular parapet fronting Castle Roads, with five guns emplaced *en barbette.* To the rear, a raised courtyard with a rectangular building is to be seen. Beyond that, a crenellated wall with two circular

84 Ibid., 161–2.
85 Ibid., 163.
86 Ibid., 279.
87 Ibid.
88 Bermuda Archives, The Fay and Geoffrey Elliott Collection.

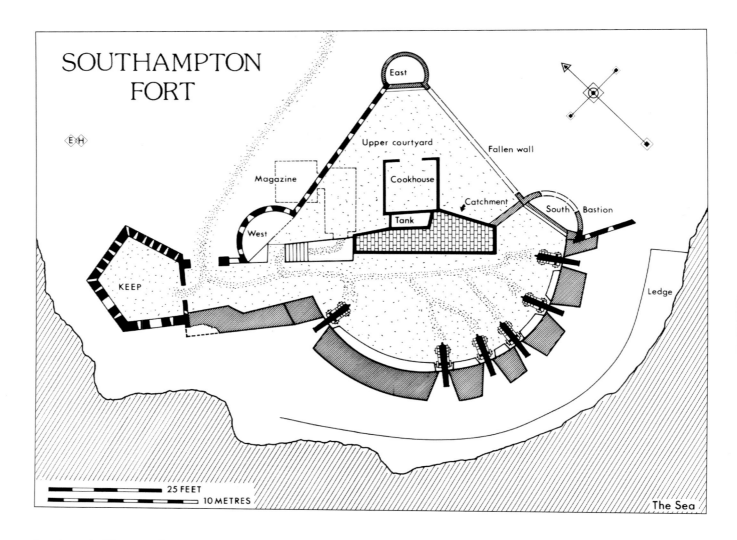

bastions is illustrated, a possible third bulwark foreshadowed by the building. To either side of these landward defences, curtain walls run out to the edge of the island. A section of wall was found on the eastern side of the work in 1984 (Fig. 3.28) and may be one of Butler's 'two curtaines.'

In the interior of the fort, according to Driver in 1816, there was a small elevated watercatch, which fed a tank about the size of a large bath-tub. Between the tank and the central bastion was a square building, with a pitched roof, described as a 'guard room.' This building may have been Butler's 'powder-house,' although it is now made of stone. To the west of this, there was an underground magazine. The gate of the fort was on the landward side to the west: it was flanked by a pentagonal masonry structure, which was roofed by 1811,[89] and contains a series of loop-holes for muskets, yet extant. Until archaeological excavation takes place, it cannot be said as to whether this is one of Butler's ravelins, or a later work.

As in 1816, the gun platform is equipped with six embrasures, interspersed by firing steps against the masonry parapet (Fig. 3.29). Given the presence of embrasures at the King's Castle, it is possible that these embrasures may be from Butler's time, but the Smith drawing shows a parapet *en barbette*. Of the landward defences, with their medieval curtains, bastions and crenellations,

FIGURE 3.28: *Southampton Fort was Governor Butler's masterpiece, having a parapet for six cannon, a water catchment, tank and cook-house in the rear courtyard, enclosed by two curtains and three half-bastions, as recorded in 1984.*

[89] PRO. Cunningham, Defence Report: 'one french 8 pr. has been placed in a Window of the Guard house the roof of which has fallen in.'

74

FIGURE 3.29: Southampton Fort from the air in the early 1990s, looking north.

there is little doubt that these features, recorded in 1816 and 1984, are the standing remains of Governor Butler's masterpiece (Fig. 3.30). Built against a landward attack from the landing place at the extreme north end of the island, the curtains had masonry or timber platforms on which the men could stand and use their muskets. Such a platform is indicated by Driver and in his day, all the features were still standing. By the 1980s, the eastern curtain and the north and eastern bastions had collapsed, although the masonry was laying on the ground in large pieces.

By the beginning of the tenth year of the colony, the Adventurers' Order in Court for the defence of Bermuda was finally brought to fruition by Nathaniel Butler's Southampton Fort, representing elements of the medieval castle, combined with newer ideas for artillery fortifications. Fortuitously overlooked, along with the forts on Castle Island, by the inexorable march of technology and saved from modern depredations by its remote location, Southampton Fort and the works on Castle Island are by a century or more the finest standing defence works of the early English colonisation of the New World.

That these works were erected at all, in the face of much adversity in the establishment of a new life in a distant and isolated island by so few people, says much for the tenacity and enterprise of Governors Moore and Butler. It is possible that we may never know the full extent of Richard Moore's works, as it seems likely that much of what appears in Smith's illustrations of the first English masonry forts in the New World was the handiwork of Butler. By these works he shall be known, but the perspicacity and statesmanship of this

FIGURE 3.30:
Archaeological volunteers at the Keep of Southampton Fort in the mid-1980s; to the right is the musketry platform and crenellated wall of the west half-bastion.

remarkable man can also be found in his speech to the first Parliament at Bermuda, held—'all of them being seated, and in quiett'—at St. George's on the first day of August, 1620.

> Fourthly, we are to endeauour and aime at the good and benefitt of our selues in perticuler. I meane at the generall good and wellfare of the inhabitants of thes Ilands wherin we liue: and herein, in the first place, we are to prouide against the attempts of all forraigne enemies, by secureinge our harbours, and places of accesse by botes or shypinge: and this is done by sufficient fortification, and well manninge of them, as also by makeing of our selues in generall to vnderstand how to defend ourselues, that is to saye, to be soldiers: otherwise, I see not with what comfort we can plant tobacco, and take paines to make it good (as we ought to doe) vnless we prouide to keepe it when we haue it. Me thincks, that euery married man that hath a childe borne to him here should (if it wer but for his childs sake) be ready to keepe it a freeman: and ther is noe earthly meanes to doe it better than this. It may be, some of you conceiue and flatter yourselues that all thinges this waye are well ynough already, and that ther needs noe more to be done than ther is. It is a deceitfull and dangerous apprehension this: and you doe noe lesse than betraye yourselues and your owne safetye by it. You heare by this barke that is newely come in vnto us from England, of the rumours and likelyhoode of great warres in Christian-doome. If it should so fall out that any soudaine breach happen betweene England and Spaine (and who knows how sone this may be), ther is not any place that it will breake out vpon soner than vpon this [island]. The pyrates, likewise, haue a longinge eye after thes Ilands, and knowe well how behoufefull [useful] they would be for them; let us, therfore, so prouide for our selues, that come an enemye when he will, and be what he will, we may be able to giue him a braue wellcome.[90]

Perhaps inspired by this, the people of Bermuda,[91] in spite of the occasional complaint, must have given Butler their full support in view of the number and complexity of the forts erected during his tenure of a little over three years, though some foundation had been made by the previous governors. Butler's strategic overview of the situation by 1622 was that (Fig. 3.31):

90 Butler, *Historye*, 195–6.
91 Estimated in 1620 to be about 1,000 souls.

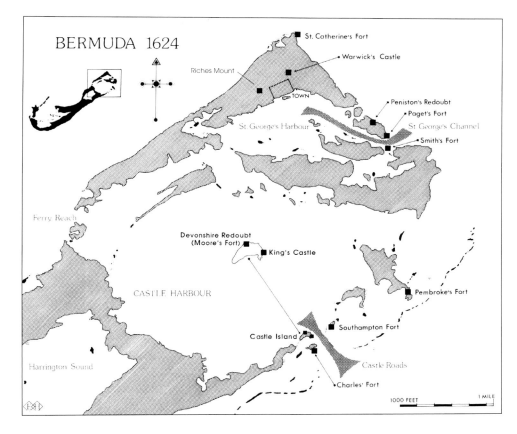

FIGURE 3.31: *A chart of the first ten masonry forts built at Bermuda 1612-22; they were the first such English forts in the New World and mark the beginning of the coastal defence of the British Empire.*

...on the west-end is Tuckers Towne, betweene which and St. Georges are erected thes peeces of fortification followeinge: first, the **kings castle,** wherin on three plattformes are mounted sixteene peeces of ordinance: nere vpon which vpon a high rock to the southwarde stands **Charles his fort,** wher are two peeces of ordinance; one of them commandeinge the landinge place vpon the castle, the other playeing of to sea: then hauve you ouer against the kings-castle, and in flauncker vnto it, **Southampton fort,** wer lie mounted five peeces of ordinance, betweene which and the castle passeth in the chanell that leadeth into the harbour; which is thus secured and played vpon by three and twenty peeces of good artillerye. From hence (the coast trendinge to the north-easte) is Coopers island, wher standeth **Pembroke Fort,** and vpon it three peeces of ordinance: thence passeinge on, more northwards, you come to the harbours mouth of St. Georges which is garded by **Pagett Fort,** and **Smithes Fort,** lieing opposite one vnto another and the channell passeing in betwixt them: in Smithes Fort are five peeces of ordinance: in Pagetts Fort six. About halfe a leauge more inwards into that harbour standeth the towne of St. Georges; which is commanded by **Warwick Fort,** wheron are placed three great peeces: and on the warfe, before the Gouernours house, lie eight more: besides one smale faulcon, planted at the foote of a trianguler frame of timber, made to looke out to the sea for discouery of shyps, called **the Mount,** beinge the warneinge peece of the fortes: and lastly, on the north side of St. Georges island, is erected vpon a rock the smale fort of **St. Katherines,** in garde of a certaine sandy baye; being the same wheron the first that euer landed in thoes partes, first set their feete, and in it are mounted two peeces of ordinance: so that the whole number of great peeces at the present vpon the fortes, and at the towne, are fiftie, many of which are whole culuerins; the rest demi-culuerins, sakers, minions, and some one or two faulcons [**emphasis** added].[92]

Thus by the end of the term of the first Governor, Richard Moore, nine defence works had been erected or begun, not counting the signal station at the Mount. This number increased to ten (mounting forty-five guns) during Butler's tenure, for he built two new works, namely, Southampton Fort, and

92 Butler, *Historye,* 106–8.

Devonshire Redoubt which replaced Moore's timbered fort on Castle Island. On that summary, Butler and Smith are in agreement, but there are the anomalies of the names 'Gates Fort' and 'Penistons Redoute.'

'Gates Fort' was mentioned by John Smith in his list of Moore's forts: 'he built and laid the foundation of eight or nine Forts, called the Kings Castle, Charles Fort, Pembrookes Fort, Smith's Fort, Pagits Fort, Gates Fort, Warwick Castle, Saint Katharines Fort, etc. mounting in them all the Ordnance he had.'[93] Gates Fort is not mentioned by Butler, but it is clear that the 'Pigeon-House' of his account refers to the 'Penistons Redoute' of the Smith map.

It has been claimed that Gates Fort and Peniston's Redoubt are one and the same, but the evidence for such a supposition is too circumstantial.[94] The use of 'Gates Fort' to describe the surviving early eighteenth-century work—in all other sources called the 'Town Cut Battery'—on the south-eastern tip of St. George's Island is certainly incorrect and may ultimately be traced to the restoration of that fort as a tourist attraction in the 1930s.[95] Although he was at Bermuda in 1609–10 as a survivor from the wrecked *Sea Venture*, Sir Thomas Gates had nothing further to do with the island and it is difficult to imagine why his name would be associated with a defensive work at Bermuda. By the time of the publication of Norwood's 1617 survey by Speed in 1627, 'Davers Fort,' ('nowhere mentioned by Butler and apparently added after his departure'[96]) appeared on the site of the Town Cut Battery, presumably named for Sir John Danvers of the Bermuda Company.[97]

Additionally on Speed's map, the site of Peniston's Redoubt has been named as 'Cavendish Fort,' again in honour of an Adventurer of the Bermuda Company—and not for Sir Thomas Gates.[98] The 'pigeon-house' is the only fort not given a name in Butler, which must have presented John Smith, whose history of Bermuda was culled largely from Butler's account, with a problem of nomenclature. He may have solved it in the first instance by adding 'Gates Fort' to his first serial list of the forts,[99] but in his final listing, it is left out, indicating an uncertainty with the name.[100] This uncertainty is reflected in his map, in which the appropriate picture ('G', Fig. 3.2) was not named 'Penistons Redoute' until the second of its three states.[101] Paget Island was for some years known as Penistone's Island and an association with the name of the island and its second fort would have been a natural progression, perhaps given to Smith (after 1624) for inclusion in the second state of his map by someone familiar with Bermuda. 'Gates Fort' is therefore accepted as misnomer produced but once by Smith and may be discounted from the discussion of the first forts at Bermuda.

• • •

[93] Barbour, *Complete Works*, Vol. II, 354.

[94] Alan Mardis, 'A battery on Bermuda,' *Fort* 15 (1987), 21–38.

[95] As late as 'The Town Cut Fort Act, 1922,' no mention is made to 'Gates Fort,' but to 'the old defence work or fortification known as "Pembroke Fort" or the "Town Cut Fort"': Thomas Melville Dill, *Acts of the Legislature of the Islands of Bermuda, 1690 to 1923* (1923), 1384.

[96] Craven, *History*, 99.

[97] The *Dictionary of National Biography* lists Danvers as 'Regicide. Knighted by James I. 1624 had papers of Virginia Company copied and entrusted to the care of Lord Southampton who deposited them at his home at Titchfield, Hants.'

[98] *DNB*. Gates was sent from Virginia to London late in 1610, returning in August 1611, to assume the Governorship. He went back to Europe in 1614 and 'thereafter to the East Indies and died there—nothing is known of his later career.'

[99] Barbour, *Works,* II, 354.

[100] Ibid., 389.

[101] Ibid., 335–7 mentions the three states and reproduces the first. See also Margaret Palmer, *The Mapping of Bermuda* (1983), 24–5.

CONCLUSIONS

The following is a summary of the construction of the first Bermuda forts (1612–22), from south to north.

1. Goat Island, **Charles Fort (by 1615)**: begun by Moore, altered by Butler, 2 guns.

2. Castle Island, **Moore's Fort (by 1614)**: built by Moore, destroyed by fire in 1619.

3. Castle Island, **Devonshire Redoubt (1620)**: built by Butler, 7 guns.

4. Castle Island, **King's Castle (1612)**: begun by Moore, altered by Butler, 11 guns.

5. Southampton Island, **Southampton Fort (1620)**: built by Butler, 5 guns.

6. Coopers Island, **Pembroke Fort (by 1615)**: built by Moore, 3 guns.

7. Governors Island, **Smith's Fort (1613)**: begun by Moore, altered by Butler, 5 guns.

8. Paget Island, **Paget Fort (1612)**: begun by Moore, altered by Tucker and Butler, 6 guns.

9. Paget Island, **Peniston's Redoubt (by 1615)**: begun by Moore, altered by Butler, 1 gun.

10. St. George's Island, **Warwick Castle (1613)**: begun by Moore, altered by Butler, 3 guns.

11. St. George's Island, **St. Catherine's Fort (1613)**: built by Moore, 2 guns.

Between Governors Moore and Butler, eleven works were constructed between 1612 and 1622, one of which was destroyed in 1619. Of the ten extant in 1622, the following was the state of affairs in the 1980s: Charles Fort had fallen into the sea due to erosion in the early 1960s; the King's Castle 'battlements, that to this daye lie out vpon the mouth of the harbour'[102] still did; Devonshire Redoubt and Southampton Fort survived largely intact; Smith's and Paget Forts and Peniston's Redoubt existed as archaeological sites, with little standing masonry; and Warwick Castle and Pembroke and St. Catherine's Forts were presumed to have been destroyed. Extraordinarily, this means that more than half of the first ten masonry fortifications constructed by the English in the New World at Bermuda have survived, albeit in various states of preservation.

The Spanish were very aware of the fortification of Bermuda and received a summation of the situation in 1620 by a Flemish pilot, Simon Zacharias, who 'has made two voyages to the said islands and had lived there for more than six months.'[103]

The major settlement is called New London [Town of St. George] which he says has some 400 colonists. It has an oblong harbour. The beach and island which the Spanish call La

102 Butler, *Historye,* 35.

103 Archivo General de Indias, Indiferente General 1528, Letter from Diego de Mercado and Simon Zacharias to the Crown. Santiago de Guatemala, January 7, 1620.

Bermuda is the larger of the islands and is six or seven leagues in length and a league and one-half or two leagues in width. The English call this island Tierra Firme and Cabeza del Condestable.[104] This island has the main [Castle] harbour where all the ships destined for this island enter, secure and anchor by way of a narrow but good entrance [Castle Roads] as is shown on the map. It is closed with a chain.[105]

The entrance to this port has three islets [Castle, Charles and Southampton Islands] nearby. The distance from one to the other would be eight hundred strides. One is on each side and one in the middle of the entrance as is shown on the map.[106] The two islets flanking the entrance each have two small fortresses with upwards to fifty pieces of cast-iron artillery that would be of twenty to thirty quintals each. In total there are five towers[107] with upwards to 160 men in garrison and artillerymen. The majority of the soldiers bear arms, and half of those are pressed into service because of crimes they committed and desire their freedom. They were exiled to the garrisons.

As previously mentioned, the entrance to the port has a heavy chain which closes the port. There is no city or town, except for the dwellings of soldiers of the garrison, on the main island. There are herds of swine and cattle. It has few prairies. Other than grazing animals, they take advantage of the cedar wood and send it, along with palm wood, to England.

To the left of the entrance is a hill towering over all five of the fortresses where a platform could be easily constructed.[108] The platform would strengthen the five fortresses; the fortresses are more important for the island's defence, as shown on the map.

The second fortified island [St. George's] is where the town of New London [St. George's] is located. The island has the same name as the town. It is two and one-half or three leagues in length and one league in width. It has a port and a shallow harbour. Its entrance is to the Northeast and is eleven feet deep, deep enough for small ships. At the entrance it has three small fortresses with fifteen pieces of cast-iron artillery and, in each tower, thirty or forty soldiers and artillerymen could be garrisoned.[109] The fortresses are supplied with men from the town of New London which is located about a league away. The town has four hundred citizens as stated previously which are all English, and in the city itself, there are three small fortresses which have eighteen pieces of cast-iron artillery of twenty quintals. These fortresses do not have soldiers garrisoned in them and guarding them, because the citizens themselves garrison them. Small ships anchor in front of these fortresses. There are two other small towers on this island. One is on the north-east coast on the bay and the other is on the north coast, as shown on the map.[110] Ships up to fifty or sixty tons can enter the bay. There are two or three pedreros and another very small piece of artillery in the extremely small tower of the fortress located on the north coast. A Master Baver, an English gentleman, lives in the tower. There are no other fortifications in any of the other islands. All the fortifications are of little consideration and very weak, because the limestone from which they are constructed is not strong. This limestone is almost like hard mud. The stone is very soft and could be breached with few rounds of fire, especially if heavy artillery were used.

Ushered in by the wrecking of the *Sea Venture* in 1609, the English involvement at Bermuda in the years to the end of the reign of King James I in 1625 saw its settlement by the Virginia, later Bermuda, Company. The colonisation was a private venture, funded by shareholders in England who expected a return on their money. This they obtained by way of land grants which comprise the original division of Bermuda into plots demarcated by Richard Norwood in his survey of 1616–17. Monetary profits were elusive, given the expenses for public works such as the forts, and with the exception of tobacco, the inability of Bermudians to produce cash crops.

The fortifications were a company matter; until the American War of

[104] Literally, the 'rock of the master gunner,' presumably Castle Island.

[105] The chain must have run between Castle and Southampton Islands: there is no other record of this defensive feature.

[106] According to Jonathan Bream, whom I thank for the translation, the map is lost.

[107] A total of five 'towers' may indicate that Southampton Fort was underway and that the Landward Fort (see Chap. 4) at the western end of Castle Island had also been started.

[108] Possibly the highest hill on the Tucker's Town peninsula where Fort Bruere was later constructed to that end (see Chap. 4).

[109] Namely, Smith's and Paget Forts and Penistons Redoubt.

[110] The three 'fortresses' at the town are presumably Warwick Castle, the Mount and the guns on the Square; St. Catherine's would be to the 'north-east on the bay,' but the north coast tower suggests another work not otherwise known.

Independence went against the English, the Crown had little military interest in Bermuda. The situation changed significantly in 1783 and is recorded in the history of the later fortifications. The first Bermuda forts were almost a family affair, put together with a little expertise and much hard work by the settlers who numbered less than a thousand souls in the first decade of the colony. The design of the forts is dissimilar from developments in continental America and represents the beginning of the coastal defence of the British Empire.

As seen in Chapter One, the forts at Puerto Rico, Roanoke and the Popham settlements, are within the European bastioned tradition. These works were composed of timber and earth, both easily obtained. Masonry forts, other than at Bermuda, did not occur for some decades, due to the expense of stone-working. At Roanoke and James Fort, an adaptation to local circumstances seems to have developed with some of the forts designed against the bow and arrow, not cannon and gunpowder. It is here that some have suggested a comparison with the fortified 'bawns' of Ireland under English colonisation.[111] With the possible exception of the rear part of Smith's Fort, the bawn example is not applicable to the Bermuda works.

None of the other American works compare well with the early Bermuda situation, for here there were no natives and no stockaded works. For whatever reason, there were no bastioned works in the island until the dockyard defences were erected in the 1820s. Instead, the Bermuda forts seem to return in part to an earlier era, that of the coastal defences of England under Henry VIII. The towers and rounded parapets at Devonshire Redoubt and Warwick Castle, along with the crenellated walls and rounded bastions at Southampton Fort can be related generally to the castles at Deal and Sandgate in Kent.[112] The four large forts, namely, Paget, Smith's, Southampton and the King's Castle all have a feature not found in the typical angular bastioned work. Each has a semi-circular gun platform adapted to the site, with the exception of the King's Castle where the platform follows the irregular natural limits of the site. These bulwarks stand free and clear with no ditches or earthen ramparts and outworks. They are largely offensive works, designed to pound the enemy's ships with as much iron as they could bring to bear in a limited context.

Perhaps Richard Moore and Nathaniel Butler had experience on the Henrican coastal forts in southern England. Perhaps impressions of such fortifications were translated to the Bermuda scene, considerably reduced in scale. At the same time, the forts, especially the citadel of the King's Castle— the strongest fort in Bermuda until the nineteenth century—were made to fit the site, organically, as the modern architect might say. These fortification patterns laid down in the first decade of the Bermuda colony persisted into the eighteenth century, as will be seen in the following chapter.

111 Paul M. Kerrigan, *Castles and Fortifications in Ireland 1485–1945* (1995), 57–84.

112 Edward C. Harris, 'Archaeological Investigations at Sandgate Castle, Kent, 1976–9,' *Post-Medieval Archaeology* 14 (1980), 53–88.

On the archaeological excavation at Bailey's Bay Battery in 1991: (standing, from left) Joe Rego, Amy Kowalski, Linda Abend, Lark Lombardo, Susan Kessaram, Mike Phillips; (kneeling, from left) Patricia Samford, Carolyn Copeland, Frances Copeland.

The Later
Colonial Works

1 6 2 3 – 1 7 8 2

But the defects of Art are abundantly supplied by Nature, who has in a manner Palisaded the Islands all round with inaccessible rocks, in most places three quarters of a mile from the Beach.
—Simon Fraser, R.A., 1806

IN THE PREVIOUS CHAPTER, THE FIRST ELEVEN BERMUDA FORTS WERE EXAMined in some detail, with the information of military activity in the first decade of the colony based mainly upon the *Historye* of Nathaniel Butler, the map published in 1624 by Captain John Smith, and archaeological information gathered from 1981–95. This chapter deals with the structures thought to have been erected after Governor Butler's time but before the end of the American War of Independence. They are presented as if on a geographical itinerary with a military officer, although some sites are chronologically out of period (Fig. 4.1).

These forts fall into the period after the end of the first decade of settlement and before the end of the War in 1783. During this time, the Spanish continued as the foremost enemy, with the French not far behind. A thousand miles from the Bahamas and further still from the other British West Indies possessions, Bermuda was not involved in the land skirmishes and sea battles of that area. As long as 'sugar was king,' the emphasis on British military fortifications in the Americas was in the West Indies and magnificent works such as Brimstone Hill Fort in St. Kitts were not duplicated in Bermuda. Rather the settlers, although under the crown upon the dissolution of the Bermuda Company in 1684, continued to build their own small and primitive variety of fortifications throughout the islands.

A discussion of the forts built in the seventeenth century and up to 1783—and many there were—should begin with an examination of the evidence in

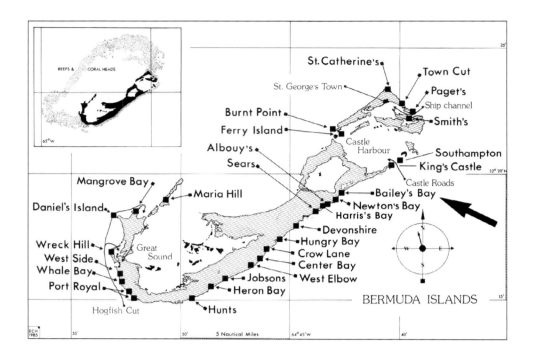

St. Catherine's

Town Cut

St. George's Town

Paget's

Ship channel

Burnt Point

Smith's

Ferry Island

Castle
Harbour

Albouy's

Sears

Southampton

King's Castle

Castle Roads

Mangrove Bay

Bailey's Bay

Maria Hill

Newton's Bay

Daniel's Island

Harris's Bay

Devonshire

Wreck Hill

Great
Sound

Hungry Bay

West Side

Crow Lane

Whale Bay

Center Bay

Jobsons

West Elbow

Port Royal

Heron Bay

Hogfish Cut

Hunts

BERMUDA ISLANDS

REEFS & CORAL HEADS

5 Nautical Miles

FIGURE 4.1: From 1612 to 1783, almost the entire south and west coasts of Bermuda were fortified, though not all the forts are represented in this drawing.

the surveys and maps of Richard Norwood, an important figure of the first decades of Bermudian history.

RICHARD NORWOOD
SURVEYOR OF BERMUDA

In 1614 at the age of twenty-three, Richard Norwood arrived in Bermuda to take up pearl fishing, although he was already a teacher of mathematics and navigation. Due to a disagreement between Governor Moore and another man, Norwood took up the survey of Bermuda, including dividing it into eight 'tribes,' or parishes. No manuscript chart has survived from this survey, but the late Jeannette D. Black, Curator of Maps at the John Carter Brown Library, has suggested that 'this must have been the map used by Captain John Smith as the central part of an engraved plate illustrating the section on Bermuda in his *Generall Historie*'[1] (Fig. 3.2). That chart is referred to as Norwood's first survey. Black also thought that the 'views of Saint George's and the forts cannot be Norwood's because they represent a situation later than his departure from the islands,' although this would only partly have been the case, as a number of the forts were probably little changed from Governor Moore's time.[2]

A few years later, Norwood was asked by Daniel Tucker, the second Governor of Bermuda, to undertake a detailed survey and division of the tribes into shares of 50 acres. Begun around late August 1616, the work was completed in April the following year, his second survey. Neither the original map, nor his 'Book of Survey,' which Norwood took to England around May 1617, have survived, but a copy fortunately appeared in print in 1627 and 'became one of the best-known maps of any part of America in the seventeenth century' (Fig. 4.2).[3]

[1] Jeannette D. Black, *The Blathwayt Atlas, Volume II: Commentary* (1975), 152.

[2] Ibid., n. 13. As suggested in Chap. 3, these views are probably the work of Governor Nathaniel Butler, not John Smith.

[3] Ibid., 152-3.

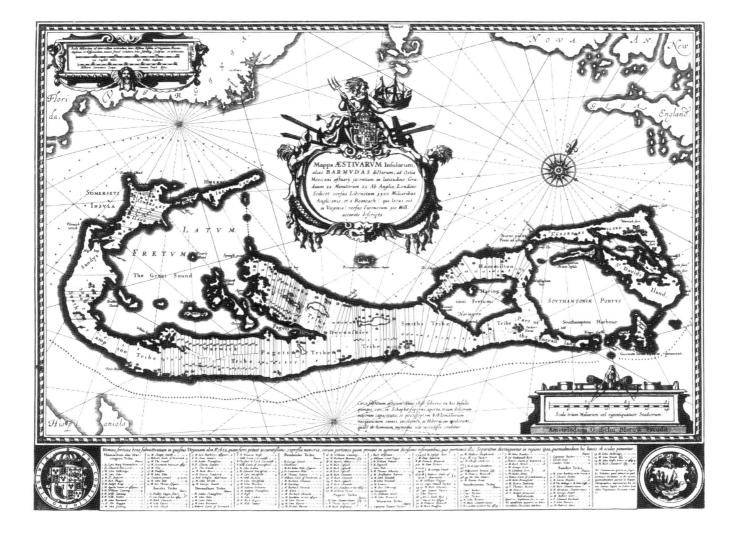

FIGURE 4.2: Richard Norwood's second survey of Bermuda was published in 1627, with the island divided into shares granted to those listed at the bottom of the map.

4 J. H. Lefroy, *Memorials of the Discovery and Early Settlement of the Bermudas or Somers Islands 1515–1685* (1981), Appendix XV.

5 The Blathwayt Atlas was reproduced in facsimile by the John Carter Brown Library in 1975.

After an absence of two decades, Norwood returned to Bermuda as a schoolmaster, where he died in 1675. A third survey, completed in 1663, was commissioned by the Company in London. The chart of this survey was never published, but one of the two original vellum maps is to be found in the Bermuda Archives, as is the survey book. The last contains detailed descriptions of the shares of land and was published in 1879.[4] The second original map, sent to England, appears to have survived as a copy of 1678 by Thomas Clarke and found its way into the 'Blathwayt Atlas,' one of the prized possessions of the John Carter Brown Library (Pl. 4).[5]

Norwood's surveys of 1617 and 1663 contain some information about the early forts. The Clarke and Bermuda Archives maps list only Paget, Smith's, Southampton and Charles Forts and the King's Castle and in this the survey book of 1663 concurs. The 1617 survey, appearing as a printed map in 1627, had been revised in 1622, as indicated in the text giving the names of the shareholders in each parish. Norwood was probably responsible for the additions, since several of the forts therein do not agree with Butler or John Smith descriptions. Those that appear in all four sources are Warwick Castle, Paget, Smith's, Pembroke and Charles Forts and the King's Castle, all of which would have been in existence during the 1617 survey. Changes of name occur in the

85

1627 version, with 'Cavendish Fort' for Peniston's Redoubt and 'Sandys Fort' standing in for St. Catherine's, the locations of these agreeing with Butler's account. Missing on the 1627 map is any named reference to Butler's two new works of 1620, Devonshire Redoubt on Castle Island and Southampton Fort on nearby Southampton Island, but the last called 'Moores Iland' has a symbol for a fort on it.

An anomaly for the eastern coast on the 1627 map is the appearance of 'Davers Fort' on the eastern tip of St. George's Island. This is the only known reference to such a fort, which, if it existed, was not counted in the 1663 survey. Later documentary evidence records the building of 'Town Cut Battery' on the site of Davers, or Danvers, Fort in 1700, but makes no mention of an earlier work. The other anomaly found in the 1627 map is the presence of cannon at six locations on the south and west coast of the main island: these positions are not found on Norwood's 1663 maps, nor are they mentioned in the 1663 Book of Survey. Butler makes no reference to any works on the main island of Great Bermuda, yet each of the cannon is found on the site of a fort known from later sources or from archaeological data.

The cannon symbols may represent forts; if so, they may be dated to 1617, the time of Norwood's survey, or at least to the first decade of settlement. Alternatively, they could have been added to the map as late as 1626, when it was engraved by Abraham Goos of Amsterdam 'to be sold by George Humble in Pops-head against the Exchainge. Ano 1626.'[6] The location of the guns on later fort sites may indicate that Norwood was responsible for placing them on this map, either from his 1617 survey, or from precise information given to him by people from Bermuda in the early 1620s.

From east to west, the guns are located on the south shore of Great Bermuda in the following shares: Smith's Tribe, share 3, western end, on the land of William Payne; Devonshire Tribe, share 6, on the land of Francis West; Paget's Tribe, share 9, on the land of Christopher Barron; Warwick Tribe, share 23, on the land of Daniel Tucker; Southampton Tribe, share 8, on the land of Sir Nathaniell Rich, and in the same Tribe, share 11, west central, on the land of George Scot. By the time of the 1663 survey, these lands were in the possession of Samuell Newton (Smith's, share 3), West's was divided between John Long and 'common land' (Devonshire, shares 7 and 8), Barron's passed to 'Leiftennant Collonell John Hinde' (Paget, share 28), Daniel's Tucker's lot belonged to Capt. George Tucker (share 23), excepting a six-acre 'parcell of common land lying at ye west end of Great Turckle bay' (Warwick, share 26), Rich's territory became that of Richard Hunt (Southampton, share 18) and the Scott property was in the hands of Thomas Murrell (Southampton, share 27).

None of the Book of Survey entries of 1663 makes any mention of forts on these lands.[7] As each gun position occupies a place where a fort is now known to have existed (excepting the two westernmost sites), the question of continuity could be answered by the assumption that they had been in existence since the very early days of the colony, as possibly inferred from the Speed map of 1627. The four eastern positions were occupied in due course by Albouy's Fort, Devonshire Bay Fort, West Elbow Bay Fort, and at the western end of

[6] The map was published in John Speed's atlas, *A Prospect of the Most Famous Parts of the World,* in 1627. It remained in print for fifty years and was copied in Amsterdam by Blaeu, Hondius and Jansson.

[7] Lefroy, *Memorials,* Appendix XV.

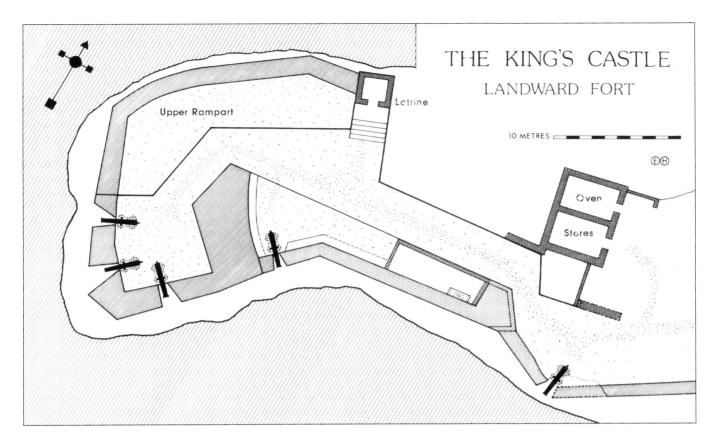

THE KING'S CASTLE
LANDWARD FORT

Upper Rampart

Latrine

10 METRES

Oven

Stores

FIGURE 4.3: The Landward Fort on Castle Island was recorded by archaeologists in 1984, the main battery fronting Tucker's Town Point is in the lower left.

Warwick Long Bay, Jobson's Fort. The two westernmost sites may be placed too far east and probably represent Church Bay East and Whale Bay Forts. It is therefore possible that some of the forts discussed in this chapter could date to the first decade of the settlement of Bermuda. Until archaeological excavations are carried out, it is difficult, faced with the paucity of early documentary references, to date these sites with any precision.

However, the general trend is obvious: after coping with the exigencies of protecting the new town and settlement at the eastern end at St. George's Island, the colonists on Great Bermuda undertook to fortify their own backyards. Small redoubts of varying shapes and dimensions were erected on most of the landing places afforded by the beaches of the South Shore. In looking at these 'mainland' features, it is appropriate first to examine the third fort on Castle Island, which fronted and protected that isle from a landward attack from Great Bermuda. This discussion will then proceed westward along the southern coast, up the west coast, over to the western end of St. George's Island, finishing the circuit on St. David's Island.

LANDWARD FORT
CASTLE ISLAND

At the south-western tip of Castle Island, there yet stands a small redoubt fronting Tucker's Town Point. Its position as a rearguard bulwark against an attack on Castle Island from the mainland is obvious. Several types of stonework indicate at least three periods of development.

FIGURE 4.4: *The Landward Fort from the air in 1994; the latrine is the small building in the centre foreground and the main battery is on the right.*

The first period consisted of a lower battery of three guns, two facing the mainland, the third firing into the bay towards Charles Island (Fig. 4.3). This was recorded by Simon Fraser in 1783.

> The nixt Battery, is on the south East end of the Rock, Consists of two Guns, & fronts a point of the Main land On the Opposite side, about a 100 yards from it, several Rocks interspersing, between some of which, small Boats can pass, from Castle Harbour, out to sea without Going threw the Ship Channel, this Battery Appears to me but of little consequence, as the Ground on the Opposite side is much higher...[8]

Westward and above the battery, a curving rampart for guns firing over the parapet connected the battery with a small masonry building of the type commonly called a 'buttery' in local architectural terminology (Fig. 4.4). The buttery at the Landward Fort proved to be a covered latrine, with the slots for a wooden seat still preserved in

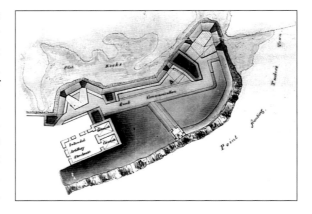

FIGURE 4.5: *This plan of the Landward Fort is one of the few in existence of the many which were drawn of the forts by Andrew Durnford, R. E., and his assistants in the 1790s (Bermuda Library).*

the stonework. To the east, the battery was linked to a curtain wall running along the southern side of Castle Island, ending at a gateway and barracks near the King's Castle. Within the fort, the curtain was pierced by three embrasures for cannon to fire into the bay towards Charles Island. Two of these were located in a small bastion by the entrance to the fort, and the third on a platform behind a parados, which formed the rear wall of the lower part of the battery.

The fort was entered from its northern end, through a defile cut out of the bedrock on one side and defined by a building, probably a cook-house, on the curtain wall of the other. Before the entrance, there once stood a barrack building, now perhaps only an archaeological feature, but a vaulted storage room and adjacent bread oven survive. A plan of the fort from 1794 by Andrew Durnford's assistant is in the Bermuda Reference Library (Fig. 4.5) and shows

[8] Scottish Record Office GD/50/185/267/12/7. Simon Fraser, Report on the Defences of Bermuda, 1783.

these features, excepting the barracks, which was not yet erected.

The fort was examined in 1811 by Thomas Cunningham, R.E., whose report is the last known description of the site: it was 'an irregular Battery, mounting one 12 and two 6 p^{rs} on good cedar platforms, and one 4 and two 9 p^{rs} on pine platforms, in a bad state. There is here a small Barracks and store for the artillery.'[9] Dating the construction of the Landward Fort will have to await archaeological excavation or the discovery of new documentary sources, although there is some suggestion from records in the Bermuda Archives that the Landward Fort was in place by the 1680s.

The forts on Castle Island remained in use until they were superseded by the new works of the 1820s on Paget and St. George's Islands. For a few years, they would have been overlooked by Fort Bruere on a nearby hill in Tucker's Town, erected in a strategic position suggested in 1620 by the Flemish pilot, Simon Zacharias, in a report to the King of Spain.

• • •

FIGURE 4.6: *Fort Bruere stood on a high hill to the east of Tucker's Town and commanded a wide beach to the south and the land approaches to Castle Island (drawn by Heather Harvey).*

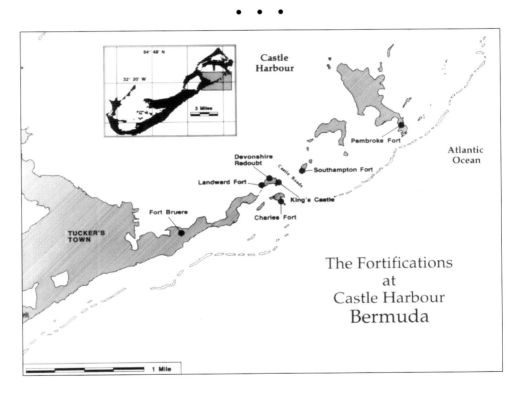

FORT BRUERE

The run of forts on the southern coast of the main island of Great Bermuda begins with Fort Bruere, on a hill just east of the site of the undeveloped 'Tucker's Town' (Fig. 4.6).[10] Fort Bruere was the last battery to be built by the local population. It is mentioned but a few times, being noted in the 1783 survey made just at the end of the American Revolutionary War by Simon Fraser of the Royal Artillery. In discussing the Landward Fort on the western tip of Castle Island, he argued that

> this Battery Appears to me but of little consequence, as the Ground on the Opposite side is much higher, And of course must command it, that seems to have Accured to the Governor & Assembly, for about half a mile further in on the land, they have Begun a

9 PRO WO 55/1551/2. Thomas Cunningham. Report on the Defences of Bermuda, 1811.

10 The name is a slight misnomer as the town was never developed.

FIGURE 4.7: *Looking north from the air, Fort Bruere is on the hill to the left, now occupied by the rectangular patio, to the right of that is the overhang protecting the door to the magazine.*

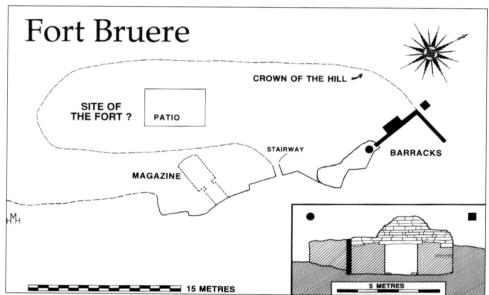

FIGURE 4.8: *The main features of Fort Bruere were recorded in 1995 and comprised an underground magazine, a small building, and traces of the fort on the hill above (drawn by Heather Harvey).*

Work of fashines [Fort Bruere], on the Highest ground there, but like all the publick Works, belonging to these Islands, is given over before tis half finished, most of the Designs of this kind here, being ill laid out, and wers Executed, from this bad management, the people are discouraged, from voting money for publick uses...[11]

The position of Fort Bruere is marked on the survey of Bermuda made by Andrew Durnford and his assistant, Henry Lauzan in 1793,[12] having been described by the former during his first time in Bermuda in the late summer of 1783 (Fig. 4.7).

The Castle and Tucker's Town Point are Separated by a Channel full of sharp Rocks about 150 yards over, and the Point is above a mile long forming the West [*sic*, south-east] Side of Castle Harbour and is a Succession of Hills. A small Oval Redoubt was begun during the War on the Top of the highest of these Hills, at about a Mile from the Castle, in order to prevent an Enemy's approaching this Point, and to command some Small Bays near it. This Work was intended for a *Barbette Battery*, but being placed injudiciously and raised

11 SRO, Defence Report. Simon Fraser completed three surveys of the defences of Bermuda, in 1783, 1806 and 1808.

12 PRO MPH 137. A Survey of the Islands of Bermuda by Captain Andrew Durnford, Royal Engineer, assisted by Mr. Henry Lauzan, Draughtsman, 1793.

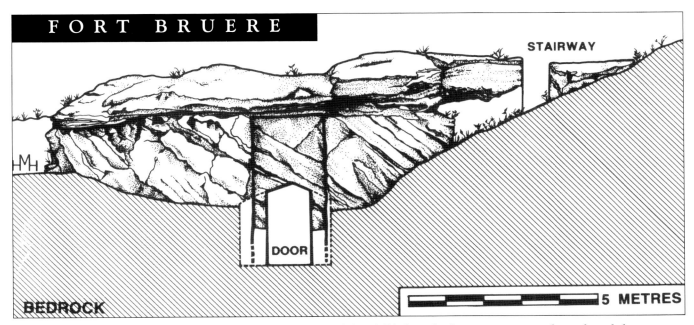

FORT BRUERE

STAIRWAY

DOOR

BEDROCK

5 METRES

FIGURE 4.9: *The magazine at Fort Bruere took advantage of the cliff below the fort; it is cut into the rock and the entrance was protected by an overhang of natural rock (drawn by Heather Harvey).*

in the front so high, as to cover an Enemy at the foot of it, I am of Opinion, A Redoubt is necessary at this Place for this purpose above mentioned, but that this Work should be levelled, and the Redoubt more retired.[13]

Nothing came of this plan and it would seem that the fort fell into ruin after the War, its construction attributed to Governor George James Bruere (1764-80) and his son, George, Lieutenant Governor, 1780–85.[14] An examination of the area in 1994 found what could be the stones of a fascined work, strewn in a circular pattern on the crescent of the hill looking out over Surf Bay (Fig. 4.8). A ruined building nearby could be part of a military accommodation, but the undeniable military structure is a fine magazine cut into the hillside and protected by an overhang of natural rock. The magazine was partly filled with sand, as were the steps leading down to it (Fig. 4.9). A house now occupies the eastern part of the hill, but the site of the fort seems to have survived largely intact.[15]

• • •

BAILEY'S BAY BATTERY

A mile to the south of Castle Island and half a mile from Fort Bruere stood Bailey's Bay Battery, upon a cliff of ragged rocks to the east of which is a small beach (Fig. 4.10). The site is mentioned in a return of 1783 as 'Tucker's Town Battery,' the officer giving the rationale for the placement of forts along the southern coast.

Thus I have mentioned all the Fortifications, from the South east End of the Islands Kings Castle, To the Ferry which is the north west, a Curve of Ten or eleven miles, but as there is other places, that are called works, (tho' Very improperly), [I] Shall likewise mention them, they are situated on the south Side of the Island. I shall first mention the natural strength and then the artificial, all along the south side of the Island, runs a reef of Rocks, about 150 yards from Highwater mark, they continue for upwards of 16 or

[13] PRO CO 37/38. Andrew Durnford. Report on the Defences of Bermuda, 1783.

[14] In August 1775, gunpowder was stolen from the magazine near Government House in St. George's and delivered to the American rebels. With good reason, Governor Bruere suspected more thefts of this sort by a faction of Bermudians, so in October 'He persuaded Captain Tollemache of the *Scorpion* to take the precious cannon on board and carry them away at his departure. Thus Bermuda was left without any defenses of any sort.' Wilfred Brenton Kerr, *Bermuda and the American revolution: 1760-1783* (1995), 53.

[15] I am indebted to Mr. and Mrs. Ross Perot, who kindly allowed Professor Norman Barka and me to look at the fort on their property. Heather Harvey drew the illustrations.

FIGURE 4.10: Bailey's Bay Battery is located to the left of the house in the centre and overlooked a cutting in the reef to the south and a landing beach to the west.

eighteen Miles, these Rocks are not Broad and flat, as in most Places, with sholes near them, they rise like a spire or steeple, one End of a ship may be on the rocks, and at the other end, fifty fathom water, all along these Brakers, vessels of any draught of water, may come alongside of them, within hail of the shore, there are Several Creeks and Bays, with small openings, between Cliffs of the Rocks, where Boats of four or five feet Draught of water, can come and land on the sandy Beach, the Works above mentioned are intended to prevent that.

I shall take them in their turn, beginning with that Two miles south of the Castle, from the point of the Main, opposite the south east Battery, formerly mentioned—The name of 'tis Tuckerstown Bay Fort, Here are Two six pounders, without Carriages side Arms or ammunition, the Guns much honey combed, there's no Embrasures, nor works here of any kind. There's a sandy Beach with a passage for Boats as Before mentioned.[16]

The fort does not appear in the 1798 survey of the local militia, but was mentioned by the Royal Engineers that year: 'The first of these Sea batteries is distant about a Mile West of King Castles called Bailey's Bay Battery consisting of a smale Guard House loop holed, enclosed by a Parapet and mounting three 6 Pdrs on a good Cedar Platform.'[17]

A final reference to Bailey's Bay Battery was in the Cunningham report of 1811, which refers to 'Bailey's Bay Battery, about two miles and a half west of the Castle Island. 'Tis a semicircular work, with a magazine in the rear…and commands this Bay and the only opening thro' the reef, where however, but one boat can pass at a time. There are two 4 pdrs mounted on cedar carriages and a cedar platform, but not in good condition.'[18]

Although the site remained in military hands until the 1920s, later references to it in the documentary records are scant. In 1928, 'The Old Battery'

16 SRO, Defence Report.

17 PRO WO 55/1551/1. Augustus De Butts, Report on the Defences of Bermuda, 1798.

18 PRO, Cunningham, Defence Report.

FIGURE 4.11: *The bottom course of the wall of the south-west corner of the magazine at Bailey's Bay Battery was found in archaeological excavations just outside the conservatory of "The Old Battery," a private home.*

FIGURE 4.12: *Archaeologists found the bottom course of stonework associated with the parapet of Bailey's Bay Battery in 1991, as well as the south-west corner of the magazine. (Drawn by Patricia Samford.)*

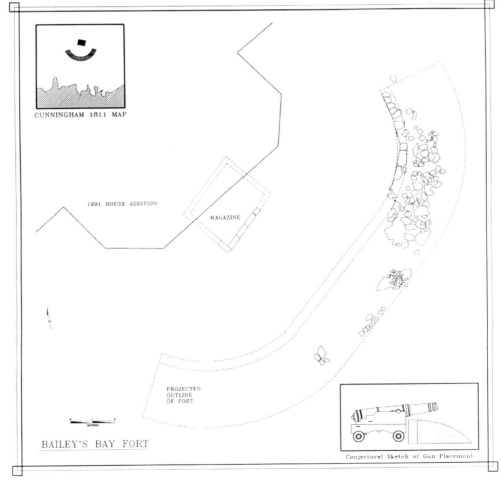

CUNNINGHAM 1811 MAP

1991 HOUSE ADDITION

MAGAZINE

PROJECTED
OUTLINE
OF FORT

BAILEY'S BAY FORT

Conjectural Sketch of Gun Placement

became the site of a stately home for Charles Blair Macdonald, designer of the nearby Mid-Ocean Golf Course. In 1992, during the rebuilding of the house, an archaeological excavation took place to ascertain what, if anything, could be found of the original fort.[19]

Immediately below the turf, sections of the lowest course of stonework for the semi-circular parapet and the magazine were uncovered, along with an array of artifacts from the eighteenth to the early twentieth century.[20] No conclusive dating material was found for the construction of the fort, but the magazine appears to have stood into the first years of this century. Only one corner of the magazine was found (Fig. 4.11), which is in accord with the small rectangular building shown in the Cunningham plan.

The fort itself proved to be a parapet with faced-stone interior (Fig. 4.12), fronted to the sea by a bank of rubble and earth, described in 1806 as 'two feet high and three feet thick, with earth thrown up against it.'[21] Behind this low mound would have stood the two guns mentioned, but by 1806, they were replaced by two English 6-pounders, the 'two 4 Pounders formerly mounted here were left at Tucker's Town Bay in the Autumn of 1805.'[22] Twenty-three years after his first survey, Simon Fraser gave a fuller description of this position.

> The Carriages are all of Wood for these Guns and are in a Serviceable State, the Platforms are Cedar both Plank and Sleepers, and in good repair. There are Six Rounds of Ammunition prepared for each piece of Ordnance on this Work, which are well secured (in a Serviceable Magazine) and in a good state. The Side Arms (the Spunges excepted, they only want coating) and Stores for the whole of the Ordnance in the Fort are complete and fit for Service. They with the Ammunition are kept in a small house or Magazine in the Rear of the Work. A Mr. Thomas Wood has the charge of the whole, as the Person that held the Commission as Captain, is lately dead, and his successor is not appointed. In case of Emergency the Guns are to be manned by the Militia, for there are no Artillery men Stationed at any of the Works West of the Ferry, as there are no Barracks or places of accommodation for men at any of them. The intention of Erecting this Work was to command a chasm in the Rock, called Pinder's Cut. Having mentioned the Shoals, it may not be unnecessary once for all to attempt (though very imperfectly) some description of them, as it's in consequence of the Rifts or openings in the Rocks, that the present as well as the Works that are to be mentioned have been built, and though they are places of no importance whatever, being untenable, for there is not one of them but what would be carried by a Boat's Crew in Ten minutes: But the defects of Art are abundantly supplied by Nature, who has in a manner Palisaded the Islands all round with inaccessible rocks, in most places three quarters of a mile from the Beach.[23]

In the 1870s, the South, or Military, Road was constructed from Tucker's Town to Church Bay in Southampton, incorporating the northern extremity of the Bailey's Bay Battery land into its path. It is possible that the site was in use as a mobile gun position from the 1880s, along with others such as West Elbow Bay.[24] Two guns were found on the site in the late 1980s, but were probably unconnected with its military use. One had a spike in its muzzle, for use as a pivot for a gun emplacement and bore the Tudor Rose and Crown cipher. The other was a 40-pounder Rifled Breech Loader of 1864, now at the Dockyard Keep, and the object of a major restoration.[25]

• • •

[19] Bermuda is indebted to Helen and Richard Fraser of 'The Old Battery' for their support of the excavations. The remodelled house included the footprint of the fort and two replica guns were installed in 1993 on the line of the original parapet.

[20] Amy Kowalski and Patricia Samford. 'The Excavations at Bailey's Bay Fort, Hamilton Parish, Bermuda,' *Bermuda Journal of Archaeology and Maritime History* 4 (1992), 1–19.

[21] PRO WO 928. Simon Fraser, Report on the Defences of Bermuda, 1806.

[22] Ibid.

[23] Ibid.

[24] Bermuda Archives. Defence of Bermuda and Construction of the South Coast Road 1853–1890.

[25] The RBL was given to the Bermuda Maritime Museum along with funds for its restoration by Helen and Richard Fraser.

FIGURE 4.13: *Newton's Bay Fort was located just to the right of the large house in the centre foreground; to the left is John Smith's Bay which it covered.*

NEWTON'S BAY FORT
(HALLS BAY FORT)

Less than a mile westwards from Bailey's Bay Battery is the site of Newton's Bay Fort, on the eastern shoulder of John Smith's Bay (Fig. 4.13). The fort is possibly the one mentioned in a return of March 9, 1756 as 'Hamilton [Parish] Fort,' having two six-pounders.[26] It appears by name a few years later as 'Jeremiah Peniston Commander, consisting of two Guns, which want Scaleing and Tarring; the Carriages insufficient; the Platform in bad order.'[27]

In his survey of 1783, Fraser lists this work as 'Half a mile south'—presumably from Bailey's Bay Battery—calling it

> Halls Bay Fort, Here are two Guns of the same size [6-pounders], and in the same Condition, without Carriages side arms or ammunition, Nor is there the smallest appearance, of a work of any Kind, the guns lying on the Rock, the hight of this is much the same with ~~Newtons~~ Harris's Bay Fort from the water, with a sort of a Beach at each of them…[28]

Little else is known about this site,[29] which may have been re-built in the 1790s, but was overlooked in the important survey of 1811 in which many of the forts were illustrated by scale drawings. It was recorded on the Ordnance Survey of 1899 as a half-moon redoubt. In the 1980s, only the south-west boundary stone of the site indicated the presence of the redoubt, as the area had been built upon.

• • •

ALBOUY'S FORT
(PINDAR'S BAY FORT)

Albouy's Fort was a short distance south along the coast from Newton's Bay Fort. Probably situated on the bluff above what is now Albouy's Point (Fig. 4.14), it may be 'Pindar's Bay Fort' of two guns, seen in an inspection report-

[26] Bermuda Archives. Map Drawer #5. If so, the fort would have been in Smith's Parish.

[27] Minutes of the Governor's Council, May 13, 1762.

[28] SRO, Defence Report. Fraser had difficulty with his listings for Halls, Newton and Harris's Bay Forts, with Newton's crossed out on several occasions. Taking his distances as correct, Newton's is the same as Halls Bay Fort at half a mile from Bailey's Bay Battery.

[29] In the Durnford Papers in the Bermuda Archives, there is reference in 1793 to a payment to 'John Albouy for building a Fort & opening Trenches etc., at Newton's Bay': this may refer to repairs at either Newton's Bay Fort or the nearby Albouy's Fort.

FIGURE 4.14: Albouy's Fort would have been located on this part of the south coast near the place called 'Albouy's Point' (left foreground) on the 1899 Ordnance Survey of Bermuda.

ed to the Governor in Council in May 1762. It is recorded in local and military surveys of 1798 as

> Albouy's Fort in barbet to the Eastward of the above, mounting two nine pounders, has a stone platform. This Fort commands two Bays, one to E'ward and the other Westward, and two more cannon will be useful, another battery is necessary on the high bluff on Hinson's Land to protect the intervening Bays.[30] The next is Harris's Bay Battery [*sic*] distant three quarters of a Mile [from Bailey's Bay Battery] cut out of the Rock for two 9 Pounrs with a Guard House, Platforms &. This Battery defends the aforementioned Bay where it is possible Boats might land after having got within the Breakers.[31]

In 1806, Albouy's was erroneously called 'Harris's Bay Fort' in the Fraser report, but a location three-quarters of a mile from Bailey's Bay Fort was stated, confirming its position.

> Is a straight Wall or Breast Work, twenty four feet long, two high, and three thick, with earth and rubbish thrown up against it. Commanded by a Captain Albouy.

> In this Fort are mounted the following Ordnance Viz: Guns—9 Pounders—2 English all of which are serviceable.

> The Carriages are all of Wood for these Guns, and in a Serviceable State. There are no laid Platforms either of Wood or Stone, and the Rock is so soft and loamy there is no traversing the Guns. Neither is there any Ammunition or Side Arms for these Guns. When the old unserviceable Ordnance were withdrawn in the Autumn of 1805, none of the Ammunition etc. for these Guns could be accounted for, though there is a serviceable Magazine for securing it. For that reason Governor Gore would not allow any to be sent for those now in the Fort.

> The Captain is a seafaring man, and often from home. What makes so many desirous of being appointed Captains of Forts is that it exempts them from Carrying Arms in the Militia. But as to faithfully discharging the duties annexed to the Command, is the least of their intention.[32]

While the descriptions of this fort do not entirely agree, the presence of the

[30] *Bermuda Historical Quarterly* 24 (1967), 134–9.

[31] PRO, De Butts, Defence Report.

[32] PRO, Fraser, Defence Report. Fraser's description for 'Harris's Bay Fort' in his survey of 1783 and 1806 are contradictory and must refer to Albouy's in the former and Harris's Bay Fort in the latter.

two nine-pounders may confirm that they refer to the same site, since it is unlikely that the guns would have been much moved about. At three-quarters of a mile from Bailey's Bay Battery, the fort would have been located at Albouy's Point in Smith's Parish but no evidence of it can be found on that coast. Clearly a work firing *en barbette*, its construction seems to have been similar to Bailey's Bay Battery, though a straight wall, rather than a semi-circular arrangement is suggested. Overlooked in 1811, no topographical survey or map of this battery seems to have survived.

• • •

HARRIS'S BAY FORT
(HARRIET'S BAY FORT, SMITH'S TRIBE FORT)

Albouy's Fort was halfway between Bailey's Bay Battery and Harris's Bay Fort, the next in line.

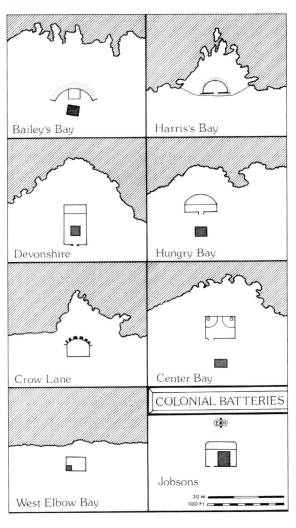

FIGURE 4.15: *Thomas Cunningham, R.E., recorded many of the small coastal batteries in his survey of 1811. Harris's Bay was the second of these on his east to west itinerary (for Jobsons read Warwick Fort; redrawn by the author).*

33 SRO, Defence Report.

34 PRO, Cunningham, Defence Report. Cunningham's confusion over the names may have arisen from a misunderstanding that some of these forts were named for the parishes, not a particular bay. The difficulty over names was noted in 1783: 'the whole is divided Into nine Parishes who have different names, sometimes They are called by one name, and sometimes by another, They are as follows, St. Georges, Baylies bay, Harris's Bay, Brackish pond, spanish point, this is so called from the Spaniards landing here first on this point, Crow Lane this parish takes its name from a great number of Crows being found here by the first settlers, Heronbay, Port Royal, and Sommerset, so term'd after Sir George Sommers' (SRO, Defence Report).

About a mile & a half south, from Tuckerstown Bay Fort, is ~~Newton's~~ Harris's [substituted] Bay Fort, here are likewise Two 6 Po[rs] unserviceable, without side arms or ammunition, Here are two Garrison Carriages wth Iron trucks, wants Very little repairs, to make them good carriages, the Work is hewn out of the rock, has no Embrasures nor Magazine, with a Pole standing by way of a flag staff the Work stands on a Rock 30 feet above the surface of the water…[33]

The next is Harris's Bay Battery, also semicircular, cut out of the rock, distant from Bailey's Bay about a mile and a half. In it is mounted an unserviceable French 8 pdr but without platform, guard house, or magazine. The object for which this Battery has been erected I could not discover, as Harris' Bay is nearly half a mile from it and commanded by Devonshire Fort.[34]

Separated by twenty-eight years, these reports see a change from two 6-pounders to a single 8-pounder, but otherwise appear to be discussing the same site. This may be the site called 'Smith's Tribe Fort' in the return of 1756, when two six-pounders were emplaced, or it may be the 'Harriet's Bay Fort, Jona Redding late Commander, consisting of two guns' of the Minutes in Council, May 13, 1762. As the crow flies, one and a half miles from Bailey's Bay Battery would land one at 'Spencer's Point,' a spit of land forming the eastern side of McGall's Bay. This promontory accords with the 1811 drawing of the fort (Fig. 4.15) and is the last projection of the coast until Harris's, or Sue Wood's, Bay proper is reached, the disparity between the name of the fort and the bay of the name being noted by Cunningham above.[35] Along with Newton's and Albouy's, all evidence of Harris's Bay Fort would seem to have been lost on the ground, although in this instance, it was recorded as a small half-moon battery by the Cunningham report.

• • •

SEARS FORT

A reference to this small work, located on what is now Pokiok Farm (Fig. 4.16) almost due south of St. Mark's Church, Smith's Parish, was made in the survey by the Bermudians in 1798. It is a short distance west of Spencer's Point, the site of Harris's Bay Fort.

> Sear's Fort in Smith's, of an half moon form in barbet, mounting one six pounder and a good carriage, has a platform. A Magazine is not necessary. This Fort is situated in a place difficult of access from the high cliffs and rugged coasts it was intended to defend.[36]

It appears to have been built by the Bermudians about 1793, when Durnford records a payment to 'William Sears for Land and Expences in building a Fort at Walkers Bay, Baileys Bay Parish.'[37] Sears Fort, if built in the 1790s, could not have been seen by Simon Fraser in 1783, when he surveyed Harris's Bay Fort.[38]

Sears Fort was recorded in the 1980s by an archaeological team (Fig. 4.17). While the site earlier caused confusion with Harris's Bay Fort, being nearby and of similar shape, they are separate structures. The fort was built of blocks of soft Bermuda stone and was partly cut into the bedrock on the seaward side. Several courses of

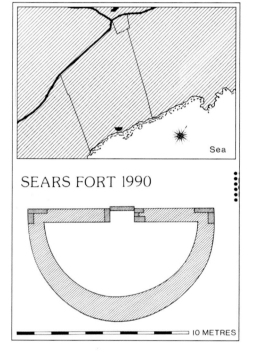

SEARS FORT 1990

10 METRES

FIGURE 4.16: *Spencer's Point, the presumed site of Harris's Bay Fort is the promontory on the right of this plan of the coastline, with Sears Fort depicted in the centre.*

FIGURE 4.17: *Sear's Fort was a small D-shaped redoubt on the south coast, seen from the air in the early 1990s.*

[35] One of these descriptions led earlier to the erroneous conclusion that Harris's Bay Battery was one and the same as 'Sears Fort.' Recorded in 1783, it seems that Sears was not built for another decade and it sits on a straight piece of coastline, although in shape a half-moon. See Edward Harris, 'Bermuda defences at the end of the American Revolutionary War,' *Bermuda Journal of Archaeology and Maritime History* 1 (1989), 96.

[36] PRO CO 37/47. Col. Jennings, Report on Defences of Bermuda, 1798.

[37] Durnford Papers.

[38] I am indebted to Owen J. J. Rogers and the late Rohan S. Sturdy for their assistance in surveying Sears Fort and to Lt. Col. Brendan Hollis for information relating to this work.

stonework have survived and it had an entry in the middle of the rear wall (Figs. 4.18 and 4.19). Its purpose was to serve as a central battery in the defence of the coast between Spencer's Point and the headland at Devonshire Bay.

FIGURE 4.18: *The parapet of Sear's Fort as it appeared after clearing of vegetation in the late 1980s, looking seaward and south-east.*

FIGURE 4.19: *The entrance to Sear's Fort was in the centre of the rear wall, seen on the right.*

DEVONSHIRE BAY FORT
(BRACKISH POND FORT)

As the 1811 survey notes, Harris's Bay itself, at the border of Smith's and the westerly Devonshire Parish, is adjacent to Devonshire Bay (Fig. 4.20). On the western side of the latter bay stood the small Devonshire Fort, referred to in the return of 1756 as 'Devon Fort' and mounting two six-pounders. In 1783, it was found to be

> Three miles west from this [Bailey's Bay Battery] (for we are now past the south Point) is Devonshire Fort, so called from the Parish in Which 'tis, this Work is hewn out of the Rock, stands on a Promontory, about fifty feet above the water, here is a Small Bay, where

FIGURE 4.20: *Devonshire Bay Fort is located under the overgrowth on the central peninsula with Devonshire Bay to the right.*

fishing Boats goes out and in, here are two 6 Po^r looks tolerably well, with Canvas apron Has two good carriages with Iron Trucks here is a watch House and Flag Staf no side arms nor ammunition For the Guns...[39]

In the local survey of 1798, it has become 'Watch House Fort in Devonshire, commanded by Capt. George Harvey, is of a square form *en barbette* and defends Brackish Pond Bay, mounting four nine pounders proved and has a good cedar platform and a very good Magazine.'[40] In the then-fashion of the Bermudianisation of the original Parish name, by 1806, the stylish 'Brackish Pond' Fort was in vogue.

Is a Straight Wall or Breastwork, fifty feet long, two high and three thick with earth and rubbish thrown up against it, exactly similar to this last mentioned [Albouy's]. Commanded by a Captain Harvey. In this Fort are mounted the following Ordnance Viz: Guns—12 Pounders—2 English all of which are serviceable. The Carriages are all of Wood for these Guns and are in a Serviceable State. The Platform of Wood, both Plank and Sleepers are Cedar and in good repair. There are six Rounds of Ammunition prepared for each Piece of Ordnance on this Work, which are well secured (in a Moveable Magazine) and in a good State. The Side Arms (the Spunges excepted who want coating) and Stores for the whole of the Ordnance in this Fort are complete and fit for Service. They with the ammunition are kept in a small house or Magazine in the rear of the Work.[41]

By 1811, the name had reverted to Devonshire Fort and in that guise was surveyed by Cunningham, whose accurate plan survives (Fig. 4.15). At that time, the armament of two twelve-pounders was unchanged. The fort was a squarish redoubt, with a parapet for firing *en barbette* and a central magazine. In 1984, an archaeological project found several of these features, and ascertained that the fort was slightly cut into the bedrock. The foundations of the magazine still existed, but all trace of the parapet had been removed. No excavation took place, but the features were largely evident after clearing the site of trees and undergrowth; the site is now a National Park.

• • •

39 SRO, Defence Report.
40 PRO, Jennings, Defence Report.
41 PRO, Fraser, Defence Report.

FIGURE 4.21: *Hungry Bay in Paget Parish could have provided a landing place and safe anchorage for a fleet of lighters from warships.*

HUNGRY BAY FORT

The next redoubt, a mile to the west from Devonshire Fort, stood on the eastern side of the mouth of Hungry Bay in Paget Parish (Fig. 4.21). This fort was missed in the 1783 Fraser survey and that of DeButts in 1798, but in the latter year it was recorded by the local militia.

FIGURE 4.22: *The remains of Hungry Bay Fort were recorded in 1990 by archaeologists from the Bermuda Maritime Museum.*

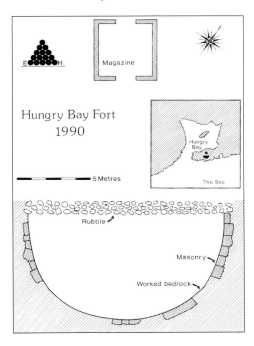

Hungrey bay Fort [was] Commanded by Capt. Francis Trimingham is of an half moon form in Barbet and requires to be backed with Stones and Earth, the platform is of Stone, and wants a Magazine. This Fort is mounted with two twelve pounders Cannon proved—the rings on the Axletrees of the Carriages are decayed—the Carriages are otherwise good.[42]

Similar to others on this coast, the fort had a parapet of eight-inch stone, two feet high and thick, with earth banked against it (Fig. 4.22). The guns were mounted in 1794 and eight years later, Capt. Trimingham was still in command and a magazine appears to have been added (Fig. 4.23).

The Carriages are all of Wood for these Guns, and are in a serviceable State. The Platform of Wood, both Plank and Sleepers are Cedar and in good repair. There are sixteen rounds of Ammunition for each piece of Ordnance in this Work which are well secured (in a moveable Magazine) the Powder good but the Paper Cartridges are much eat by the Cockroaches. The Side Arms (the Spunges excepted that want coating) and the Stores for the whole of the Ordnance in the Fort are Complete and fit for service, and with the Ammunition, kept in a Small House or Magazine in the rear of the Work.[43]

Unusually, a painting exists of one of these small south coast forts and shows the magazine with two storeys (Fig. 4.24).[44] The guns were unserviceable by the time of 1811 survey. Thereafter the fort passes from mention in

42 PRO, Jennings, Defence Report.

43 PRO, Fraser, Defence Report.

44 I am indebted to Mr. and Mrs. Robert Tucker for allowing me to record this fort and to Mr. and Mrs. Durham Stephens for the photograph of the Hungry Bay Fort painting.

FIGURE 4.23: *Hungry Bay Fort and its magazine to the rear still stand in the 1980s, as seen from the air looking seaward.*

military surveys, but due to its remoteness on a small promontory, protected at the rear by a mangrove swamp, it has survived. It was surveyed in 1990 but no archaeological excavation has taken place, which might date its construction.

• • •

FIGURE 4.24: *One of the few known paintings of a south coast fort depicts the two storeys of the magazine at Hungry Bay Fort with its gabled roof (courtesy of Durham Stephens).*

CROW LANE FORT
(NEW PAGETTS FORT)

On a small parcel of land, now a National Park, at the eastern end of Elbow Bay, was the easternmost of three forts which guarded its long beach (Fig. 4.25).[45] Variously called, this structure, some 50 feet above the beach, was for a time named for 'Crow Lane,' otherwise Paget, Parish. In a return of 1756, as New Pagetts Fort, it mounted four guns, two each of 6- and 3-pounders,[46] and was commanded by James Dickinson, the guns 'want scaleing and Tarring.'[47] The earliest structural description is from Andrew Durnford's survey of 1783, which recorded it as 'semi-circular...sunk in the Rocks with Seven Embrasures, but only 4 guns.'[48] A more fulsome view was supplied near the turn of the century.

> Pagets Easternmost Fort Commanded by Capt. William Lightbourn has Embrasures for Seven Guns, it is mounted with two six pounders, and one supposed a nine pounder, proved, and good Carriages, and one proved Cannon dismounted and a good Carriage belonging thereto. This Fort requires a Magazine, that will serve for the other Fort, the embrasures of this last Fort had best be filled up and constructed in Barbet by building a wall with large block Stones, four feet within the outer one, and the intermediate spaces filled up with Earth, and the front part backed with Stones and Earth, there are plenty of proper stones for the purpose on the adjoining Beach. It is necessary to observe that these Forts were designed to defend a long Bay, the most accessible of any other part of the Southside Coast, by reason that Ships of burthen can anchor within half a mile of the Shore, and therefore should be attended to.[49]

[45] I wish to thank Dr. A. C. H. Hallett, former President of the Bermuda College and Mr. William Mulder, General Manager of the Stonington Beach Hotel for information on Crow Lane Fort.

[46] PRO CO 37/18. Inventory of March 9, 1756.

[47] Minutes in Council, May 13, 1762.

[48] PRO, Durnford, Defence Report.

[49] PRO, Jennings, Defence Report.

FIGURE 4.25: Crow Lane Fort was located on the rise above the end of the beach on the left hand side of this aerial view of the 1980s.

By 1806, it was known as East Elbow Bay Fort, in the command of a Captain Butterfield. The strengthening of the walls seems to have taken place, but 'from no Guns being fired here, they are not shaken.' The guns had been upgraded to two 12-pounders, but the ammunition was kept two miles away 'at the Speaker of the Assembly's Store in Crow Lane.' This was the site 'marked on the map Crow Lane Battery' by Cunningham five years later (Fig. 4.15).[50]

Nothing could be seen of the original Crow Lane Battery above ground in the 1980s; without archaeological investigations its exact position cannot be proved. The site is overgrown, but the upper parts of several concrete expense magazines of the 1880s are to be found. These would have served a mobile battery of guns, probably brought from Prospect Camp near the City of Hamilton, and are also found at the rear of West Elbow Bay Fort.

• • •

CENTRE BAY FORT
(MIDDLETON'S BAY FORT)

Halfway along Elbow Beach was the aptly named Centre Bay Fort, so noted by Durnford in 1783 as 'half a mile east [of West Elbow Bay Fort] is another Small Battery, quite open with one Gun,' although Minutes in Council for 1762 refer to it as Middleton's Bay Fort, mounting a six-pounder in 1756 (Fig. 4.15).[51] The fort was rebuilt about 1802,[52] which must explain the presence of guns on traversing carriages. By 1806, it was in the charge of Captain Godet with two French 36-pounders, and in an unkempt state.

> The Carriages are all of Wood for these Guns and are in a Serviceable State. (In 1801 they cost the Public of Bermuda Two Hundred Pounds, Sixteen Shillings and some pence Currency). There is no Platform, as the Carriages may be said to be both Carriage and Platform, being so constructed as to traverse with the greatest ease in every direction. There are ten rounds of Ammunition prepared for each piece of Ordnance in this Work, which are well secured (In a Moveable Magazine) but never being aired, the Paper Cartridges are much eaten by Vermin. The Powder is good. The Side Arms and Stores for the whole of the Ordnance in the Fort are complete (Spunges excepted the wool having dropped off) and fit for service, are, with the Ammunition, kept in a Small House in the rear of the Work, which serves as a Storehouse or Magazine.[53]

When seen by Cunningham in 1811, these guns were on traversing platforms—the only fort on this coast to have such elaboration— in a rectangular enclosure 40 feet by 30 feet, the magazine to the rear being 7 by 12 feet. The guns were also the largest mounted in any of the South Shore forts.

The site of Centre Bay Fort has not been located. It may be buried in an area of active sand dunes, or conversely has been destroyed in the building of a major hotel.

50 PRO, Cunningham, Defence report. To the contrary, his surviving maps mark it as 'East Elbow Bay Battery.'

51 Minutes in Council, May 13, 1762 and PRO CO 37/18.

52 PRO CO 37/52. I am grateful to Dr. A. C. H. Hallett for this reference.

53 PRO, Fraser, Defence report.

FIGURE 4.26: *In this aerial view of the Coral Beach and Tennis Club, West Elbow Bay Fort can be seen just to left of centre next to the main building.*

WEST ELBOW BAY FORT

The western extremity of Elbow Beach was guarded by West Elbow Bay Fort, which was probably the site of two guns (6-pounders in 1756) mentioned in 1762 under the command of William Brereton (Fig. 4.26).[54] The site may be of some antiquity, as a drawing of a cannon, taken to depict a fort, appears on Share 9 of Paget Parish in Norwood's 1617 survey.[55] West Elbow Bay may therefore be one of the earliest forts to have been built on the main island of Bermuda. At the end of American hostilities in 1783, it was 'a Small Battery sunk in the Rock, quite open in the Rear for two Guns, and a little Building in the East Angle for a Magazine' (Fig. 4.27).[56]

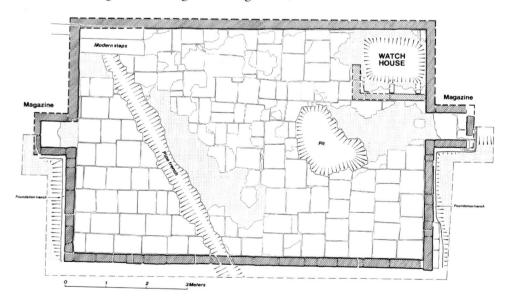

FIGURE 4.27: *West Elbow Bay Fort was recorded in 1989 and had a flagstoned floor, two expense lockers and a magazine in the rear (drawing by Fred Aldsworth).*

[54] Minutes in Council, May 13, 1762 and PRO CO 37/18.

[55] F. G. Aldsworth, 'Excavations at West Elbow Bay Fort, Paget, Bermuda,' *BJAMH* 2 (1990), 61–70.

[56] PRO, Durnford, Defence Report. Fraser in 1783 mentioned a gun buried in the sand off this site, probably that often reported on the beach after storms.

It may be necessary to observe that great reliance is placed on this and the two last mentioned Works—Viz: Centre Fort and East Elbow Bay Fort—by the inhabitants in this part of the Island. Opposite to them for the space of nearly three miles, is most Excellent

FIGURE 4.28: The flagstoned floor of West Elbow Bay after archaeological excavations; the small arched expense locker is in the centre of the side wall.

FIGURE 4.29: This is the continuation from Figure 4.15 of Cunningham's 1811 itinerary of the south and west coast forts (for Heron Bay read Jobson's Cove Fort; redrawn by the author).

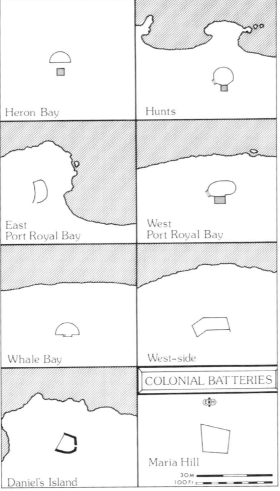

Anchoring Ground for Vessels of any draught of Water outside of the Shoals. In the Centre Work are placed the heavy Guns, on the East and West Sides are the Flanking Batteries, and some Experiments made by General Beckwith in 1801 from the 36 Pounders [in Centre Fort]. It was ascertained that the situation of ships in that Anchorage would be very hazardous, as the Shot reach much further than where Vessels usually anchor.[57]

A few decades ago, a hotel was built in the area, but West Elbow Bay Fort was retained as a ruin. Thus it was possible in 1989 to carry out the first archaeological excavation on one of the South Shore batteries. The original walls of the fort were uncovered and to the east and west, they incorporated a small expense locker (Fig. 4.28). Evidence for the magazine recorded by Cunningham was found in the flagstone floor of the redoubt. No artifacts were found which would assist in dating the construction of this fort.[58]

A small carronade, probably a 12-pounder, was located at the site and remounted in 1990. The walls of the fort were restored and the original flooring, not removed in the excavations, was covered for protection with modern paving stones. West Elbow Bay Fort thus became the only South Shore battery to have been restored and on view to the public.

[57] PRO, Fraser, Defence Report.

[58] Aldsworth, 'Excavations…' Bermuda is indebted to George and Claudia Wardman and the Coral Beach and Tennis Club for their restoration of West Elbow Bay Battery in the 1990s.

• • •

WARWICK FORT
(WATCHHOUSE OR HERON BAY FORT)

Two miles from Elbow Beach lies another long strand facing Great Turtle Bay, now Warwick Long Bay. By 1762, 'Warwick and Jobson's Cove Forts, John

Darrell Commander, consisting of five Guns' were emplaced at the east and west ends of this beach. That to the east went under the name of Warwick Fort, or the Watchhouse Fort.[59] Its exact location is not known, but it was probably on the rocky foreshore which marks the eastern end of Great Turtle Bay. A general description comes from one of the 1783 surveys.

> West from this [Elbow Bay] about two miles, stands Warwick Fort, this is the only place I have come too, that has the appearance of a Work, 'tis twenty four feet by Eighteen, is three feet high in front, and four in rear, is Built in the face of a Hill or Rock, about forty feet above the Beach, has a watch House & flag staf, the Ordnance here, is two 6 Po[r.] mounted on Garrison Carriages, Both of which appear to be good, the Beach & landing is much the same, as the others before mentioned—I had almost forgot to mention, that there's no Embrasures Here, the work being all of an equal hight[60]

In the Durnford report of the year above, he wrote that Great Turtle Bay was 'Defended at the…East End of the Bay is a Watchhouse with an Old Battery under it, for Two Guns, where the Militia in Wartime were used to keep Guard.' Some years later, it was called Watch House Fort, and at the beginning of the nineteenth century, Heron Bay Fort. It is presumably the fort erroneously called 'Jobsons' in Cunningham's 1811 survey (Fig. 4.15).

> Watch-house Fort, Commanded by Capt. Darrell, has a breast work of palmetto Logs with five embrasures, mounting one Eighteen pounder, one twelve pounder and one nine pounder and good Carriages, platform laid with wood, very good and properly sloped, it has the necessary implements belonging to the Cannon, a very good Magazine appertains thereto—this Fort likewise co-operates with the aforementioned Forts by a cross fire to sweep Common Land Bay. [61]

> Heron Bay Fort, in Warwick Parish about 2 miles West of West Elbow Bay—Is a Semicircular Work, or rather a Rough dry Wall, built of 6, 8 and 10 Inch Stone, not even laid with Mortar, and as may be supposed in a very ruinous state, for Walls built in that manner are never durable, as the rain falling swells the Stones and causes the Wall to burst asunder. There is Earth and Rubbish thrown up against it, over which the grass has grown. The late John Darrell was Captain of the Fort. Since his death the Honourable William Smith has taken charge of the Stores. In this Fort are mounted the following Ordnance Viz: Guns—18 Pounders—2 English, all of which are serviceable. The Carriages are all of Wood for these guns and are in a Serviceable State. The Platforms are Wood Viz: Pine Plank laid on Cedar Sleepers, the former very much decayed. There are Six Rounds of Ammunition prepared for each piece of Ordnance on this Work, which are well secured (in a Moveable Magazine) and in a good State. The Side Arms (the spunges excepted, who like the others want coating) and Stores for the whole of the Ordnance in the Fort are complete and fit for Service. They with the Ammunition are kept in a small Storehouse or Magazine in the rear of the Work, the Roof of which is much injured in the East and West Sides by the Gale of the 17th September last…NB. the three old Guns formerly mounted here, Viz: one 18, one 12 and one 9 Pounder lay in the vicinity of the Work, not being brought to St. Georges.[62]

The descriptions are contradictory, but it is possible that the site evolved from a rectangular to a semi-circular work. The inventory of guns in 1798 and 1806 would seem to confirm the same fort in different structural guises.

• • •

GREAT TURTLE BAY BATTERY

Between the Watch House Fort and Jobson's Fort, at least in 1798, there was another structure, recorded in the Bermudian survey that year as a:

59 The names of the forts on Great Turtle Bay were used erroneously in several cases. The arrangement given here is the best that can be done without further documentary evidence.

60 SRO, Defence Report.

61 PRO, Jennings, Defence Report.

62 PRO, Fraser, Defence Report.

Redoubt to the Eastward of said Fort [Jobson's Fort], on an eminence with a Breast work of stone, being designed a defence for Musquetry and mounted with two three pounders—this breast work with the several Forts, under the Command of Ingham, Lightbourn and Tucker, are calculated to defend Common Land Bay aforesaid, and their situations are judiciously contrived to sweep the said Bay, conjointly by a cross directed fire and can all be brought to bear at one point; this Bay is of great length.[63]

Little else is known of this work, which for sake of reference, will be called here 'Great Turtle Bay Battery.'[64] It does not appear in any written survey, other than that conducted in 1798 by Col. Jennings and reported to the Governor in Council. That survey listed, from east to west, 'Watch House Fort,' 'Redoubt' [Great Turtle Bay Battery], 'Jobson's Fort' and 'Jobson's Cove Fort.' Of these four sites, two—probably Jobson's Fort and Jobson's Cove Fort—existed until the Ordnance Survey of 1899 and are recorded on it.

• • •

JOBSON'S FORT

When seen by Col. Jennings in 1798, Jobson's Fort mounted one 6-pounder and two 4-pounders, which had been proved. Its late construction and purpose were recorded by the Royal Engineers that same year, with details noted by Simon Fraser of the Royal Artillery in 1806 (this is not the 'Jobsons' in Fig. 4.15).

The next practicable landing Place for small Craft is called Great Turtle Bay, the intermediate space between these several Bays or Batteries may be deemed inaccessible along this shore. Great Turtle Bay is nearly half a mile in length flanked by two Batteries on barbette with a Curtain or Intrenchment, which however is filled up in some places by the drift of the Sand. A New Battery has lately been thrown upon a raising ground between called Jobson's Fort to protect this Bay & prevent the possibility of a Landing. [65]

Jobson's Fort in Warwick Parish about 1/2 mile West of Heron Bay [Warwick] Fort—Is not formed into any kind of Work, the Guns being placed on the Rock, without any Breastwork thrown up. Commanded by Captain Thomas Tucker, an infirm old man incapable of leaving his room. In this place are mounted the following Ordnance Viz: Guns—9 Pounders—2 English, all of which are serviceable. The Carriages are all of Wood for the Guns, and are in a Serviceable State. There is no Platform but the Rock. There are Six rounds of Ammunition prepared for each piece of Ordnance on this work, which are well secured (in a Moveable Magazine) and in a good State. The Side Arms, (the spunges excepted who want coating) and Stores for the whole of the Ordnance in the fort, are complete and fit for Service, and with the Ammunition are kept in a small Storehouse or Magazine adjoining the Work. NB. at a small distance from this Fort are three Old guns formerly mounted here Viz: one 9, one 4, and one 3 Pounder.[66]

When Thomas Cunningham visited the site in 1811, there were two 12-pounders at Jobson's Fort and the 'two lower batteries, with an entrenchment between them are entirely in ruins, and the guns, two 4 pdrs, unserviceable.'[67] Such entrenchments for musketry fire also existed at Church Bay, joining two batteries commanding a landing beach.

The general location of Jobson's Fort may be the area indicated on the Ordnance Survey of 1899 near the South Road, where some stonework, not readily identifiable as a military structure, could be seen in the undergrowth in the late 1980s.

[63] PRO, Jennings, Defence Report.

[64] This name appears for one of the four forts in this area on a copy of the Durnford land survey of 1788–93 in the Vaughan Library, Acadia University (see Chap. 5).

[65] PRO, De Butts, Defence Report.

[66] PRO, Fraser, Defence Report.

[67] PRO, Cunningham, Defence Report.

JOBSON'S COVE FORT
(BASCOME'S FORT)

In 1756, Great Turtle Bay was defended by Jobson's Cove Fort to the west and Watch-house Fort to the east, sharing two 6-pounders, one 4- and two 3-pounders between them. This fort is mentioned in the Minutes of the Governor in Council in May 1762, and is almost certainly the site next to Jobson's Cove seen on the 1899 Ordnance Survey.[68] Writing his first report on the defences of Bermuda in 1783, Andrew Durnford described it as 'a Small Battery *en barbette* for two Guns sunk in the Rock.' Another report in 1783 seems to describe the same fort, but under another name.

> Something more than a mile west from this, Stands Bascome's Fort, so called from the Captain that commands it, here is one nine Po[r] & one six, both without Carriages, almost buried in the sand, quite Unserviceable, here is not the appearance of a work of any kind, there's what they call a watch or lookout House, wanting the Roof, situated on a high Clif of Rock & sand.[69]

That 'Bascome's Fort' is one and the same with Jobson's Cove Fort is supported by the distance given, and the east to west progression of Simon Fraser's itinerary. It appears in the same position in the survey of 1811 by Cunningham, but he refers to it as 'Herron Bay or Warwick Battery,' both being erroneous as they are the other names for Watchhouse Fort on the eastern side of Great Turtle Bay.[70] The distinction between the two Jobson's forts is made in the survey by the Bermudians in 1798, which also confirms the presence of five guns, but of different calibre from the 1756 report, being now one 6- and five 4-pounders.

> Jobson's Fort on an eminence, and Jobson's Cove Fort in a line below, are both in Warwick and Commanded by Capt. Tucker; they are sunk in the rock, en Barbet, and stone platforms, the former mounted with one six pounder and two four pounders proved and good carriages, with a Magazine and implements for the Cannon; the latter Fort is mounted with two four pounders proved, and the above Magazine answers for both Forts.[71]

According to Cunningham's illustration, Jobson's Cove Fort was a half-moon redoubt, thirty feet in diameter with a 10 feet square guardhouse at the rear. Curiously, he does not indicate the nearby shoreline, as he did for the other forts at the waters edge (Fig. 4.29, but called 'Heron Bay'). Thus the two long bays of Elbow and Great Turtle were defended by three main forts, one central and two on the flanks, with an additional fort at the latter. The period of construction of most of these remains obscure, but on the Norwood map of 1617, the symbol of a cannon appears at both Elbow and Great 'Turkle' Bay, perhaps an indication of a presence of some of these forts in the first decade of settlement (Fig. 4.30).

FIGURE 4.30: *Jobson's Cove Fort was located on the outcrop at the end of the long Great Turtle Bay, now called 'Warwick Long Bay.'*

68 PRO CO 37/18 and Minutes in Council, May 13, 1762.

69 SRO, Defence Report.

70 PRO, Cunningham, Defence Report. The mistaken use of Heron Battery for Jobson's Cove Fort appears on his sketch plans of the South Shore forts.

71 PRO, Jennings, Defence Report.

• • •

HUNT'S FORT
(HUNT'S POINT, LIGHTBOURN'S OR COMMON LAND BAY FORT)

A short distance along the coast from Jobson's Cove Fort stood two other works, that nearest the sea being Hunt's Fort and the other slightly inland, Ingham's (Fig. 4.31). One of these may have been the 'Southampton Fort,' which had three guns in 1738, one four and two 6-pounders.[72] Called 'Common Land' and 'Hunt's Point' forts in 1756, they had two 3- and two 6-pounders and were under the command of Thomas Hunt.[73] The purpose of these forts was given by Durnford in 1783.

FIGURE 4.31: *Common Land (Horseshoe) Bay, was defended by Hunt's Fort on the centre peninsular between it and Cross Bay to the left.*

The next Bay near it [Sinky Bay], is Cross Bay, where are the Remains of an Old Intrenchment, which is also Scoured by a small Circular Fort distant about a quarter of a Mile called Hunt's Fort, which defends another Bay called Common Land Bay close under it, and Port Royal Long Bay [Horseshoe Bay] on the other side. Here are also Remains of Intrenchments made Last War but filled up with sand.

In other reports, given below in chronological order, the fort is variously named and a drawing made of it in 1811 (Fig. 4.29).

FIGURE 4.32: *From the air, Hunt's Fort appears as a small circular cutting just to the east of the Whaler Inn of the Southampton Princess Hotel.*

A mile west from this, is Cumberland [*sic*] Bay Fort, the form of 'tis Round about fourteen feet in Diameter, is hewn out of the Rock, about 2½ feet deep, has no Embrasures being of an equal hight all Round, here is a flagstaf, with two Guns no ascertaining What they are, being so much defaced with rust, this work stands on the top of a Hill fifty feet above the Water[74]

[72] CO 37/13. Return of August 25, 1738.

[73] Minutes in Council, May 13, 1762 and PRO CO 37/18 and Bermuda Archives, Map Drawer # 5, Inventory 1756.

[74] SRO, Defence Report.

[75] PRO, Jennings, Defence Report.

Lightbourn's Fort on a steep rock in a line below Inghams, is of an oval form dug in solid Rock en Barbet, stone platform, wanting cannon and every other utensil, two six pounders will be sufficient for this Fort and Inghams Magazine answers for both.[75]

Common Land Bay Fort, in Southampton Parish about a Mile West of Jobson's Fort—Is a circular Work on an Eminence, in the form of a cock pit, has a Breast Work built of 8 and 10 Inch Stone, two feet high, with Earth and Rubbish thrown up to a level with the top of the Wall. Commanded by a Captain Samuel Lightbourn. In this Work are mounted the following Ordnance Viz: Guns—12 Pounders—1 English, which is unserviceable. The Carriage is of Wood for this Gun and in a Serviceable State. The Platform is Stone and in good repair. There is neither Ammunition nor Side Arms for this Gun. The

Storehouse or Magazine in the rear of the Work, in which they were kept, was broke open in 1802, the door and everything carried off, and there has been no Order for replacing them.[76]

Hunt's Fort, about three quarters of a mile from Herron Bay, commands an apparently good opening thro' the breakers, and flanks a fine bay about 300 yards wide. 'Tis an irregular barbette work in which are two unserviceable French 8 pdrs on good cedar carriages, and stone platform. The magazine in the rear has been dismantled.[77]

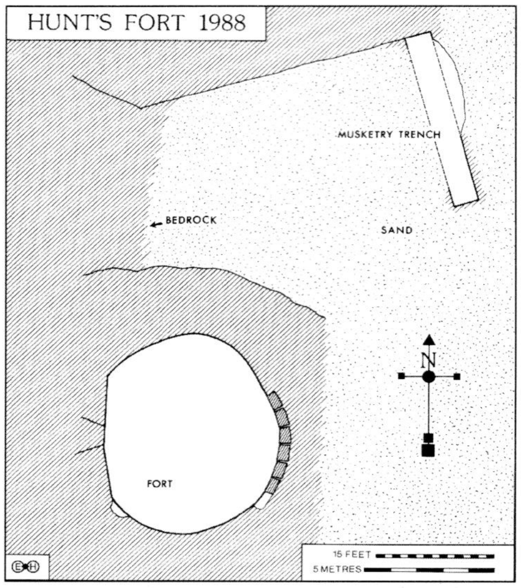

Hunt's Fort is to be found on the hill on the eastern side of East Whale Bay (Fig. 4.32), and its position was recorded on the Ordnance Survey of 1899. It was drawn by an archaeological team in the late 1980s (Fig. 4.33). A musketry or rifle entrenchment, of an undetermined date, is located just to the north-east of the fort.

HUNT'S FORT 1988

MUSKETRY TRENCH

BEDROCK

SAND

N

FORT

15 FEET
5 METRES

FIGURE 4.33: *The plan of Hunt's Fort was recorded in the 1980s and includes the circular redoubt and a nearby entrenchment of uncertain date.*

• • •

INGHAM'S FORT
(COMMON LAND OR SOUTHAMPTON FORT)

This fort, as noted in 1798, was in a line above Hunt's Fort, and the position is preserved on the Ordnance Survey of 1899. To have survived as an emplacement into the present century, must mean that it had some substance, but Ingham's Fort is only mentioned in the Bermudian report of 1798.

Inghams Fort at the westernmost end of Common Land Bay at the extreme of Southampton is on a high hill, sunk in the rock in barbet, of a half moon form and stone platform mounted with one eighteen pounder and one nine pounder proved and good carriages and has a Magazine and necessary implements for said cannon.[78]

The actual site of Ingham's Fort has not been located, but it may survive on the bank to the south of the coast road, although some of the bank was removed in the 1960s to make a tunnel under that road to East Whale Bay.

The Fort in 1783 received some additional support from a nearby gun, situated on a point of land between Sinky and Hunt's Bays, where a major hotel now takes precedence.[79] The defences of the South Shore, which began with Bailey's Bay Battery are completed by two forts to the west of Ingham's, near St. Anne's, the parish church of Southampton.

• • •

CHURCH BAY EAST FORT

In 1738, the two structures at Church, or Port Royal, Bay were referred to as 'Tucker's Forts,' mounting four guns each, which almost twenty years later were 4-, 6-, 9- and 18-pounders.[80] By 1762, the forts were in the command of Henry Todd. According to Durnford, the 'East Fort is under a Rock, cut

[76] PRO, Fraser, Defence Report.

[77] PRO, Cunningham, Defence Report.

[78] PRO, Jennings, Defence Report.

[79] PRO, Durnford, Defence Report.

[80] CO 37/13. Return of August 25, 1738 and PRO CO 37/18.

out for two Guns *en barbette*. Round the Bay are the Remains of two Intrenchments made last war, but at present [filled] up with sand.'[81] In 1798, two 9-pounders were mounted in Church Bay East Fort and the two forts kept 'communication by an entrenchment from the one to the other.'[82] A later survey describes the site in some detail.

> Church Bay East, in Southampton Parish, about two Miles from Commonland Fort—Is a Semicircular Wall, two feet high, and one and a half thick, built of 8 and 10 Inch Stone, not laid in Mortar, but coated over after it was built with mortar. There is some Earth and Rubbish thrown up, but not to a level with the top of the Wall, as most of them are. Commanded by Captain Francis Dickinson. In this Work are mounted the Following ordnance Viz: Guns—9 Pounders—2 English, all of which are Serviceable. The Carriages are all of Wood for these Guns and are in a Serviceable State. The Platforms of Stone and in good repair. (In the Autumn of 1805 when these Guns were mounted here, they like the other Works, were supplied with Six Rounds of Ammunition for each piece of Ordnance. At present there are only Nine Rounds for both, and the Captain can give no Account in what manner the other three were expended.) The remaining nine Rounds are well secured (in a Moveable Magazine) and are in a good state. The Side Arms (the Spunges excepted whose defects are the same as those so often mentioned) and Stores for the whole of the Ordnance in the Fort are complete and fit for service. They with the Ammunition, are kept in a small Storehouse or Magazine at West Church Bay Fort—there being no Magazine at this Work. NB. The Guns formerly mounted here, Viz: one Twelve, and two Nine Pounders, lay in the rear of the Work.[83]

The fort is illustrated by one of Cunningham's drawings (Fig. 4.29) as Port Royal Bay Battery, East, an irregular half moon, 26 feet in diameter. Its location is indicated on the 1899 Ordnance Survey and its exact position was known in the 1970s, at which time it was buried to preserve it. A couple of snapshots confirm the semi-circular shape of the fort.[84] One of the guns from the fort lies in the water nearby and is often found by swimmers.

• • •

CHURCH BAY WEST FORT

When seen in 1783 by Durnford, this fort was a 'sunk' Battery with five embrasures, also recorded that year by Simon Fraser and in further detail by him in 1806.

> West from this about a mile & a half is Church Bay Fort, so called from 'tis being, in the neighbourhood of a Church, this work stands very low, has five Embrasures, in form of a half moon, here's one 18 Po[r] one nine d[o] & one Six d[o] without Carriages, there's likewise six four Po[r] Mounted on ship Carriages, most of them wanting trucks, and all of them Beds & Coins, but the Whole is quite unserviceable, there's no magazine...[85]

> Is a circular Wall, two feet high and two feet thick, built of 10 Inch Stone. This Work is Commanded by Captain Francis Dickinson, the person who has charge of Church Bay East. In this Fort are mounted the following Ordnance Viz: Guns—12 Pounders—2 English, all of which are serviceable. The Carriages are all of Wood for these Guns and are in a Serviceable State. The Platform is of Stone, much too soft for that purpose, as the Trucks sink in running out the Guns. There were Six Rounds of Ammunition prepared for each Piece of Ordnance on this Work (at present there is only six for both remaining, and like those deficient at Church Bay East, cannot be accounted for). The remainder are well secured (in a Moveable Magazine) and in a good State. The Side Arms (the Spunges excepted who want coating) and Stores for the whole of the Ordnance in the Fort, are complete and fit for service. They with the Ammunition are kept in a Small Storehouse or Magazine in the rear of the Work. NB. The two old nine Pounders formerly mounted here lay in the rear of the Work.[86]

[81] PRO, Durnford, Defence Report.

[82] PRO, Jennings, Defence Report.

[83] PRO, Fraser, Defence Report.

[84] I wish to thank J. Hubert Jones for this information and the photographs of East Church Bay Fort and for his support of the preservation of fortifications in Bermuda.

[85] SRO, Fraser, Defence Report.

[86] PRO, Fraser, Defence Report.

111

The Cunningham Survey shows the site as 'West Port Royal Bay,' an irregular oval, 20 feet wide and about 35 feet long, with stairs into this sunken work on the eastern side (Fig. 4.29). A magazine, 10 by 15 feet was situated at the rear and the fort is positioned on the Ordnance Survey of 1899. Nothing is now evident of the site above ground, but given its sunken nature, it may survive as an archaeological feature below the modern ground level.

Thus at the turn of the nineteenth century, the south coast of Bermuda from Tucker's Town Point to Church Bay was defended by no less than nineteen forts of varying sizes and calibre of guns. The coastline being about twelve miles long between those points, there was almost a fort every half mile. Run by the local government and militia, it is obvious from the surveys that most of these structures were of a simple construction, generally in disrepair with their guns in various stages of decay.

• • •

FORT NEWBOLD
(WHALE BAY FORT)

After Church Bay, the coast trends west and northwards, turning to the eastwards at Wreck Hill and Elys Harbour. A channel for small boats, Hogfish Cut, parallels the coast and was defended by several local shoreline batteries, the first being Whale Bay Fort or Fort Newbold, recorded in the surveys of 1798 and in 1806.

> Whale Bay Fort Commanded by Capt. William Newbold, about two hundred yards Eastward of the above [Westside Fort], is of an half moon form en Barbet, has a good platform of wood mounted with one Eighteen pounder and two six pounders proved... The Magazine at West Fort answers also for this—these two Forts act conjointly by a cross fire to guard the Entrances into Hogfish Cut and protects West side and Whale Bay.[87]

> Two miles and a Quarter Westward is Whale Bay Battery mounting two 6 Pdrs & this Work is useless as the Coast is here totally impracticable making a tremendous appearance from the Sea—but it seems the system of the Bermudian Engineers to erect Batteries on every projection or head Lands whether accessible or not.[88]

> Fort Newbold in Southampton Parish about 2 miles West of Church Bay West—Is a Semicircular Wall or Breast Work two feet high and two feet thick, built of Eight and Ten Inch Stone, with earth and Rubbish thrown up to a level with the top of the Wall. Commanded by Captain William Newbold. In this fort are mounted the following Ordnance Viz: Guns—9 Pounders—2 English, all of which are serviceable. The Carriages are all of Wood for these Guns and are in a Serviceable State. The Platform of soft Stone, in every respect like that last mentioned. There were Six Rounds of Ammunition prepared for each piece of Ordnance on this Work—at present only four—two are said to be expended on the King's and two on the Queen's Birthday. The Remainder are well secured (in a Moveable Magazine) and in a good State. The Side Arms (the Spunges excepted that want coating) and Stores for the whole of the Ordnance in the Fort are Complete and fit for Service. They with the Ammunition are kept in a Small House or Magazine at West Side Fort, (which is in a very improper State, having been stowed full of Pork, Flour and Corn, Picked up from some Wreck) there being no Storehouse of any kind at this Work. NB. the Three 6 Pounders formerly mounted here, lay in the vicinity of the Work.[89]

[87] PRO, Jennings, Defence Report.

[88] PRO, De Butts, Defence Report.

[89] PRO, Fraser, Defence Report.

FIGURE 4.34: Fort Newbold was a small D-shaped redoubt high on the cliff overlooking West Whale Bay; the straight rear wall appears in this picture.

In 1811, when Thomas Cunningham visited the site, the 9-pounders were still in place and a plan was made of the small redoubt (Fig. 4.29). Still exhibiting its half moon shape, Fort Newbold survives relatively intact, as it was not destroyed in the building of Whale Bay Battery in the 1870s, which lies adjacent to the north-east (Fig. 4.34). It is connected to that much larger work by a passage cut in the rock, which may be original or may date to the 1870s, indicating the last days of Fort Newbold may have been as an observation outpost for Whale Bay Battery. In February 1996, investigations by the Parks Department revealed the flagstoned floor of the fort, as had been found at West Elbow Bay Fort, perhaps indicating a consistent pattern of design.

• • •

WEST SIDE FORT

Directly opposite the entrance to Hogfish Cut Channel stood West Side Fort, which around 1762 was in the command of William Burrows and had six guns, one each of 12- and 9-pounders, and two 6- and two 4-pounders.[90] Aside from defending the channel entrance, its place in a general defence system was explained in 1783 to Lt. Col. Morse, 'Chief Engineer in America,' by Andrew Durnford (Fig. 4.35).

> The South Side of these Islands from Elies Harbour to Tucker's Town Point, near the King's Castle, is nearly a Strait Line, without any Harbours or Great Bays, full of Rocks, and generally a great Swell, and at all times very difficult for an Enemy to land upon. There are however some Small Bays, with Openings between the Rocks, where Boats might occasionally land. To Prevent which, several Small Batteries, have at different times been built, at the Expense of the Island. First of these batteries is the West Side Fort about two Miles East of Elies Harbour opposite Hogfish Cut, which it was built to defend. It is a Semicircular Battery sunk in the Rock, partly raised in the Front, with a thin Parapet & seven Embrasures, open in the Rear.[91]

By the turn of the century, the fort was commanded by Captain J. Burrows, 'Jun[r],' mounting two six and two 18-pounders. It had 'a platform of wood that has not sufficient slope towards the breastwork, which causes the cannon to recoil over the platform,' needless creating difficulty under fire.[92]

By 1806, command of the site had passed from the Burrows' and the fort was recorded in a Royal Artillery survey.

> West Side Fort, in Southampton Parish about 1/4 mile from Fort Newbold—Is a Semicircular Wall or Breast Work, two feet thick and Twenty inches high, built of 8 inch Stone with Earth and Rubbish thrown up to the level of the Wall. Commanded by Captain Leycraft, an old infirm man, entirely worn out. In this Fort are mounted the following Ordnance Viz: Guns—18 Pounders—2 English, all of which are serviceable.
>
> The Carriages are all of Wood for these Guns, and are in a Serviceable State. The Platform is of Stone and in good repair. There were Six Rounds of Ammunition prepared for each Piece of Ordnance on this Work. At present there are only four, two are said to have been

[90] Minutes in Council, May 13, 1762 and PRO CO 37/18

[91] PRO, Durnford, Defence Report.

[92] PRO, Jennings, Defence Report.

FIGURE 4.35: *West Side Fort sits on a point of land only a few feet above the water and guarded the entrance into a boat channel along the western coast of Bermuda.*

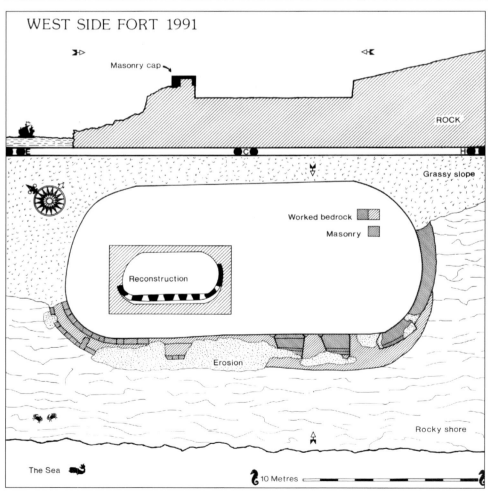

FIGURE 4.36: *West Side Fort is an oval, mostly cut into the bedrock but surmounted by a masonry parapet with embrasures for seven guns.*

expended on the Queen's Birth, and two on an Alarm. The remainder are well secured (in a Moveable Magazine) and in a good State. The Side Arms (the Spunges excepted which want coating) and Stores for the whole of the Ordnance in the Fort are complete and fit for Service. They with the Ammunition are kept in the Magazine, (whose state is above mentioned [see entry for Fort Newbold]) in the rear of the Work. NB. The two old 18 Pounders formerly mounted here, lay some distance from the Work.[93]

Cunningham, writing in 1811 (Fig. 4.29), states that the magazine for the fort was a considerable distance 'in the interior': this may have been the Watch-house '100 yards' to the rear, noted by Simon Fraser in 1783. The Magazine has not been found, but the fort itself is still swept by the Atlantic, laying, as it does, but a few feet above the sea. The fort itself was recorded by archaeological survey in 1991 (Fig. 4.36) and proved to be an oblong structure, cut into the bedrock, with embrasures raised in stone on the sea front. The interior of the fort was filled with sand and no excavation took place.

• • •

WRECK HILL FORT

Halfway up Hogfish Cut Channel is the eminence of Wreck Hill, so named from its use as a lookout for ships in distress on the western reefs, which there extend several miles out to sea. In 1783, the site was a ruin, 'where formerly there was two guns, at present there's none, they are supposed to have been taken, by some Vessel For Balast, for like the rest they are said to have been Fit for nothing else, there's no work here of any kind—This Rack Hill, is the first land, that is seen by ships at Sea, from the southward or westward, being Very high.'[94] This geographical fact led to the call for a lighthouse at Wreck Hill in 1798, but the scheme was not carried out.[95] The structure was recorded in 1806.

> Wreck Hill Fort, in Sandys Parish about 3 Miles Northwest from West Side Fort—Is a Circular Wall or Breast Work, built of 8,10 and 12 Inch Stone laid in Mortar, two feet thick and Eighteen Inches high, with Earth and Rubbish thrown up against it. Commanded by Captain Jeremiah Burrows. In this fort are mounted the following Ordnance Viz: Guns—18 Pounders—2 English, all of which are serviceable.
>
> The Carriages for these Guns are all of Wood and are in a serviceable State. The Platform is of soft Stone laid in Mortar in a very irregular manner. There were Six Rounds of Ammunition prepared for each Piece of Ordnance in this Work. At present there are only five (two were expended 4th June 1806) which are well secured (in a Moveable Magazine) and in a good state. The Side Arms (including the Spunges) and Stores for the whole of the Ordnance in the Fort are complete and fit for Service. They with the Ammunition are kept in a Small Storehouse in the rear of the Work.[96]

In 1811, 'the last work on the main island' was listed as a circular redoubt, some 32 feet in diameter. Being sunk in the rock, its outline appears to have survived into modern times. In its centre are several concrete footings for American works during the Second World War.

To Wreck Hill Fort goes the ignominy of being the site of the only invasion of Bermuda by foreign forces: this occurred in June, 1777.

> We have just now received Intelligence…That the *Fair American* [Charles Morgan] and *Experiment* [Francis Morgan], however, went into the Western Harbour [Elys] the 13th, were fired at from the Fort, mounting 5 Cannon, to which they returned a Broadside; That upon preparing to give a second Broadside, the Fort was abandoned; which the

93 PRO, Fraser, Defence Report.

94 SRO, Defence Report.

95 PRO, De Butts, Defence Report. 'I here beg leave to observe that as this is generally the first land made by Vessels bound to the Island it would be of the greatest Utility, not only to these but to Navigators of all Stations, trading to and from the West Indies—obliged to cross this latitude—to have a light-house built upon it, which from its elevated situation &c it is in every respect well calculated for.'

96 PRO, Fraser, Defence Report.

Captains Morgans observing, they landed some Men, took Possession of it, demolished the Embrasures, dismounted and spiked the Cannon, and destroyed the Carriages; and remained there Six Days.[97]

To add local insult to this public injury, it seems that the 'rebel privateers' were skippered by two Bermudians from South Carolina: several of the guns were also stolen from the fort, which were 'private property.' A few days after the attack, the Governor, George James Bruere, used the occasion to press his case for moneys to be granted for the forts from the reluctant Council and Assembly.

> I have called you together to take up and renew the Militia Bill now lying at Council Board, fallen by a Dissolution of the General Assembly. I am very sorry that two Rebel Privateers should arrive at the West End of these Island and Insult Government in the manner they have at this Critical Time…Gentlemen of the Assembly, I have repeatedly requested some supply to be granted for the Repairs of the Fortifications, which I hope you will now take into your consideration, and likewise promise me your assistance in the case of any attack or further Insult on these Islands by the Enemies of Great Britain.[98]

• • •

DANIEL'S ISLAND FORT

Guarding a bend in Hogfish Cut Channel, where it turns to the east towards Long and Mangrove Bays, was a small fort named for the island on which it stood, the boats having to pass directly under its guns (Fig. 4.37). Daniel's Island Fort also was the only one 'Commanding the Chub cut Channel, which was little known but by the Island Pilots and seldom made use of except by vessels in distress.'[99] The site was overlooked by both Durnford and Fraser in their 1783 surveys, which might suggest it was built thereafter (Fig. 4.29). A reference of 1738 to a gun at 'Cow Ground Point' (Cow Ground being an area of shallow water and reefs just off Daniel's island), however, may indicate its earlier presence. The fort and the bursting of its cannon was recorded in 1798.

> Darrells [sic] Island Fort in Sandys, Commanded by Capt. John Gilbert Junr, is a square at two sides sunk in the solid rock, the other two sides are built with stone en barbet, but

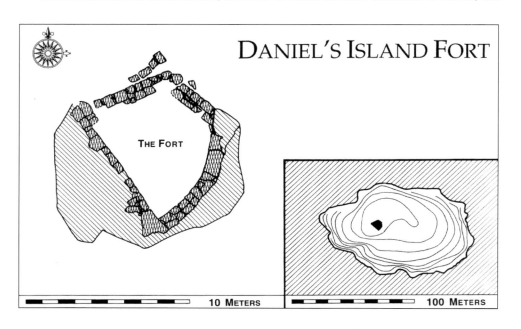

FIGURE 4.37: Daniel's Island Fort controlled the bend in the Hogfish Cut Channel leading into Mangrove Bay (drawn by Heather Harvey).

97 William James Morgan (ed.). *Naval Documents of The American Revolution* 9 (1986), 194.

98 Journal of the House of Assembly, June 24, 1777.

99 PRO, De Butts, Defence Report.

FIGURE 4.38:
Archaeological excavations took place at Daniel's Island Fort in 1991 and revealed an irregular D-shaped redoubt.

100 PRO, Jennings, Defence Report.

101 Bermuda is indebted to Professor Norman F. Barka of the College of William and Mary and the archaeological team for their work on Daniel's Island Fort. The excavation was conducted with the blessing of the National Parks Commission and with considerable support from Col. William Cook, U.S.M.C. (ret.), the then-Assistant Director of Parks and his team from the Department of Agriculture, Fisheries & Parks. Peter Forster and his group from the Land Survey Division of the Ministry of Works & Engineering were of invaluable assistance in the mapping of the site.

on proving a Cannon, the explosion bursted the Stone Work. The said Fort has no Cannon at present, and is capable when repaired to mount three six pounders—there remains a new Carriage of Cedar for a six pounder that bursted in proving—the said Fort has no Magazine nor Flag-Staff. This Fort is situated to annoy an Enemy passing round Somerset, and acting conjointly with Jones' [Mangrove Bay] Fort and sweeping Long Bay.[100]

Daniel's Island is a National Park and in 1992 an archaeological examination of the site took place in a joint field school of the Bermuda Maritime Museum and the College of William and Mary (Fig. 4.38). The excavation revealed an irregular half-moon fort, with the straight side of the work, unusually, fronting the sea. The northern flank of the building had been rebuilt, presumably after its walls were 'bursted' upon the exploding of the cannon, which quite dramatically did not come up to proof. Several holes, which may have been formed by the explosion, were found to be filled with rubble, possibly from the demolished stonework. By extraordinary happenstance, part of the muzzle of the gun which burst was found in that fill in 1992. Unfortunately, the artifacts from the site shed little light on the date of construction of the fort.[101]

MANGROVE BAY FORT

A short distance north and east of Daniel's Island Fort is Long Bay, near which stood another small redoubt, named not for the waters it protected, but for the bay on the eastern side of this part of Somerset Island. There is only one clear reference to this work, but as it comes from the 1798 survey by the local militia, it has some credibility.

> Mangrove Bay Fort Commanded by Capt. Thomas Jones is of an Oval Form sunk in the Rock and a Breast Work en barbet, there are two insufficient platforms, in place of which, the platform requires to be extended to two thirds of the Oval of the Fort in order to traverse

the Cannon to necessary directions—there are two six pounders Cannon provided for this that are good, the Carriages are insufficient, being calculated for Ship use. Here is also wanting a Flag-Staff; Spunges, Worms &ca. are provided for the said Cannon, but no Ammunition. A magazine is unnecessary, there being a Store at hand equal to the preservation of the Powder. This Fort is well situated to annoy an enemy passing round Somerset and sweeps Long Bay.[102]

The logical site for this fort would be at the northern end of Long Bay, where the beach terminates in a small headland. No evidence of the structure can be found in that position, or on the southern perimeter of the beach. A survey of 1798 refers to a 'large unfinished Work intended for the Defence of Long Bay on the West—and Mangrove Bay on the East, which is to be completed and Guns mounted in it,'[103] and Cunningham in 1811 speaks of the ruins of an unfinished work 'in Long Bay.'

Since the local survey was made in the same year as that which describes an unfinished fort which would cover both Long and Mangrove Bays, it would seem that they refer to two different works, as Mangrove Bay Fort appears to be a completed structure. Given the topography, it would be difficult for that fort to 'sweep Long Bay,' as well as Mangrove Bay, if it was located in the position suggested. The evidence would thus support the presence of a new work under construction in 1798, located in the area of King's Point at the north-western tip of Somerset. The guns from such a site could cover Mangrove Bay and the approach to Long Bay, but would not cover the beach at the latter. For the sake of identification, this presumed work may be referred to as 'King's Point Redoubt,' to distinguish it from the known structure of Mangrove Bay Fort. It would have straddled, defensively speaking, a small peninsular, serving much the same function as did Maria Hill Fort on Ireland Island to the north-east.

There are no known plans or topographical maps which show the positions of either of these forts at Long and Mangrove Bays in Sandys Parish.

• • •

MARIA HILL FORT

To the north-east of Somerset are the islands of Watford, Boaz and Ireland, which after 1809 became part of the Royal Naval lands at Bermuda. In the southern half of Ireland there was an unusually high area, shown in some exaggerated early nineteenth century prints as a sugar-loaf hill dominating the countryside. This land at some time apparently belonged to a Mr. Neriah Hill, from whence it was named by corruption, Maria Hill. The earliest reference to a military structure comes in the local survey of 1798:

> Fort on the high Hill of Ireland [Island] commanded by Capt. John V. Seymour is of a square form, sunk in the Rock and constructed en Barbet. Some part of the platform, which is Stone, is found to be soft and therefore will require to be laid with wood; here are nine Twelve pounder Cannon, as good as new, unmounted, and new carriages, with Spunges, Ladles and Worms. A sufficient Magazine will be necessary, and one or more large Tanks to supply water in Case of Siege. This Hill is well-situated to annoy an Enemy passing round Ireland and should be rendered capable of defending the passage into the Great Sound.[104]

This information should be compared with the British military survey of

[102] PRO, Jennings, Defence Report.

[103] PRO, De Butts, Defence Report.

[104] PRO, Jennings, Defence Report.

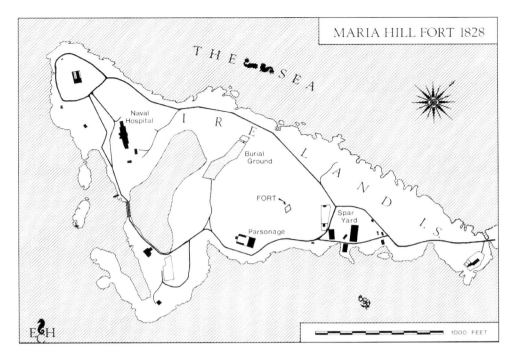

FIGURE 4.39: *Maria Hill Fort stood on the high ground of Ireland Island South and remained in existence into the 1820s.*

FIGURE 4.40: *This aerial view of the topography shown in Figure 4.39 of Ireland Island South was taken by the Canadian Forces in the early 1990s.*

1806, with particular attention to the description of the guns, which were 'as good as new' to Col. Jennings' inspection team.

> Is a Circular Wall or Breast Work in every respect like that just mentioned, but of a greater extent. Commanded by Captain Henry Harvey. In this Fort are mounted the following Ordnance Viz. Guns—9 Pounders—7 English, all of which are unserviceable.
>
> The Carriages are all of Wood for these Guns and are in a Serviceable State. The only Platform is the Rock, rather soft for that purpose. There were, during the Alarm in June 1804, Eighteen Rounds of Ammunition supplied for each piece of Ordnance on this Work, well secured in four whole Powder Barrels, as there is no Moveable Magazine here. At present there are only Eighty seven for the whole, kept at the Captain's House, two miles from the Work. The Side Arms (the Spunges excepted who want coating) and Stores for the whole of the Ordnance in the Fort are Complete and fit for Service, kept in a small Storehouse a little to the Westward of the Work.

The Guns on this Work were raised in the Summer of 1795, from the Wreck of the *Lord Amhurst*, Ordnance Transport, lost here in February 1777 returning from Jamaica, and all attempts to clear their Cylinders have proved unsuccessful. They are so much corroded and full of barnacles, there is no getting a Shot or Cartridge of the proper Calibre home. The reason of their not being withdrawn, and new guns sent, is that the Work is placed in an improper situation, being in the Interior part of the Island, and not near the Channel where the Ships must pass.[105]

By 1811, perhaps with the establishment in 1809 of the Dockyard at the northern end of Ireland Island, the guns had been upgraded to five 18-pounders and 'two new 32 pdrs on iron carriages…lately added.'[106] A drawing was also made of it in 1811 (Fig. 4.29) showing the fort to be diamond-shaped, roughly 40 feet to a side. Maria Hill Fort was one of the few of the colonial batteries to be surveyed after 1811 and perhaps due to its proximity to the Dockyard, it is recorded as extant in a map of 1828 (Fig. 4.39 & 4.40).[107]

• • •

LATER FORTIFICATIONS IN ST. GEORGE'S PARISH

From Ireland Island to the western end of St. George's Island, the northern coast of the Bermudas was undefended by fortifications until the nineteenth century. Between those points, the reef extends in an arc up to ten miles from the shore. This natural defence was cut by several channels for small boats, but these egresses were known only to a few local pilots. The north shore of the main island, Bermuda, was therefore not fortified from Maria Hill Fort until one reaches the Ferry at the western tip of St. George's Island.

Aside from the first eleven forts built in St. George's Parish, some other identifiable works were constructed by the colonial government in the eastern district of the islands up to 1783, when the British military began to take over the defence of Bermuda. The following section describes the forts in existence in 1783 in the parish, when they were surveyed by Andrew Durnford and Simon Fraser; some were later modified by Durnford in the 1790s and those changes will be mentioned in the next chapter.

• • •

BURNT POINT FORT
(FERRY POINT BATTERY)

At the western extremity of St. George's Island, a small and somewhat barren peninsula juts into the sea (Fig. 4.41). At its tip stands a small work known as Ferry Point Battery, or Burnt Point Fort. When seen in the 1980s (Fig. 4.42), it was a small half-moon work with five embrasures, matching the last description of it, given by Cunningham in 1811. In 1783, it was a less substantial structure, mounting more guns as then recorded.

The Defence of the Ferry, is an Old Battery, in a very ruinous Situation, being circular for 9 Embrasures with a Parapet about 18 inches thick, and totally unserviceable. As this Battery is advanced on a Low Point, and very much commanded, am of Opinion, it should be levelled, and a good defenceable Fort erected upon a rising Ground about 100 yards in the rear of it. At the Ferry is Stationed a Company of the Royal Garrison Battalion, where is a good Quarter for the Officers, and Barrack with Births for 70

[105] PRO, Fraser, Defence Report. Fraser was often scathing in his views of Bermudians and their military enterprise. His description of Maria Hill Fort ends with an anthropological touch: '[Ireland Island] is inhabited at present by a few families, who can hardly be said to be human, extremely poor, but still not attended with the same degree of misery, as those suffer in similar situations, who live in Colder Climates.'

[106] PRO, Cunningham, Defence Report.

[107] Bermuda Maritime Museum Archives. 'S. W. End of Ireland Island. Surveyed and drawn by W. B. Delves Broughton, Lt. Royal Engineers, July 1828.'

FIGURE 4.41: *Burnt Point Fort is located at the southwest tip of St. George's Island near the later Martello Tower, left foreground.*

Men, and a good Cistern for water.[108]

The narrow parapet in Bermuda stone is evident at the site, as are four blocked embrasures, which, added to the existing five (Fig. 4.43), would give the 1783 total of nine such gunports. Of the other forts at Ferry Reach, being works on Ferry and Coney Islands, no mention is made in either 1783 report and those works are presumed to date to the 1790s.

FIGURE 4.42: *Seen from the air, Burnt Point Fort is a D-shaped redoubt with walls of Bermuda stone forming merlons filled with rubble.*

FIGURE 4.43: *There were several periods in the design of Burnt Point Fort, as seen by the infilled embrasures and earlier and narrower parapet wall.*

108 PRO, Durnford, Defence Report. Fraser in his 1783 report mistakenly gives eleven embrasures.

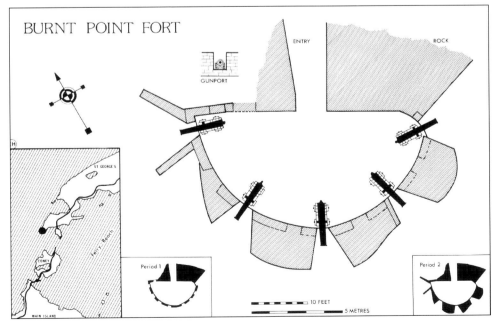

BURNT POINT FORT

ENTRY

ROCK

GUNPORT

ST GEORGE'S

Ferry Reach

CONEY

Period 1

Period 2

10 FEET

5 METRES

MAIN ISLAND

FORT CLINTON & NEW REDOUBT

Moving east from Burnt Point Fort, Simon Fraser listed two works in the central northern part of St. George's Island, structures overlooked by Durnford in 1783.

> To the South West of this [Fort St Catherine], near a mile Distant is what they call the **New Redoubt**, where There's two platforms but no Embrasures, it stands on the top of a Hill, about two 100 yards south of this stands **Fort Clinton** On the top of another Hill, the new Redoubt and this Fort, may be said To be inland forts, if I may be allowed the Expression, this place appears to me but of little Consequence, tho it may be said to command, both The Town & Harbour of St. Georges, being not Three 100 yards distant from them, but an enemy Could March, in to Town at the bottom of the Hill, and they in the Fort, could not make a gun To bear on them, 'tis now in ruins, there being neither Embrasure nor platform remaining, there was Barracks for three officers and some men, but there's not the smalest vestage of them lest, the Cistern is Stile standing, but of no use at it leaks, & never no magazine of any kind nor never has…[109]

These works must be on two of the sites of the later 'Town Redoubts,' discussed in the following chapter and suggested by Durnford as a 'dérnière Resource' at the rear of the town. Fraser's is the only reference to a Fort Clinton in Bermuda, which was probably the work named later by Durnford for the King—Fort George—occupying a high hill just west of the Town, formerly the site of Riches Mount of the 1620s and called by the locals in the 1750s 'Fort St. George.' Other works seen in 1783 were Fort St. Catherine (see Chapter 5) and the 'Powder Magazine…near the Governor's House, excavated in the Rock, probably at the site of the Western Redoubt, from whence was stolen the powder handed over to the Rebels in America in 1777.'[110] Two companies of the Royal Garrison Battalion, under a Major Anstruther, were quartered in the town, some in the jail, and new buildings were being erected for their accommodation in 1783.

Other sites mentioned in various returns for 1718, 1738 and 1756 suggest the following emplacements, which may or may not have been forts. The guns stood at 'Tobacco Bay Fort' on the north side of St. George Island; 'St. Catherine's Point Fort,' and 'St. Catherine's Bay Fort,' 'Eastside Fort' and 'Buildings Bay Fort' on the east coast: one of the last may also be known as 'Amberfish Hole Fort.'[111] A final work, the Old Town Cut Fort, or 'Old Town Fort,' was found at a small boat channel at the south-eastern tip of St. George's Island.

• • •

TOWN CUT BATTERY

In 1783, the 'Old Town Cut Fort' had 'four Embrasures Hewn out of the rock,'[112] and according to Durnford, four guns were mounted but the 'Old Battery' was quite useless for the purpose intended. This was to defend a channel for small craft between St. George's and Higgs Island, the latter standing between the former and the southerly Paget Island (Fig. 4.44).

Town Cut Battery was erected around 1700, possibly replacing an earlier structure known as Davers Fort; its appellation of 'Gates Fort' has been discussed in Chapter Three (Fig. 4.45). By 1800, it mounted three 12-pounders, had a blockhouse, or barracks for the Artillery and a wall for musquetry extended to the west on the southern side of the work:[113] 'There is a small

109 SRO, Defence Report.

110 PRO, Durnford, Defence Report.

111 PRO CO 37/10, 37/13 and 37/18. I am very grateful to Mr. Ronald Biggs for his research at the Public Record Office on the eighteenth century forts.

112 SRO, Defence Report.

113 PRO, De Butts, Defence Report.

house, in the ground floor of which they are kept, in the upper Room the Artillery man lodges, the Cooking Place is at some distance, and serves also for a Guard House for a Corporal and three men of the Royal Artillery that mount Guard at this Place.'[114] This was the site found in 1811 by Cunningham, but

FIGURE 4.44: Town Cut was excavated in this century and replaced a small boat channel to St. George's, which was defended from 1700 onwards by Town Cut Battery just to the right of the stern of the ship.

FIGURE 4.45: The guardhouse at Town Cut Battery had gunloops for musketry fire and would have had a roof.

his survey map mistakenly shows only two embrasures, probably an error in drafting.[115] The site now has four embrasures (Fig. 4.46), reflecting the rebuilding of the fort by Andrew Durnford (see Chap. Five).

Town Cut Battery is now part of the National Parks System and several pieces of historic ordnance are mounted on reproduction cast iron garrison standing carriages. In another National Park, a short distance to the south on St. David's Island is to be found another eighteenth-century fort flanking to the entrances to St. George's Harbour, called 'Fort Popple.' That work was supported in the 'late war' by a virtually unknown fort on Paget Island.

FIGURE 4.46: The plan of Town Cut Battery was recorded in the early 1980s and shows the guardhouse and the embrasured parapet for four guns.

114 PRO, Fraser, Defence Report.
115 PRO, Cunningham, Defence Report. Plan of Town Cut Battery.

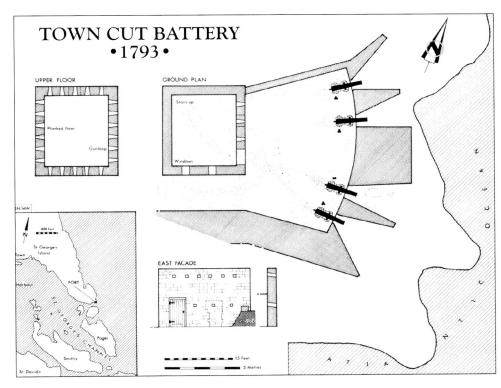

TOWN CUT BATTERY
•1793•

PAGET FASCINE BATTERY

Mentioned in Andrew Durnford's report of 1783, it is clear that a little-known fort was erected on Paget Island during the American Revolutionary War, here called the 'Paget Fascine Battery.'

> About One hundred yards in the Rear of Fort Paget, is a rising Ground on which a Fascine Battery for three Guns was made last war, to fire at Shipes on the Bar, with Barracks for 15 men & a Quarter for an Officer, with a Cistern to contain [about] 30 Hogsheads of water, and the Flag Staff. On this Ground a New Fort [should] be constructed for the Defence of St. George's Harbour (the best in this Island) in the rear of the Present Battery, which is absolutely defenceless. The Present Powder Magazine is situated on the Declivity of the hill, between the Fascine Battery and Fort Paget, It is cut out of the Rock containing about twenty Barrels, totally out of Repairs, not being [lined?] & very damp.[116]

The physical evidence for this battery of three guns was lost, presumably in the construction of Durnford's Upper Paget Fort in the 1790s, but certainly all trace would have been removed in the erection of Fort Cunningham thirty years later. As with Fort Bruere, the building of a fascine battery represents a quick solution to the circumstances which would have impinged on the security of Bermuda during the war in the American mainland colonies.

• • •

FORT POPPLE

Looking north towards Five Fathom Hole, this fort was excavated out of the hillside at Little Head on the northern end of St. David's Island by Governor Alured Popple in the 1730s; it is in effect one large sculpture, with a little masonry added later on to block some embrasures. It was recorded by Durnford and Fraser in 1783 as having nine gunports, a figure supported by the remains of the parapet (Fig. 4.47). The best description of it is to be found in Fraser's second report on the defences of Bermuda.

> Fort Popple...Is on the East side of David's Island, an Oblong Work rather inclining to a Semicircle—has six Embrasures in good repair, cut out of the Solid Rock, as the whole of this Work is from South to North 64 feet, from East to West 35 feet. Commanded by Captain Francis Hinson. In this Work are mounted the following Ordnance Viz; Guns—9 Pounders—2, 6 ditto 2} Dutch, weighed from a wreck in 1792, all of which are unserviceable.

> The Carriages are all of Wood for these Guns, and are in a Serviceable State. There is no Platform or flooring of any kind, but the Solid Rock. There are Twelve Rounds of Ammunition prepared for each piece of Ordnance in this Work, which are well secured (in a Moveable Magazine) and in a good State. The Side Arms and Stores for the whole of the Ordnance in this Work are complete and fit for Service—they along with the Ammunition are kept in the small House on Smith's Island formerly mentioned. There are two small places dug out of the Rock—one 7 feet by 8 the other 10 feet square, for placing the Ammunition and Stores in, but so damp and were they dry, are so much exposed to depredation, nothing can be kept in them, as there are no Troops stationed here. There is no Cistern or building of any kind at this Work—The reason assigned for Erecting this Work during Governor Popple's administration was that Vessels coming from the South side of the Island to five Fathom hole, where they can Anchor when the wind is unfavourable for entering St George's Harbour must come through a Channel, within the reach of the Guns of this Work, But from some Experiments made in 1793

[116] PRO, Durnford, Defence Report.

FIGURE 4.47: *The remains of Fort Popple were surveyed by archaeologists in the 1980s, several blocked embrasures being noted.*

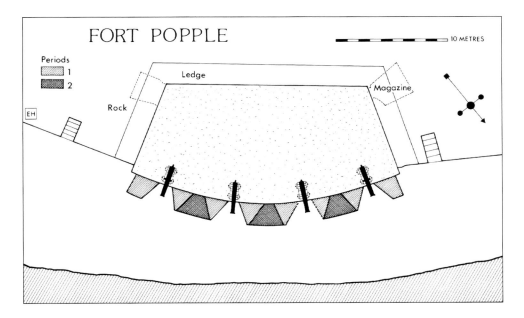

FIGURE 4.48: *Fort Popple as seen from the air in the early 1990s was quarried out of the bedrock.*

by Governor Hamilton, placing a large Cask in the Ship Channel, we were convinced the distance was too great for the Shot materially to injure a Vessel passing.[117]

The site was surveyed by Cunningham in 1811 and his drawing concurs with Fraser's description. Presumably during Andrew Durnford's tenure in the 1790s, three of the embrasures were blocked up with masonry, as seen in the 1980s (Fig. 4.48). The fort bears the distinction of being one of the two, which were named after the Governor of Bermuda at the time of their construction; the other, Fort Bruere, probably being the last colonial work to be erected prior to 1783.

[117] PRO, Fraser, Defence Report. This 1806 report is the most detailed description of the Bermuda forts prior to the building of the Dockyard in 1809.

CONCLUSIONS

The colonial forts and batteries from 1612 to 1783—the end of the American War of Independence—may now be summarised.

The first decade of settlement (1612-22) saw the building of eleven forts, ten in stone, and one in timber (being the only one ever constructed in wood in Bermuda) on the islands forming the eastern perimeter of the chain. In the successive decades, but possibly starting as early as 1617, a series of not less than twenty-seven batteries were built on the south and west coasts. At various dates, some undetermined but all before 1783, at least nine other redoubts were built on St. George's Island, with the Paget Fascine Battery being founded on Paget Island, Fort Popple on St. David's Island and the Landward Fort on Castle Island. This gives a total of about fifty colonial forts in the Bermudas at the turn of the military epoch in 1783.

Starting an itinerary on Castle Island and working west along the south coast of Great Bermuda, up the west coast to Somerset and Ireland Islands and then east to St. George's, the later group of thirty-nine forts discussed in this chapter may be summarised by their parish, name and approximate number of guns in position towards the end of the eighteenth century.

ST. GEORGE'S PARISH (2)
Landward Fort, 6 guns
Fort Bruere, none

HAMILTON PARISH (1)
Bailey's Bay Battery, 2 guns

SMITH'S PARISH (4)
Newton's Bay Fort, 2 guns
Albouy's Fort, 2 guns
Harris's Bay Fort, 2 guns
Sears Fort, 1 gun

DEVONSHIRE PARISH (1)
Devonshire Bay Fort, 2 guns

PAGET PARISH (4)
Hungry Bay Fort, 2 guns
Crow Lane Fort, 4 guns
Centre Bay Fort, 2 guns
West Elbow Bay Fort, 2 guns

WARWICK PARISH (4)
Warwick Fort, 2 guns
Great Turtle Bay Battery, 2 guns
Jobson's Fort, 2 guns
Jobson's Cove Fort, 2 guns

SOUTHAMPTON PARISH (6)
Hunt's Fort, 2 guns
Ingham's Fort, 2 guns
Church Bay East Fort, 2 guns
Church Bay West Fort, 4 guns
Fort Newbold, 2 guns
West Side Fort, 4 guns

SANDYS PARISH (5)
Wreck Hill Fort, 2 guns
Daniel's Island Fort, 3 guns
Mangrove Bay Fort, 2 guns
[King's Point Fort], none
Maria Hill Fort, 7 guns

ST. GEORGE'S PARISH (12)
Burnt Point Fort, 5 guns
New Redoubt, 2 guns
Fort Clinton, 5 guns
[Tobacco Bay Fort], 1 gun
[St. Catherine's Point Fort], 1 gun
[St. Catherine's Bay Fort], 2 guns
[Eastside Fort], 1 gun
[Amberfish Hole Fort], 1 gun
[Buildings Bay Fort], 1 gun
Town Cut Battery, 3 guns
Paget Fascine Battery, 3 guns
Fort Popple, 7 guns

This gives a total of ninety-seven guns for the small coastal works. In the mid-eighteenth century, the forts still in use from the first decade of settlement mounted the following: Old Castle (Charles Fort), two guns; King's Castle, twenty-four; Southampton Fort, five; Smith's Fort, seven and Paget Fort, ten guns, for a combined total of one hundred and forty five pieces of ordnance. By the end of the American War of Independence, the Americans had stolen the guns from Wreck Hill, and Governor Bruere dispatched the remaining thirty he possessed in the *Scorpion,* as he feared the Bermudians would steal them for sale to the American rebels, given the earlier theft of the government's gunpowder.

So ended one hundred and seventy one years of fort-building and armament by the Bermudians at the end of the war in 1783. Fifty-odd forts capable of mounting three times as many guns had been erected to fend off the Spaniards and other enemies. As will be seen in the next chapter, the American victory in the war forever changed the local military scene, as the British forces moved into Bermuda to make up for the strategic loss of naval bases on the eastern seaboard of the former mainland colonies.

■ ■ ■

The Corps of Royal Engineers erected many of the forts at Bermuda: pictured here are men of the 36th Company, R.E., probably at Fort Hamilton in the late nineteenth century.

5

Andrew Durnford &
The Corps of Royal Engineers

1 7 8 3 – 1 8 0 8

Agreeable to your Orders of the 13th May [I] Shall attempt a description of the different Forts the most of which are rather nominal than real, Being places of no defence, but what art is Defficient in, nature has abundantly supplied, having as 'twere, Palisaded the Islands with inaccessible rocks all round...

—Simon Fraser, R.A., 1783

IN 1775, THE PEACE OF THE BRITISH OVERSEAS POSSESSIONS WAS SHATTERED at the place where the empire of colonies began in 1607 in North America. All of the thirteen colonies on the eastern seaboard were eventually involved in this civil war which saw their independence from England in 1783. The Bermudians used both sides to their advantage in the conflict and went as far as to steal gunpowder from the magazine at St. George's for sale and barter to the 'Americans.'[1] They remained loyal to the British Crown and deigned not to join their mainland cousins in a new state of 'Independence.'[2] The war was won in part because of a temporary supremacy of the seas by the French Navy, a fact not lost on the thinking of the British forces. So it was that as the war ended, the British military looked to Bermuda as a possible replacement for the lost naval bases of the eastern seaboard of the new United States of America. Several officers were sent to Bermuda and later stationed there, foremost of whom was Andrew Durnford of the Corps of Royal Engineers.

By the 1980s, the Durnford family of Hampshire, England had accrued nearly 200 years of service in the British Army, with five successive generations serving in the Corps of Royal Engineers. Andrew Durnford was in the first generation, being a younger brother of Elias who joined the Royal Engineers in 1759 and was Lieutenant-Governor of West Florida in 1769. Andrew was born on April 24, 1744 and obtained his commission in the Royal Engineers on July 28, 1769. The following year, he took part in the demolition of the

[1] Wilfred Brenton Kerr, *Bermuda and the American Revolution: 1760–1783* (1995).

[2] Two hundred years on, in August 1995, Bermuda voted to remain a colony, making the island the oldest such entity in the British Commonwealth.

fortifications at Dunkirk, owing 'his selection for this work to his well-known talents as a draughtsman.'[3] After a stint on the forts at Plymouth, he embarked for America in 1776, serving there throughout the War of Independence. Spending a few months in Bermuda in 1783, he returned to the United Kingdom to be Chief Engineer at Chatham. In 1788, he was ordered to Bermuda to re-fortify the island: there he died on September 10, 1798, at the age of 54 with the rank of Major.[4] He was the first member of the Corps of Royal Engineers, 'purveyors of technology to the empire,' to be stationed at Bermuda and his achievements here reflect the extraordinary standards of that division of the British Army.

During his time in Bermuda, Durnford was much involved in local politics, becoming the first Mayor of St. George's and building a fine home and warehouse for himself on the western edge of the Town. Working first under the affable Governor Henry Hamilton, he ran afoul of his replacement, Crauford, who dismissed Durnford in 1795. His last three years were spent under 'Suspension from Rank & Pay…Promotion stopt in the Corps of Engineers, & every Mortification that can be accumulated on the head of a Military Man—I have felt'; the matter was only resolved by his untimely death.[5] His home became known as the 'Fifth Fort,'[6] a reference to the four new redoubts he built to the north and west of St. George's. Because of associations of impropriety between the building of house and forts, some writers have tended to treat Durnford's career in Bermuda with derision.[7]

Yet, as will be evident below, Andrew Durnford was extremely active and a more detailed study than the present would underline his many achievements. By 1793, he had completed a land survey of the islands, albeit not in the detail a modern historian would desire. He assisted the hydrographer, Thomas Hurd, in his monumental survey of the Bermuda reefs and aside from his civic duties, including a second family, Durnford altered, repaired or built anew a number of the East End fortifications, in addition to the building of the four 'Town Redoubts.'[8]

Durnford first came to Bermuda as a replacement for a Lieutenant Slack, R.E., who had been employed on a reconnaissance of the fortifications early in 1783. Slack sailed with his report to New York on HMS *Mentor* in the late Spring with the officers and all but one of the crew of HMS *Cerberus*—herself lately wrecked at Bermuda—but all hands were lost without trace.[9] Sent out from New York on September 4 following, on the 'Transport Brig Joseph,' Lieut. Durnford arrived at St. George's on the 16th and on the 20th of the next month, his report was submitted to Lt.-Col. Morse, Chief Engineer in America. The study dealt with the harbours, channels and the natural defences of the extensive reefs; the existing fortifications and their armaments were also described, although several forts were missed.[10] An independent survey had already been sent to the Royal Artillery by Simon Fraser, R.A.,[11] and the two reports are the foundation of much of the knowledge of the fortifications at Bermuda in the third quarter of the eighteenth century. The plans of the fortifications which accompanied Durnford's report have been lost.

In 1788, Durnford stated that those plans could not be taken as accurate

[3] J. W. Lydekker, 'A Soldier Family,' *Royal Engineers Journal* (1933), 428-38.

[4] Ibid., Durnford was married in 1772 and had two sons in England: the sixth generation to carry the name of one son, Andrew Montague Isaacson Durnford, was born in Canada in 1983, where that branch of the family survives. The Rev. Percival Durnford Burrows of that line kindly provided information on the family.

[5] Bermuda Archives, Durnford Papers, May 26, 1798.

[6] 'Durnford House' still stands as a private home, and the 'Queen's Warehouse' is in the possession of the Corporation of St. George's.

[7] Terry Tucker, 'The Honourable Major Andrew Durnford of the Corps of Royal Engineers,' *Bermuda Historical Quarterly* 25, 4 (1968), 111.

[8] Durnford had a family of four sons and two daughters in Bermuda. His relict, 'my dear friend Elizabeth Lucas late of Great Britain but now resident in town of St George & known by that name only' (*BHQ* 25, 4 (1968), 112), sold their land where Fort George stands for £900 in 1818.

[9] H. G. Middleton, 'The Loss of HMS *Cerberus*,' *BHQ* 24, 4 (1967), 125.

[10] PRO, CO 37/38. Andrew Durnford, Report on the Defences of Bermuda, 1783.

[11] Scottish Record Office GD/50/185/267/12/7. Simon Fraser, Report on the Defences of Bermuda, 1783. Fraser remained in Bermuda as Commissary of the Royal Artillery.

as they 'were made from other drafts' and that a 'minute survey' should be made before 'a system of defence be laid down for Bermuda.'[12] Thereupon he was ordered to Bermuda by the Duke of Richmond to make a special survey to include the land and shores; soundings also were to be taken to fix the positions of the rocks and shoals, 'so as to make ye survey as complete as possible.' When all that was done and reported, he was to proceed to Grenada.[13] With Henry Lauzun, his draughtsman assistant, Captain Andrew Durnford embarked on July 18, 1788, taking with them the equipment necessary for the 'Intended survey of the Islands of Bermuda. One Large Theodolite, One Spirit Level with Telescope, One small Theodolite to fill up with, Two Station Staves, a Protractor, a Sextant, a Three Foot Telescope, a Brass Scale of Equal Parts, One Hundred Foot Chain, One Fifty Foot Chain.'[14] Arriving on September 11, Lauzun and Durnford set to work examining the existing fortifications and making plans for alterations and new buildings. Three of their plans survive, one of Smith's Fort on Governor's Island and two of Castle Island. What would have been an important set for historic purposes was still in Bermuda in the early 1840s, when Governor Reid learned to his distress that 'a mulatto woman,' formerly the Durnfords' cook, had recently sold forty plans of forts and defences to the Colonel of Engineers of the U.S. Army.[15]

Durnford's first task was to carry out a survey of Bermuda, which was completed five years later (Pl. 5).[16] For this job, several local boats were purchased, which were also used in raising guns from the wrecks of *My Lord Amherst*, Ordnance Transport (lost 1778) and HMS *Cerberus* (lost 1783). This was to be the first general survey of the Bermudas since Norwood's of 1663 and the original map is not known to have survived. A copy giving a date of 1793 in its title, but annotated 'Copy Tho. Arrowsmith' is to be found in the Public Record Office[17] and a copy 'corrected from a plan of Genl. Hodgsons in 1833' exists in a Canadian archive.[18] The latter copy is somewhat corrupted and most of the detail of land holdings found in the London document have been lost in transcription. Curiously, the Canadian map has the sites of a number of the forts marked with an X, a feature not apparent in the PRO version. In addition (noted by their absence on the PRO map), this copy records batteries at Maria Hill, and Daniel's Island, and by name, Whale Bay Battery, Common Land Battery,[19] and Great Turtle Bay Battery.

Durnford makes no mention of the use of any earlier surveys and it is probable that he was not aware of the 1663 Norwood map. Taking the PRO chart as reminiscent of the original work, Lauzun and Durnford surveyed the entire coastline noting the general position of some of its batteries by name. Of interest to a topographical history a number of the shares of land are delineated, with some buildings shown. This monumental task was carried out at a time when Durnford had also begun to renovate several of the major fortifications at the eastern end of the islands.

A summary of his work on the forts begins with repairs to the King's Castle, Devonshire Redoubt and Southampton Fort and by the middle of 1790 a new work was begun on Castle Island. In 1791, Paget Fort was repaired, Town Cut Battery rebuilt and the 'Great Battery' at Devonshire Redoubt on Castle Island completed. The year 1793 saw repairs at Fort St.

[12] Royal Engineers Library, Connolly Papers.

[13] Ibid.

[14] BA, Durnford Papers, Book 2, 9 June 1788.

[15] Henry C. Wilkinson, *Bermuda from Sail to Steam* (1973), 551.

[16] A copy was sent to the Duke of Richmond, Master General of the Ordnance, on November 24, 1793. See *BHQ* 25, 4 (1968), 121.

[17] PRO MPH 137. A Survey of the Islands of Bermuda by Captain Andrew Durnford Royal Engineer assisted by Mr. Henry Lauzun, Draughtsman. 1793.

[18] Having the same title as PRO MPH 137, this map is from 'The Library of George, 9th Earl of Dalhousie, Governor of Nova Scotia, 1816–1819, and of Canada, 1819–1828. Wm. Inglis Morse Collection.' Vaughan Library, Acadia University.

[19] Misplaced, along with 'Cross Bay,' a mile too far West.

Catherine and Fort Popple, Burnt Point Fort was rebuilt and works were started at the King's Castle, Southampton Fort, on Paget, Smith's and Ferry Islands, and on the South Shore at Newton's Bay and Walker's Bay (Sears Fort). In 1794, new works were begun on Coney Island to the west side of the Ferry and on four redoubts to the north of the Town of St. George.

CASTLE & SOUTHAMPTON ISLANDS

Shortly after his second arrival in Bermuda, Durnford visited Castle Island and a letter of late November 1788 confirms the presence of the Captain's House at the King's Castle 'in great want of immediate repair'; the nearby Bakehouse (discovered again in 1993) had had its roof blown off in 'a gale of Wind' and the adjacent Cistern had a leak.[20] Writing to the Duke of Richmond late in 1790, Durnford noted that the 'Officers Quarters' and the 'upper Sea Battery' at the King's Castle had been repaired, with the parapet thickened towards Charles Island. Extensive work was undertaken in the main work below.

> The lower Sea Battery has been considerably thickened, the useless Embrasures filled up, the Rock upon which it stands being cracked, has been made good with Masonry, the Stone Platform repaired, a Banquette made where necessary, New Cross Walls at the entrance of the Battery and the Passage widened & made capable of giving Shelter to a considerable Number of Men in case of attack from Tuckers' Town point.[21]

FIGURE 5.1: *Castle Island from the south-east; the men in the boat in Figure 5.2 are mid-channel, centre foreground in this aerial view.*

FIGURE 5.2: *In this water-colour of 1814, the Great Battery at Devonshire Redoubt shows its strategic position; on the right are the Captain's House, Cookhouse and batteries of the King's Castle (Bermuda National Trust).*

[20] *BHQ* 25, 4 (1968), 115. The transcriptions of the Durnford papers in this Journal are not reliable: the originals have been quoted where possible

[21] BA, Durnford Papers, Book 4, November 1, 1790.

Removing to the centre of the island (Fig. 5.1), Durnford 'repaired by thickening and raising the Parapet' of the 'old Tower' at Devonshire Redoubt, built in 1621 by Governor Nathaniel Butler.[22] Below this, a new work to be called the 'Great Battery' (Fig. 5.2)

> …has been begun & will be soon defenceable, round the old Tower for Eight Guns & the two 10 Inch Howitzers inclosing the lower Battery [part of Devonshire Redoubt] towards the Harbour & Powder Magazine. This work is *En Embrazure* with walls of Bermuda Masonry 2 feet thick filled with Earth, and the Parapet towards Tuckers Town Point and the Entrance of the Harbour most exposed to fire [i.e., towards Charles Island] will be about 20 feet thick…[23]

FIGURE 5.3: *Devonshire Redoubt and the Great Battery from the air in 1994; a large magazine is protected by Durnford's redan on the left.*

22 In a return for the month of December, 1790 (BA, Durnford Papers, Book 9), Durnford had employed on the repair works 'an Overseer, a Toolkeeper, 2 carpenters, 8 Black and 19 White Labourers,' the last receiving equal pay for the period of £3/12s. One of the labourers was a James Whitecross, probably the great-great-great grandfather of the author.

23 BA, Durnford Papers, Book 4, November 1, 1790.

24 BA, Durnford Papers, Book 4, October 1, 1791. Normally, an abatis is a 'defence formed by placing felled trees lengthwise one over the other with their branches towards the enemy's line' (*OED*). Perhaps the Bermudian equivalent of prickly pear-bush may masquerade as an *abatis passif*, serving 'as a mere obstacle.' Cornélis De Witt Willox, *A French-English Military Technical Dictionary* (1917).

The new work was protected by anti-personnel planting for in 1791 a 'few Labourers have been also kept upon pay & employed at the King's Castle particularly, in weeding & removing the prickly Pear-Bush to the Front of the great Battery, where an *Abbatis* of them has been formed about 20 feet wide.'[24] The large magazine at Devonshire Redoubt was also repaired and a Redan was added to the East of it for protection against fire from ships in the channel (Fig. 5.3).

The Great Battery at Devonshire Redoubt is indicative of the fine quality of work carried out by Andrew Durnford; it is the only one of his works to survive intact. The original Devonshire Redoubt was designed to fire into Castle Harbour: Durnford's new work reversed the emphasis to fire to seawards in protection of the southern side of Castle Island. To the north the rock forms a cliff, but the southern side of the island being low to the sea had to have a rampart erected on it to heighten its defences. The Great Battery, with its seven guns, fired over this and covered the bay against an attack from a landing force in small boats.

It is clear from Durnford's notes that several structures on Castle Island were in existence at his arrival. The curtain wall or rampart on the south side, the barracks near his new gate and the large magazine at Devonshire Redoubt all pre-date his work. The dates of construction for these interesting features is not known, but they are certainly eighteenth- and in some aspects may be seventeenth-century.

The work towards Tucker's Town was not neglected and by November 1790, Durnford had thickened and raised its parapet, along with that of the nearby 'Small Battery' and the curtain wall facing Charles Island (see Fig. 3.18). A new traverse—one of several planned—was being erected on the curtain to prevent its enfilade. The line of the musketry curtain was broken by a 'New Entrance to the Castle…near the Barracks with Strong Gates, where the old Guard house stood, which being in ruins was pulled down and several useless Embrazures in this Line' were filled up in passing.[25] A stone wharf at the new entrance was completed in the Spring of 1793,[26] but was utterly destroyed in a violent storm on October 23, when 'the Sea rose in a few minutes so high as to cover the Wharf at least three feet and in a short time took the greatest part of it away.'[27]

In the same period, Durnford had been 'employed in Repairing, thickening and raising the Parapet of the Sea Battery at Fort Southampton,' as well as making repairs to the 'Tower,' 'Guardhouse,' cistern and the gate.[28] The existing cannon parapet on Southampton Island (see Fig. 3.28) may thus be assumed to be the 1621 work of Governor Butler, overlain by additional bolstering masonry by Andrew Durnford.

Neither Castle nor Southampton Islands seems to have been altered since Durnford's time, which is fortuitous for history. The two islands, with their four standing forts, dating from 1612, 1621 and the 1790s must therefore be seen to be two of the most important early English military sites in the New World.

• • •

PAGET, GOVERNOR'S & ST. DAVID'S ISLANDS

One of the first places visited by Durnford was Paget Island and repairs to Fort Paget were begun late in 1789, but in a severe gale on January 22, 1790, all of the work effected on the 'old Sea Battery' was overturned. Convinced that it was pointless to attempt to rearm that position, Durnford recommended to the Governor that he 'thicken the Walls, and fill up with Earth the area of the Dungeon in order to mount 3—12 Prs. belonging to the *Cerberus*,' which work was well advanced, but discontinued in June 1791,[29] being completed two years later. It is presumed that the 'dungeon' was the ditch, which was found to be filled by archaeologists in the 1980s (see Fig. 3.5). Nothing of Fort Paget survives above ground, except a few mortar traces of the base courses of some of the walls (Fig. 5.4).

25 BA, Durnford Papers, Book 4, November 1, 1790.

26 *BHQ* 26, 3 (1969), 83.

27 *BHQ* 25, 4 (1968), 116–7. This must have been a blow to Durnford's pride, having but a few months previously informed the Master General of Ordnance that the wharf 'stood the last Winter in an unfinished state, to the astonishment of many people who did not conceive from the great Surge always going, that it was a practicable Undertaking; not being accustomed to see a work of such strength constructed before' (BA, Durnford Papers, Book 4, April 30, 1793).

28 *BHQ* 26, 1 (1969), p. 23–4.

29 BA, Durnford Papers, Book 4, June 1, 1791.

FIGURE 5.4: *In this aerial view of the 1940s, Fort Cunningham occupies the site of Upper Fort Paget, with Paget Fort on the point next to eighteenth century musketry trenches (author's collection).*

FIGURE 5.5: *Paget Island has been home to five fortifications: Peniston's Redoubt, Paget Fort, Paget Fascine Battery and Upper Fort Paget, the last being supplanted by Fort Cunningham.*

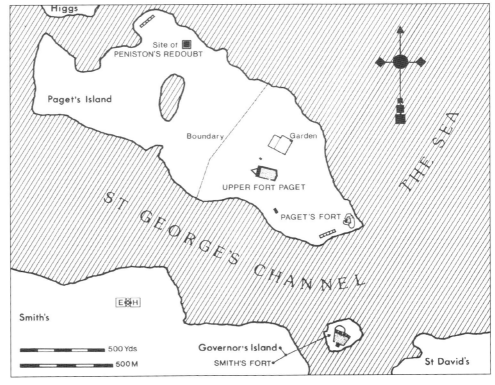

30 BA, Durnford Papers, Book 4, April 30, 1793.

31 PRO WO 55/1551/2. Thomas Cunningham. Defence Report. 1811.

In the Spring of 1793, Durnford was ordered by the Governor to begin a 'new Work for a Barbette Battery at the Flagstaff on Paget Island, together with some considerable improvements to the Works at Catherines Point.'[30] The work, to be called 'Upper Fort Paget,' was situated on the top of the rise to the north-west of Paget Fort and was recorded in the 1811 survey (Fig. 5.5).

Upper Fort Paget is advantageously situated upon a rising ground 170 yards from the lower battery. Its form is nearly a parallelogram. The front and sides towards the entrance of the Harbour has a parapet 12 inches high and 12 feet thick, with an excellent platform of cedar on which two Dutch 24 pdrs, four English—two 4-pdrs and one 8-inch Howitzer. The south side is occupied by a building which contains a barracks for 50 men, officers' quarters, and Artillery House, and the rear is closed by a wall 3 feet high.[31]

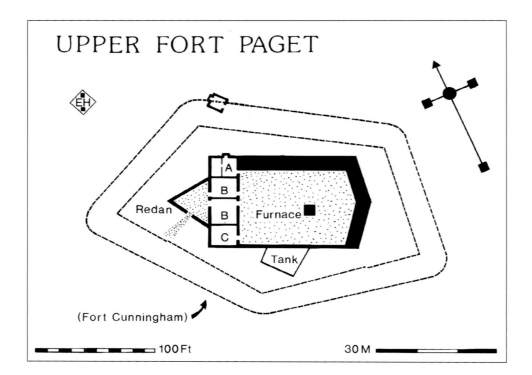

FIGURE 5.6: *This plan of Upper Fort Paget is from Cunningham's 1811 survey and shows his proposed ditch for what became Fort Cunningham (redrawn by the author).*

The building has Durnford's stamp on it, with the thick parapet for six guns, possibly firing through embrasures consistent with his other works. At the rear it was divided into four rooms and the entrance was protected by a redan. All of this would have been swept away in the construction of Fort Cunningham in the late 1810s, for the 1811 survey upon which Figure 5.6 is based already contained the outline of the new work which Thomas Cunningham had in mind.

Upper Fort Paget played across the channel into St. George's Harbour and thus worked in concert with the old Smith's Fort on Governor's Island. Writing to the Duke of Richmond in July 1793, Durnford mentioned that a 'new Fort is also far advanced on the Island called Smith's [*sic,* Governor's] Island, at the Entrance of St. George's Harbour.'[32] Cunningham describes it in his 1811 survey (Fig. 5.7).

> The south side of the entrance of the ship channel which is about 170 yards inside is formed by a small island on which is Smith's Fort. The embrasures are in ruins from the first firing of the guns owing to the wretched execution of the work, the merlons being only faced with stone 9 inches thick and filled with rubbish. In front is a low circular work with a parapet 4 feet thick and eight embrasures now built up. The roof of the guard house some time since fell in. There are three 18 pdrs in this work on stone platforms, but not in good condition.[33]

The rear of Smith's Fort in the 1980s was inaccessible under poison ivy, but little seemed to remain above ground. Durnford's new battery could be seen and was similar in construction to the Great Battery on Castle Island. The merlons are about 15 feet thick and there were four emplacements for guns firing *en embrasure.* The D-shaped sea battery from the 1620s was presumably reconstituted with a parapet four feet thick and mounting eight guns (Fig. 5.8).

32 BA, Durnford Papers, Book 4, July 15, 1793.
33 PRO, Cunningham. Defence Report.

FIGURE 5.7: *Governor's Island was overgrown with brush and poison ivy in the 1980s, but the face of Durnford's battery was evident.*

FIGURE 5.8: *This plan of Smith's Fort was recorded in 1985 and shows the relationship of the upper (Durnford's) and lower batteries to the original two-bastioned work of 1612, part of which may survive below ground.*

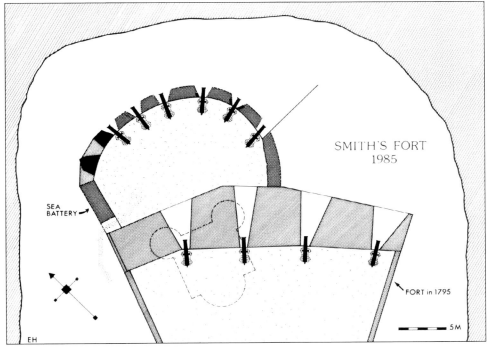

34 *BHQ* 26, 3 (1969), 86.

35 BA, Durnford Papers, Book 2, February 10, 1795.

Repairs were made to Fort Popple in 1792,[34] the purpose of that fort 'being to annoy Vessels coming round the head, in going over the Bar, or lying in five fathom hole, or coming from the northward round the point of breakers and flanking the East side of St. George's Island between Fort Paget and Catherines point...'[35] While Durnford repaired Fort Popple, he was later of the opinion that it should be rebuilt on higher grounds as he did in the instance of Paget Fort on the opposite island. His work on Paget, Governor's, and St. David's Islands thus reconstituted the defences for the protection of the only ships' channel into St. George's Harbour and was the first major renovation of some of those sites since they had been built in 1612–22.

ST. GEORGE'S & CONEY ISLANDS

The defences of St. George's Island and the much smaller Coney Island, at the western approaches to the former at the Ferry, also received Durnford's attention. Starting on the eastern coast, Durnford largely made over a fort built in 1700, itself possibly on an earlier structure (see Fig 4.46).

> The Town Cut Battery at the East End of St. George's Island has been rebuilt for 4, 6 pors: belonging to the Cerberus and are now mounted. A New Building in the rear to serve as an Ordnance Store for the Carriages &c. with a Guard Room over it has been likewise built being in *Crenaux*[36] is intended to serve as a Block House for the Guard to retire into. This work…is of great consequence to the protection of the Town as all vessels from the Eastward must be seen from this place.[37]

The battery also covered a shallow channel between St. George's and Higgs Island to the south, which could be used by small boats. The structure, known locally as 'Gates Fort' is thus almost two centuries later than has generally been thought. In order to improve communications, a new military road was in place by June 1791 from St. George's to the Town Cut Battery and from thence along the coast to Fort St. Catherine.[38]

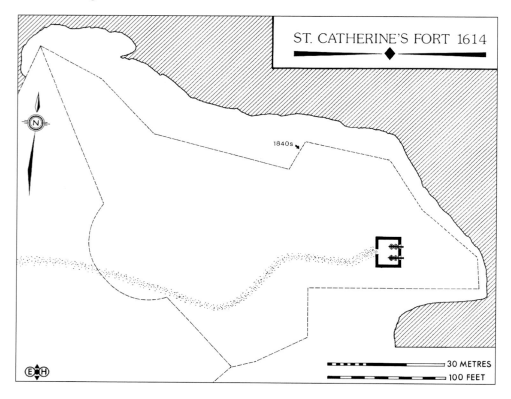

ST. CATHERINE'S FORT 1614

1840s

30 METRES
100 FEET

FIGURE 5.9: *The original St. Catherine's Fort is presumed in this drawing to have been positioned on the eastern headland at St. Catherine's Point.*

Fort St. Catherine had one of the longest histories of all the Bermuda defence works. The site began life in the first years of the colony when a small fort was erected (Fig. 5.9). At some point, the fort was rebuilt and assumed the shape described in 1783 by Simon Fraser, R.A. in his report to London.

> Stands Fort St Catherine, on a promontory under the Guns of which, all the Ships that come down the North side of the Island must come, that being the Only channel, that leads to the entrance of the Harbour by Pagett Isd., This Fort has seven Embrasures Is Sixty feet from right to left, & forty five from the rear to the utmost point in front,

[36] Probably in the sense of *créneaux d'étage*, being loopholes through a wall, as occurs at this site, in the Tower at Fort Southampton, and the latrine building at the Landward Fort on Castle Island.

[37] BA, Durnford Papers, Book 4, June 1, 1791.

[38] *BHQ* 26, 3 (1969), 73.

'tis certainly In the power of this Fort, to annoy ships when passing Very much were it fortified, but like all the other Works of this Island, in its present situation is good For nothing, there's no magazine Cestern nor Barrack Here...[39]

This is not the fort described and drawn by Cunningham in his 1811 report, but must be the one surveyed by Andrew Evans, R.N., prior to Durnford's remodelling of the site. In the Evans drawing (Fig. 5.10),[40] a hexagonal fort is shown with indications of the embrasures. Just east of the main work is a small squarish building, which may be the only

FIGURE 5.11: Andrew Durnford rebuilt Fort St. Catherine as two separate batteries connected by a sunken communications passage in the 1790s.

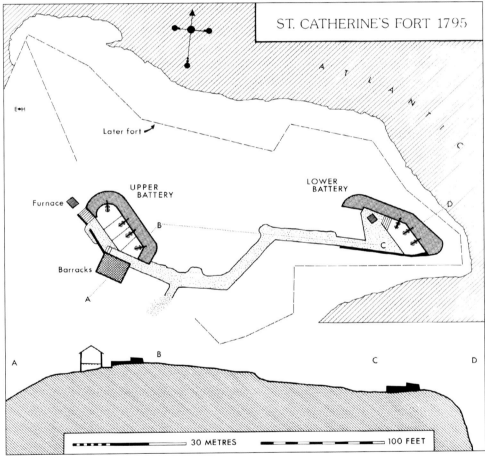

[39] SRO, Defence Report. I am grateful to David J. Brown of the SRO Historical Search Room for a copy of this important report.

[40] Public Archives Canada, National Map Collection, NMC 8789. I thank Ed Dahl, Curator of Maps for his assistance.

topographical evidence known of the original St. Catherine's Fort. Durnford's new works are recorded in Cunningham's plan (Fig. 5.11), from which the following scenario may be suggested.

On the point, Durnford removed what may have been the original fort on the site and replaced it with a thick parapet fronting the channel, probably not

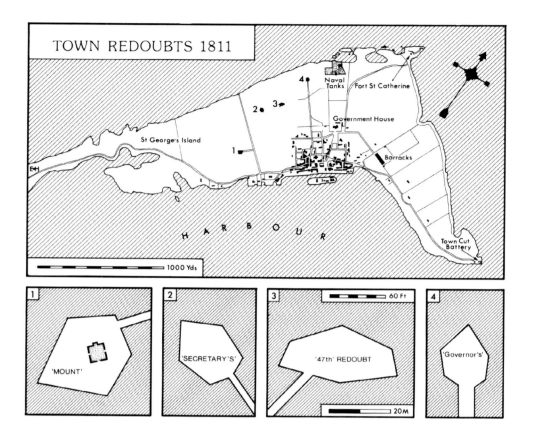

FIGURE 5.12: *Redrawn from the 1811 Cunningham report, this plan shows the location and design of the four Town Redoubts built by Andrew Durnford.*

unlike the works on Smith's Fort and Devonshire Redoubt. In 1811, this forward battery mounted three 24-pounders. It is presumed that he removed the work recorded by Evans and in its place erected a new redoubt on an irregular D-shape. To its rear was a barracks and the two batteries were joined by a communications trench cut into the bedrock. In his own words:

> The old Battery on the point was strengthened and a new Battery in the rear of it has been made with three Redoubts to the Westward along the Shore to prevent an Enemy from landing in Tobacco Bay and to support any of his Majesty's Ships of War drawn up to defend the passage round Catherines Point; for this reason these Batteries being upon high situations were made *en barbette* that the Guns may be turned to any part of the Channel. The Redoubt on the Mount hill where is the Signal house is more immediately to command the Approach to the Town by the land from the Ferry.[41]

The other works became known as the 'Town Redoubts' (Fig. 5.12). By August 1794, they were in 'great forwardness' and would shortly be ready to receive their armament. Durnford sent the Duke of Richmond 'Plan 33,' to inform him of the situation.[42]

> Besides the works already mentioned for the defence of the Harbours, there are works immediately surrounding the Town of St. George's, consisting of four Redouts thrown up on the summit of as many hills, for the defence of the town towards the land side.
>
> No. 1 or St. Georges Redout is of a pentagonal figure from 50 to 80 feet each side, the parapet raised 2½ feet above the terraplain, the superior Talus taking nearly the natural slope of the hill, and revetted with a dry wall. In many parts totally decayed. There are two 24 p^{rs} and two 18 p^{rs} mounted in this work, but no platforms.

[41] BA, Durnford Papers, Book 2, February 10, 1795.

[42] *BHQ* 26, 3 (1969), 90. At least 34 plans are mentioned in the Durnford letters on the progress of the works, but none appear to have survived.

No. 2 or Secretary's Redout is a work of a similar construction to No. 1 only smaller, and distant from it about 400 yards. In this work are two 18 p^{rs} but no platforms.

No. 3, about 200 yards to the East of No. 2 by which it is commanded, is an irregular hexagon of from 30 to 60 feet each side, also similar in construction to the other two. In this work are two 18 p^{rs} in a very decayed state but no remains of either carriages or platforms.

No. 4 or Governor's Redout, is a small hexagonal work similar in construction to the others, now completely in ruins. 'Tis also commanded by No.2 at the distance of between 4 and 500 yards.

Redoubt No. 1 eventually became Fort George: it is the highest point on St. George's Island and was used as a signal station from the earliest days, as Riches Mount. No. 2 was on the 150 feet elevation of Secretary's, later Cemetery, Hill and it commanded No. 3 and 4 at about 100 feet above the sea. These were irregular works, dug into the bedrock and not given the emphasis displayed by Durnford at his coastal positions at St. Catherine's Point, the Town Cut, Paget and Smith's Forts and Devonshire Redoubt to the south. Nothing survives above ground of these fortifications, which were to work with those at the Ferry to defend the rear approaches to the Town:[43] 'I have been employed by his Excellency the Governor, in strengthening the several Works at the Ferry, & establishing a Chain of Redoubts on the North side of this Town for its better security.' [44]

FIGURE 5.13: A Ferry connected St. George's with Great Bermuda across the channel in the left foreground via Coney Island in the centre foreground.

At the Northwest end of St. George's Island is another Entrance into St. George's and Castle Harbour called the Ferry [Fig. 5.13] for Vessels drawing about 10 feet Water, but there is no Communication except by small Boats between the Ferry and Castle Harbour on account of sunken Rocks and shoals throughout it. The Defence of the Ferry consists of three unfinished Works, two on this or St. George's and one on the opposite side.

The first is an old Sea Battery [Burnt Point] sometime repaired last year, the Parapet 6 feet high and five feet thick with three Embrazures towards the Entrance of the Ferry Channel and two for the North shore towards Whalebone bay. This Work was much damaged and the Merlons shaken by the explosion of its Guns in firing a Salute not long ago and I must here remark the Bermuda Stone which is only concreted and is by no means calculated for the checks or soles of Embrazures differing materially from the Europa Stone at Gibraltar which the longer it is exposed to the weather the harder it

[43] It is a pity that history has unfairly associated Durnford with these four minor works, rather than the significant fortifications he renovated or rebuilt.

[44] BA, Durnford Papers, Book 2, August 20, 1794.

FIGURE 5.14: Ferry Island
Fort from the air in the
1990s, looking south-west.

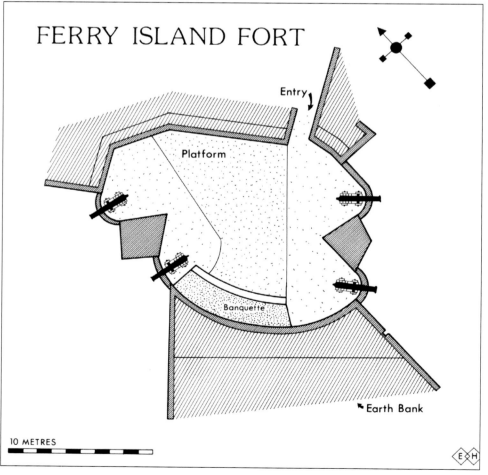

FERRY ISLAND FORT

Entry

Platform

Banquette

Earth Bank

10 METRES

FIGURE 5.15: Ferry Island
Fort was recorded by
archaeologists in the 1980s:
this is the only known plan
of the work, which probably
dates to the 1810s.

becomes whereas the Bermuda Stone from its porous quality imbibes a considerable quantity of Moisture and consequently soon Moulders away unless constantly washed over with slacked lime. The other Work [Ferry Island Fort] is well situated for the defence of the Entrance and Passage of the Ferry on an insulated Mound its form is semi-circular mounting three 12 Pounders en barbette but from the lowness of the Parapet about 2½ feet it is entirely exposed to and commanded by the Hill on the opposite shore this might easily be avoided by raising the parapet and putting the Guns on embrazures. The third Redout [Coney Island Fort] remains unfinished it is a barbette hexagonal Battery of 250 feet in Circumference erected on a Sandy hill to defend the approach to the Ferry on the West side.[45]

Figure 5.16: In 1811, three works protected Ferry Reach at the western end of St. George's Island, with two Martello Towers proposed.

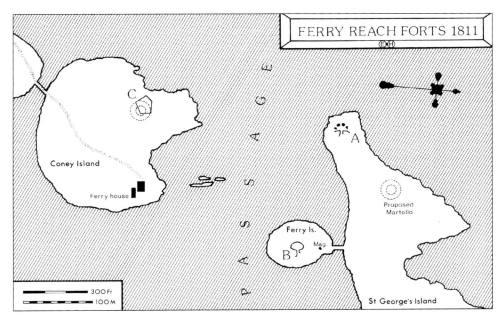

The evidence of Durnford's repairs to Burnt Point Fort are obvious, as he increased the width of the merlons of the embrasures by some four feet and this could be seen in the stonework in the 1980s (see Fig. 4.43). The guns were a bigger calibre and the embrasures commensurably reduced from nine to five openings.

Ferry Island Fort is described in several of the Royal Engineers' defence reports as being circular, *en barbette*, with a parapet no higher than three feet.[46] This is not the work found at the site in the 1980s (Figs. 5.14 and 5.15), which is a developed structure, clearly of a later date. It must be assumed that Durnford's Ferry Island Fort was destroyed in the process of building this existing work for four guns firing through embrasures. Unfortunately, no documentary reference can be found to this interesting and unusually shaped structure, but it must pre-date the nearby Martello Tower, itself completed in 1824. This fort is therefore probably the only one built in Bermuda between Durnford's death in 1798 and the beginning of the major new fortifications associated with the establishment of the Royal Naval Dockyard at the western end of the islands.

On Coney Island (Fig. 5.16), the southern landing of the Ferry just off the eastern extremity of Great Bermuda, Durnford built an hexagonal battery to work the channel with Burnt Point and Ferry Island Forts. In the 1811 survey, this seemed to have been in ruins, or was simply not finished in Durnford's time: in the 1980s nothing of note could be found of this fort.

[45] PRO WO 55/1551/1. Augustus DeButts. Bermuda Defence Report 1798.

[46] BA, Durnford Papers, Book 10, July 31, 1793. This year finds Durnford 'rebuilding the Old Fort on Burnt Point at the Ferry, and building a Barbette Battery with a Guard house on Ferry Island…'

CONCLUSIONS

In 1795, Major Andrew Durnford was suspended after disagreements with Governor Crauford and this disgrace must have played a part in his early death three years later. His work over the ten years to 1798 may be summarised. On Great Bermuda, he caused Sears Fort to be erected, along with repairs to another small work at Newton's Bay (see Chap. 4). On Castle and Southampton Islands he made major repairs and on the former built a considerable new work at Devonshire Redoubt, thus effecting the rearming of the Castle Roads channel into Castle Harbour. He then reasserted control of the channel to St. George's Harbour with repairs at Forts Popple and Paget, and the construction of two new works, Upper Paget Fort and Smith's Fort. Another major reworking at Town Cut sealed the boat channel leading into St. George's Harbour from the north-east, which was supported by a new work replacing earlier versions of Fort St. Catherine. Westwards from there he planted four new Town Redoubts, leading to works at the Ferry. The last covered the Ferry Reach Channel and the rear approaches to the Town of St. George. Burnt Point Fort was repaired and two new works, Ferry Island Fort and Coney Island Fort were brought into existence. In total, seven existing forts were extensively repaired and thirteen were either new or virtually new works.

Adjusting for works already mentioned in the previous chapter, namely, Town Cut Battery and Sears Fort, but including the pre-1790s Fort St. Catherine, twelve new works may be added to the total number of forts in existence before the Durnford period. This brings the number of forts at Bermuda by 1809 to sixty-two installations and 135 guns, with the additions (all in St. George's Parish) listed below:

DEVONSHIRE REDOUBT
(1790s) 8 guns

SMITH'S FORT
(1790s) 4 guns

UPPER PAGET FORT
7 guns

FORT ST. CATHERINE
(pre-1790s) 7 guns

FORT ST. CATHERINE
(1790s) 6 guns

TOWN REDOUBT, NO. 1, MOUNT HILL
4 guns

TOWN REDOUBT, NO. 2, SECRETARY'S HILL
2 guns

TOWN REDOUBT, NO. 3
2 guns

TOWN REDOUBT, NO. 4, TOBACCO BAY
3 guns

FERRY ISLAND FORT
(1790s) 3 guns

FERRY ISLAND FORT
(post-1790s) 4 guns

CONEY ISLAND FORT
none

Thus ended the first half of the period after 1783 which led into the establishment of the Dockyard at Ireland Island in 1809. The time between Andrew Durnford's passing in 1798 and that date saw a replacement for his Ferry Island Fort erected; no other new works are known to have come into existence in those years. On the strategic side, the threat of the Spanish had subsided as the eighteenth century progressed, but they were replaced by the upcoming French. After Trafalgar in 1805 and Waterloo in 1814, the French ceased to be a force to be reckoned with, but they in turn were replaced by the new American nation.

The new threat from the United States of America was the major reason for the building of Royal Naval Dockyard at Bermuda after 1809 and for all its attendant military works to come into being, as discussed in the next three chapters. In the twentieth century, the Americans became staunch allies of England and in Chapter Nine the tables were turned as the U.S. forces assumed responsibility for the coastal defence of Bermuda in the Second World War.

■ ■ ■

The forts protected the Floating Dock, Bermuda (built 1869), which was the essence of the Bermuda Dockyard (Bermuda Archives).

6

Bermuda Dockyard
& its Consorts

1809–1864

...for though Bermuda is a place of no trade, having no Staple, and can never produce any revenue to the Mother Country, being a mere barren Rock, were it ever to fall into the hands of an Enemy, would be the severest stroke over West India trade ever experienced, as ships of War and Privateers may be at Anchor in St. Georges Harbour, and in twenty minutes [be] at Sea in the very track where all our Ships must pass, and in the case of a rupture with America, [holding Bermuda] would prove of the utmost consequence in annoying their trade, both to Europe and the West Indies, and even their coasting trade would severely feel the bad consequences of such a neighbour.

—Simon Fraser, 1806

A T THE END OF THE AMERICAN WAR OF INDEPENDENCE, THE ROYAL NAVY lost all of its significant bases and harbours on the eastern seaboard of the new United States of America. Canada was retained following the war and the base at Halifax became a major factor in the revised strategic plan for the Western North Atlantic. To the south, the West Indies islands remained in the British fold and bases at Antigua, Jamaica and St. Lucia contributed to holding the southern sector of a new defensive line. Halfway between Canada and the West Indies stood Bermuda, which became the object of British military interest after 1783 and the new centre of that line.

As seen in Chapter Five, the Royal Engineers were sent to Bermuda to survey and renovate the fortifications. At the same time, Lieut. Thomas Hurd, a hydrographer of the Royal Navy, completed in 1792 a study of the reefs and anchorages, discovering 'Hurd's,' or the 'Narrows,' Channel in the process.[1] Various sites for a dockyard were considered and in 1795, the Admiralty approved the purchase of the westerly Ireland Island. The wheels of bureaucracy turned slowly and it was not until 1809 that work begun on the new naval base. After the Battle of Waterloo, the French threat was diminished, but work

[1] Jack Arnell, 'Bermuda as a Strategic Naval Base,' *Bermuda Journal of Archaeology and Maritime History* 5 (1993), 126–134.

on supporting fortifications for the Dockyard at the western end of Bermuda had already begun. The construction of the Dockyard itself was advanced greatly in 1823 by the importation of convicts from England, who remained the labour force until their removal in 1864. Writing but two years before the departure of the Royal Navy after two hundred years and the American Navy after 54 years, a maritime historian summed up the situation created by the advent of the British forces at Bermuda.

> As a naval base, Bermuda claims a lengthy and illustrious history, and even yet boasts an ongoing strategic importance. However, in the classic era of *Pax Britannica*, 1815–1914, the colony assumed a special value that can be seen in the massive surviving works of Ireland Island. These stone creations testify to Whitehall's resolve to construct a fulcrum of authority of undoubted strategic value…For Bermuda as an imperial concentration of power constituted nothing less than a fist in the middle of the Western Atlantic, a political projection of force that was a direct implementation of Britannia's power, and of the design of statesmen and Boards of Admiralty to counter potential and real challenges to their authority in the Western Ocean.[2]

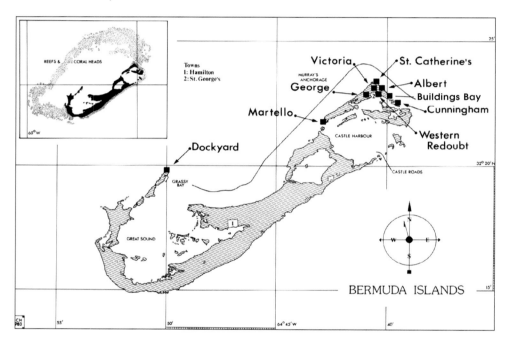

FIGURE 6.1: *Nine new fortifications were built at Bermuda between 1815 and 1865, seven at the eastern end of the island (Buildings Bay Battery not shown).*

By the end of the first era in that long peace, the fist comprised nine entirely new fortifications. The Dockyard stood as one of the last bastioned works ever constructed by the British; a fashionable Martello Tower defended the back door of St. George's Island, with six other works at the eastern end of that island and one on Paget Island. Five of the latter were constructed on the new 'polygonal trace' design for fortifications, while Fort St. Catherine perhaps straddles several styles; the design of Buildings Bay Battery is unknown. These were also the last forts to be built at Bermuda for the employment of smooth-bore cannon, an artillery method that had remained unchanged for over three centuries (Fig. 6.1).

In this chapter, the Martello will be discussed first, followed by the forts defending St. George's Harbour and the Narrows Channel and ending with the fortifications of the Bermuda Dockyard. Much of the information relating to the

[2] Barry Gough. 'Bermuda, Naval Base of the Early *Pax Britannica,* Origins, Strategy and Construction,' *BJAMH* 5 (1993), 135.

Bermuda Forts of this period is to be found in the existing fabric of the buildings and in two espionage documents of the United States Army. Few British plans of the Bermuda works during this period have survived. The forts were much altered after the 1860s and the sketch plans by the Americans are of considerable help in understanding their arrangement and armaments before that time.

• • •

AMERICAN SPIES IN BERMUDA

The first known survey of Bermuda by an American was by Albert Fitz, selected as a secret agent because he had some familiarity with the West Indies. He managed to visit all of the sites in Bermuda and produced plans of them (Fig. 6.2), excepting the Martello Tower and Fort George, under construction in 1842: '…I found the utmost caution was necessary; for the Bermudas being of limited extent, an important Naval Depot, and having but a small trade, strangers are looked upon with suspicion and distrust.'[3]

FIGURE 6.2: *Secret agent Albert Fitz's sketch plans of Bermuda forts in 1842.*

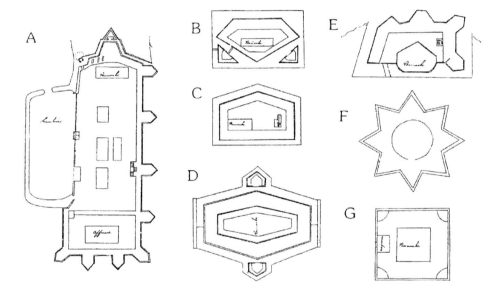

[3] Anthony M. Brescia, 'The Naval and Military Strength of the British West India Islands in 1842,' *BJAMH* 6 (1994), 195–6.

[4] Ibid., 197. Original report: National Archives and Records Service, DNA, Record Group 59, Records of the Department of State, Communications from Special Agents, 1785–1908.

[5] Ibid., I am very grateful to Anthony Brescia for bringing the Fitz material to my notice.

[6] Ibid.

[7] Taking a cue from history, it has been used effectively as modern fencing at the Dockyard Keep, now the Bermuda Maritime Museum.

Fitz was unable to determine the armament of the Dockyard, but ascertained that the Martello Tower had a 24-pounder; Fort Cunningham 'the oldest and feeblest permanent work upon these islands'[4] mounted twelve 24-pounders; Albert had seven 32-pounders, while adjacent Victoria had eighteen and two 32-pounder carronades; St. Catherine claimed '…sixteen thirty-two and sixty-four [*sic*, sixty-eight] pounders, and has a furnace for heating shot.'[5] The Western Redoubt has begun and is called a 'star battery' and nearby Fort George is also under construction, its landscaping taking shape.

> The hill upon which it stands is of a conical form and so smoothly graded, that, like the famed hill forts of the Deccan, it is a task of great difficulty to ascend it; and when the Prickly Pear, which is thickly sown upon the glacis of this Fort, and also of Fort Victoria, has attained its growth, the ascent will be almost impracticable.[6]

This technique of using cactus as anti-personnel planting is confirmed in other reports and would have been extremely effective.[7]

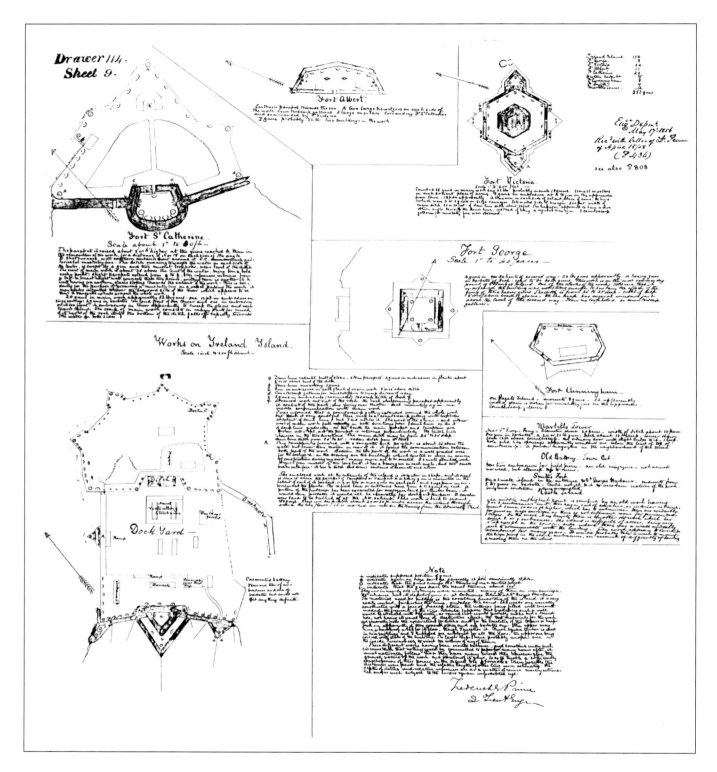

Another collection of American documents relates to the activities of two officers of the Corps of Engineers at Bermuda in 1842, 1849 and 1852. Three drawings and six letters tell the story of covert operations by Capt. Minor Knowlton and Lieut. Frederick Prime to record the forts being erected for the defence of the Bermuda Dockyard. After the War of 1812, it was an American practice to send officers abroad to collect military information, or to encourage them to use their leave, including those for reasons of health, to that end.

FIGURE 6.3: Lieut. Frederick Prime's plans of the fortifications at Bermuda in 1852 (National Archives, Washington, D.C.).

Knowlton, in fact, appears at one point on health leave as an *aide-de-camp* to French forces in Algeria.[8] Many such visits could not thus be considered as espionage, but the Bermuda trips made under the cover of health leave, were undoubtedly spying operations.

Capt. Knowlton, for example, came to Bermuda in 1842 and 1849 and, eschewing friendships and 'entertainments altogether,' sought to give the 'impression everywhere that my sole object in travelling was health.'[9] Frederick Prime, who came in 1852 is as explicit about the covert nature of his walks about Bermuda. 'These different works [the forts] having been visited but once and sometimes under such circumstances that nothing would be committed to paper for many hours after, it must naturally follow that they [the sketches: Fig. 6.3] have many errors.'[10] Both men reported to General Joseph G. Totten, the Chief Engineer, at Washington, who, over a long professional career ending in 1864, took a great interest in design of coastal fortifications.[11]

Two letters by Knowlton survive, as does a plan of the Dockyard which may be associated with him. In his second letter (June 25, 1849), Knowlton promises to submit a report on the fortifications, but there is no record that it was ever received. As a portent for invasion plans, he tested the tone of public feeling towards the United States. Perhaps disappointedly, Capt. Knowlton found the Bermuda population of ten thousand to be 'universally loyal.' In his view, 'the blacks strongly prefer the English government to our own, and for reasons too obvious to mention. The whites…because of the great artificial importance given to the colony by the government and the great expenditures of money made in it in the attempt to make it the great military and naval depot for this part of the world.'[12]

Another item in the National Archives, Washington, D.C., is a plan of the Bermuda Dockyard in 1831, which bears the signature of George Taylor, Edward Holl's successor as Surveyor of Buildings to the Navy Board, 1824–37. Taylor was involved with Holl in the design of the great Commissioner's House at the Bermuda Dockyard,[13] and presumably worked on other projects for the yard.[14] The drawing is annotated as received at the Engineering Department, Washington, December 2, 1848. It is therefore possible that Knowlton (or another spy)[15] obtained the plan from a friendly clerk in the Bermuda Dockyard during his first visit in 1842. The drawing gives the general configuration of the Dockyard defences as they would have been in the 1840s. Aside from such paperwork he may have carried out of Bermuda, Minor Knowlton took home two blocks of Bermuda stone 'as specimens of the type of stone used in the fortifications…which may be advantageously shattered by hollow shot under some circumstances.' He promises to hand them to Major Richard Delafield,[16] to West Point, or to any other place Gen. Totten should wish them deposited.

February 1852 found Lieut. Frederick Prime reporting on sick leave at Bermuda. Presumably after his fevers abated, he wrote to Washington: 'They are erecting a splendid Dockyard here and appear to be lavish with their money.'[17] Four years later, Prime was at Alcatraz Island when he made a report on Bermuda. He suggests a plan for the invasion of Bermuda[18] and includes a

8 Dale E. Floyd, 'U.S. Army Officers in Europe, 1815–61,' *Proceedings of the Citadel Conference on War and Diplomacy* (1977), 28. My thanks to the author for bringing this material to my attention.

9 National Archives. Record Group 77, K220/221. Messrs. Michael Musick and Richard Smith at the National Archives were most helpful with inquires on these sources.

10 NA, Record Group 77, Dr. 114, sht. 9. Sketches of Works at the Bermuda Islands.

11 E. R. Lewis, *Seacoast Fortifications of the United States* (1979), 38. I am grateful to Ray Lewis for his discussions in Bermuda on fortifications.

12 NA, Record Group 77, K220/221.

13 Jonathan G. Coad, 'The building of Commissioner's House, Bermuda Dockyard,' *Post-Medieval Archaeology* 17 (1983), 167. Bermuda is indebted to Jonathan Coad for his interest in this building and in the fortifications.

14 Comparing the signature with that on several of the Commissioner's House drawings leaves little doubt that it is an original drawing by Taylor.

15 NA, Record Group 77. Document B4272 was missing in 1985, but is dated March 21, 1849. If consistent with other records, the 'B' is the first letter of a surname, suggesting the presence of another spy in Bermuda in the 1840s.

16 Delafield was involved in spying activities and was in contact with Prime about the Bermuda fortifications.

17 NA, Record Group 77, D4393.

18 Ibid., P436.

copy of an Admiralty chart of the islands.[19] The idea took his imagination, for he wrote again to Gen. Totten in 1860, giving extracts from the *United Services Magazine* and a book on Bermuda, which confirmed his opinion of the weaknesses in its defences.[20] The most valuable part of the Prime report, however, is his drawing containing sketch plans and notes on all the major fortifications at Bermuda in 1852, excepting the Martello Tower.

The Prime drawing (Fig. 6.3) has plans of the Dockyard and Forts Victoria, Albert, George, Cunningham and St. Catherine. The value of the illustration lies in the fact that few other drawings of these fortifications survive from the period 1815–65. All of these forts were considerably altered in the later nineteenth century, destroying or obscuring details of their first period of construction. Plans exist for some aspects of later works on the sites, which combined with Prime's drawing and the evidence of extant structures allows for reconstructions to be made of the first period of these forts. Lieut. Frederick Prime's record was thus of great help in the 1980s survey of Bermuda forts, as it sharply illuminated a little known period in the history of fortifications at Bermuda. It is a fine example of espionage in the service of archaeology and history.

• • •

FIGURE 6.4: *The Martello Tower at Ferry Reach from the air in the 1940s (BMM Archives).*

THE MARTELLO TOWER AT FERRY REACH

As a fort design, the 'Martello Tower' came into vogue in the early nineteenth century. In 1794, at Cape Mortella on the island of Corsica, a small tower mounting one 6-pounder and two 18-pounders repulsed an attack by HMS *Fortitude* (seventy-four guns) and HMS *Juno* (thirty-two guns) for two days before surrendering with its garrison of thirty-eight men. The British were impressed with this type of work, which they called 'Martello Towers.' During the next few decades, one hundred and three martellos were built in Britain. Others were erected in Ireland, the Orkneys, the Channel Islands, South Africa, Canada, and Mauritius. Towers were also built on Barbuda and Jamaica in the West Indies; the last example was erected in 1873 at Key West, Florida.[21]

19 Ibid., Dr. 114, sht 8.

20 Ibid., P808.

21 Sheila Sutcliffe, *Martello Towers* (1972).

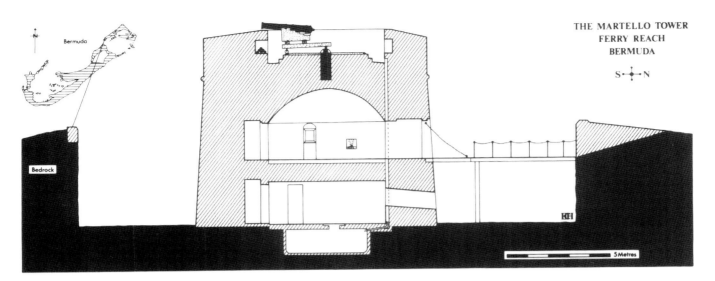

THE MARTELLO TOWER
FERRY REACH
BERMUDA

S ··+·· N

Bermuda

Bedrock

5 Metres

FIGURE 6.5: A cross-section of the Martello Tower at Ferry Reach.

In 1822, a martello tower was built at Ferry Point, St. George's Island, Bermuda and was noted by Prime as having one gun *en barbette*. The tower was overlooked in Sutcliffe's classic volume, *Martello Towers*, and no plans of it survived in 1982 when the Bermuda Maritime Museum undertook a study of the site.[22]

The tower was built at the south-western tip of St George's Island at the place called 'Ferry Point' (Fig. 6.4) and resembles the design of those on the

FIGURE 6.6: The Martello Tower was entered by a drawbridge across a ditch.

south coast of England between Folkestone and Seaford. It is set in a ditch eighteen feet wide (Fig. 6.5), about half the width of the ditches of the south coast martellos. The only entry is positioned ten feet above the floor of the ditch and was reached by a drawbridge (Fig. 6.6), evidence of which survives in brass fittings in the stonework of the doorway. These features conform to the original design of 1804 for the south coast towers, as does the height of the building, which is thirty-four feet from foundation to parapet.[23]

The south coast towers were almost all built of brick and stucco.[24] The Ferry Point tower is built of 'hard-stone,' being the older and more indurated form of aeolian limestone native to Bermuda. The works at the Dockyard, and the 1820s

22 Dr. Jack Arnell and Jane Downing kindly assisted in various aspects of the study.

23 Sutcliffe, *Martello,* 56.

24 Sandgate Castle is an exception: Edward Harris, 'Archaeological Investigations at Sandgate Castle, Kent, 1975–9,' *Post-Medieval Archaeology* 14 (1980).

periods of Forts St. Catherine and Cunningham were also made with hard-stone.

> The Stone for Building is of two kinds. That which is used by the people generally is a sand Stone varying much in quality. The best is very good for Parapets. The effect of Shot upon it being much the same as on soft brick, but as it may be used in large masses, it is less liable to splinter and is more firm. On being taken from the Quarry, it may be cut with a Hand Saw but exposure to the weather hardens the surface greatly. It lasts many years without decaying even when not attended to (as is shewn by the Old Batteries here which are in general wretchedly built) but when the surface is well rubbed with a soft Stone and Lime (called rendering) the weather has scarcely any effect on it. The Limestone [hard-stone] is about equal in hardness to that at Plymouth, it is quite impervious to the wet and is therefore well-suited for the Martello Towers, and as it may be worked with great exactness, repairs will not be required for years. It is in great quantity at Ireland [Island] but is coarse in parts and unsound from sand holes. The Works there will be faced with it entirely. That obtained from a Quarry [Shorehills] near St. Georges is very excellent, but is now scarce. The Ferry Tower is built of it.[25]

The Ferry Point tower has the characteristic ovoid shape of a typical south coast martello. It has been noted that martello walls were usually nine feet thick in front, five feet at the rear, enclosing a terreplein, or gun level, twenty-six feet in diameter.[26] By comparison, the Ferry Point tower has a terreplein of nineteen feet, with wall thicknesses of ten feet six inches and six feet six inches. The smaller internal diameter and thicker walls of the Ferry Point tower probably compensated for the missing central pillar.

The thickening of the front wall of martello towers allowed for the insertion of stairs to the roof, without losing the strength of the masonry. The ground floor was usually reached by a trap-door and ladder from the first floor. In the Ferry Point tower, stairs to the ground floor were placed within the thickness of the front wall. The ground floor of the Ferry Point tower (Fig. 6.7) is in accord with the original design for the south coast martellos. It was divided into magazines and a storeroom; under its floor was a cistern for rainwater fed by a lead pipe from the terreplein which served as a catchment. The storeroom was lit by a single window and the floor was further ventilated by a series of flues.

The first floor (Fig. 6.8) was wooden, the remnants of the joists and planking being seen in the late 1960s by the writer. The flooring was founded on solid masonry, which formed the vaulted ceilings of the magazines and storeroom below. In the usual pattern, a fireplace existed on the first floor and there were two windows placed at ninety degrees to either side of the entrance; it was intended to house six men.

At roof level (Fig. 6.9) can be found three recesses for shot and the iron rail for the gun carriage. A narrow well serves as a walkway between the traversing platform and the wall of the parapet. This arrangement does not seem to be typical, as the outer traversing rail usually abutted the face of the parapet. A series of iron rings on the north-eastern section of the parapet may have been anchors for the stays of a signal mast facing the Fort George.

According to the date-stone over the entrance the tower was erected in 1823, in the third year of the short reign of King George IV, but it was not completed until 1828. Its only gun was mounted on the roof in 1828, which formed a well so that the gun could traverse a complete circle. In 1857, the

25 PRO WO 55/1551/3, Thomas Blanshard. Report on the Defences of Bermuda, 1823.

26 H. P. Mead, 'The Martello Towers of England,' *The Mariner's Mirror* 34 (1948).

FIGURE 6.7: *The ground floor of the Martello Tower contained the powder magazines and a water tank fed from the roof.*

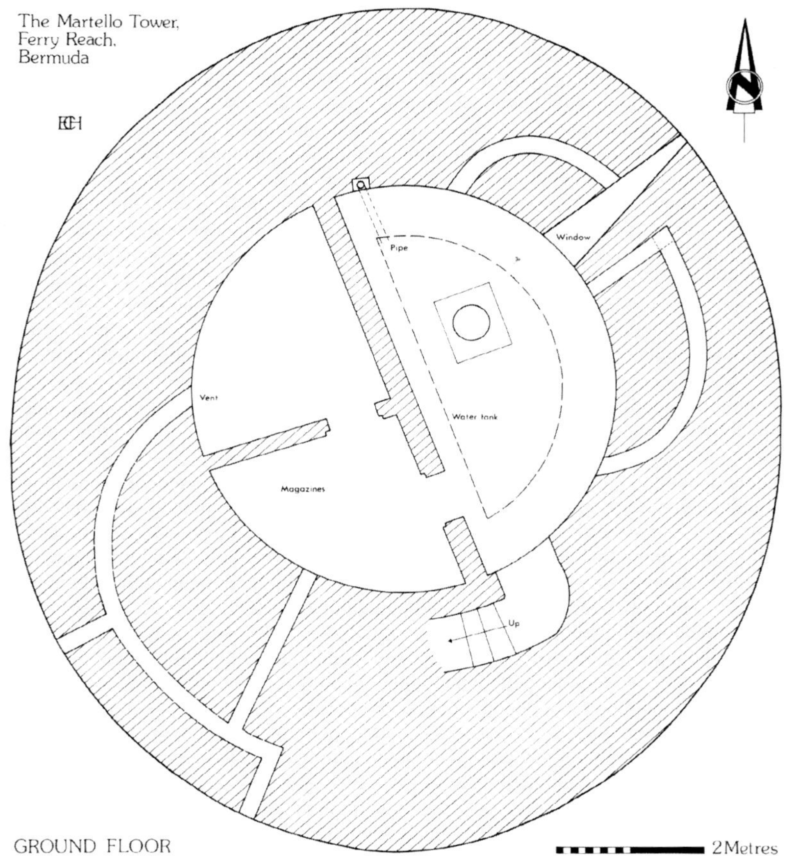

The Martello Tower,
Ferry Reach,
Bermuda

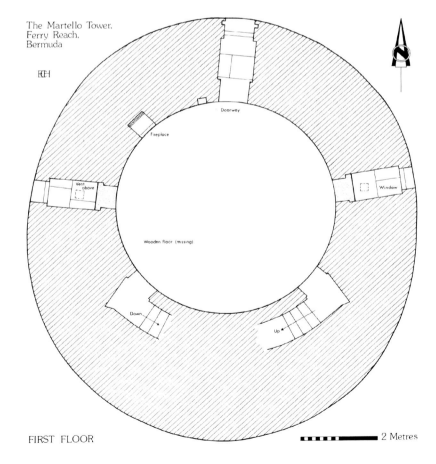

GROUND FLOOR   2 Metres

FIGURE 6.8: *The first floor of the Martello Tower housed the living quarters and its windows with ceiling vents seconded as gun ports.*

The Martello Tower,
Ferry Reach,
Bermuda

FIRST FLOOR   2 Metres

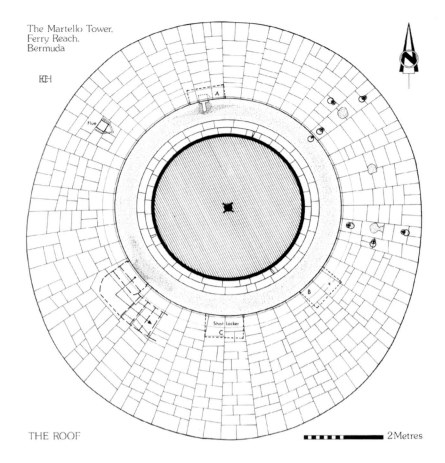

The Martello Tower.
Ferry Reach.
Bermuda

THE ROOF

2 Metres

FIGURE 6.9: *The roof well of the Martello Tower contained the emplacement for a single gun.*

FIGURE 6.10: *Major Blanshard's powder magazine was built near the Martello Tower in 1828.*

gun was an 18-pounder, firing over the parapet: 'This tower is to prevent an enemy crossing from the principal to St. George's Island, to keep up the communication between them and to command the passage from St. George's and Castle Harbour into the [Murray's] anchorage.'[27] Should the Martello Tower fall, the next line of defence for St. George's and the eastern forts would have been Fort George just to the west of the town.

Near the Martello Tower, a powder magazine (Fig. 6.10) was constructed by Major Blanshard in the late 1820s, apparently on a design of his predecessor, Captain Thomas Cunningham.

• • •

27 PRO, Blanshard, Defence Report.

FIGURE 6.11: *Forts St. Catherine, Victoria, Albert and Cunningham protected the entrance to the Narrows Channel.*

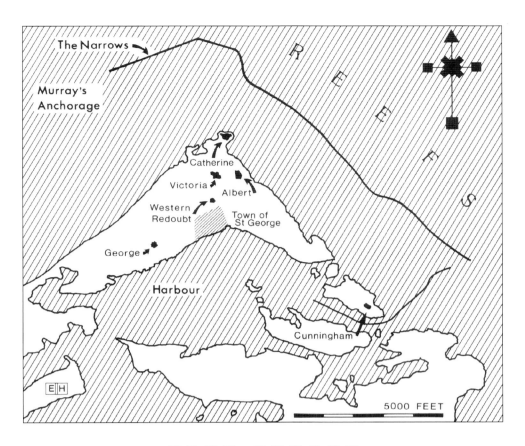

FORT GEORGE

Fort George was erected on the hill where Bermuda's first signal station stood, known in 1622 as Riches Mount (Fig. 6.11). The site had been modified in the 1790s, when Andrew Durnford added an irregular work, seen in relation to the fort to be built in the late 1830s (Fig. 6.12). The site was proposed by Col. Edward Fanshawe, R.E., who arrived in Bermuda on HMS *Blanche* in September 1826 on a reconnaissance visit under instruction from the Duke of Wellington, Master General of Ordnance.

> St. Georges Hill is about 1100 yards from Retreat Hill, and 160 feet high, on the Western side of the Town, commanding the Harbour and the entrance from the Ferry. It sees the reverse of Secretary's Hill, another eminence of the original position for the defence of St. George's, which rises to a similar level 400 yards from St. Georges and within 800 yards of the forward position. St. Georges Hill is mainly precipitous on two sides; a small work on it would add to the security of Retreat Hill. It would be difficult to reduce it, and no attack could be made on the other works from this side whilst it held out.[28]

Fanshawe's recommendations were approved by the Duke in November 1826, who instructed that: 'Major Blanshard will also send the necessary Drawings and Estimate for occupying this Post with a small Work that shall be well Covered and secure from assault and capable of the following objects— that of Commanding the approach from the Ferry, the Harbour and the Reverse of Secretary's Hill so that neither that eminence may be occupied nor any attack made on the position from this side whilst St. George's Hill holds out.'[29] Work must have commenced shortly thereafter.

Lieut. Prime, the American, visited the site in 1842, by which time it had

28 PRO WO 55/929. Edward Fanshawe. Report on the Defences of Bermuda, 1826.

29 National Army Museum, Report on the Defences of Bermuda, 1826–1827 (Acc. no. 6807-169).

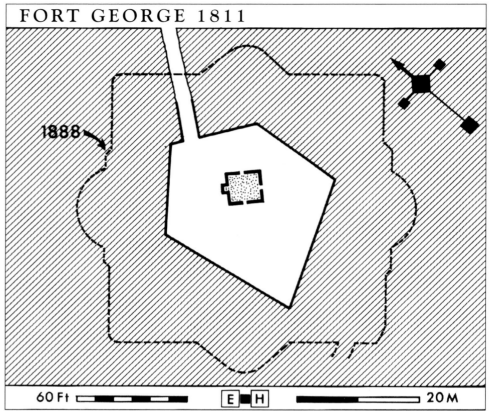

FIGURE 6.12: Fort George as built by Durnford and surveyed by Cunningham in 1811, with the outline of the 1830s fort added.

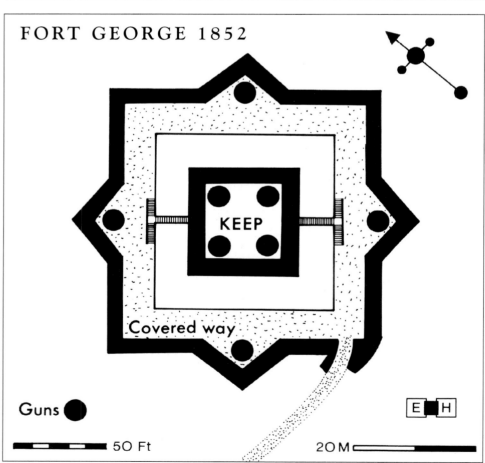

FIGURE 6.13: A schematic plan of Fort George in the smooth-bore period, with cannon mounted in its covered way and on the roof of the Keep.

been largely completed; he left a sketch (at a scale of 1 inch to 40 paces) and gave this description as an observant spy:

> 4 guns in salients of covered way—32 lbs guns apparently: 4 heavy guns en barbette on Keep: said to be 60 lbs guns. This work is on the most commanding point of St. George's Island. One of the clerks of the works told me that it was feared that building was not strong enough to sustain the effect of the firing of these heavy guns. The ditch is from 20' to 25' deep—crest of Keep 8' or 10' ft above crest of glacis. The Keep has several windows just about the level of the covered way—I saw no loopholes, or counterscarp galleries.[30]

All trace of this work on the roof of the Keep has been buried in the construction of a radio station in the 1970s. On the covered way, two great 11-inch Rifled Muzzle Loaders were emplaced in the 1870s to the north and south, with smaller guns to the east and west. The general plan of the fort survives and with the Prime evidence and other documents, it was possible to reconstruct the arrangement of the fort in the 1840–50s (Fig. 6.13).

The fort was entered at the south-east corner, but there is no evidence of a drawbridge. The Keep had two entrances via drawbridges to the north and south. It had three floors (see Fig. 7.4) and access to two counterscarp galleries was by way of a tunnel under the ditch from the ground floor (see Fig. 7.4). The casemated upper floor supported the guns in the roof well above, while a middle floor serves as barrack accommodation. With the exception of the roof details, the interior floors and the galleries are largely intact as built in the late 1830s. The exterior walls of the Keep and its ditch remain much the same. The site was described by a British officer in 1857, the final report before its conversion for Rifled Muzzle Loaders.

> Fort George is a work of similar capacity to that of the Western Redoubt, about 177 feet above the level of the sea, and 1000 yards Southwest of Fort Victoria. The town of St. George's lies in a hollow between it, Fort Victoria, and the Western Redoubt. It commands the Western land approaches from St. George's Ferry, St. George's Town and harbour, up to its entrances by the East and West ferries, and Castle Harbour, and at long range, Murray's Anchorage, and part of the channel leading to the Dockyard, but its fire on the latter is considerably masked by an unoccupied hill called Secretary's Hill which detracts much from its power on that side. It carries 2 24-pounder guns en barbette, on iron traversing platforms on its keep, and 4 8-inch guns on iron traversing platforms in its covered way.[31]

Thus in its last days as an artillery fortification for smooth-bore weapons, the guns on the roof of the Keep had been reduced to two 24-pounders, perhaps in relation to the fears of larger guns shaking the soft Bermuda stone masonry of that building. On the terreplein or covered way, the guns were increased to 8-inch (68-pounders) the largest in the British arsenal at the time. Col. Hemphill in 1857 recommended that 32-pounders be put on the roof and that three 10-inch mortars be added for plunging fire 'to shell ships attempting to take up positions at extreme ranges.'

A fine series of illustrations by Gaspard Le Marchant Tupper[32] contain several views of Fort George (see Plates), including one of the southern side of the structure. In that view the drawbridge is shown, along with a 68-pounder on a cast iron traversing carriage. A large flagstaff is supported by guy wires, one of which

[30] NA, Record Group 77, Dr. 114, sht. 9.

[31] Bermuda Archives. A. J. Hemphill. Report on the Defences of Bermuda, 1857.

[32] These drawings were originally identified as the work of Sir John Gaspard Le Marchant, Lieutenant Governor of Newfoundland 1847–1852. Subsequent research in 1995 by Jean Trapido-Rosenthal of the Bermuda National Gallery revealed them to be the handiwork of his nephew, later Lieut. General, Gaspard Le Marchant Tupper, who was posted to Bermuda with the Royal Regiment of Artillery, from November 1856 to April 1858.

is presumed to have been anchored to the cascabel of a gun found in the 1980s buried at an angle just to the west of the entrance of the fort.

• • •

WESTERN REDOUBT
(FORT WILLIAM)

In his report of 1823, Major Blanshard recommended several new works, the one on Retreat Hill to the rear of Fort St. Catherine becoming Fort Victoria. The erection of that work became the justification for another.

> As this work [Fort Victoria] is prevented by land intervening from commanding the [St. George's] harbour and is at some distance from the main barracks, a redoubt [Western Redoubt] appears necessary. On a hill below it from this Hill there is a good command of the Harbour and of the ridge on which the Barracks are situated which the redoubt would connect with Retreat Hill. This work which is completely dependant on Retreat Hill would also take in reverse an enemy approaching it on the South, as Fort St. Catherine would on the North. According to the plan proposed, this work would be sufficiently spacious for three traversing guns, a casemated barracks and stores for 40 men and a small magazine.[33]

This proposal was later approved by the Duke of Wellington, with work beginning in the 1830s. Located some eight hundred yards east of Fort George, the Western Redoubt[34] is almost identical in plan to it, but was completed some years later. Albert Fitz, the American 'special agent,' commented in 1842 that 'a Star Battery has been commenced, but the work is at present discontinued for the purpose of completing forts deemed of more importance.'[35]

Western Redoubt is probably on the site of Warwick Castle, built in the first decade of the colony and its construction would have destroyed any trace of the earlier building. Fort George defended the landward approach from the west to the town of St George, Murray's Anchorage to the north and covered the harbour. Western Redoubt protected the harbour and coastline to the south-east. It was finished in 1853 and was described in the 1857 report.

> The Western Redoubt, recently completed, but not yet armed is a square Masonry bombproof Tower of 3 Stories, constructed to carry 4 heavy guns on its summit, which is at an elevation of about 138 feet above the level of the Sea, and to accommodate 2 Officers and 71 Men, with Tank, Magazine, provision, and Artillery Stores. It is surrounded by a deep ditch flanked by Reverse fires, with covertway and Glacis. On its Western side there is an epaulment for 4 other guns. The objects of this work are to command the town, and harbour of St. George's and approaches to the latter both from the East and West ferries, and distantly part of the main channel leading to Murray's Anchorage, and to enfilade the Ravines affording cover for approaches against the Northern and Southern sides of Fort George which is 800 yards distant, and the high ground to its North. It also commands the Barrack Hill, and the Naval Tanks. It is supported and commanded by Fort Victoria at 220 yards.

> Proposed armament: Upon the joint recommendation of the Commanding Officers of Artillery and Engineers in 1852, an Armament of 8—24 Pounder Guns en barbette on traversing platforms was approved, the pivots for which were sent out, but owing to its recent construction, the masonry has not been considered sufficiently dry to receive the Guns. We conceive that a more suitable armament for the tower would be 4—32 p^{rs}, but that no change is necessary in the Guns [on the epaulment] for the shorter ranges of about 800 yards towards Fort George.[36]

[33] PRO, Blanshard, Defence Report.

[34] Sometimes referred to as 'Fort William'; the 'Eastern Redoubt' became Fort Albert.

[35] Brescia, 'The Naval and Military...', 197.

[36] BA, Hemphill, Defence Report.

FIGURE 6.14: *The Western Redoubt after its completion in 1857 was almost a carbon copy of Fort George, with the exception of the epaulment.*

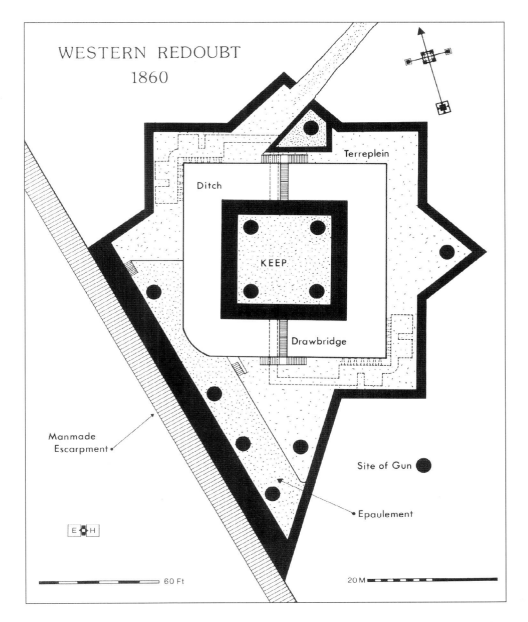

This then was the 'Star Battery' seen by Fitz at the beginning of its construction and in operation by the late 1850s, as its guns approached obsolescence (Fig. 6.14). The fort was entered from the north; but for the epaulment, its shape would have mirrored that of Fort George. In its centre was a small Keep with four guns on its roof. Access to the Keep was across north and south drawbridges, and the ditch was protected by two counterscarp galleries.

The addition of the epaulment confused the regular arrangement of guns on the covered way: at Fort George there was one in each salient. At the Western Redoubt, only the eastern salient was occupied. The salient to the north is bisected by the gate and its gun would have been off centre. The western salient is incorporated into the epaulment which had four guns, as was the southern, where a gun was emplaced in advance of the normal position.

The Western Redoubt has the only *épaulment* at Bermuda, described in a military dictionary as a 'parapet or gun bank.' The *OED* notes it as 'a covering

FIGURE 6.15: Forts George, Victoria, Albert and St. Catherine and the Western Redoubt from the air in the 1940s (BMM Archives).

mass raised to protect from the fire of the enemy.' At this fort, the epaulment is a parapet situated on top of a man-made escarpment, formed by the quarrying away of the western slope of the hill occupied by the redoubt. This artificial cliff faces the expected line of attack from Ferry Point and is a massive front protecting the entire Western Redoubt from that sector. Thus a normal parapet and the artificial escarpment

FIGURE 6.16: The Western Redoubt from the air in the 1980s; the Keep and ditch were roofed over in the 1890s.

FIGURE 6.17: *Brick skin walls were added to the ditch at the Western Redoubt to convert it to a powder magazine; a new access was pierced through the north-west flanking gallery.*

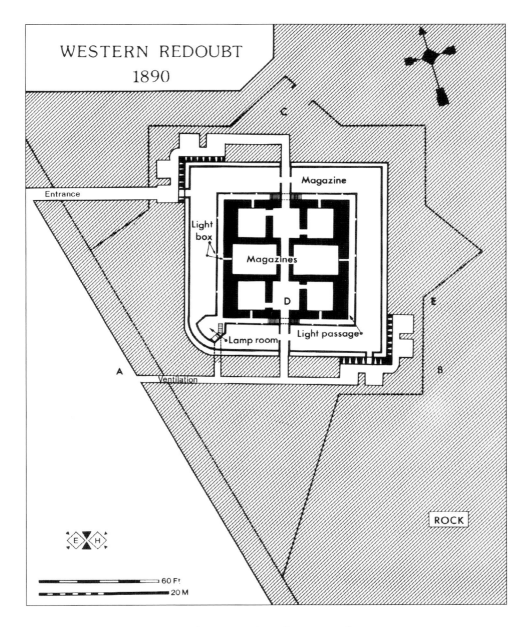

presumably became an epaulment, rather than an ordinary rampart.

The interior of the Western Redoubt has survived and is perhaps identical to the plan of Fort George. It contains three floors for barracks and stores and would have had a magazine at the ground level of the ditch. Tunnels under the ditch from the basement led to the counterscarp galleries.

The fate of the fort as a defensive work was sealed in a report of 1869, which recommended that 'the *Western Redoubt*, a small work about 200 yards south of *Fort Victoria*, need not be armed. It is, however, of use for storing munitions of war, and should be retained for this purpose.'[37]

In the late 1880s, that intention was carried out in a spectacular way when the Western Redoubt was converted into an enormous powder magazine by roofing over the ditch and the Keep (Fig. 6.15). The roof well of the Keep was filled in the process. All that could be seen from the air in the 1980s was the

[37] BA, F. E. Chapman. Report on the Defences of Bermuda, 1869.

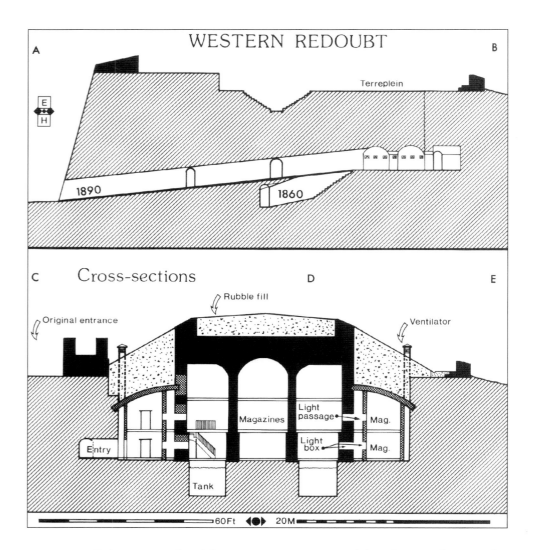

WESTERN REDOUBT

FIGURE 6.18: *A cross-section of the Western Redoubt demonstrates the 1890s access and roofing over of the ditch and Keep.*

square roof thus created, with one corner truncated by the epaulment, the southern run of which survives in the undergrowth (Fig. 6.16).

Within the fort, two skin walls of brick were built around the sides of the old ditch and against the counterscarp a space was left for ventilation (Fig. 6.17). A slightly larger space against the wall of the Keep was used as a light passage, from which kerosene lanterns could be placed in glass-fronted light-boxes to illuminate the magazines in the space that once was the ditch. The magazines in the ditch were two storeys, with an extra storey in the Keep, which was also turned over for exclusive use for munitions storage.

Two passages were pierced through at ditch level through the cliff and epaulment which form the western limit of the fort (Fig. 6.18). The northern passage became the entrance to the Western Redoubt in the 1890s. The conversion of the site into a powder magazine by sealing it off from the outside world has created an ideal space for a military museum: perhaps that will be the final and fitting use for this building which saw but a year or two of usage as intended. Redundant before its mortar was dry, of the forts built for the defence of the Dockyard 1809–65, only it and the Martello Tower were not converted for reuse in the RML era to follow.

• • •

FORT VICTORIA

Several hundred yards north-east of the Western Redoubt was Fort Victoria, which came to be the citadel of the defences of St George's Island. Fort Victoria was begun in the late 1820s and survived until the early 1960s, when it was unfortunately degraded in the building of a hotel, though much of value and interest remains. The site was first proposed in 1823 by Major Thomas Blanshard in his report to the Inspector General of Fortifications.

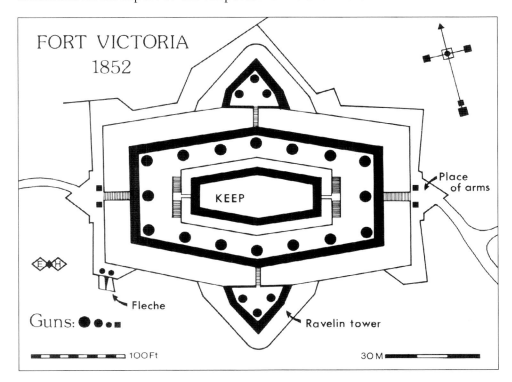

FIGURE 6.19: *A schematic plan of Fort Victoria during the smooth-bore era, mounting several dozen guns.*

For the further security of the high ground North East of St. George's on which the sovereignty of the Island so greatly depends, a permanent work on Retreat Hill is essentially necessary. This work would completely protect Fort St. Catherine and would command the ground round it particularly the ridge on which the Barracks are situated which, with a respectable garrison might be made a very strong position. The summit of the Hill is very small even for a work with reverse fires but by placing a casemated barrack in the rampart on the North side where it is not exposed, accommodation and stores for 2 officers, 100 men and a magazine would be obtained. Five guns and traversing platforms may be mounted—4 of which would assist in commanding the channel. The summit of Retreat Hill is 160 feet above the level of the sea.[38]

London must have replied suggesting the work as inadequate, for three years later a new plan had emerged for Retreat Hill, giving the dimensions of the first period of the later-named Fort Victoria.

Major Blanshard has, in obedience to your Grace's instructions, projected a larger work than was originally intended for Retreat Hill. It is an hexagonal Redoubt of 30 yards at either end and 50 yards each side, adapted to the figure of the hill, with a keep and Reverse Fires for the defence of the Ditch, but as this hill is small and its slope too steep to be formed as a Glacis, it has been thought expedient to circumscribe the counterscarp [of the Keep] by an envelope [the gun terreplein] which by means of collateral defences will see the slope of the hill.[39]

[38] PRO, Blanshard, Defence Report.

[39] PRO, Fanshawe. Defence Report.

The hexagonal fort was approved later in 1826 by the Duke and construction began soon thereafter. In the Bermuda Archives, there is a 'Plan of the Fort now erecting on Retreat Hill, 9 February 1831,' which is one of the very few plans of the Bermuda forts for the period to 1815–65. Written in another hand is the instruction that 'the Main Bridges to be of the same dimensions as the Bridge of the Couvre Porte at Ireland Island.' No drawings survive of the Couvre Porte bridge, but the 1831 plan indicates fixed bridges connecting to drawbridges in the middle of each of the four axis of the Retreat Hill fort.

FIGURE 6.20: Fort Victoria from the air in the 1940s before the demolition of the Keep and covering of the inner ditch (BMM Archives).

Perhaps the Couvre Porte bridge was another of Thomas Blanshard's innovative designs for drawbridges (as mentioned for the Dockyard Ravelin Tower below).

The 1831 plan shows two ravelin towers, with three guns each, and reverse fires with secondary ditches in the four corners of the main ditch, the last presumably buried in the 1960s. The fort was entered from the east and west. Positions for four guns are indicated on the terreplein. Two other bridges carried men over the second and inner ditch around the Keep.

FIGURE 6.21: The southern Ravelin Tower at Fort Victoria in the 1930s; the central building was added in the 1880s (Bermuda Archives: Roger Willock Collection).

Some of those details are seen in Figure 6.19, which also incorporates some information from the plan by Lieut. Prime in 1852. By 1842, according to Albert Fitz, Fort Victoria was 'a complete bomb-proof work, of the first class, and great strength; mounting eighteen thirty-two pounders, and two thirty-two pound Carronades.'[40]

FIGURE 6.22: The terreplein, inner ditch and Keep at Fort Victoria in the 1930s: the parapet of the Keep was cut down to terreplein level around 1905 (Bermuda Archives: Roger Willock Collection).

The definitive description of the final version of Fort Victoria in the smooth bore period is given in the British defence report of 1857.

> *Fort Victoria* is about 2191 yards from Fort Cunningham, and from its commanding position (about 52 feet above Fort Albert) in every direction may be considered the citadel, of St. George's with reference to either Land or Sea Attack. Its form is an irregular oblong with a ravelin to each of its two long North and South faces, it contains bombproof cover for 6 Officers and 194 Men; with Tanks, Powder Magazines, provisions and Artillery Stores, &c. separated by a deep ditch flanked by reverse fires from an envelope, carrying on its ramparts and Ravelins (again surrounded by deep ditches covertways, and good glacis), 18—24 Pounders, 2—18 Pounders, and 2—8 inch Mortars, the guns (except in the 2—

40 Brescia, 'The Naval and Military…', 197.

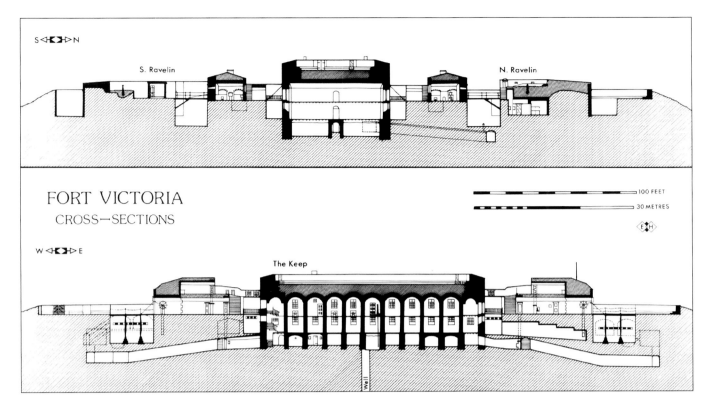

FORT VICTORIA
CROSS—SECTIONS

100 FEET
30 METRES

FIGURE 6.23: Fort Victoria was the most complex fort in Bermuda with its large central Keep, or barracks, and double set of ditches and flanking galleries.

18 Prs which are on ground platforms) all mounted on iron traversing platforms, and bearing in every direction; seawards, on the Ship Channel at a minimum distance of about 1000 yards, up to the eastern entrance at about 2500 yards, on part of Murray's Anchorage at about 1800 yards; and the Naval Tanks at about 500 yards; on the town and St. George's Harbour, up to its inner entrance by Fort Cunningham. With Fort Albert, which it commands at 248 yards; it commands and supports Fort Catherine at 400 yards. It also commands the Western Redoubt at 220 yards, and the Barrack Hill and crosses its fire with that of Fort George (1000 yards) on St. George's Harbour; and it sweeps the whole tongue of land forming the eastern end of St. George's Island, up to Fort Cunningham.[41]

An apt description of a magnificent building (Fig. 6.20): Fort Victoria was without a doubt the most elaborate fortification in Bermuda in the 1850s. When seen by Roger Willock in the early 1930s, it was very much the building designed by Thomas Blanshard. Its South Ravelin (Fig. 6.21) was well preserved as were many other features. The casemated roof of the Keep (Fig. 6.22), however, had its parapet removed and the level of the roof was reduced to the terreplein level in the early twentieth century.

The complexity of the original building is seen in Figure 6.23, disregarding the buildings added in the RML period. In its centre stood the Keep, which was a bombproof barrack for six officers and wives and 194 men and all their necessaries, the former occupying part of the uppermost floor (Fig. 6.24).

On the middle level (Fig. 6.25) were to be found additional barracks, stores and the 'jail.' The floor of this level was equal to that of the ditches and the counterscarp galleries appear in play.

The basement (Fig. 6.26), below the ground level of the ditches, contained the magazines and shell stores. The tunnels to the flanking galleries also appear

41 BA, Hemphill, Defence Report.

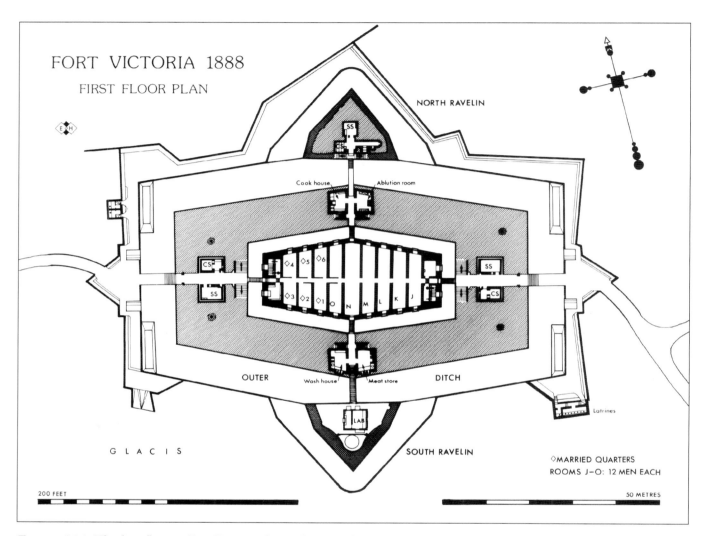

FORT VICTORIA 1888

FIRST FLOOR PLAN

NORTH RAVELIN

EXH

SS

Cook house   Ablution room

CS   SS

SS   CS

◇4 ◇5 ◇6

◇3 ◇2 ◇1 O N M L K J

OUTER   DITCH
Wash house   Meat store

LAB

Latrines

G L A C I S   SOUTH RAVELIN

◇MARRIED QUARTERS
ROOMS J–O: 12 MEN EACH

200 FEET   50 METRES

FIGURE 6.24: *The first floor at Fort Victoria shows the eight drawbridges which gave access to the terreplein and the Keep.*

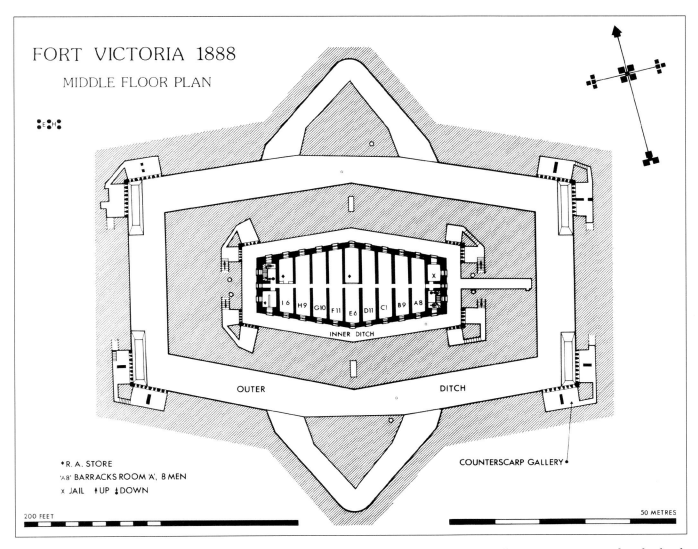

FORT VICTORIA 1888

MIDDLE FLOOR PLAN

R. A. STORE
'A8' BARRACKS ROOM 'A', 8 MEN
x JAIL ↑UP ↓DOWN

COUNTERSCARP GALLERY

OUTER   DITCH

INNER DITCH

I 6 H 9 G10 F 11 E 6 D11 C1 B 9 A 8

X

200 FEET

50 METRES

FIGURE 6.25: *The middle floor at Fort Victoria contained barracks and the jail; the flanking galleries were operational at this level.*

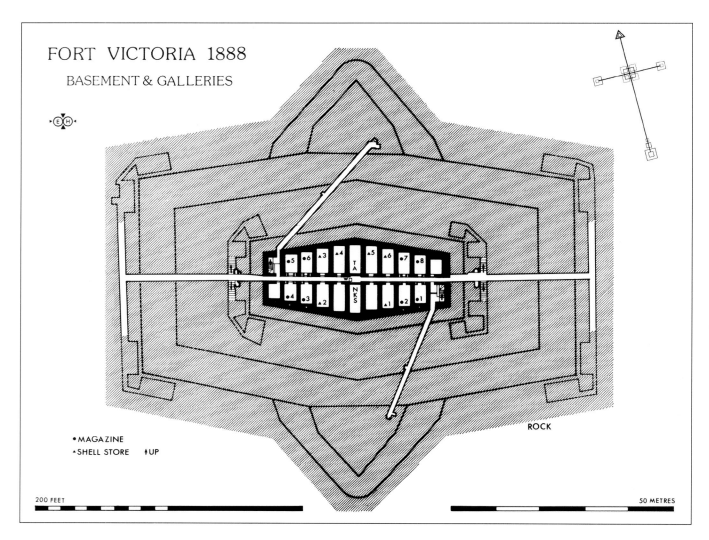

FIGURE 6.26: *The basement floor at Fort Victoria housed the magazines and the tunnels to the flanking galleries.*

at that level. A well was excavated to sea level in the centre aisle of the basement: 'This well was 5 feet in diameter at the mouth, which was gradually reduced to 4 feet at a depth of 20 feet. This last remained unaltered for the rest of the depth = 133 feet 6 inches. The water stood at best about 4 feet high at the bottom, depending on the rise and fall of the tide, which, acting through this very porous rock, bore the fresh water above it.'[42]

The roof of the Keep was clearly intended to play its part in the close defence of Fort Victoria as it was provided with a banquette for riflemen (see Fig. 7.6), not unlike the Casemate Barracks at the Dockyard. The terreplein, or gun level, formed the ground between the inner and outer ditch and it was probably provided with firing steps between the guns, as at the Keep at Dockyard.

• • •

42 R. Nelson, 'Engineer Details,' *Professional Papers of the Corps of Royal Engineers* 4 (1840), 154. This phenomenon occurs in other places and is Bermuda's only source of ground water.

FIGURE 6.27: A view of Fort Albert in the nineteenth century from the south-west shows external guns on cast iron garrison standing carriages (Bermuda Archives).

FORT ALBERT
(EASTERN REDOUBT)

Between Major Blanshard on site and Colonel Fanshawe and the Duke of Wellington in England, the stage was set for the final arrangement of forts on St. George's Island in late 1826. After Fanshawe's visit to Bermuda that year, he recommended several more works in addition to those proposed by Blanshard. One of these was to be on

> a small hill about 300 yards Eastward from the summit of Retreat Hill, commanding the Southern approach to Fort St. Catherine and capable of affording collateral assistance to the other works of the position, as well as an additional Battery on the ship channel…I also think that the occupation of the Eastern Hill by a work under the command of Retreat Hill with a heavy Sea Battery would materially strengthen that side of St. Georges, and co-operate in the defence of the Narrows.[43]

In the Duke of Wellington's Minute on the defences of Bermuda in November 1828, this site was approved and named the 'Eastern Redoubt,' in relation to Retreat Hill (Fort Victoria) and thus also arose in relationship to the latter, the Western Redoubt described above. At the death of King William IV, in June 1837, Victoria became the monarch of Great Britain: in honour of this event, the work on Retreat Hill was named for the new Queen. Three years later, Queen Victoria married Prince Albert of Saxe-Coburg and in 1841 permission was given to call the Eastern Redoubt, 'Fort Albert,' although according to Albert Fitz, it was not quite finished a year later when he made his undercover inspections of the Bermuda works (Fig. 6.27).

The purpose of the fort was clearly stated by the Duke in his Minute.

> In addition to the above Works it has been decided to construct a Redoubt with an Escarp of 30 feet and Reverse fires for the defence of the Ditch at the end of the Eastern Hill about 300 Yards from the Summit of Retreat Hill, 400 Yards from the Western Redoubt and 500 Yards from the Barracks. The objects to be attained by this Work are to direct the fire from Seven heavy Guns on Traversing Platforms to be mounted on two of its sides upon the Ship Channel to command the Southern approaches to Fort St. Catherine and to afford collateral assistance to the other Works of the position.[44]

Lieut. Prime's drawing of Fort Albert in 1852 is the only one we have of

[43] PRO, Fanshawe. Defence Report.

[44] NAM, Defence Report.

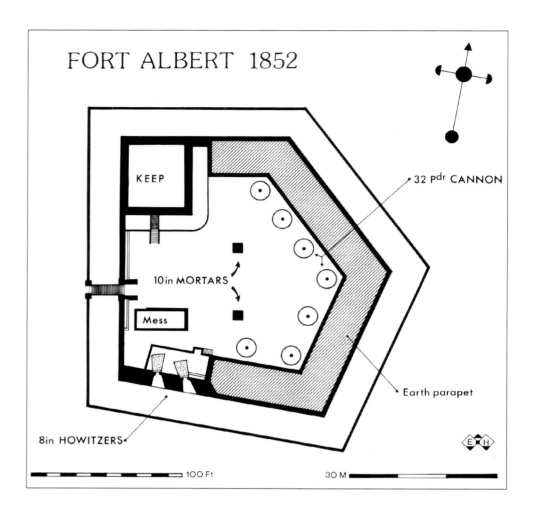

FORT ALBERT 1852

KEEP

32 pdr CANNON

10in MORTARS

Mess

Earth parapet

8in HOWITZERS

100 Ft   30 M

FIGURE 6.28: *A schematic plan of Fort Albert in smooth-bore times, when it mounted mortars, howitzers and cannon, the classic artillery trio.*

that time, as no British drawings have been found before the 1880s. With his information and data from later drawings, the first period of the fort in the 1840s can be reconstructed in a partly schematic plan (Fig. 6.28). Fortunately, the survey of 1857 by a combined committee of the forces (Col. A. J. Hemphill, 26th Regiment, Commanding the Troops; Col. Monty Williams, R.E.; Lt. Col. H. A. Turner, R.A., and John Parsons, Master R.N.) gives an excellent description of the site as its days as a smooth-bore fortification drew to a close.

> Proceeding up channel, Fort Albert stands at an elevation of about 114 feet above the level of the Sea, and is a Pentagonal Masonry Redoubt, with escarp and ditch of ample height and width flanked by reverse fires, covered by a glacis, and mounting behind earthen parapets 7—32 Pounders on iron traversing platforms, bearing on the channel, and 2—8 inch howitzers on ground platforms, flanking the land approach from the South East. It also mounts 2—10 inch Mortars and has an Addison's furnace for heating shot. A bombproof Barrack or Keep in one of the rear Angles, with separate ditch and drawbridge will accommodate 1 Officer and 34 Men and it has a Tank and Stores in its basement. It perfectly Commands and supports Fort Catherine 74 feet below it, and 487 yards distant from it. It commands the Ship Channel (at a minimum distance of from 900 to 1000 yards) eastward, as far as its guns can range; and westwards, until masked by Catherine's Point.[45]

Fort Albert was about half the size of Fort Victoria and was surrounded by a dry ditch (Fig. 6.29). A drawbridge on the western side of the fort was the

---

[45] BA, Hemphill, Defence Report.

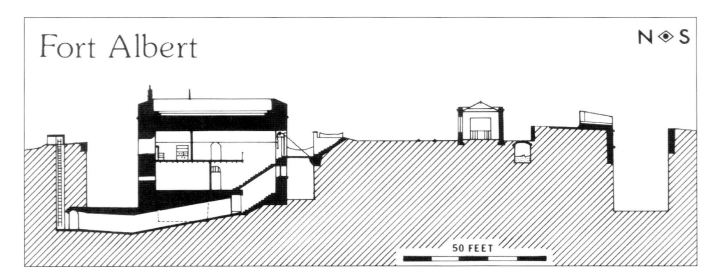

Fort Albert

N ◈ S

50 FEET

FIGURE 6.29: *Fort Albert had a Keep and a deep ditch with flanking galleries, in accord with the design of polygonal trace artillery fortifications.*

only entrance. The small Keep had two storeys; from the lower, a single tunnel led to the three counterscarp galleries. The roof of the Keep was formed by the parapet into a well with firing steps for riflemen.

It is presumed that the unusual earthen parapet was fronted by a stone wall on the top of the escarp, with a similar retaining wall on the interior face of the bank. If this was so, it may explain the earthen bank in front of the RML guns, installed at the site in the 1870s. Such a bank was an early sign of the movement away from stone parapets towards the use of an earth glacis in front of the guns, as seen at other sites in Bermuda.

All of the forts built in the second round of works in the last decades of the smooth-bore era on St. George's Island were built of the local soft stone; only, for example, in the cheeks of the howitzer embrasures at Fort Albert does the Bermuda hard-stone appear. Thus Fort St. Catherine before 1825, the Martello Tower and Fort Cunningham were in hard-stone, some from the Shorehills quarry in St. George's, but most probably from Ireland Island. The later Fort St. Catherine, the Western Redoubt, Forts George, Victoria and Albert and presumably Buildings Bay Battery were all in soft stone, except for details, such as embrasures and door lintels.

The soft stone was mostly obtained from each site, for it can be easily sawn by hand into blocks. The excavation of the ditches would have produced much of the stone and rubble necessary for each work. Using the soft stone would have been much faster than working with the hard-stone and it may well have been that as the Dockyard advanced the hard limestone was no longer generally available for the other fortifications. St. George's in the late 1820s and throughout the 1830s and early 1840s, must have been the scene of great activity with the works in progress on five new forts. No doubt most of the locals benefited from these imperial enterprises, but the economic history of British military activity in Bermuda has yet to be written.

• • •

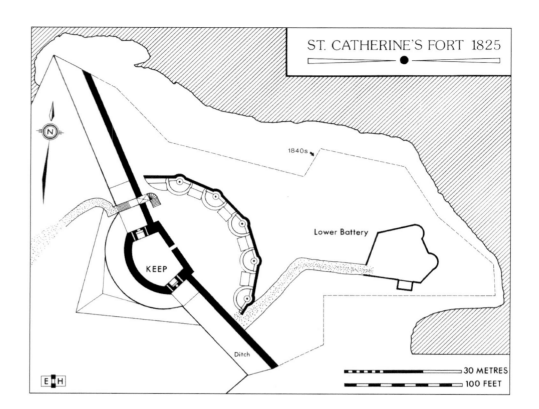

FIGURE 6.30: In 1825, Fort St. Catherine consisted of a Keep and a semi-circular redoubt for five guns, the lower battery retained from an earlier period.

FORT ST. CATHERINE

In the 1820s, as a part of the defensive system to protect the Dockyard, Fort St. Catherine was again rebuilt. A new design had been proposed by Cunningham in 1811; it consisted of a curtain wall across St. Catherine's Point, broken by an artillery store and barracks. To the seaward of the buildings was to be a substantial parapet for four guns in embrasures.

Given the present configuration of Fort St. Catherine, it was assumed that Cunningham's plan had not been carried out. His design was eventually built, but for some time during the research for the present volume it escaped detection, since the site was twice built over thereafter. The key lay in Blanshard's report of 1823 and a surviving plan of the site at the Public Record Office in London.

> Fort St. Catherine has been constructed on a more expensive scale than was at first intended [by Cunningham]. The Gorge is enclosed by a Ditch and Parapet instead of a simple Wall. The Barracks which flanks the Ditch will contain 100 Men. In the lower storey there is a casemated Magazine for 300 Barrels of Powder and 2 large Store Rooms. The Upper Battery is now laid out for Five 24 Pors (one more than at first proposed) and in the lower Battery two 24 Pors are to be mounted, all on Traversing Platforms.[46]

The plan of the fort, annotated 'See Capt. Walkers letter to Lt. Genl. Mann dated 23 Feby 1821,'[47] indicates that the Lower Battery had been built. It was a replacement for Andrew Durnford's Lower Battery and is shown to overlap the latter on the plan. The Lower Battery conforms exactly with Cunningham's plan for the new works at this site,[48] and must be assumed to have been built by him before 1816.

The Upper Battery proposed on the plan of February 23, 1821, along with

---

[46] PRO, Blanshard, Defence Report.

[47] PRO MPH 468.

[48] PRO, Cunningham, Defence Report.

a ditch and keep, in the form it later assumed, was a major revision of Cunningham's plan (Fig. 6.30). Those features are presumed to have been built by Captain Walker prior to Blanshard's arrival in 1823.[49] The ditch cut St. Catherine's Point in two and the fort was entered by a drawbridge and decorated doorway, still extant (Fig. 6.31). The Keep was entered from the east and faced the five gun emplacements (Fig. 6.32). The ditch was covered by cannon gunports and musketry loops from the Keep.

FIGURE 6.31: The draw-bridge entrance to Fort St. Catherine with the Keep on the right was built in the early 1820s.

FIGURE 6.32: In the 1840s, the interior facade of the Keep at Fort St. Catherine had a drawbridge over a ditch, later covered over.

Fort St. Catherine of 1825 was thus the fourth or fifth defence work of that name, but it was not the one, or only in part, seen by the American spy Lieut. Frederick Prime in 1852. The fort seen in the 1980s was also only in part the fort seen by Prime, as all of its parapet was buried under RML emplacements of the 1870s. From Prime's plan, it has been possible to reconstruct the Fort St. Catherine of the 1840s (Fig. 6.33), as there are no known British plans of the time. It was a building which deviated considerably from Blanshard's plan, approved by Lt. Col. Fanshawe during his 1826 inspection and seconded by no less an authority than the Duke of Wellington.

This fort is to be [finished in a] manner for eleven heavy Guns on Iron Traversing Platforms; Two Guns at the extreme point—Five Guns in the Battery in front of the Tower—One additional Gun on each flank as proposed by Major Blanshard—The present Roof on the Tower to be removed and the upper Walls constructed of sufficient thickness to support an arch, on which two Guns are to be mounted.[50]

From that simple directive, the design was fundamentally changed and the new structure that was built in the 1830s defines the limits of the existing work to seaward. The five-gun battery was swept away, although the hill on which it sat was partly retained as a natural parados in front of the Keep. A ditch was added to the seaward facade of the Keep and access was by a small drawbridge. A great irregular, but angular, rampart encompassed the entirety of the point of land in masonry very similar in style to the Dockyard. Behind the new parapet some twenty guns were mounted, to be supplied with heated shot from a furnace protected by a U-shaped enclosure. A stone roof was added to the Keep to carry the weight of three guns. A ditch, covered by a flanking gallery, was cut in front of the Keep and a magazine was excavated in the rock off the gallery passage (Fig. 6.34).

In 1857, the fort mounted twenty-six guns: three 24-pounders on the roof

[49] Royal Engineers Library, Conolly Papers, vol. XI, 32. Capt. A. Walker, R.E., arrived in Bermuda in December 1819 and left in July 1822.

[50] NAM, Defence Report.

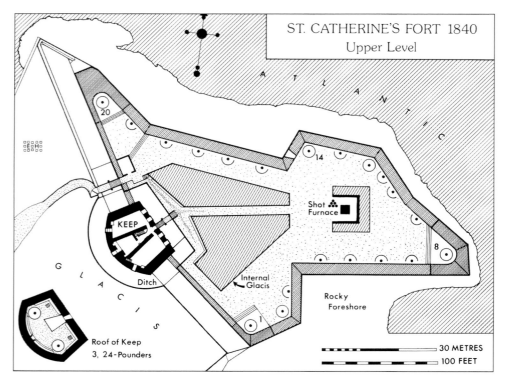

FIGURE 6.33: A reconstructed plan at terreplein level of Fort St. Catherine in the 1840s in its last configuration as a work for smooth-bore cannon.

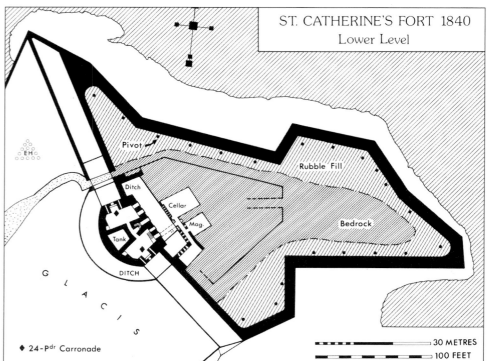

FIGURE 6.34: A reconstructed plan at ditch level of Fort St. Catherine in the 1840s, the magazine was found in 1986.

of the Keep; two 24-pounder carronades flanking the main ditch from the basement of the Keep, and around the ramparts facing the sea, seven 8-inch guns, twelve 32-pounders and two 24-pounders. Fort St. Catherine's function was to protect the head of the Narrows Channel where it makes a turn before opening up into Murray's Anchorage (Fig. 6.35): 'Heavy Ships could approach sufficiently close to bring an irresistible fire on this Fort, and its stone parapets are rather thin for present requirements; but they would be exposed to such a

FIGURE 6.35: A 1940s aerial view of Fort St. Catherine before the removal of the central parados and the emplacement of guns from Fort Albert in the 1960s.

FIGURE 6.35: A 1940s aerial view of Fort St. Catherine before the removal of the central parados and the emplacement of guns from Fort Albert in the 1960s.

concentrated fire from the three Forts (two of which being at good elevations, and well covered by Glacis, would be but little liable to damage from Shipping) that the operation would be one of great hardihood...'[51]

Along the coast to the south-east, Buildings Bay Battery and Fort Cunningham also helped to guard the Narrows Channel.

• • •

BUILDINGS BAY BATTERY

In 1865, Bermuda was visited by W. Drummond Jervois, Deputy Director of Fortifications and in his report of June 10 that year, he made the only known reference to 'Buildings Bay Battery,' presumably on the site of what became Alexandra Battery. His report, accurate in other respects, states as follows.

> 2. A battery about 800 yards North-west of Fort Cunningham, at Buildings Bay, for five 68-prs. above [*sic*] 30 feet above the sea, with a small guard house, not bomb-proof, at the gorge.

> 3. A battery about 1,000 yards North-west of Buildings Bay [Battery], called "Fort Albert" for seven guns, at present only 32-pounders; about 100 feet above the sea; with a bomb-proof keep at its gorge for one officer and 22 men.[52]

This description places the fort at the site of the later Alexandra Battery (see Chap. 7), which four years later was being erected for five 9-inch RMLs with iron shields. As the entry for Buildings Bay Battery appears under the heading of 'Existing Defences,' it must be assumed that it was extant during the Jervois visit. If it were a part of the alterations of the site which had taken place by 1869, its description should have reflected a state of upheaval and construction. In the 1857 Defence Report, it was recommended that two forts, one at Buildings Bay, be built in the long interval of 2,000 yards between Forts Cunningham and St. Catherine. Buildings Bay Battery must be an expression of those recommendations, though little else is known of this work.

As Jervois said in his report, the Narrows Channel was defended by four forts, from north to south: Fort St. Catherine, Fort Albert, Buildings Bay Battery and Fort Cunningham. All of these were extensively modified in the later 1860s and in the 1870s to take the new heavy guns of the Rifled Muzzle Loader period.

• • •

[51] BA, Hemphill, Defence Report, 1857

[52] BA. Wm. F. Drummond Jervois. Report on the Defences of Bermuda, 1865.

FORT CUNNINGHAM

In the 1790s, Captain Andrew Durnford raised an entirely new work on the hill on the southern half of Paget Island, which he called Upper Paget Fort. It was a rectangular structure with a barrack attached to the north side and in 1798 mounted one 8-inch howitzer, two 18-pounders and four 12-pounders. Upper Paget Fort, of which nothing remains, was perhaps similar to Durnford's other works, such as the Great Battery at Devonshire Redoubt. While his works were a decided improvement on the old batteries erected by the Bermudians, they bear little comparison to most British works of the period, such as the monumental fortress at Brimstone Hill in St. Kitts in the West Indies.[53]

Although the American War of Independence had irrevocably changed the political spectrum of the Western North Atlantic, during Durnford's time the pendulum of interest and financial investment had not yet fully swung from the cockpit of the West Indies to the north, to Bermuda and Halifax. While the Americans were in the throes of nationhood, the French continued as a force to be reckoned with to the south and it was there

FIGURE 6.36: *Fort Cunningham on Paget Island protected the mouth of the Narrows Channel.*

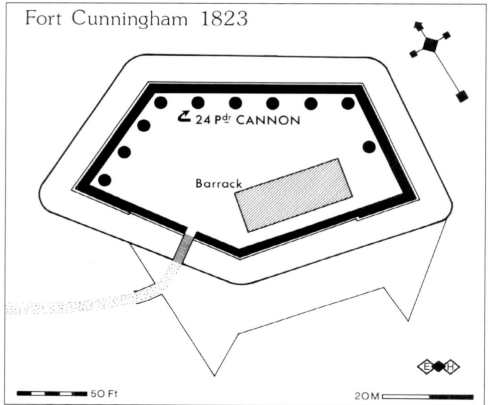

Fort Cunningham 1823

24 P^{dr} CANNON

Barrack

50 Ft   20 M

FIGURE 6.37: *A schematic plan of the first Fort Cunningham mounting ten 24-pounders in its arrangement of the early 1820s.*

[53] Victor T. C. Smith, 'Brimstone Hill Fortress, St Kitts, West Indies. Part one: history,' *Post-Medieval Archaeology* 28 (1994), 73–109.

FIGURE 6.39: The arched masonry in the ditch belongs to the first Fort Cunningham, completed in the early 1820s: the gun level dates to the 1870s and later.

FIGURE 6.38: Archaeological excavations in 1991 revealed the lower reaches of the ditch of the first Fort Cunningham of the 1820s.

54 Durnford's records contain many references by name to his workers, free and slave, black and white: see Cyril Outerbridge Packwood, *Chained on the Rock: Slavery in Bermuda* (1975) for discussions of slave labour in the building of the Dockyard where ' "The places of highest trust" were held by the Bermudian Blacks.'

55 PRO, Blanshard, Defence Report.

that the British military concentrated their forces. At Bermuda, Durnford worked largely alone, with some help from the small garrison, but employing mostly local labour.[54]

The shift to the north came irreversibly after the purchase of Ireland Island and the beginning of the Bermuda Dockyard in 1809. Two years later, Captain Thomas Cunningham, R.E., was dispatched to the island and his report set the stage for the erection of great works suitable for the task at hand of the defence of the Dockyard and the eastern channel to it through the reefs. It is fitting perhaps that the fort (Fig. 6.36) which guarded the entrance to the Narrows Channel bears the name of that talented Royal Engineer, completed and so named in 1823 'by order of the late Governor.'[55]

Fort Cunningham commanded the eastern entrances into St George's Harbour, the channel into Murray's Anchorage and the anchorage in Five Fathom Hole, and it did away with the necessity of maintaining Fort Popple, Paget Fort, Smith's Fort and the Town Cut Battery. Based on Frederick Prime's drawing and surviving features on the site, a schematic plan of the site can be made (Fig. 6.37). At terreplein level in 1823, there were ten 24-pounders on traversing platforms, a barrack with stores below and a casemated magazine for three hundred barrels of powder. The latter may be the two rooms still found within the flanking galleries in the south-east corner of the site.

The fort was a pentagonal redoubt set in a ditch: 'The defence of the ditch

FIGURE 6.40: *The ditch and arched masonry of the east facade of Fort Cunningham date to the 1820s; the upper works and iron front are from the 1870s and early 1900s.*

FIGURE 6.41: *Fort Cunningham was entered via a drawbridge on its western facade; the entrance masonry dates to the 1870s.*

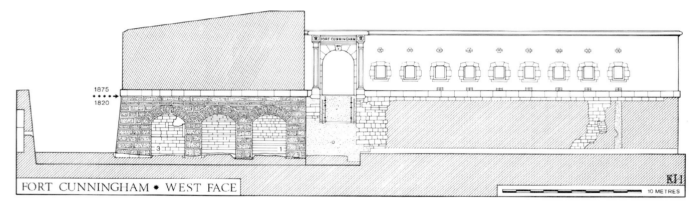

FORT CUNNINGHAM • WEST FACE

10 METRES

[would be] by Casemates in the angles of the counterscarp, which can be executed without any difficulty, and little expense, as the rock, though much more calculated for the purpose is nearly as easily cut as chalk, and does not require casing. The ditch will also be cut out of the rock, and consequently save the expense of rivetting.'[56]

In the late nineteenth century, the ditch was filled up with rubble to form a glacis for new guns: this filling was removed in archaeological excavations in 1991 (Fig. 6.38).[57] All of Fort Cunningham above the decorative cordon of the parapet had been removed in the 1870s, but the stonework below at ditch level was retained and later mostly buried. The excavation revealed it to consist of Bermuda hard-stone carved into blocks with scabbling and drafted margins, the whole arranged, not as a normal wall, but as a series of arches, later (though some contemporaneous) infilled (Fig. 6.39). Such arches exist, for example, at the Halifax Citadel, but they are on the interior of the fort and serve as doorways to workshops and storage rooms. Their appearance at Fort Cunningham on the escarp of the ditch is difficult to explain. The deeper, secondary ditches in front of the counterscarp gallery gunloops were also

56 PRO, Cunningham, Defence Report.

57 Directed by Professor Richard Gould and the author, with volunteers from EARTHWATCH: I am indebted to Dr. Gould for his assistance with the interpretation of the site.

FIGURE 6.42: The fixed portion of the drawbridge at Fort Cunningham was made of cast and wrought iron and is still standing from the 1820s.

found in the excavation, suggesting that they may exist at sites such as Fort Victoria, Albert and George (Fig. 6.40).

The entrance to the fort was on its western facade (Fig. 6.41), where three of the arches just mentioned may also be seen. In the 1830s, Major Blanshard designed a new drawbridge for the site, the fixed portion on the counterscarp yet existing (Fig. 6.42). The structure was another of his revolutionary designs for drawbridges, published by an anonymous author in the *Professional Papers of the Corps of Royal Engineers* in

FIGURE 6.43: The cast iron grating and stanchions of the fixed bridge date to the 1820s; the upper part of the entrance to Fort Cunningham is from the 1870s.

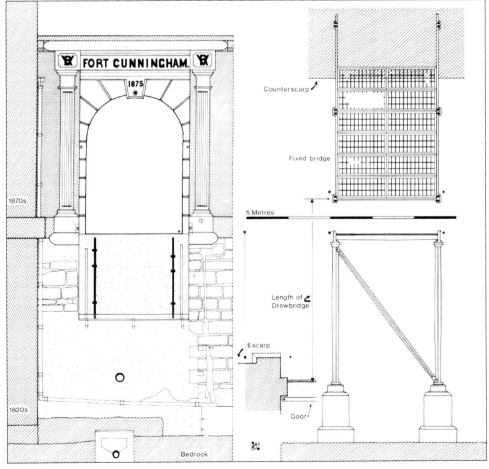

1847 in a paper called 'Draw-Bridges at Bermuda.' The 'draw' part of the Fort Cunningham bridge did not so do, but rather fell forward and downward into a space provided in the escarp wall. This action was effected by drawing back towards the doorway a long bolt, the end of which seated in the fixed bridge and held the 'drawbridge' in place. In the 1870s, the fixed bridge was retained, but the original drawbridge was replaced by an 'equilibrium bridge,' which fell backwards and downwards into the original space now modified with rails for rollers on the inboard end of the bridge (Fig. 6.43).[58]

The extension modification of Fort Cunningham in the 1870s removed most of the upper level of work designed and partly executed by Thomas Cunningham. The reasons for its renovation to contain the largest RMLs ever mounted at Bermuda and two continuous iron fronts in the Gibraltar Shield tradition is cogently expressed in the Hemphill Report.

> The Position of St. George's (on the maintenance of which the possession of the Colony mainly depends) covers the entrance from sea to the Channels leading to Murray's anchorage and the Dockyard, as well as the entrance to St. George's Harbour. The most important work as commanding both these (and therefore requiring the utmost attention) and the first for hostile ships attempting this main gate, to come in contact with, is Fort Cunningham on Paget 's Island, near the extreme East end of Bermuda. It is a pentagonal Redoubt mounting 10—24 Pounders on iron traversing platforms, 9 of which bear on the Channel entrance from Sea, and one on the entrance to the Harbour of St. George's. It is about 74 feet above the level of the Sea, well covered by its Glacis, but without bombproof cover for its garrison, and its Escarp being but 24 feet high, is not so secure against escalade as that of so isolated a Work should be. Considering the paramount importance of the objects it has to fulfil, it appears far too weak both in the number and calibre of its guns, and incapable in itself under any circumstances, of adequately protecting either of the entrances it commands.[59]

All of the foregoing works had but a single purpose: to prevent the fall of the strategic eastern end of Bermuda, which, should it succumb to the enemy, the Dockyard despite its extensive works could not but follow in short order.

• • •

DEFENCES OF THE BERMUDA DOCKYARD

The Bermuda Dockyard was established in 1809 with the purchase of Ireland Island from local landowners. The yard was begun at the eastern half of the island, centred on a small cove known as Grassy Bay (Fig. 6.44).[60] Storehouses, residences and other buildings were soon constructed in timber and soft Bermuda stone. These buildings were eventually demolished as the entire yard was rebuilt in hard Bermuda limestone in the 1820–50s.

The first Commodore Superintendent was Captain Andrew Evans, who was at Bermuda yard from 1811–17. At the Hydrographic Office there are two plans of the first Dockyard, which were made by Evans in 1813,[61] on which Figure 6.45 is based. Evans showed a proposed martello and ditch on the western side of the Dockyard. This proposal can be attributed to Cunningham, as it first appears in a plan in his 1811 report on the Bermuda defences.[62] There is no evidence that the tower was ever built.

58 D. A. Wood, *An Illustrated Guide to Victorian Forts and Equipment* (1989).

59 BA, Hemphill, Defence Report.

60 I. Stranack, *The Andrew and the Onions, the Story of the Royal Navy in Bermuda, 1795–1975* (1978).

61 Hydrographic Office. Accessions 214/1 and 214/2.

62 PRO, Cunningham, Defence Report.

FIGURE 6.44: *Seen from Spanish Point, ships of the Royal Navy lie at anchor in Grassy Bay before the fortifications of the dockyard in the later nineteenth century (National Army Museum, 7511-26).*

FIGURE 6.45: *The plan of the Bermuda Dockyard in 1811 showing the proposed site of a Martello Tower and defensive ditch (redrawn by the author).*

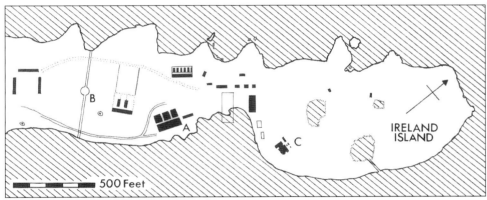

63 REL, Conolly Papers, Vol. XI, 30.

64 PRO, Cunningham, Defence Report.

65 Ibid.

66 PRO, Blanshard, Defence Report.

67 Coad, '…Commissioner's House…'.

Captain Thomas Cunningham, R.E., arrived in Bermuda in July 1811,[63] under orders to report 'upon the measures that may be necessary to take to secure the permanent military possession of the Bermuda Islands.'[64] His report was completed in November that year and contained the first proposals for the local defences of the new Dockyard. Against a landward attack, a ditch was to be cut across Ireland Island, which would be enfiladed by carronades from the windows of a martello tower on the crest of the hill in the centre of the ditch. To cover the eastern extremity of the island and the nearby anchorage, on the site of the present Commissioner's House, Cunningham proposed a three-gun tower, 'such as are now building on the Coast of Essex.'[65] He knew of these towers only by hearsay and requested a plan if his scheme was approved.

Cunningham's tour of duty at Bermuda ended in August 1816. His proposals for the Dockyard had been allowed, but in 1823 only 'the excavation of the Ditch [was] in a forward State.'[66] Except for the ditch, none of Cunningham's other proposals were carried out. By 1823, the foundations of the great Commissioner's House were being laid on the site of his proposed three-gun tower,[67] and Major Thomas Blanshard, R.E., had arrived with his own ideas for the Dockyard defences.

Blanshard came to Bermuda in March 1822 and remained (with a year of leave 1824–25) until February 1830.[68] In September 1823, he reported on the defences at Bermuda, including suggestions for changes and additions to the fortifications. He noted that since Cunningham's time, it had been decided to expand the Dockyard and to construct a large breakwater. The excavation of stone for the breakwater, if properly managed according to Blanshard, could form an escarp in those parts which required one. This would allow the fortifications to be built at a reduced cost. The Commissioner fell in with this scheme, and 'by the plan adopted the whole Coast will be properly flanked.'[69] Blanshard then proposed two batteries on Commissioner's Point and for the entrenched line on the west, a barrack 'en caponiere,' as more advantageous than a martello tower (Fig. 6.46).

FIGURE 6.46: The Bermuda Dockyard, North Yard, from the air in the 1940s; the South Yard was added early in the twentieth century (BMM Archives).

These proposals were not taken up, although work proceeded on the excavations for the escarp of a land front. From later reports, it is clear that Blanshard was working on a much larger plan for the Dockyard defences. Accordingly, Colonel Edward Fanshawe, R.E., proceeded to Bermuda in the summer of 1826, under orders from the Duke of Wellington to examine the plans for the Dockyard and the state of the works on St. George's Island. His report (September 16, 1826) recommended a 'Couvre Porte' for the Dockyard gate; a casemated barrack on the western hill which could be used for musketry fire over the Dockyard; the cutting off of the breakwater by a rampart, 'thus enclosing the Dockyard on all sides except from the basin, the entrance to which will be closed by a boom and subject to a heavy fire.'[70] The eastern point of Ireland Island was to be separated from the Dockyard by a wall: this, Fanshawe suggested, could be constructed 'to bring a fire upon the interior of the Yard, and together with the Casemated Barracks already spoken of and the enclosed Bastion on the North side, will effectively command the whole Arsenal from where it is possible for an enemy to force a landing from the Basin.'[71] This 'wall' became the six-acre site known as the 'Keep'—the largest fort in Bermuda—now the Maritime Museum.

Fanshawe's report was considered and opinions on it were noted in the Duke of Wellington's Minute of November 27, 1826.[72] The Minute mentions the 'Right Advance' of the Land Front and other features, probably proposed earlier by Blanshard in reports now missing. With various recommendations, it set the stage for the construction of the massive defences of the Dockyard, as illustrated in Figure 6.47. The Minute also instructed Major Blanshard to

[68] REL, Conolly Papers, vol. XVI.

[69] PRO, Blanshard, Defence Report.

[70] PRO, Fanshawe, Defence Report.

[71] Ibid.

[72] NAM, Defence Report.

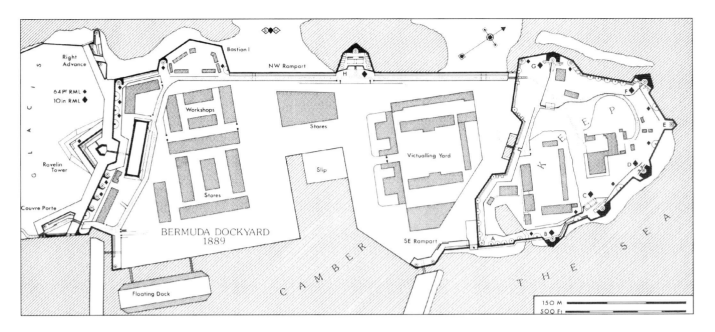

FIGURE 6.47: *The Bermuda Dockyard was surrounded by fortifications on three sides, leaving only the camber towards Grassy Bay exposed (BMM Archives, redrawn by the author).*

proceed forthwith on plans, or construction, for Fort George, a work on Retreat Hill (Fort Victoria) and the Eastern (Fort Albert) and Western Redoubts (Fort William) on St. George's Island.

By 1829, work was well advanced in the Dockyard under Blanshard's direction. With the exception of the Right Advance (not completed until 1843), all the major features of the defences were in place, if only perhaps in an outline form.[73]

Construction of the defences

The building of the Dockyard defences took a little over twenty years, from Blanshard's arrival in 1822 until the completion of the Right Advance in 1843. In October 1828, Lieutenant Richard Nelson, R.E., joined the supervisory force at Dockyard, staying until July 1833. Over his five years at Bermuda, he collected details on the construction of the Dockyard, particularly on the deployment of labour and aspects of masonry work, including the use of diving bells for the wharves and boat slip. Nelson published his notes in 1840 in a didactic paper for engineers involved in major construction works elsewhere in the Empire.

He noted that the Bermuda rock varied from a soft stone to a compact limestone, called 'hard-stone,' the two comparable respectively to the softest Bath Stone and a second-rate Portland Limestone. The rock at St. George's was generally soft, while Ireland Island was mostly hard-stone. The best stone at Ireland Island was in the yard; that of the defences more irregular. In consequence of sand-flaws in this stone, 'high and massive masonry...is apt to crack down the face; and thus, though seldom productive of serious consequences, gives an undeserved character of bad workmanship to one's performances.'[74]

Another flaw in the limestone was the existence of caves: 'such caverns may at any time occur in the field allotted to the exertions of the Engineer, without the slightest indication above, of their existence beneath, and consequently,

73 PRO WO 78/406. A plan of 1829 by Blanshard shows these details.

74 Nelson, 'Engineer Details,' Page 136–197.

without the slightest blame being imputable for the necessary alterations in, not faults of, his original estimate.' As a result at Dockyard, one curtain wall was retired several times.[75] On the other hand, they were used to advantage: for example, the moat of the Keep is the residual lagoon of a cave.[76]

From 1823, the primary workforce was composed of convicts from Britain and local labour, including slaves, and was supervised by military and naval personnel.[77] Much of the work on the construction of the Dockyard and its defences was carried out by the convicts. Over a forty-year period from 1823, a little over 9,000 men were sent to the hulks at Bermuda, a quarter of whom died here as a result of the conditions of service.[78] They were employed in many aspects of the work, from 'jumping' rock, to the making of ashlar blocks and the building itself. The working of the hard-stone meant blasting and all other methods used for monumental stonework. Aside from the first period of Fort Cunningham, the Martello Tower, Fort St. Catherine and works of detail, such as embrasures on other forts, the Dockyard was the only place in Bermuda where the hard-stone was used extensively. Ireland Island is one of only two places in Bermuda where this stone appears at the surface in amounts which could be economically quarried, which was fortuitous for the purpose at hand.[79] The resulting buildings and defence works are thus splendid architectural monuments, unlike any other buildings in Bermuda. Had they been built in the local soft stone, little would remain of these great Imperial works.

It is difficult to give a precise schedule of the construction of the defences of the Bermuda Dockyard. The excavation of the ditch was obviously begun in the early 1820s, but was still being excavated in Lieut. Nelson's day. It seems that the Keep was started shortly after 1823 and was completed by the end of the decade. The Couvre Porte was probably started in 1827 and the Ravelin Tower and Land Front a short time later. The long Northwest Rampart may have been started late in the 1820s and the doorway to Bastion H on this line has a datestone of 1835. The Right Advance appears to have been the final work, dating to the early 1840s. The following descriptive study of the Dockyard defences is given in a topographical, rather than chronological order, beginning with the gateway and proceeding eastwards. Notes on the armament of each structure are based on the 1857 defence report.[80] The garrisons associated with the Dockyard and other fortifications have been discussed in Col. Roger Willock's classic work, *Bulwark of Empire*.[81]

• • •

THE COUVRE PORTE

The Dockyard was entered from a road on the eastern side of Ireland Island. Until early in this century, it was not connected by bridges to the mainland, although a ferry was in operation from Watford Island later in the nineteenth century. The road only served Ireland Island south of the Dockyard, most traffic being directly by boat into the basin.

At the Dockyard, the road passed over a drawbridge into the Couvre Porte, an irregular outwork surrounded by a ditch, except to the east where it stood

[75] Ibid.

[76] Jane Downing and Edward Harris, 'Excavations at Her Majesty's Dockyard, Bermuda,' *Post-Medieval Archaeology* 16 (1982), 201–216.

[77] Stranack, *Andrew*, 134.

[78] Ibid.

[79] The other was the Shorehills quarry, on the site of the ESSO Bermuda oil tanks in the 1980s on St. George's Island.

[80] BA, Hemphill, Defence Report.

[81] Roger Willock, *Bulwark of Empire, Bermuda's Fortified Naval Base 1860–1920* (1962).

FIGURE 6.48: *The entrance to the Bermuda Dockyard was protected by two drawbridges, a detached work called the Couvre Porte and the South Orillon.*

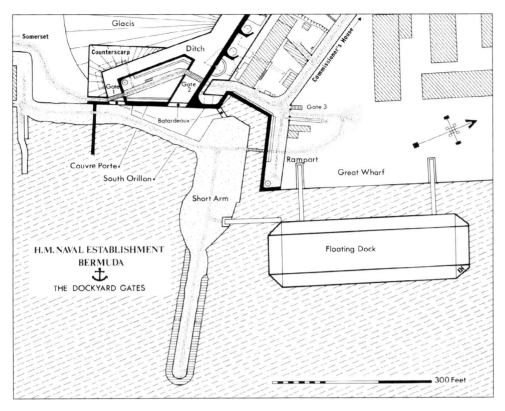

FIGURE 6.49: *The South Orillon had three gunports facing the Short Arm and was connected to the Couvre Port by a batardeau blocking the eastern end of the Land Front ditch (BMM Archives).*

originally on the waters of the Grassy Bay. The ditch at the drawbridge was defended by reverse fires from a counterscarp gallery under the eastern end of the glacis. The glacis extended from the Couvre Porte to the western side of Ireland Island, in front to the ditch of the Land Front and the other outworks. Another drawbridge to the north connected the Courve Porte to the gate in the South Orillon. The ditch around the Couvre Porte was terminated by batardeaux on Grassy Bay and joined the Land Front ditch to the west (Fig. 6.48).

The western and eastern ramparts of the Couvre Porte had firing steps for musketry. In the south-west corner of this outwork a cannon was located, which covered the roadway. This salient mounted a 24-pounder in 1857.

The Couvre Porte was never re-armed in the RML period and was demolished in the construction of the South Yard in 1901–7.

THE SOUTH ORILLON

The eastern end of the Land Front formed the South Orillon, which fronted Grassy Bay and was later joined to the Short Arm Breakwater by a batardeau. It contained a casemate for three 24-pounder carronades and on the roof were two positions, probably for 24-pounder cannon (Fig. 6.49).

A little to the north-east of the South Orillon, 'a short line of rampart for 2 guns [was] thrown out to bring a flanking fire on the Eastern shore southwards and on the entrance of the basin, the foundations of this which are in the water, having partially settled, the guns have not been mounted.'[82]

In front, or south, of this Great Wharf Rampart was a moat open to the sea (Fig. 6.50). A drawbridge connected the Short Arm with the Dockyard via an archway in the Rampart. A firing step was located on the terreplein of the Rampart, and on the curtain between it and the South Orillon. The curtain wall was all that survived above ground in the 1980s of the South Orillon and the Great Wharf Rampart, which were destroyed in the South Yard works about 1905. There is no evidence that the South Orillon or the Great Wharf Rampart were re-armed after 1865 with RMLs.

• • •

THE RAVELIN TOWER

The central outwork of the Land Front was the Ravelin Tower and its Counterguard (Fig. 6.51). The tower was entered at first floor level from the southern side of Casemate Barracks, through a tunnel in the Land Front, and across a bridge; another bridge joined the tower to the Counterguard. These bridges were not the typical drawbridges, but an invention by Thomas Blanshard.

> Few officers of Engineers can have looked at the ordinary draw-bridges of fortifications without remarking that little change has been made in their construction during a period in which every other application of machinery has undergone very great improvement. The rolling bridge designed for Fort Regent, in Jersey, by Mr. John Le Sueur, foreman of works at that station…and a suspension bridge invented by Colonel Blanshard, and applied at Bermuda, of which the defences were chiefly designed by him, appear to be the only exceptions to this remark…[83]

FIGURE 6.50: *This view of the Dockyard gate from the 1890s shows the Great Wharf Rampart, the South Orillon and the Couvre Porte beyond (BMM Archives).*

82 BA, Hemphill, Defence Report.

83 [A Royal Engineer]. 'Draw-bridges at Bermuda' *Professional Papers of the Corps of Royal Engineers* 9 (1847), 40–49.

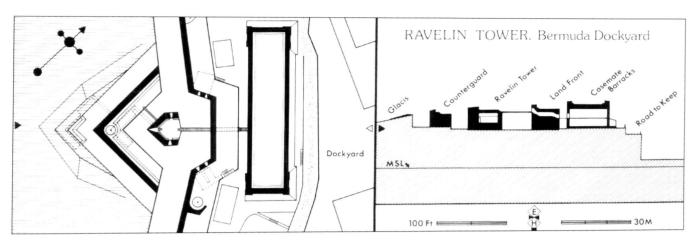

Glacis Counterguard Ravelin Tower Land Front Casemate Barracks Road to Keep

Dockyard

MSL

100 Ft   30M

FIGURE 6.51: *The Ravelin Tower was the central outwork of Dockyard Land Front and was itself covered by a Counterguard, both demolished about 1905.*

FIGURE 6.52: *This rare view of the Ravelin Tower shows a ladder to the Counterguard and the later fixed bridge to the Tower itself (Wendell Hollis Collection).*

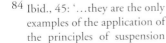

84 Ibid., 45: '...they are the only examples of the application of the principles of suspension bridges to draw-bridges.'

In a diagram published in 1847, the bridge looks like a simple suspension structure and there were two of them at Bermuda, both at the Ravelin Tower.[84] The dimension of forty-two feet given for the illustration of one matches the gap between the Tower and the Land Front. Instead of being drawn up, like a normal drawbridge, Blanshard's suspension bridge was designed to be dropped into the ditch. After the enemy were thus spilled into the ditch, the bridge could be winched back into position from the Ravelin Tower. Another advantage of this design was the removal of the usual impediment caused by the stanchions of a fixed bridge in the ditch. The bridges may have been difficult to maintain and later in the century seem to have been replaced by a fixed arrangement (Fig. 6.52).

The Ravelin Tower was a casemated irregular hexagon. It was built to hold twenty-two men and had a 24-pounder in each of its flanks. In the casemates were four 24-pounder carronades flanking the ditch to the east and west. The

Counterguard mounted one 24-pounder in its salient and had reverse fires in its counterscarp, covering the ditch of the Ravelin Tower. These galleries were entered from the tower by a tunnel under the western run of its ditch. From those galleries, another tunnel under the ditch of the Counterguard led to further counterscarp galleries under the glacis, the remains of which were discovered in 1986 (Fig. 6.53-54). With the exception of those archaeological traces, all evidence of the Ravelin Tower and its Counterguard was removed in the extension of the Dockyard in 1901–07.

FIGURE 6.53: *The western tunnel and stair of the flanking gallery for the Counterguard of the Ravelin Tower was found in demolition work in the 1980s.*

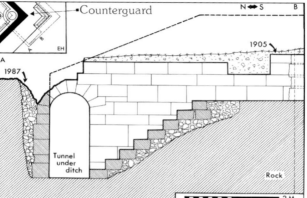

FIGURE 6.54: *An archaeological record of the elevation of the tunnel and stairs to the flanking gallery of the Counterguard of the Ravelin Tower.*

• • •

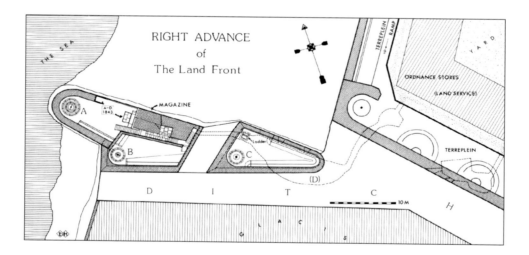

FIGURE 6.55: *The Right Advance was the western outwork of the Dockyard Land Front, a work of three tiers for as many guns.*

THE RIGHT ADVANCE

The last of the three outworks of the Land Front was the Right Advance. It was a structure of three tiers, entered by a tunnel under the ditch of the Land Front from the yard of Casemate Barracks. The tunnel passed through a cave (Fig. 6.55, Emplacement 'D'), the mouth to the north being walled up for two gunports, thus forming a largely natural casemate. These were for 24-pounder carronades to flank the western face of the North-west Rampart and Bastion 'I'. At the western end of the cave, a ladder gave the only access to

FIGURE 6.56: The Right Advance and the Land Front from the air, looking east, in the early 1980s.

Emplacement 'C' above. This emplacement was for a single 32-pounder on an iron traversing platform and a banquette ran around the eastern side of the emplacement for musketry fire into the Land Front ditch.

A secondary ditch separates Emplacement 'C' from 'B', its floor being about ten feet above the Land Front ditch. Under this minor ditch, a tunnel ran from the cave below to steps leading to Emplacements 'A' and 'B'. Emplacement 'B' is the central work of the Right Advance and mounted a 32-pounder cannon. It had a firing step facing the ditch and glacis to the south-west. Emplacement 'A' was arranged in a similar fashion and also carried a 32-pounder in 1857. The magazine for the Right Advance was located at the rear of Emplacement 'A', its door protected by a small parados with a date-stone of 1843. The ditch to the south of the Right Advance was flanked by an oblique casemate for two guns, probably 24-pounder carronades, under the terreplein of the western half-bastion of the Land Front.

The purpose of the Right Advance was to enfilade the western shore of Ireland Island, to bear on the small boat channel from the westward, and to flank the sea face of the North-west Rampart (Fig. 6.56). Neither the Right Advance nor the Ravelin Tower were rearmed in the RML period.[85]

• • •

THE LAND FRONT

The Land Front extended across Ireland Island and in front of it was a defensive ditch; on Grassy Bay, it terminated at the South Orillon and Couvre Porte. In its eastern half-bastion above the South Orillon, it mounted five 24-pounders, the upper four being terraced to match the fall of the ground. The western half-bastion of the Land Front, which ended at the Right Advance, carried three 24-pounders, and probably on its westernmost emplacement, a 32-pounder.[86]

The flanks of the Land Front facing the Ravelin Tower each mounted two 24-pounders carronades, with a like number in casemates below. The hill on which the Front stands is about ninety feet above the sea, giving it good command of the southern part of Ireland Island. The glacis of the Land Front extended about one hundred yards beyond the Ravelin Tower and was considered to be steep. In the rear of the Land Front was the bombproof Casemate Barracks, built for thirteen officers and 307 men. On the flanks of the barracks were bombproof magazines for 2,500 barrels of gunpowder.

[85] In 1985, the Right Advance was threatened with demolition in the construction of a new prison on the western part of the glacis. Through the efforts of the Bermuda National Trust and the Bermuda Maritime Museum, this impressive outwork was saved and recorded.

[86] Bermuda Maritime Museum Archives. Forster Cooper Collection. Plans of dockyard defences (Acc. no. BMM 81.237).

THE NORTH-WEST RAMPART

Connecting the defences of the Land Front with the Keep at the north-east point of Ireland Island was the North-west Rampart (Fig. 6.57). The terreplein of the Rampart also served as the only road to the Commissioner's House and the upper grounds of the Keep until the early twentieth century when a road was cut from the Keep Yard. At the northern end of the Rampart, the road passed over a rolling bridge into the Keep, to the west of which was a batardeau. On the western side of the Rampart, a firing step was provided along most of its length. It was interrupted by Bastion 'H' in the middle of the Rampart and terminated on the northern edge of Bastion 'I'.

Bastion 'I', next to the Land Front, was open in the rear. In the late 1850s, it mounted seven 32-pounders on iron traversing platforms. The central work, Bastion H, had a small moat at its gorge. It contained a casemated barrack for twenty-two men, water tanks and powder magazines. On its terreplein were carried five 32-pounders on iron platforms, the two in the rear could traverse to sweep the interior and basin of the Dockyard. Two additional 32-pounders on ground platforms covered the flanks of the Rampart. Two 10-inch mortars completed the armament of Bastion 'H' in 1857.

• • •

THE KEEP OF THE DOCKYARD

At the eastern end of Ireland Island was the 'Keep,' or citadel, of the Dockyard defences. It was a six-acre fort, with seven irregular bastions, named 'A' to 'G'.[87] The lower ground, or Keep Yard, contained the Sea Service stores, which in 1857 comprised two bombproof magazines for 6,540 barrels of powder, a shell store, a filling room and a shifting house. Lighters from the Keep Pond served the fleet at anchor in Grassy Bay with munitions from these stores, or removed them thereto if a ship was under repairs in the Dockyard.

The majority of the emplacements in the Keep were interspersed with

FIGURE 6.57: *Looking from Bastion 'I', the North-west Rampart joined the Land Front to the Keep of the Dockyard defences to the north (BMM Archives).*

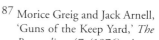

[87] Morice Greig and Jack Arnell, 'Guns of the Keep Yard,' *The Bermudian* 47 (1976) give a general outline of the defence periods of the Keep.

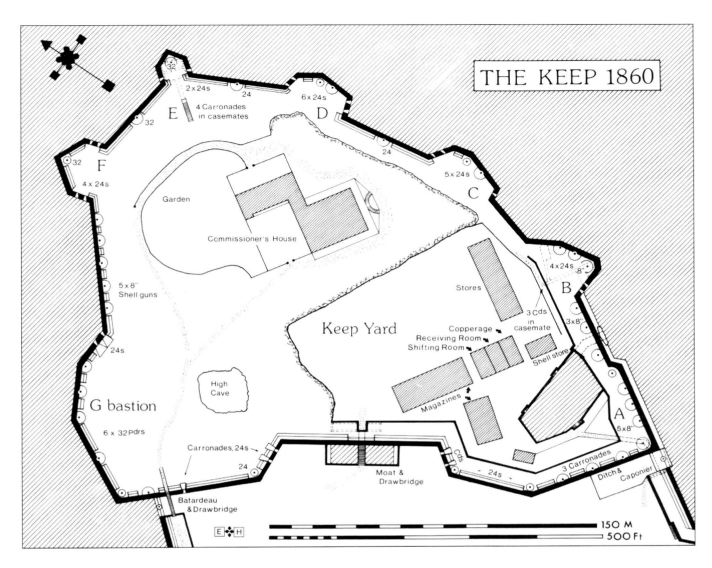

THE KEEP 1860

32

2 x 24s

24

6 x 24s

E

4 Carronades
in casemates

D

32

24

F

32

5 x 24s

4 x 24s

C

Garden

4 x 24s

Commissioner's House

B

3 x 8"

5 x 8"
Shell guns

Stores

3 Cds
in
casemate

24s

Keep Yard

Copperage
Receiving Room
Shifting Room

Shell store

High
Cave

Magazines

A

G bastion

5 x 8'

6 x 32 Pdrs

Carronades, 24s

24

Cds

3 Carronades

24 s

Ditch & Caponier

Moat &
Drawbridge

Batardeau
& Drawbridge

E ✦ H

150 M
500 Ft

short runs of a firing step. Working counter-clockwise from the moated entrance, the armament of the Keep in the late 1850s was as follows (Fig. 6.58). The entrance was flanked by four 24-pounder carronades, with a 24-pounder in each salient. On the curtain approaching Bastion 'A' were a 24-pounder and three 24-pounder carronades. Bastion 'A' carried five 8-inch shell guns, and on the curtain towards Bastion 'B', were three more guns of that calibre.

Bastion 'B' (Fig. 6.59) mounted one 8-inch shell gun and four 24-

pounders, with three 24-pounder carronades in case-mates flanking the watergate to the Keep Pond, and the curtain to Bastion 'C'. At that spot, five 24-pounders could be brought into action, supp-orted by an additional 24-pounder in its northern curtain. Bastion 'D' mounted six 24-pounders and also had a 24-

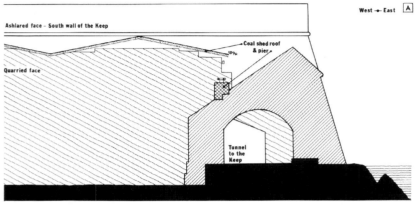

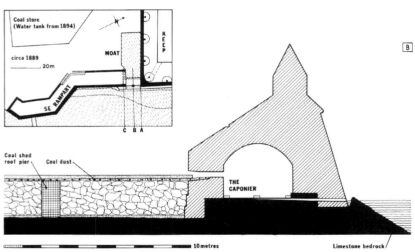

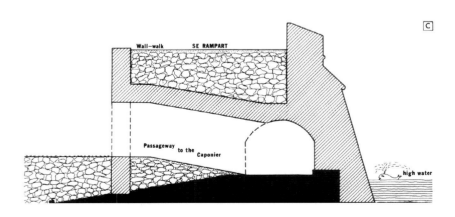

FIGURE 6.60: *The ramparts of the Keep from Grassy Bay with the Commissioner's House above in the 1980s.*

FIGURE 6.61: *Elevations of the Caponier of the Dockyard Keep and the adjacent South-east Rampart fronting the North Breakwater.*

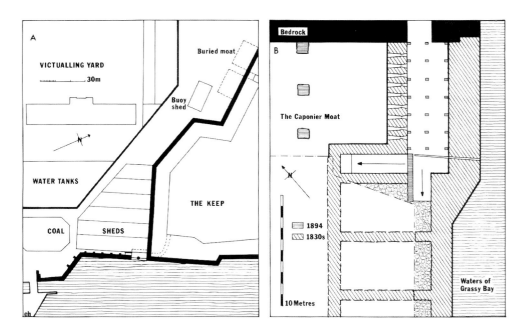

FIGURE 6.62: *This plan shows the Caponier of the Dockyard Keep after the South-east Rampart had been partly demolished in order to build coal sheds in the 1890s.*

pounder in the curtain shared with Bastion 'E' (Fig. 6.60).

Bastion 'E', marking the tip of Ireland Island, had a 32-pounder and two 24-pounders on the terreplein, and four 24-pounder carronades in casemates below. These flanked the 30-foot high walls towards Bastions 'D' and 'F'. Another 32-pounder was mounted in the flank towards Bastion 'F', which was armed with four 24-pounders and a 32-pounder in its salient.

The curtain between Bastions 'F' and 'G' held five 8-inch shell guns, and on its southern flank were two 24-pounders on ground platforms. Bastion 'G' mounted six 32-pounders, and on the far side of the drawbridge to the Northwest Rampart was to be found a 24-pounder carronade in an embrasure.

Above all these emplacements and ramparts rose the three storeys of the large Commissioner's House of the 1820s, much to the annoyance of the Royal Engineers. In 1857, it was proposed to place a 'cavalier casemated barrack'[88] to the east of the House, shown with five guns in a pencilled addition to Blanshard's 1829 plan:[89] the scheme was not carried out.

The western entry was by way of the rolling bridge from the North-west Rampart. The central entrance into the Keep was across a drawbridge and moat (the residual lagoon of a cave) filled by the sea seeping through the rock. The eastern entrance led into the Caponier of the Southeast Rampart, and from thence into the lower yard of the Keep (Figs. 6.61-62).

Flanking the southern corner of the Keep was the Southeast Rampart, which also covered the drawbridge to the breakwater (Fig. 6.63).[90] This rampart was intended for four guns, two in the face, and two in the flank. In consequence of the slight settling of this work into the seabed, these guns were not mounted, but the 1857 report recommends that they be so. That report also noted that the Duke of Wellington approved a battery in the north-east angle of the breakwater, 'to afford a flanking fire on the Eastern shore, and along the water line of the breakwater, which we strongly recommend should

[88] BA, Hemphill, Defence Report.

[89] PRO WO 78/406.

[90] Downing and Harris, 'Excavations,' Fig. 3.

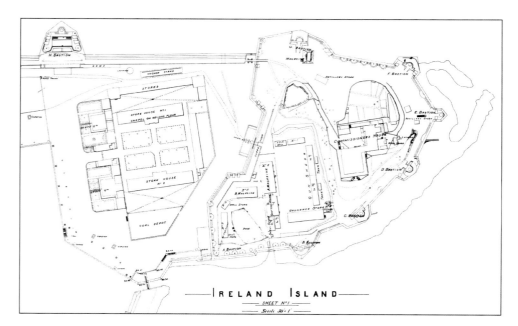

FIGURE 6.63: *The South-east Rampart fronted the North Breakwater and through it ran a gateway protected by a drawbridge (BMM Archives).*

be carried out; its armament should consist of 3—32 pounders on dwarf traversing platforms with embrasures.'[91] The foundations for this battery appear to have been laid, but the work was not completed (Fig. 6.64).

• • •

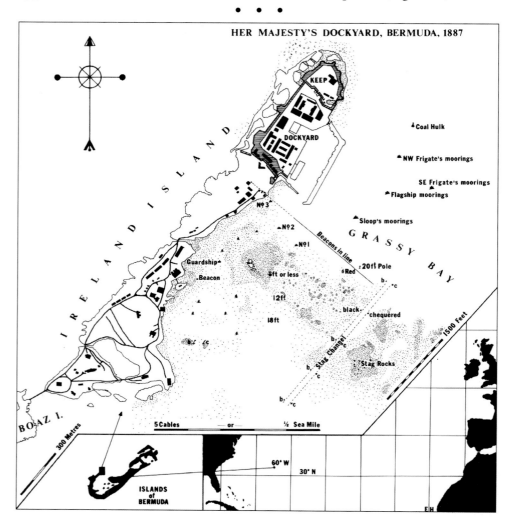

FIGURE 6.64: *This chart of Bermuda Dockyard towards the end of the nineteenth century shows the moorings of the fleet and storage hulks.*

[91] BA, Hemphill, Defence Report.

CONCLUSIONS

As the 1850s drew to a close, the fortifications built in Bermuda in the previous five decades reached their maturity, particularly regarding their armament, which represented the best and the largest guns at the apogee of the smooth-bore era, which began in the late Middle Ages.

The total number of guns at Dockyard in the late 1850s stood at 123: forty-eight 24-pounders, twenty-seven 32-pounders, fourteen 8-inch guns, and thirty 24-pounder carronades and four 10-inch mortars. The total at the forts around St. George's at the same period was ninety-three guns: three 18-pounders; forty-one 24-pounders; twenty-six 32-pounders; two 24-pounder carronades; fifteen 8-inch guns; two 8-inch howitzers, and two 10-inch and two 8-inch mortars, as listed in the Table.

Fort/Gun	18 pdr	24 pdr	32 pdr	68 pdr (8")	Carronade (24 pdr)	Mortar	Howitzer	Totals
Cunningham	–	10	–	–	–	–	–	10
Buildings Bay	–	–	7	–	–	–	–	7
Albert	–	–	7	–	–	2, 10-in.	2, 8-in.	11
Catherine	–	5	12	7	2	–	–	26
Victoria	2	18	–	–	–	2, 8-in.	–	22
Western Redoubt	–	4	–	4	–	–	–	8
George	–	4	–	4	–	–	–	8
Martello	1	–	–	–	–	–	–	1
Dockyard	–	48	27	14	30	4, 10-in.	–	123
Totals	3	89	53	29	32	8	2	216

An overall total of 216 pieces in 1857 tallies with a sum of 206 guns at Bermuda in 1861, when there was considerable concern over the defences of the island during the American Civil War and immediately following the Trent affair in November 1861.[92] If, as indicated, the guns at the Western Redoubt were never mounted, the tally would be 208 guns in 1857 and only two less four years later.

Thus in 1857, the number of guns had increased by eighty-one from the 135 in position at the beginning of the nineteenth century. Thereafter the numbers would decline as the calibre and power of the new Rifled Breech, and Muzzle Loading guns came into being in the late 1850s and early 1860s. The efficiency of rifled artillery was amply demonstrated during the American Civil War in 1861–5. Coupled with the building of iron-hulled ships, with the French *Gloire* (1859) and the British *Warrior* (1860), shortly to be steam-driven with screw propulsion, the armaments of war changed forever and the unending arms race began. This fundamental sea-change was reflected in a new round of Bermuda fortifications after 1865.

■ ■ ■

92 R.A. Courtemanche, *No Need of Glory, the British Navy in American Waters 1860–1864,* (1977), 53.

Bermuda Maritime Museum benefactors, Island Construction Services, excavating the ditch at Fort Cunningham in 1991. A 38-ton RML is next to the machine.

7

Fortifications in the RML Period

1 8 6 5 – 1 8 9 8

Deservedly high in importance to Great Britain as Bermuda has ever been held as a well-placed sentinel over her West Indies and South American interests and possessions; as a refuge and depot for her fleets and ships in that particular ocean where her envied naval supremacy is in most danger of disputes; and in close proximity to an increasingly powerful and impulsive nation [U.S.A.], scarcely deigning to disavow its disregard of any rights found to interfere with long cherished schemes of aggrandizement and acquisition; and hitherto unable, if not unwilling, to control among its people a wild spirit of aggression dangerous to the maintenance of peace...

—Hemphill Report 1857

AFTER THE DIFFICULTIES PRESENTED BY THE AMERICAN CIVIL WAR AND WITH major changes in weaponry and shipping in progress, the British military in 1865 reassessed the defences of their overseas stations. Bermuda was deemed to be 'the most important of our naval stations in the Atlantic. Its central position in that ocean, within three days steaming distance of the shores of North America, its dockyard, and capacious deep-water harbours, together with its natural capabilities for defence, contribute to render it the citadel of our naval power in the western world. There is reason to believe that the desire of the Americans for its possession is in proportion to its value to this country.'[1] Accordingly, the British sent Col. Drummond Jervois, R.E., Deputy Director of Fortifications, to Bermuda to inspect the existing works and make recommendations for the future.

His main interest was the Dockyard and the four forts facing the Narrows Channel. Since the Report of 1857, the guns had been upgraded at Fort Cunningham to three 110-pounder rifled Armstrongs, four 68-pounders and two 8-inch pieces, the last probably shell guns. The only other changes on the Channel were at Fort St. Catherine, now mounting seven 110-pounder

[1] Bermuda Archives, Wm. F. Drummond Jervois, Report on the Defence of Bermuda, 1865.

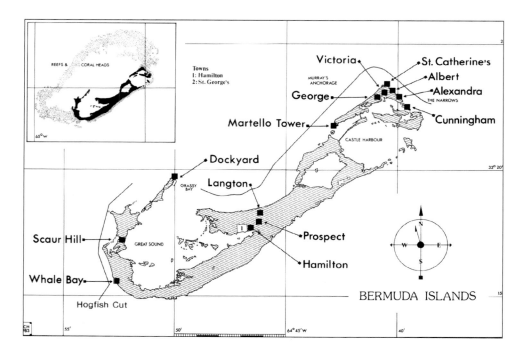

FIGURE 7.1: *Six new fortifications were built at Bermuda between 1860-1890, one at the eastern end, two at the western end and three in the central parishes.*

Armstrongs, and nine 68-pounders. Regarding the Dockyard defences at Ireland Island, Jervois thought that its fortifications were not a match for the new technology. In his view, a similar situation pertained at the Narrows, where 'the existing batteries are all well-placed, but having been constructed only to oppose sailing men-of-war, built of wood, they are not sufficiently powerful, either as regards the nature of their construction or their armament, to stop iron-plated steam vessels armed with the powerful ordnance of the present day. They are built of masonry of a character which could not resist the battering of the most modern heavy ordnance; the parapets are also of masonry, and their guns being nearly all *en barbette* would be easily silenced by the fire of rifled ordnance.'[2] Suggestions for improvements were made.

Fort St. Catherine was to become a battery for thirty guns in two tiers, one in a casemate and one on the roof, to be constructed adjacent to the existing work. The parapet of the old work was to be changed to accept iron shields, which should also be applied to Buildings Bay Battery (soon to become Alexandra Battery) and Fort Cunningham (Fig. 7.1). The other forts on St. George's Island could be left as they were except to add some slightly bigger guns. Moving towards the Dockyard, Jervois referred to a line of works to the west of the Admiral's house at Spanish Point. Those were to stop an enemy from bombarding the Dockyard from that range, as recommended in 1857, but he moved the forts to the east, to the 'Prospect Hill Position.' Further west, his recommendations for the Hog Fish Cut channel later took shape as Whale Bay Battery. To cut off an overland approach to the Dockyard, what became Scaur Hill Fort was proposed for Somerset Island between Ely's Harbour and the Great Sound.

These plans, which were carried out, more expansively than originally anticipated, over the next two decades, are the subject of this chapter. The eastern forts will be examined first, followed by the Prospect Hill Position, Whale Bay and Scaur Hill, and finally the remodelling of the Keep at the Dockyard.

2 BA, Jervois, Defence Report, 1865.

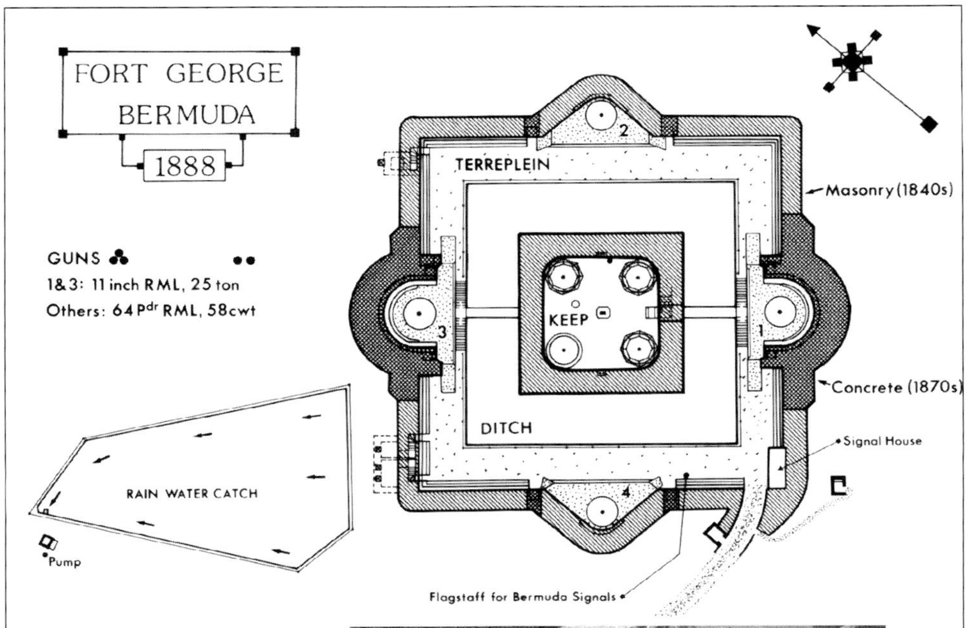

FIGURE 7.3: In the 1870s, Fort George was renovated for RML guns, four on the terreplein and four on the roof of the Keep.

FORT GEORGE
BERMUDA
1888

GUNS ♣ ••
1&3: 11 inch RML, 25 ton
Others: 64 Pdr RML, 58cwt

TERREPLEIN

KEEP

DITCH

RAIN WATER CATCH

Pump

Masonry (1840s)

Concrete (1870s)

Signal House

Flagstaff for Bermuda Signals •

FIGURE 7.2: Two 11-inch Rifled Muzzle Loaders of 25 tons were added to Fort George in the 1870s.

FORT GEORGE

The Martello Tower was not altered in the Rifled Muzzle Loader era and went out of use towards the end of the nineteenth century; this was due in part to the rearming of Fort George in the 1870s (Fig. 7.2). The dates of the reconstruction of the fort are not known precisely, but the work had not begun by the time of the 1869 Defence Report.[3]

The Keep seems to have been changed the least, with only the roof platforms being altered to take four 64-pounder RMLs of 58 cwt (Fig. 7.3). To the north and south, the terreplein was slightly remodelled for two 64-pounder RMLs of 58 cwt. To the east and west, it was extensively remade for two 11-inch RMLs of twenty-five tons. Below these guns, the terreplein had to be excavated for the insertion of shell and cartridge stores (Fig. 7.4), supplied from the magazine and stores in the ground floor of the Keep.

Fort George was not rearmed in the Breech Loader period and its massive 11-inch RMLs are the only such guns left and mounted in their original positions in Bermuda (Fig. 7.5). The Western Redoubt, or Fort William,[4] was not rearmed in either the RML or BL periods and by the time of the latter, it had been roofed over for conversion to a powder magazine.

• • •

[3] I have drawn extensively on the plans of PRO WO 78/4645 for my illustrations of Fort George at this period.

[4] So referred to in 1888 on a chart in the group of plans PRO WO 78/4645.

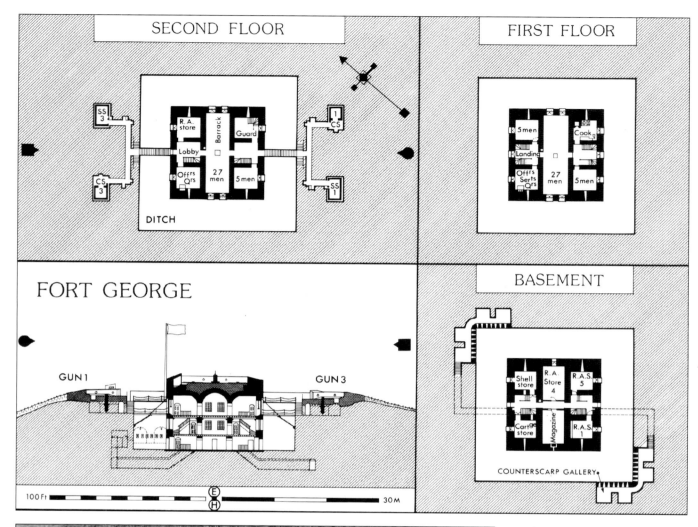

SECOND FLOOR

FIRST FLOOR

FORT GEORGE

BASEMENT

FIGURE 7.4: Shell and cartridge stores were added under the terreplein of Fort George in the 1870s, the Keep being kept as built in the 1830s

FIGURE 7.5: Volunteers from the St. George's Rotary Club clear the western 25-ton, 11-inch RML at Fort George in the 1980s.

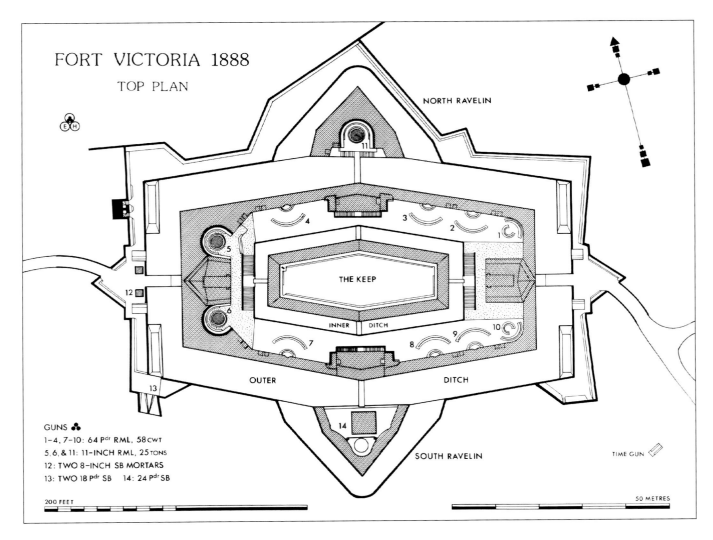

FORT VICTORIA 1888

TOP PLAN

NORTH RAVELIN

THE KEEP

INNER DITCH

OUTER DITCH

SOUTH RAVELIN

TIME GUN

GUNS ♣
1-4, 7-10: 64 P^{dr} RML, 58 CWT
5, 6, & 11: 11-INCH RML, 25 TONS
12: TWO 8-INCH SB MORTARS
13: TWO 18 P^{dr} SB   14: 24 P^{dr} SB

200 FEET

50 METRES

FIGURE 7.6: *The terreplein, or gun level, at Fort Victoria was altered in the 1870s to take two 11-inch Rifled Muzzle Loaders of 25 tons.*

FORT VICTORIA

At Fort Victoria in the 1870s, it was the 'envelope,' or the gun terreplein, and North Ravelin which were altered for the emplacement of RML guns. The South Ravelin was made redundant and a testing laboratory was built within its walls. The North Ravelin was converted to take an 11-inch RML of twenty-five tons (Fig. 7.6, no. 11). Two other 11-inch RMLs of twenty-five tons were fitted into the modified western parapet of the terreplein (Fig. 7.6,

FIGURE 7.7: *Fort Victoria from the air in the 1980s; the Keep has been roofed over to the west and replaced by a swimming pool to the east.*

203

nos. 5 & 6). This arrangement makes it clear that the main area to be covered by Fort Victoria was Murray's Anchorage and the land approaches to Fort St. Catherine and Retreat Hill (Fig. 7.7). The remainder of the terreplein was made to conform with the emplacement of eight 64-pounder RMLs of 58 cwt (Fig. 7.6, nos. 1–4 & 7–10). Work had not yet begun, but it is clear from a report in 1869, that though the guns were smaller than recommended, the general scheme of modification had been adhered to.

FIGURE 7.8: Emplacement no. 6 for an 11-inch RML survives at Fort Victoria, its pivot being an obsolete smooth-bore cannon.

FIGURE 7.9: The dapper "Bird" (probably Lieut. G. Hughes) sits on a 25-ton RML at Fort Victoria in 1902; the shell hoist is folded back on the barrel and the gun is camouflaged (Bermuda Archives: Hughes Album).

Fort Victoria.—A small permanent fort with outworks, forming the keep of St. George's Island, and having an extensive command over both land and sea. The present smooth-bore armament is obsolete, and it is proposed to replace it by a lesser number of rifled ordnance, comprising three 12-inch guns to fire on the deep water channel, and on Murray's Anchorage. The old parapets and traverses will require improvement. These modifications, if approved, may be commenced during the ensuing year.[5]

Some of these features have survived, such as the emplacement for gun no. 6 at the western end of the fort. In standard fashion, a redundant gun, probably a 32-pounder, has been buried to within a foot of its muzzle (Fig. 7.8). A spike from the RML carriage served as a pivot and as a means of imparting some of the recoil of the gun to the buried piece. One of the 25-ton RMLs was to be found in the 1980s partly buried in the western run of the ditch and was moved to Fort St. Catherine in the early 1990s. A turn of the century photograph (Fig. 7.9) shows that the 11-inch RMLs were painted with irregular spots for the purpose of camouflage.[6]

• • •

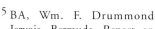

[5] BA, Wm. F. Drummond Jervois, Bermuda, Report on the Defences 1869.

[6] BA, Gerald R. Hughes Album. As Lieutenant, Hughes was with the 1st West India Regiment at Bermuda in 1902.

FIGURE 7.10: *Seen from the air in the 1980s are the four emplacements for 18-ton, 10-inch calibre Rifled Muzzle Loaders at Fort Albert.*

FORT ALBERT

The renovation of Fort Albert for the Rifled Muzzle Loader phase of armaments began in April 1865, and took eleven years to complete (Fig. 7.10). The work was assessed late in 1869, when it was suggested that the guns be placed on disappearing carriages.

> *Fort Albert* stands at the foot of the glacis of *Fort Victoria* overlooking the Narrows. The magazines are nearly completed, but no progress has as yet been made in the battery. The Defence Committee recommended that four 9-in. guns on Moncrieff carriages should be mounted here, besides two light guns. In consequence, however, of the delay which would ensue if the commencement of the gun emplacements were postponed until the precise details of the Moncrieff carriages for the heavier natures of guns are known, as well as from the height of the battery, 87 feet above the sea, and from its not being against the sky-line, it is submitted that it is unnecessary to incur the expense of constructing the work to receive Moncrieff carriages, and that the guns should be mounted *en barbette*, in which case the work would be ready for its armament during the ensuing year. A design for this mode of completion had been prepared and, if adopted, it is submitted that, owing to the commanding position of the work, it would be desirable to arm it with the most powerful guns obtainable; four 12-inch guns are therefore proposed for the armament of the battery. The two light pieces on the right flank of the work might be dispensed with.[7]

The estimate for the job was £7,000 and the actual work was calculated at £6,996.[8] The old 32-pounders were removed (or used as pivots for the new guns) and replaced by four 10-inch RMLs of 18 tons (Fig. 7.11). These were mounted on pedestals of concrete, with local hard stone forming the base for the iron racer track for the slide and carriage (Fig. 7.12).

The features at the rear of the fort, namely the Keep, the howitzer platforms, ancillary buildings and the drawbridge remained intact (Fig. 7.13). In the centre of the Fort, however, excavations were made several storeys deep, the upper part becoming shell hoists below each gun (Fig. 7.14). These connected through ammunition shafts to a new magazine complex below (Fig. 7.15).

In the early 1960s, all of the RMLs were still in position at Fort Albert, but they were moved to Fort St. Catherine when it became a 'tourist attraction.'

• • •

[7] BA, Jervois, Defence Report, 1869.

[8] Plans of Fort Albert are held by the Bermuda Archives and from these was obtained much of the information in my illustrations.

FIGURE 7.12 (left): A
detailed view of one of the
emplacements for an 18-
ton, 10-inch Rifled Muzzle
Loader gun at Fort Albert.

FIGURE 7.11 (above): Two
10-inch Rifled Muzzle
Loaders were still emplaced
at Fort Albert in the 1930s
(Bermuda Archives: Roger
Willock Collection).

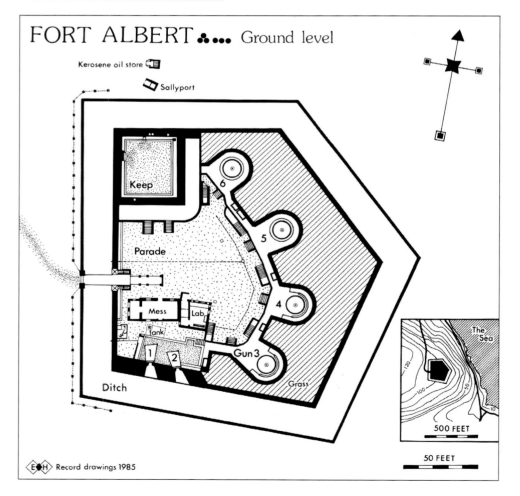

FIGURE 7.13: Fort Albert
was altered in the 1870s for
the insertion of four large
guns, the original emplacements being buried under
the new glacis.

FIGURE 7.14: *In the 1870s, a second bridge was added to the Keep at Fort Albert and shell hoist rooms were placed below the guns.*

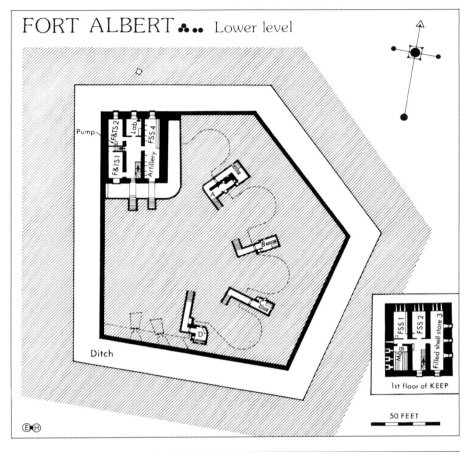

FIGURE 7.15: *New magazines were made at basement level at Fort Albert in the 1870s; the original flanking galleries were entered from the Keep.*

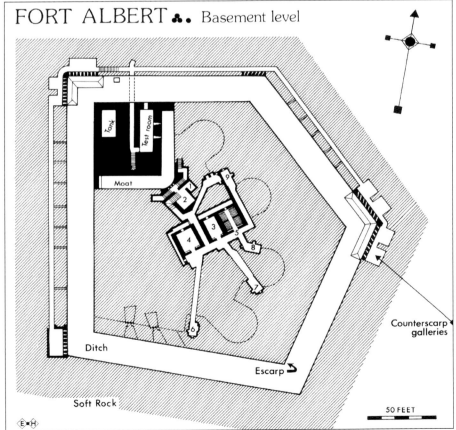

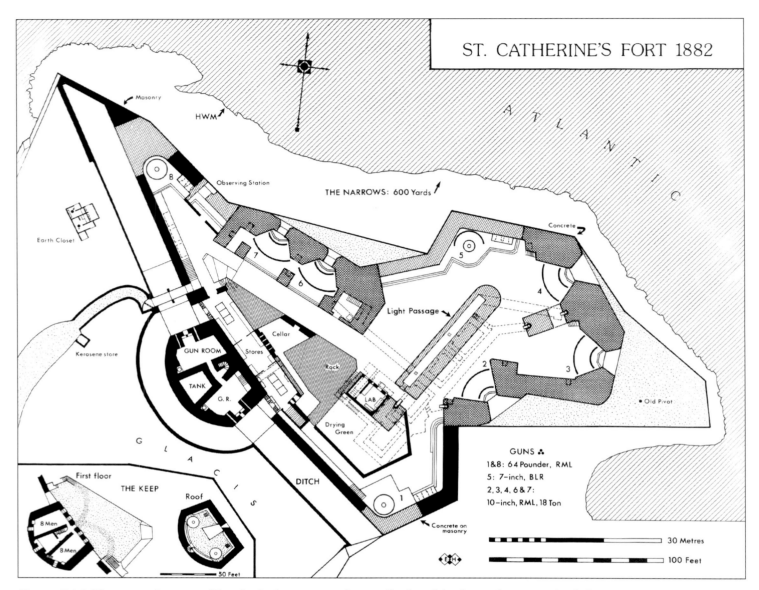

ST. CATHERINE'S FORT 1882

Masonry

HWM

Observing Station

THE NARROWS: 600 Yards

Concrete

Earth Closet

Kerosene store

GUN ROOM

Stores

Cellar

TANK

G.R.

Rock

LAB

Light Passage

Old Pivot

Drying Green

GUNS ♣

1 & 8: 64 Pounder, RML

5: 7-inch, BLR

2, 3, 4, 6 & 7:

10-inch, RML, 18 Ton

First floor

THE KEEP

Roof

8 Men

8 Men

DITCH

Concrete on masonry

50 Feet

30 Metres

100 Feet

FIGURE 7.16: The seaward portion of Fort St. Catherine was substantially altered for the emplacement of Rifled Muzzle Loaders in the 1870s.

FIGURE 7.17: A Haxo casemate for two 10-inch RMLs was added to the seaward of the Keep at Fort St. Catherine in the 1870s.

FORT ST. CATHERINE

The most powerful single fort with twenty-six guns at the end of the smooth-bore period and the northern guardian of the Narrows Channel, it was important that Fort St. Catherine be rearmed in the RML era. Four years after his 1865 visit, Col. Jervois made another trip to Bermuda for a further assessment.

> *Fort Catherine.*—An old work commanding the turning point of the *Narrows Channel* where the navigation is most intricate and difficult. A project for mounting six guns on Moncrieff carriages has been approved by the Defence Committee. Owing, however to the limited interior space of the old work, it has been found impracticable to mount more than three guns on the Moncrieff principle in such a manner as to obtain from them the most useful effect. It is therefore recommended that the revised armament should consist of three guns so mounted, supplemented by two in casemates firing on the channel adjoining the turning point. A design for carrying out this proposal has been prepared. The magazines are already in course of construction.[9]

That plan was not carried out and none of the larger Moncrieff carriages were ever employed at Bermuda. The final RML arrangement was recorded in the Goodenough Report of 1889, which gave consideration to additional alterations: 'This is an old Masonry fort with Keep. This Keep is not only of no value to the defence, but a source of danger. It should be removed. Two of the guns are in casemates, the remaining three are behind embrasures' (Fig, 7.16).[10]

FIGURE 7.18: *Concrete and brick emplacements were devised for 10-inch RMLs at Fort St. Catherine in the 1870s; the guns are from Fort Albert.*

By 1894, less than a decade from their obsolescence, five 10-inch RMLs of eighteen tons had been installed at Fort St. Catherine. Two were under the concrete cover of a Haxo casemate (Fig. 7.17) and the others in large concrete and brick embrasured emplacements which took up much space in the terreplein (Fig. 7.18). Emplacements 2 and 3 were protected from enfilade from the north by a large parados (unfortunately removed in the 1960s). Two 64-pounder RMLs were situated in the two western extremities of the fort, while a 7-inch Rifled Breech Loader stood on the northern parapet between the Haxo casemate and the other large RMLs. On the southern side of the fort, a major excavation produced an area for a large magazine of five rooms (covered by the parados above), light passages and passages to shell and cartridge hoists to the guns above.

At some point, possibly during World War Two, the barrels of the big RMLs were dumped into the sea, where they lay in the 1990s. So ended the development of Fort St. Catherine, which began in 1612 and ran through at least seven periods of development or replacement. The site was not rearmed at the end of the RML period and thus was in use as a military site for almost three centuries.

• • •

9 BA, Jervois, Defence Report, 1869.

10 PRO CAB 11/11, W. H. Goodenough, Report of Inspection in the West Indies by the Inspector-General of Artillery, 1889.

FIGURE 7.19: *Alexandra Battery from the air after the removal of the 1900 glacis from the surviving RML emplacement, centre foreground.*

ALEXANDRA BATTERY

The coming of iron-plated ships and rifled artillery in no manner changed the strategic importance of the Narrows Channel at the east end of Bermuda. The subject was discussed by Col. Jervois in his 'turn of the tide' report in 1865, as it was by then obvious to some that the days of the sailing navy were over.

> ...it will be clear that an enemy would not have effected the capture of Bermuda unless he had possession of the Channel of the Narrows, for so long as we have in our hands the power of passing large ships of war to the inner waters whilst that power is denied to him, we could overcome any naval force that he might have succeeded in passing through the minor channels in the reefs. Either the silencing or the capture of the defences of the Narrows Channel must therefore be accomplished before he could obtain actual possession of the island. If measures recommended for the improvement of the batteries bearing on the Narrows, and arming them with powerful ordnance capable of smashing iron-plated vessels be carried into effect, it will be impossible for him to silence those batteries from seaward. He would be sunk in the attempt.[11]

Jervois then discussed ways of securing the rears of the various forts, but the emphasis in the new works was to the seaward. This was especially the case with Buildings Bay Battery, renamed 'Alexandra Battery,'[12] which was without any rear defences at all (Fig. 7.19). The old work was swept away and in its place arose Bermuda's first fort with iron-plated gun ports. The task was rapidly undertaken, for in 1869 it could be reported that *Alexandra Battery, Buildings Bay*, has been prepared for five 9-inch guns protected by iron shields. With the exception of a small barrack in connection with the gorge, and some further work in the magazines, the battery is complete. Four of the iron shields are in position, and three of the guns have been mounted.'[13]

The new work (Fig. 7.20) inscribed an arc to the east and south from the side of a small hill just east of Buildings Bay. The first embrasure was made of

[11] BA, Jervois, Defence Report, 1865.

[12] Presumably named for and perhaps in honour of the marriage in 1863 of Alexandra, daughter of Christian IX of Denmark, to Edward, son of Queen Victoria, later (1901) King Edward VII.

[13] BA, Jervois, Defence Report, 1869.

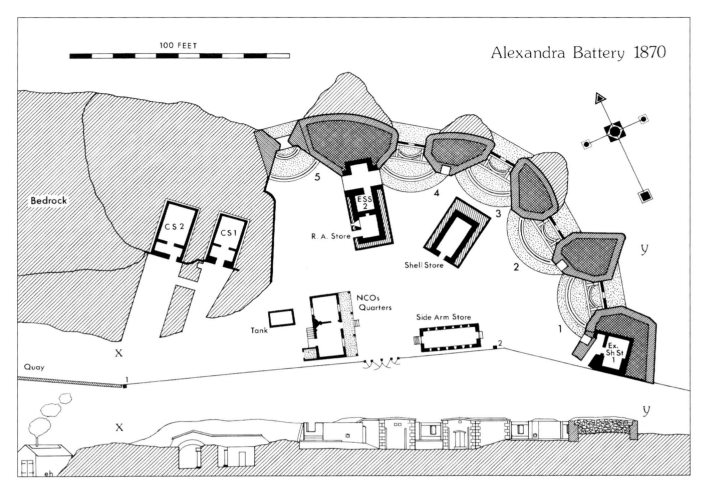

100 FEET

Alexandra Battery 1870

Bedrock

CS 2

CS 1

5

ESS 2

R. A. Store

4

3

Shell Store

2

y

NCOs Quarters

Tank

Side Arm Store

1

Ex. Sh St 1

X

2

Quay

1

X

y

eh

FIGURE 7.20: *A plan of Alexandra Battery in the 1870s shows four iron and one stone gunports, all except no. 1 were completely buried or destroyed in the new works of 1900.*

stone, perhaps indicating the lack of a fifth shield. The other gunports comprised sections of wrought iron plates, connected the one to the other by an intervening mass of hard stone masonry, possibly filled with earth and rubble. Two magazines had been excavated into the hill and a shell store was inserted under the southernmost masonry bulwark. All of the emplacements were open to the rear, with no evidence of casemates. Four small buildings were erected within the half-circle inscribed by the arc of the five emplacements.

The shields themselves (Fig. 7.21)[14] consisted of three plates of wrought iron, held together by flush-headed bolts, the nuts appearing at the rear. Two H-beams reinforced the shield top and bottom. A triangular arrangement of riveted iron plates and angles formed supports on each side of the shield; these in turn were fastened to horizontal beams which extended beyond the first racer to be joined with another at right angles. The surface of these beams appears at ground level, but the lower parts are buried in the concrete floor of the emplacement. Over the gunport was a bar for hanging a rope mantlet, of which several examples survived in 1994 at Gibraltar. This type of gunport is called a 'Gibraltar Shield,' presumably as they were first put into service at that important outpost.[15]

At the turn of the century, the site was modified to take two 6-inch BL rifles and the RML works were buried in the process. Emplacement no. 1 was only covered to seaward by the 1900 glacis, so that the interior of the shield

14 This drawing and others pertinent were based on PRO WO 78/4300 and 78/3816.

15 Quentin Hughes and Athanassios Migos, *Strong as the Rock of Gibraltar* (1995), 106.

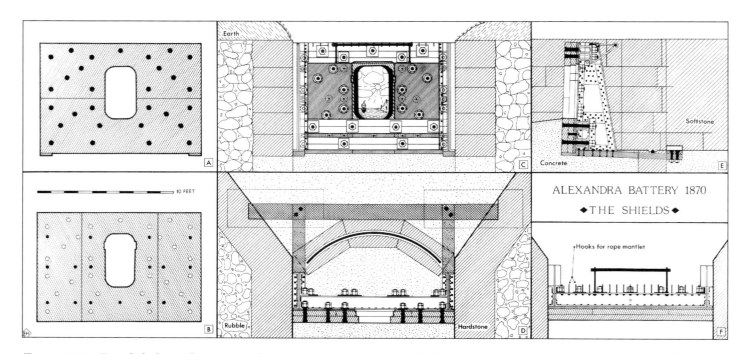

FIGURE 7.21: *Detailed plans, elevations and cross-sections of one of the RML wrought iron emplacements at Alexandra Battery.*

was exposed in the 1980s (Fig. 7.22). Working with the Department of Parks, the Bermuda Maritime Museum undertook a small archaeological project in 1985 to remove the glacis in front of the emplacement, which was exposed and restored (Fig. 7.23).[16] There was no evidence that the shield was capped with a masonry wall or casemate, but was left open to the elements. As a part of the restoration, a 9-inch RML, the right calibre for the site, was placed on exhibit at Alexandra Battery with the permission of the Board of Trustees of the Bermuda Maritime Museum. It lacks its slide, which one day may be replicated (Fig. 7.24).

Alexandra Battery added

FIGURE 7.22: *Emplacement no. 1 at Alexandra Battery was exposed in the rear but covered to seaward by the 1900 glacis of soil and sand.*

FIGURE 7.23: *Emplacement no. 1 at Alexandra Battery after the removal of the glacis and the addition of a 9-inch RML from the collection of the Bermuda Maritime Museum.*

16 My thanks go to Edward Manuel, then-Director of Agriculture, Fisheries and Parks, without whose support this project would not have taken place.

FIGURE 7.24: *The seaward face of wrought iron emplacement no. 1 at Alexandra Battery after cleaning and painting in the 1980s.*

FIGURE 7.24: *The seaward face of wrought iron emplacement no. 1 at Alexandra Battery after cleaning and painting in the 1980s.*

a powerful new work to the defences fronting the Narrows Channel, but it also presaged the changing nature of fortifications. It had no ditch or a wall enclosing its rear: it was undefendable from a landward attack. As such, it was almost forty years ahead of its time, for the change from fortified positions to gun emplacements in the landscape did not occur until the turn of the century, exemplified at this site by its conversion to Breech Loaders around 1900.

The other three forts on the Narrows Channel, St. Catherine, Albert and Cunningham, being conversions of existing works, retained the sense of defendable sites, with existing features such as deep ditches with reverse fires from the smooth-bore era.

• • •

FORT CUNNINGHAM

The fort on the summit of Paget Island, begun around 1815 by Captain Thomas Cunningham, who correctly identified the site as crucial for the defence of the mouth of the Narrows Channel, was a departure from the old bastioned method of fortifications, in use for several hundred years in England, Europe, the West Indies and elsewhere. The Dockyard defences and Fort St. Catherine were the last Bermuda forts to use the bastioned trace, possibly among the last examples in the British Empire to be so designed.

The Fort Cunningham design became known as the 'polygonal trace' and the Bermuda work may be one of the earliest examples of a system that proliferated in the 1860s.[17] A fort conformed to various polygonal shapes. Fort Victoria, for example, was hexagonal, or six-sided; Fort Cunningham was pentagonal, or five-sided, as was Fort Albert; Fort George and the Western

[17] Andrew Saunders, *Fortress Britain* (1989), 248.

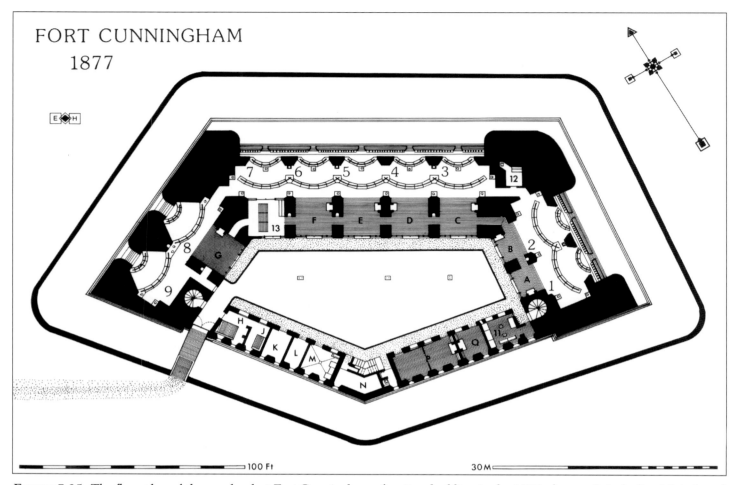

FORT CUNNINGHAM
1877

FIGURE 7.25: *The floor plan of the gun level at Fort Cunningham after its rebuilding in the 1870s for two 9-inch, five 10-inch and two 12.5-inch Rifled Muzzle Loaders.*

Redoubt were quadrangles, with four sides. Rather than having projecting bastions to cover the flanks and curtain walls, the polygonal forts were set within deep ditches. At the appropriate corners, reverse fires, or flanking galleries for riflemen were excavated into the counterscarp, and entered by tunnels from the fort and under the floor of the ditch. From the galleries, the riflemen could shoot at the enemy in the ditch; some forts, such as Prospect, also had cannon for grapeshot in these galleries. Caponiers in the ditches added further coverage. At Fort Cunningham, the flanking galleries were carried over into the RML period.

The works at gun level from the original Fort Cunningham were allowed no such rebirth, but were entirely removed in the RML renovations of the site, commenced about 1866 and much advanced four years later.

Fort Cunningham, which commands the southern end of the Narrows Channel, as well as the entrance to *St. George's Harbour*, has been re-modelled for the reception of nine heavy guns in casemates, seven of which are to be wholly iron-fronted. The iron-work for two of these casemates is already on the way to Bermuda; and that for the other five is now standing in a complete state in the Atlas works at Sheffield.[18] The magazines are nearly ready, and the gorge buildings will shortly be commenced. It is expected that this powerful work will be ready for its armament during the ensuing year.[19]

[18] This is a rare reference to the place of construction of the shields and it is possible that those for Alexandra Battery were made at Sheffield as well.

[19] BA, Jervois, Defence Report, 1869.

214

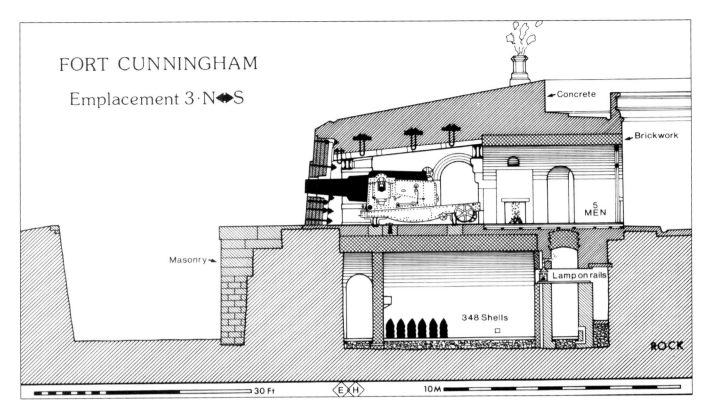

FORT CUNNINGHAM

Emplacement 3·N⬌S

←Concrete

←Brickwork

5 MEN

Masonry→

Lamp on rails

348 Shells

ROCK

30 Ft   ⟨E X H⟩   10 M

FIGURE 7.26: A cross-section of emplacement no. 3 for a 12.5-inch, 38-ton Rifled Muzzle Loader firing through a wrought iron shield about three feet thick.

This new work was the most modern and heavily armed of the works constructed at Bermuda in the RML period. The whole of the upper works built by Cunningham and his successors prior to 1823 was swept away. In their place arose a armoured fort for nine guns (Fig. 7.25). This was not to be a masonry structure with shields, such as Alexandra Battery, but a fort with an entire wrought iron design.

> These were built where it was necessary to place a work in a waterway because of the limited range of the guns of the time made it impossible to close the water gap by batteries on each shore. It followed from their position that an attacking ship might be able to come quite close, and thus the works had to be as strong as possible. Four such works were built, together with three that were cross-breeds—masonry on the landward side and armour on the seaward side, since their proximity to the shore and the position of sandbanks and reefs ensured that no warship would be able to get behind them and attack the masonry face.[20]

All four completely iron forts and two of the cross-breeds were in England; the other cross-breed was Fort Cunningham. These works may be attributed to the energy of Col. Jervois, said to be 'bound and determined to erect on any barren rock or parcel of land on which the Union Flag has been raised a lasting memento to his gifted skills wherein expense seemed a secondary consideration.'[21] The cost of the iron shield and armoured forts was immense, 'while the defences of Bermuda were such that one exasperated MP stood up in Westminster to ask, of the kingpin of the Bermudan defences, "Is Fort Cunningham made of gold?" '[22]

At Fort Cunningham, Emplacements 1 through 7 were behind two continuous iron shields, but unlike the circular structures such as the Plymouth Breakwater Fort, these were straight fronts. Similar to the shields at Alexandra

[20] Ian V. Hogg, *Coast Defences of England and Wales, 1856–1956* (1974), 64.

[21] Ibid., 46.

[22] Ibid., 68.

Battery, the Cunningham wrought iron walls are almost twice as thick and substantially stronger, having interior reinforcing of teak and solid iron beams. All of the emplacements were casemated with wrought iron plate ceilings capped with several feet of concrete (Fig. 7.26).

FIGURE 7.27: An interior view of emplacement no. 3 for a 12.5-inch, 38-ton RML of the 1870s; the carriage rails were exposed by removing a later concrete floor.

FIGURE 7.28: Seven RMLs were found in the ditch at Fort Cunningham in 1991; five were 10-inch of 18-tons and two 12.5-inch of 38 tons.

The first two emplacements looked towards St. David's Head and Five Fathom Hole, protecting as well the channel into St. George's Harbour, between Paget and Smith's Island: here were to be mounted 10-inch RMLs of 18 tons. Emplacements 3 and 4 were to house the largest calibre guns ever mounted in a Bermuda fort, namely, 12.5-inch RMLs of thirty-eight tons. A concrete screed laid over the floor of Emplacement 3 was removed in 1991 to reveal the tracks and part of the bronze quadrant for this position (Fig. 7.27).

Emplacements 5, 6, and 7, on the same face as the 12.5-inch pieces, had the same purpose, namely, to cover the entrance to the Narrows Channel. They mounted 10-inch RMLs of eighteen tons. Facing north and covering the shoreline towards Alexandra Battery were Emplacements 8 and 9, in stone and brick casemates for 9-inch RMLs of twelve tons, sometime mounted but removed apparently in the late 1880s. At the rear of the guns and the casemate, the area was used for barracks, including fireplaces. Across the courtyard to the rear of the fort were the Officers' Quarters and ancillary rooms for the garrison. Apparently retained from the earlier work were two fine newel staircases to the magazines and counterscarp galleries.

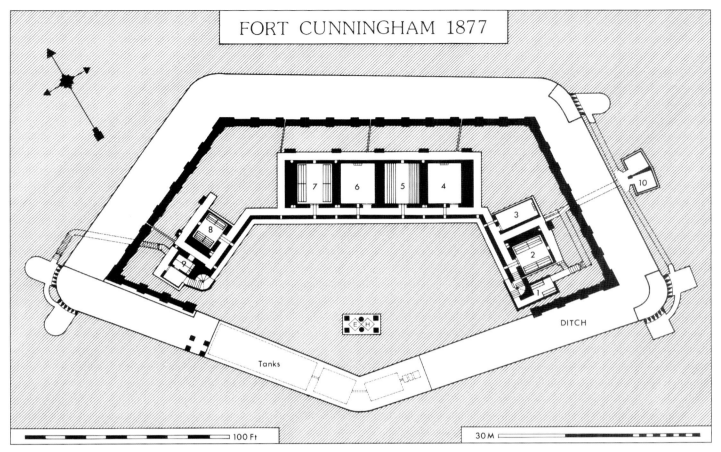

FORT CUNNINGHAM 1877

DITCH

Tanks

100 Ft

30 M

FIGURE 7.29: *The magazines at Fort Cunningham were extensively remade in the 1870s, with additions in 1900; the flanking galleries are 1820s originals.*

In the early 1900s, the fort was converted for the last time, in this instance for the installation of two 6-inch BL guns on the roof above Emplacements 2 and 7. Below the new guns, a massive pillar of concrete was placed to carry their weight, which filled parts of the RML emplacements, including the gunports. On breaking through the concrete in Emplacement 7 in 1991, the gun room was found to be almost in pristine condition from the 1890s (the other emplacements being altered and painted in later decades).

In the first years of this century, the guns from Emplacements 1 to 7 were taken from their positions and moved into the courtyard. From there, they were lifted onto the roof over Emplacement 8 and pushed into the ditch (Fig. 7.28). One of the 10-inch barrels was cracked and another lost its cascabel when they struck bottom. The guns were found in 1991 under the backfilling of that section of the ditch, which occurred around 1905. They were in remarkably good condition; the two 38-ton guns are very rare, there being only six known examples in the world.

At ditch level, the stonework of Cunningham's fort was retained, but within the enceinte of the work, major excavations were made in the bedrock for the insertion of new magazines (Fig. 7.29). These were accessed by two newel staircases in local hard stone in the north-west and south-west corners of the

FIGURE 7.30: *Fort Cunningham from the air in 1993 after the excavation of the ditch.*

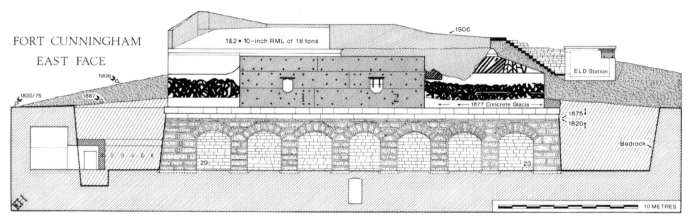

FORT CUNNINGHAM

EAST FACE

courtyard. There were nine rooms in the magazines for various functions and they will be discussed in a later work.[23]

In 1991, a team led by Professor Richard Gould of Brown University excavated the ditch, which had been infilled on two sides of the fort (Fig. 7.30). Archival research indicated that the ditch had been infilled on two occasions. The first occurred during the RML period in the late 1880s and was an attempt to create a continuous glacis to seaward of the two iron fronts. Concrete blocking walls were built across the ditch at its north corner near Emplacement 7 and in the southern run of the ditch where the 1820s stonework ends. Into the latter was constructed a new flanking gallery to replace that in the south-east corner of the ditch, soon to be buried. Access to the new gallery was had by putting a door in the western gallery to be buried and forming a tunnel from there to the new 'counterscarp' (Fig. 7.31). At the same time, a three-feet thick layer of concrete was laid on the masonry in front of the iron shields, to give further protection to both.

A second infilling took place around 1905 (Fig. 7.31), at which time the concrete bulwark to the right of Emplacement 2 was partly destroyed and overlain by the concrete of the new 6-inch BL emplacement. The concrete dripped over the edge of the shield and consequently the shutter for

FIGURE 7.31: *A cross-section and elevation of the east facade of Fort Cunningham with the wrought iron shield for gunports no. 1 and no. 2; the masonry buttresses to either side were camouflaged, the ditch was backfilled in the 1880s and a glacis added around 1905.*

23 For the results of the archaeological work see the two articles by Richard A. Gould, Edward C. Harris and John R. Triggs in vols. 3 and 4 of the *Bermuda Journal of Archaeology and Maritime History* (1991 and 1992).

FIGURE 7.32: The north-east facade of Fort Cunningham after the excavation of the ditch: camouflage paint is on the central buttress and the arched stonework is from the 1820s.

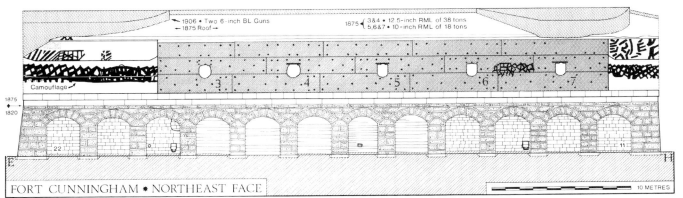

FORT CUNNINGHAM • NORTHEAST FACE

FIGURE 7.33: An elevation of the north-east facade of Fort Cunningham with a continuous wrought iron shield for gunports no. 3 through no. 7. The masonry buttresses to either side were camouflaged as was the shield itself, probably in the late 1880s; two 6-inch Breech Loaders were added at roof level around 1906.

Emplacement 2 was preserved intact. To the north, the RML guns were dropped into the ditch to the west of the 1880s blocking wall; they were then covered by a talus from the 1905 infilling which went from the bottom of the ditch to the top of the BL emplacements. Gunports 1, 3–6, 8 and 9 were retained for windows and ventilation, for these RML casemates became living quarters after 1906.

After the late 1880s alterations and infilling, the exposed frontage of Fort Cunningham was camouflaged (Figs. 7.32–33). The masonry bulwarks were painted with thick, erratic black lines on the vertical faces and on the sloping roofs, geometric red strips were the order of the day. The iron fronts were also painted in the former style. The masonry was then embellished with a yellow-green wash, not unlike the colour of the Bermuda landscape in a dry summer. On the north and south facades (Figs. 34-35), false gunports were painted on the concrete walls, all of this camouflage being preserved under the soils and sands of the glacis of the 1905 remodelling of the fort.

By the mid-1870s, the new works and rearmament of older forts at the eastern end of Bermuda was well advanced, for the protection of the Narrows

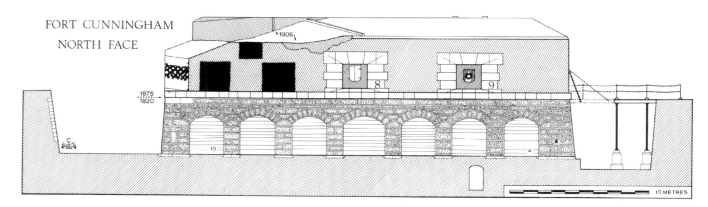

FORT CUNNINGHAM
NORTH FACE

FIGURE 7.34: *The elevation of the north facade of Fort Cunningham with its concrete and masonry ports for guns no. 8 and no. 9. In the 1880s, at least three false gunports were painted on the facade and in 1906 a concrete emplacement was added to the roof for a new 6-inch BL rifle.*

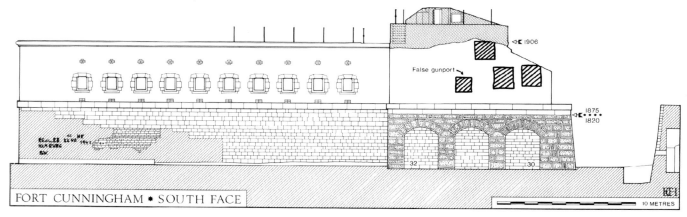

FORT CUNNINGHAM • SOUTH FACE

FIGURE 7.35: *The elevation of the south facade of Fort Cunningham. Some four false gunports were painted on the facade in the 1880s and in 1906 a concrete observation post was added at roof level. The ten windows were for the officers' quarters at the rear of the fort, above World War Two graffiti.*

Channel was paramount to the defence plan of the island. Attention was then turned to the proposed new works near the City of Hamilton, to the west in Southampton Parish and Somerset Island, and lastly to the Dockyard.

• • •

THE PROSPECT HILL POSITION

In his 1865 Report, Col. Jervois discussed the possibility of a landing by an enemy on the south shore beaches, who would then proceed overland to attack the Dockyard.

> In this case, his first object would be to get some guns into position and fire into the dockyard from Spanish Point, which is at the extremity of a peninsula jutting out to the westward from the main island of Bermuda and only about 3,000 yards from the Naval Establishment. To prevent this, it has often been proposed to construct a line of works in front of the Admiral's house [Fig. 7.36], and thus cut off access to Spanish Point, but this line would be too near the dockyard, for the enemy might take up a position outside it, from whence he might effect his object. It is recommended that, in order to provide against a bombardment of the dockyard from this direction, a very favourable position about 7,000 yards distant from it, the principal point of which would be Prospect Hill

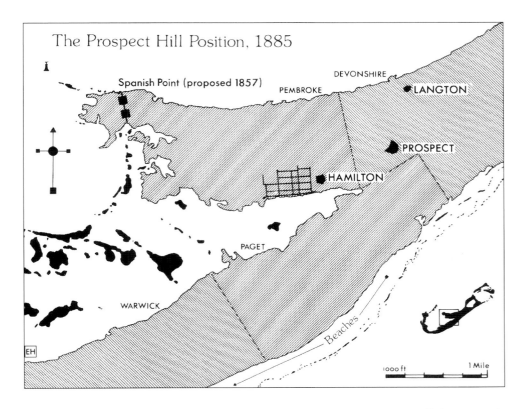

The Prospect Hill Position, 1885

should be occupied by a defensive line only about a mile long, cutting off the peninsula between the head of Hamilton Harbour and the north shore of the island.[24]

The mile-long cordon became known as the 'Prospect Hill Position,' which comprised, from south to north, Forts Hamilton, Prospect and Langton. The first two were wholly land fortifications, whereas Fort Langton was divided, with sea defences to the north and land to the south. Of the three sites, Fort Langton was demolished in the 1980s, Fort Prospect is a water catchment and tank for the City of Hamilton, while Fort Hamilton is a plant nursery, with some public access.

• • •

FORT HAMILTON

FIGURE 7.37: *Fort Hamilton from the air in the 1980s, looking south-west.*

24 BA, Jervois, Defence Report, 1865.

This fort guards the southern flank of the Prospect Hill position and is a pentagonal work erected in the late 1870s (Fig. 7.37). It faces into the head of Hamilton Harbour and across to the Paget shore and easterly to cover the ground between there and the northerly ground towards Fort Prospect. It is a single-period fort and was never rearmed or altered from its original form.

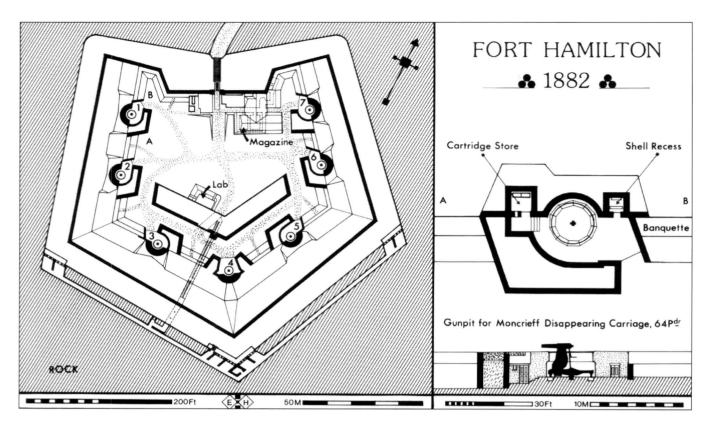

FORT HAMILTON
♣ 1882 ♣

There are seven gun emplacements for 64-pounder converted RMLs on Moncrieff disappearing carriages. The disappearing gun was a new scheme by which the enemy was denied an easy fix on the gun. When it was fired, the force of the recoil forced the piece down into the gun pit, while raising a counterweight on the carriage. The gun was loaded under cover and upon the release of the counterweight, it swung up into the firing position.

This was the smallest type of the Moncrieff carriage and Bermuda has the only known examples of some parts of a typical carriage. Two of the cheeks of the carriage were at Fort Hamilton in the 1960s, but their purpose was not known and they were discarded. The gun pits were later considered somewhat unsatisfactory for once an incoming shell entered the space, it could not easily 'escape' (Fig. 7.38). The magazine for the work was at the rear to the east of the entrance.

FIGURE 7.38: Built in the 1870s, Fort Hamilton was designed for seven 64-pounder Rifled Muzzle Loaders on Moncrieff disappearing carriages.

The original plan for Fort Hamilton called for 'an armament of six guns on Moncrieff carriages, with eight flanking pieces. The plans have received the approval of the Defence Committee, but certain modifications suggested on the occasion of my recent

FIGURE 7.39: The entrance to Fort Hamilton in the late nineteenth century; concrete RML projectiles decorate the capitals of the pillars (author's collection).

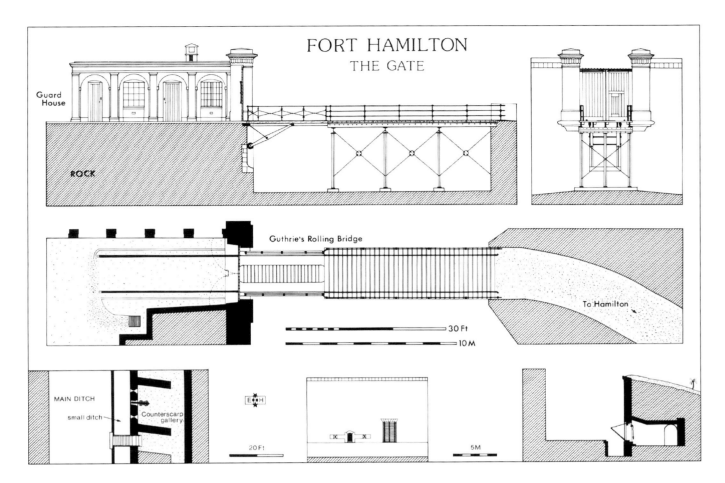

FORT HAMILTON
THE GATE

Guard House

ROCK

Guthrie's Rolling Bridge

To Hamilton

30 Ft
10 M

MAIN DITCH

small ditch

Counterscarp gallery

20 Ft

5M

FIGURE 7.40: *The ditch at Fort Hamilton was spanned by a fixed bridge and a drawbridge, which was a 'Guthrie's Rolling Bridge,' horizontally retracted.*

visit, appear desirable, and plans embodying them are now being prepared.'[25] Out of the changes must have come the design for seven guns, the flanking weapons being reduced or removed. In the 1970s, the three RMLs from Fort Langton were moved to this site and incongruously erected on concrete pillars within the Moncrieff gun pits.

The entrance to the fort was on its northern side (Fig. 7.39) and it was surrounded by a deep ditch, protected by flanking galleries. Exceptionally, one of the flanking galleries had a very small entrance and drawbridge across the secondary ditch of the gallery: this gave access from the fort into the ditch. The flanking galleries were designed for the use of cannon, as well as rifle fire.

The main entrance also had a drawbridge—'Mr. Gutherie's patented "Rolling Bridge"' (Fig. 7.40). This device allowed for the horizontal retraction of the movable part of the bridge into the fort, as opposed to the usual method of the drawing up of the structure. The rolling bridge met a fixed bridge on cast iron pillars, which extended across two-thirds of the width of the ditch.

• • •

[25] BA, Jervois, Defence Report, 1869.

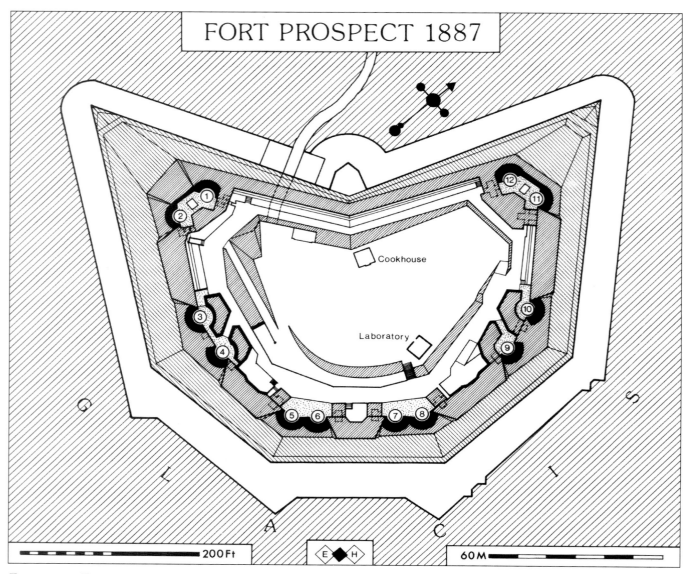

FORT PROSPECT 1887

FIGURE 7.41: *Fort Prospect was erected in the 1870s and mounted twelve 64-pounder RMLs on Moncrieff disappearing carriages.*

FORT PROSPECT

This work was the largest of the trio that made up the Prospect Hill Position. Although on a much smaller scale, its design can be seen to have derived from the forts which had been erected in England as a result of the 1859 Royal Commission on the defences of that country. The polygonal shape of Fort Prospect, in this case a heptagon, is similar, for example, to Fort Wallington near the great Portsmouth naval base.[26]

Fort Prospect was in an advanced state by the time of the Jervois visit of 1869 and was intended to mount twelve 64-pounder RMLs on Moncrieff disappearing carriages in double emplacements of three different types. Guns 1 and 2, and 11 and 12 were centred on the rear east and west salients, with no rear cover; guns 3 and 4, and 7 and 8 occupied the next salients towards the front of the fort and had a small parados behind each gun. Guns 5 through

26 Saunders, *Fortress*, 179.

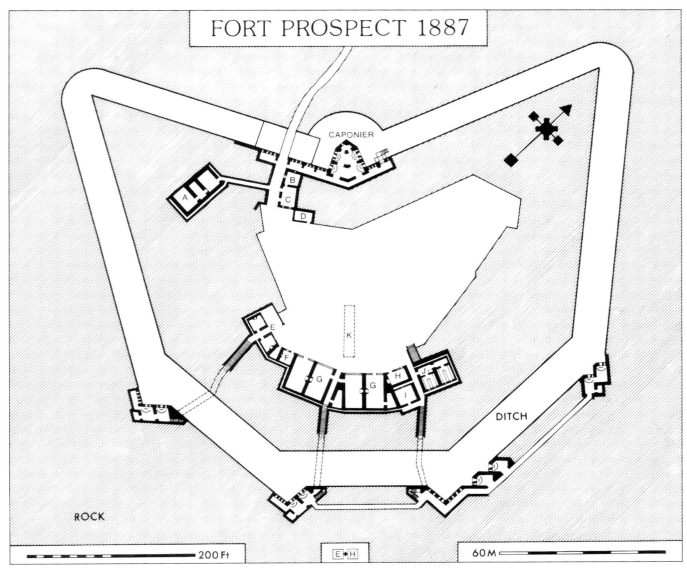

FORT PROSPECT 1887

CAPONIER

DITCH

ROCK

200 Ft E◆H 60 M

FIGURE 7.43: *Fort Prospect's heptagonal ditch was protected by gunports in a caponier at the entrance and four flanking galleries.*

FIGURE 7.42: *The counter-weight for a 64-pounder RML on Moncrieff disap-pearing carriage at Fort Prospect; at the rear is the emplacement for Gun no. 7.*

27 PRO CAB 11/11, T. C. Lyons, Bermuda Defence Scheme, January 1894.

8 were in a line facing the front of the work, but each set of two was separated by a central bulwark of masonry; there was no protection to the rear (Fig. 7.41). While no evidence was found for the Moncrieff carriages, one of the counterweights was still on the site in the 1990s (Fig. 7.42). By 1894, the number of RMLs mounted was only half the complement for which the fort was designed.[27]

At ground level, a number of chambers were excavated in the

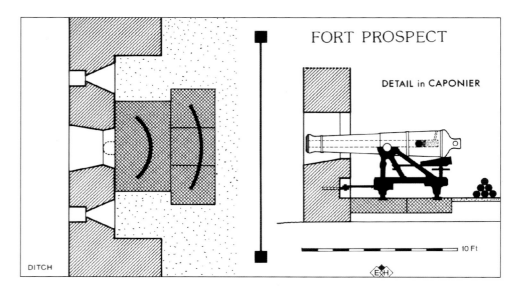

FIGURE 7.44: *The caponier and flanking galleries of the ditch at Fort Prospect contained cannon gunports as well as rifle gunloops.*

bedrock below Guns 4 through 8; from these rooms, three tunnels lead to the flanking galleries, all of which had cannon and rifle ports (Figs. 7.43-44). Instead of flanking galleries, the two rearward runs of the ditch were covered by a caponier, with two cannon on each flank. The caponier also gave protection to the entrance, which may have had a draw-bridge across a deeper, secondary ditch in front of the gate (Fig. 7.45). In all, twelve cannon could be brought to bear on the floor of the ditch from the caponier and flanking galleries.

Shortly after the Second World War, Fort Prospect was turned into a large water catchment, and was white-washed over most of its surface (Fig. 7.46). The main ditch was partly used for water tanks and the ditch at the entrance was filled up.

FIGURE 7.45: *The entrance to Fort Prospect in the 1980s, its secondary ditch is presumed to have been filled up.*

FIGURE 7.46: *Fort Prospect was turned into a water catchment some decades ago and its emplacements were partly filled up and cemented over.*

• • •

FORT LANGTON

FIGURE 7.47: An aerial view of Fort Langton prior to its demolition in 1984, landward gun emplacements on the right, seaward to the left.

The Prospect Hill Position terminated at Fort Langton near the North Shore of Devonshire Parish (Fig. 7.47), where in 1869 it was 'proposed to mount an armament of five guns on Moncrieff carriages, besides three of very heavy calibre to fire on the ship channel to Ireland Island. The ditches will be flanked by 12 small pieces. Plans for this work are now in progress.'[28] Work on the fort commenced in the 1870s and if the date-

FIGURE 7.48: Fort Langton was built in the 1870s and mounted three 10-inch RMLs for coastal defence (nos. 5-7) and four 64-pounder RMLs on Moncrieff disappearing carriages for landward firing.

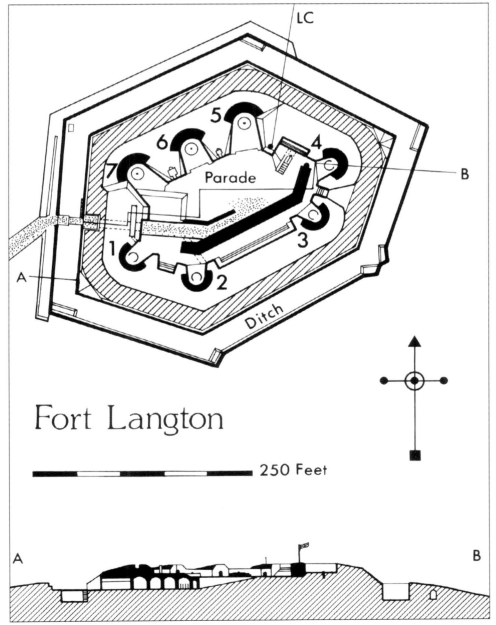

Fort Langton

250 Feet

28 BA, Jervois, Defence Report, 1865

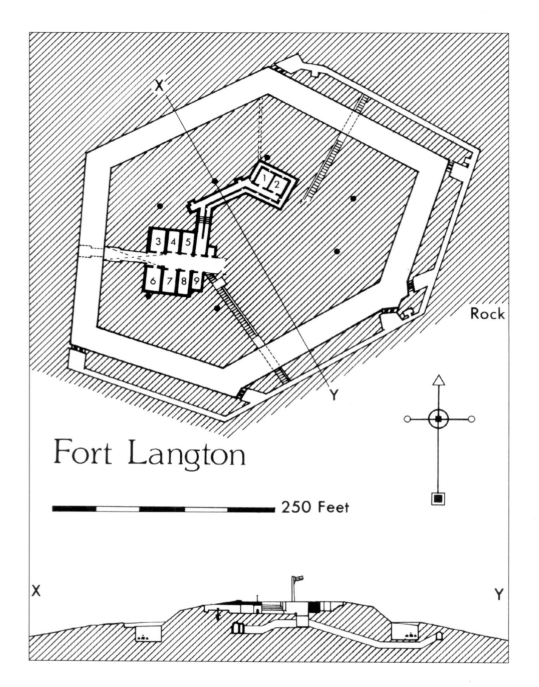

Fort Langton

250 Feet

stone at the gate is any indication, it was completed in 1881.

Unlike Forts Hamilton and Prospect, which were land forts, Fort Langton was both a land and a coastal battery. To the landward and looking down the Devonshire valleys to cross with the coverage from Fort Prospect were four emplacements for 64-pounder RML guns on Moncrieff disappearing carriages. To the seaward, there were three 10-inch RMLs of eighteen tons, firing *en barbette* (Fig. 7.48). When giving a talk to American troops of Battery 'A', 214th F. A. Battalion at the fort in August 1942, Bermudian Col. Thomas Melville Dill was able to pinpoint the first and last firing of these guns.

I assure you that I deem it a great privilege to have the opportunity of having a short talk with you today about the defence of this small group of islands, and about the defence

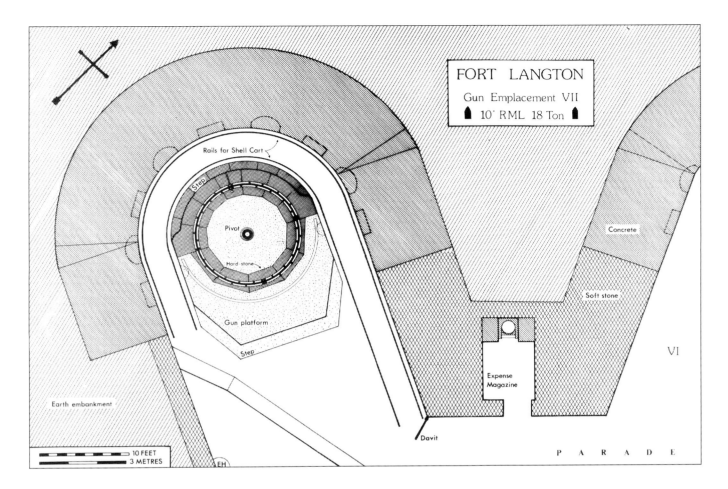

FORT LANGTON

Gun Emplacement VII

10ʺ RML 18 Ton

FIGURE 7.50: Unlike other RML emplacements at Bermuda, the 10-inch guns at Fort Langton were equipped with rails for a shell cart.

work in and about which you are now encamped, as, ancient as it may look, I, sad to relate, am still more ancient. If I can't recollect its beginning I can very well remember its completion. And I have a very distinct memory of the first and last rounds fired from the fort; the first I watched in 1884 when I was a nipper of something over seven, and the last in 1901 when I was G.G.C. of a group of 10-inch RML guns. So short an active life had this expensive fort.[29]

The lower works at Fort Langton consisted of some nine rooms for magazines, stores and related matters (Fig. 7.49). Two flights of stairs and tunnels led to the flanking galleries, which covered each run of this hexagonal fortification. Every position was supplied with a cannon port, as well as loops for riflemen.

In 1984, the local government determined upon the demolition of Fort Langton and archaeologists were allowed to make some detailed records. The 10-inch RML positions were probably the last to be built at Bermuda and they reflect the development of the design (Fig. 7.50). The gun sat on a raised pedestal, to the rear of which was formed a step and standing platform. An expense magazine was located between adjacent emplacements and had a shaft whereby the charges were brought from the magazines below. A corner davit loaded the shells onto a trolley cart, which passed to the front of the gun on iron rails. Recesses were formed in the wall of the emplacement for men to stand aside and as cupboards. The central pivots were 32-pounder smooth bore cannon: these were excavated out of the concrete during demolition and

29 Bermuda Maritime Museum, Edward A. Tomasiewicz Collection.

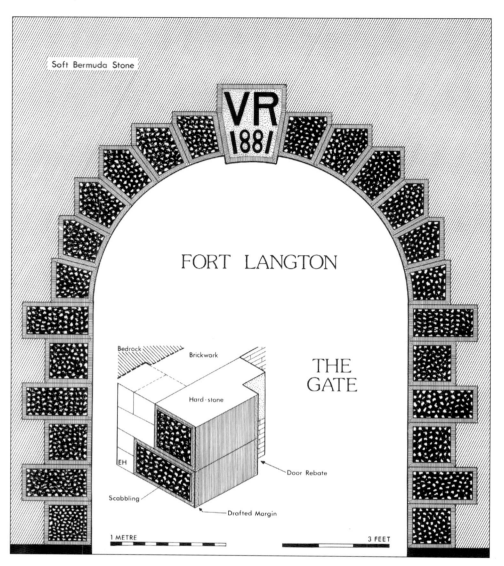

Soft Bermuda Stone

VR
1881

FORT LANGTON

THE
GATE

Bedrock

Brickwork

Hard-stone

EH

Scabbling

Door Rebate

Drafted Margin

1 METRE

3 FEET

FIGURE 7.51: *The entrance to Fort Langton was completed in 1881 and was composed of blocks of finely carved hard Bermuda limestone.*

FIGURE 7.52: *In the demolition of Fort Langton in 1984, the entrance stonework was saved.*

taken to the Dockyard Keep, where they now adorn the ramparts on replica garrison standing carriages.

The rails for the gun carriage and slide were founded on ashlar blocks of Bermuda hard-stone, the material being used in the stones of the gate (Fig. 7.51). When the fort was demolished, the stones of the entrance were saved and are now in the custody of the Maritime Museum at the Dockyard Keep (Fig. 7.52).[30]

Summing up the situation as a result of his visit in 1889 was the Inspector of Artillery, W. H. Goodenough.

> *Prospect.*—This is a line of forts, Langton, Prospect, and Hamilton, the intervals of which are to be filled by field defences in wartime for the defence of Hamilton and to deny Spanish Point to the enemy. The Forts are protected by such enormously deep and wide ditches that they are practically invulnerable. Siege operations, involving considerable time and work, would be required to reduce them.
>
> One must not grumble too much at having an article too good for the purpose for which it is required, but I must say that the expense of construction of these works, from their enormous and costly ditches down to the speaking tubes with their china mouthpieces, was lavish in the extreme, and far beyond what was necessary.[31]

From the central parishes, the Royal Engineers turned their attention to westwards and the defence of the rear of the Dockyard.

• • •

WHALE BAY BATTERY

In considering the seven minor passages through the Bermuda reef platform during his visit in 1865, Col. Jervois came to the view that all, excepting Hog Fish Cut, were too far from shore to defend with fortifications.[32] He recommended that, if necessary, they could be filled up 'by the deposit of stone after the mode in which the Portland Breakwater and the foundations of the Holyhead and Alderney Breakwaters are formed.'[33] The Hog Fish Cut runs along the western coast leading to the Dockyard and was of value to local shipping, hence Jervois' opinion on this channel, although no fort was ever added at Wreck Hill.

> The Hog Fish Cut, which is stated to be available for vessels drawing 13 feet of water, is narrow and might be easily blocked up, but it having been represented that it is desirable to keep open one channel to the westward for trading vessels, and this cut being within 600 yards from the shore, it is proposed to defend it by batteries on the sites of those which formerly existed at 'Whale Bay' and 'Wreck Hill,' adding in time of war such obstacles as might be rendered available.[34]

By 1869, nothing had happened and Jervois made a further recommendation that three 9-inch RMLs be mounted on the site of the old Whale Bay Battery (Fig. 7.53). Wreck Hill was again proposed, with another site further up the channel towards the Dockyard on Daniel's Island. His plan for Whale Bay was put into action and the fort was completed in the mid-1870s.

Whale Bay Battery was a relatively simple work and was not in the polygonal tradition seen at the Prospect Hill Position. To the seaward, it had a rudimentary

30 The demolition of the only land/coastal fortification in Bermuda is to be regretted. Such was the low state of knowledge of the forts in the island in 1984, that no one could cogently argue for its preservation.

31 PRO, Goodenough, Report of Inspection, 1889. A penned marginal note reads 'Hear Hear'!

32 Notwithstanding, there is in the Bermuda Archives a plan for the construction of a battery on North Rock, the only land permanently above water on the edge of the reefs.

33 BA, Jervois, Defence Report, 1865.

34 Ibid.

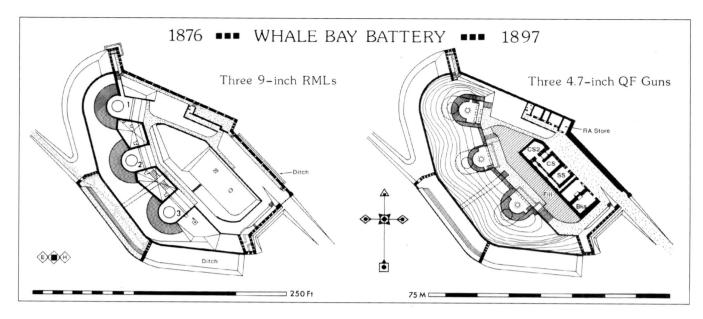

1876 ■■■ WHALE BAY BATTERY ■■■ 1897

Three 9-inch RMLs

Three 4.7-inch QF Guns

250 Ft

75 M

FIGURE 7.53: In the 1870s, Whale Bay Battery was constructed for three 9-inch Rifled Muzzle Loaders, later changed to 4.7-inch Quick Firing guns.

FIGURE 7.54: Whale Bay Battery from the air in the 1980s showing the emplacements for the QF guns of 1905.

but shallow ditch and to the rear, none at all. The ditch was divided into three parts by two looped cross-walls, left and right of a central passage or tunnel running under the guns from the interior of the fort. The central area of the ditch so defined had a banquette on the counterscarp. Caponiers formed the ends of the ditch and could also fire back into the countryside. An irregular curtain wall at the rear of the fort, through which the entry passed, connected the two caponiers and it had a number of loopholes for riflemen (Fig. 7.54).

The work, like Alexandra Battery, is a forerunner of the demise of the fort as a defendable unit. Its three guns, 9-inch RMLs of twelve tons, were mounted *en barbette* in concrete emplacements. Several magazines and stores were located to the rear of the guns; there were apparently no lifts and all ammunition was moved by hand up to the guns. A date-stone over the magazines gives the year 1876. There was no evidence of a drawbridge and in the 1980s, the surviving hinges suggested that the fort had only a large wooden door of two panels.

The guns faced the Hog Fish Cut channel and would have easily been bypassed by an enemy force marching inland towards Somerset Island and the Land Front of the Dockyard.

• • •

FIGURE 7.55: *Scaur Hill Fort had a ditch which ran from shore to shore on the southern neck of Somerset Island.*

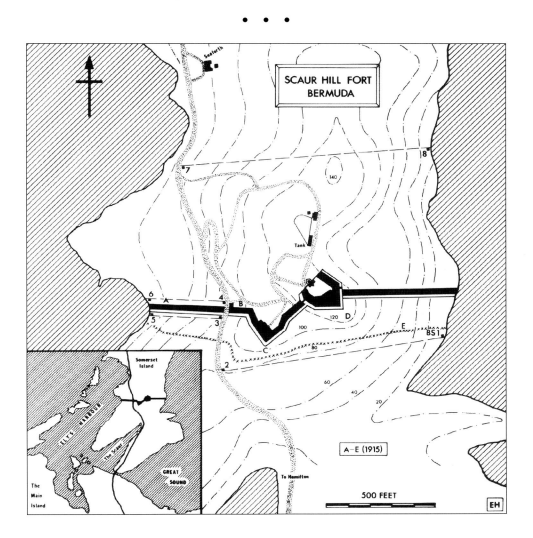

THE SOMERSET POSITION

In his 1865 report, which changed the face of Bermuda's fortifications, Col. Jervois, when considering the advance of an enemy force to Spanish Point in the east, also looked at the approach to the Dockyard from the south.

> It would also be necessary to cut off the approach of an enemy towards the dockyard from the S.W. The most convenient point for opposing him in this direction is near the southeast end of Somerset Island, where there is a good position only a few yards in extent [Somerset Bridge], which it is recommended should be secured by a permanent redoubt on the high ground between Elies Harbour and the Great Sound.[35]

By 1869, the plans were being prepared for the 'Somerset Position,' 'being

35 Ibid.

FIGURE 7.56: *Scaur Hill Fort from the air in the 1970s, looking west (Bermuda News Bureau).*

only 500 yards in extent, may be most advantageously defended by a continuous ditch and parapet from shore to shore, with a small keep in the centre, to prevent the position being turned.'[36] Driving across Somerset Bridge in the 1990s and looking north, one could see on the summit of the nearby hill the trim outline of Scaur Hill Fort, the result of these plans (Fig. 7.55).

The site had two main components, the fort itself and the extensive ditch. The latter was seen in 1878 by the editor of *The Bermuda Almanack*: 'A ditch or cutting of great length has been commenced and apparently now about half completed, extending from the Great Sound on the East to the waters of Ely's Harbour on the West—crossing the main road and almost the very top of Morgan's Hill—thus dividing Somerset in twain.'[37] The following year, he noted that 'the road is carried over a portion of the trench,' indicating the presence of a bridge across the ditch.[38]

The ditch was formed by quarrying into the hillside, in several places to a depth of twenty feet. From the east, it ran at a right angle from the shoreline

FIGURE 7.57: *The flanking galleries at Scaur Hill Fort contained cannon gunports as well as gunloops for rifles, which were protected by deeper secondary ditches.*

36 BA, Jervois, Defence Report, 1869.

37 *The Bermuda Almanack* (1878), 157.

38 *The Bermuda Almanack* (1879), 167.

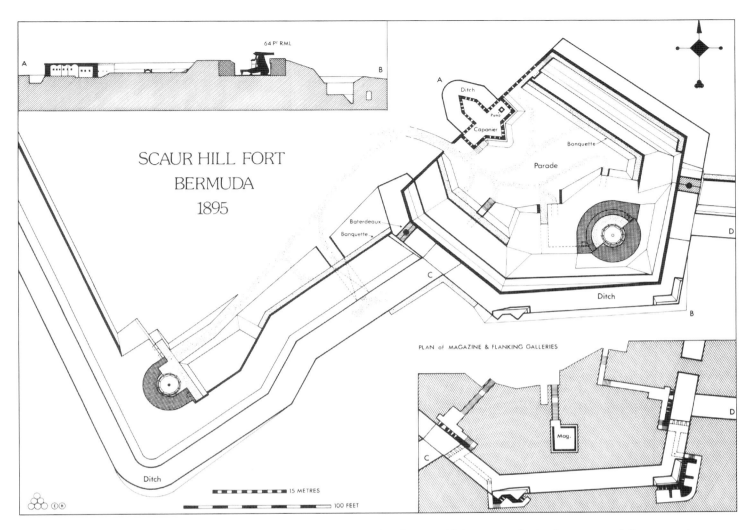

64 Pr RML

SCAUR HILL FORT
BERMUDA
1895

A

Ditch

Caponier

Pump

Banquette

Parade

Baterdeaux

Banquette

C

Ditch

B

D

PLAN of MAGAZINE & FLANKING GALLERIES

Mag.

C

D

Ditch

15 METRES

100 FEET

FIGURE 7.58: *The armaments at Scaur Hill Fort were two 64-pounder RMLs on Moncrieff disappearing carriages, one in the fort and one in a detached position.*

of the Great Sound up to the fort itself (Fig. 7.56). It then turned for several angles around the fort and its western gun emplacement, thereafter continuing west in a straight line down to a small beach on Ely's Harbour. On the latter run, it cut the only road to the Dockyard in two, but the carriageway passed over a wooden bridge at that point. The road in the 1990s was carried over solid ground, the ditch being filled up at some time in the twentieth century. A plan labelled the 'Scaur Hill Position,' dated 1875, is in the Bermuda Archives and a bridge at the road appears on it.

Two defensive features protected the ditch, the first being a rampart on its northern side, which was supplied throughout its length with a firing step for the infantry men. At the fort, two flanking galleries for rifles and cannon fired down several runs of the ditch, while secondary galleries for rifles only added to the protection (Fig. 7.57). Two sections of the ditch by the fort were closed by batardeaux, which were blocking walls but not caponiers as they did not contain any gun loops for riflemen.

Scaur Hill Fort itself is a hybrid work, which has features of the old polygonal system of fortification combined with the coming era wherein 'forts' became but guns in the landscape and any sense of a defensible building was ultimately lost. John Triggs has pointed out that the fort was designed on the 'polygonal trace,' or 'the Prussian System developed during the early nineteenth century by German engineers,'[39] This method was advertised for English engineers in *An Essay on the Modern System of Fortification*, using German examples built after 1815.[40] Fort Cunningham at Bermuda was designed in 1811 and may thus claim to be one of the earliest British forts in the polygonal trace method.[41]

FIGURE 7.59: *The floor of the gun pit in Scaur Hill Fort for a 64-pounder RML on a Moncrieff disappearing carriage was discovered in the 1980s.*

The designers of Scaur Hill Fort had Fort Cunningham and the later examples, such as Fort Prospect, to draw on in planning the single work of the Somerset Position. Nonetheless, Scaur Hill Fort, though contemporary with the works of the Prospect Position is not one with them (Fig. 7.58). It represents, in brick and stone, the struggle between the soon to be outdated polygonal system and the new method of the fort as nothing more than a glorified gun emplacement. Most of the polygonal trace features at Scaur Hill are atrophied, or stunted, versions of the system, demonstrating that it was on the wane. The features suffer from an 'inferiority of size'; the batardeaux are less than a third the mass of those at the Dockyard. The caponier at Scaur Hill is a shrunken version of that at Fort Prospect and the adjacent ditch and entrance are similarly but shadows of a former proud method. The fort at Scaur Hill points the way forward towards the new system exemplified at St. David's Battery, Bermuda, built twenty-five years later. As such a transitional work, it is of considerable interest in the history of British artillery fortifications.

The guns, which formed the excuse for building the almost useless fort, also in part suggest the changes of the next generation. The western emplacement is nothing more than a gun behind a parapet and ditch; this became at St. David's Battery and elsewhere, guns behind a continuous glacis formed by the surrounding countryside. Both pieces were converted 64-pounder Rifled Muzzle Loaders on Moncrieff disappearing carriages. These were set in an open-backed emplacement for the western gun and in an enclosed pit for the gun at the fort (Fig. 7.59). Two cheeks of the carriages were found in the nearby woods in the 1980s by the then Curator of Scaur Hill Fort, Lance Furbert, whose research and enthusiasm did much to revive the understanding and appreciation of this interesting work.[42]

Although American guns were positioned to the north-west of the site in the Second World War, no alterations were made to Scaur Hill Fort after the RML period. In 1957 through the efforts of the Trade Development Board and the Bermuda Historical Monuments Trust, it became one of the first fortifications in the island to be opened to the public. Such restoration for the Dockyard, the back door of which it protected, did not begin for almost three more decades.

• • •

[39] John R. Triggs, 'Excavations at Scaur Hill Fort, Bermuda,' *BJAMH* 1 (1989), 131–142.

[40] Lieut.-Colonel I. H. Humfrey, *An Essay on the Modern System of Fortification adopted for the Defence of the Rhine Frontier* (1838).

[41] This seems not to have been adopted generally until Col. Jervois' time in the late 1860s. See Ian V. Hogg, *Coast Defences of England and Wales, 1856–1956* (1974), 47.

[42] Lance Furbert and Edward Harris, 'Scaur Hill Fort,' *The Bermudian* 54 (1984).

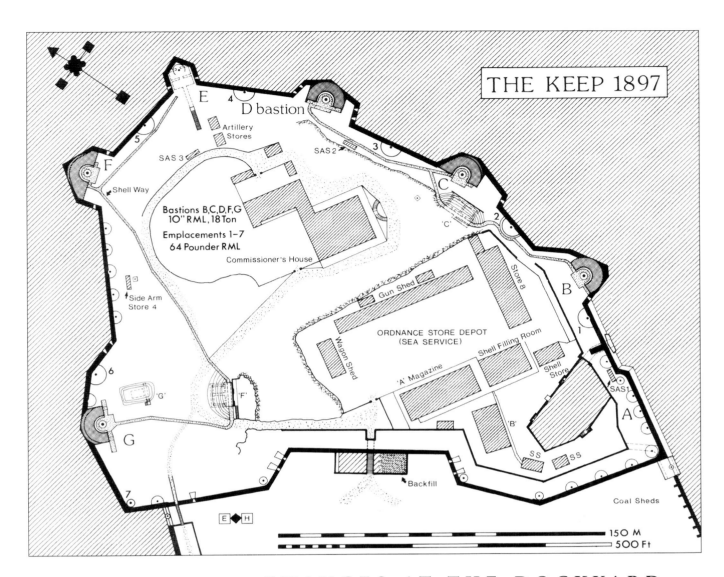

THE KEEP 1897

FIGURE 7.60: *The Keep of the Bermuda Dockyard mounted five 18-ton, 10-inch and seven 64-pounder Rifled Muzzle Loaders during the late nineteenth century.*

43 BA, Jervois, Defence Report, 1865.

CHANGES AT THE DOCKYARD

As a part of his 1865 report, which marked the change from smooth bore to rifled artillery for the Bermuda fortifications, Colonel Jervois reviewed the defences of the Dockyard.

> These consist of bastioned lines of masonry enclosing the Naval Establishment, except on the eastern side, where there is a basin in which ships lie alongside the dockyard. On the sea faces the escarps are necessarily exposed, but on the land side to the southward the escarps are covered by a counterscarp and glacis. The northern portion of the works is cut off by a bastioned line with the intention of forming a keep to these fortifications. The works are substantially constructed and in good state of repair, but, except to prevent the actual capture of the Naval Establishment, they are now of no great use; for if an enemy succeeded in passing iron-plated vessels of war through the reefs, or in landing a force in Bermuda, guns mounted on Ireland Island would not, considering their close proximity to the Dockyard, suffice to protect it from destruction.[43]

His recommendations at that time did not involve the rearming of the Dockyard defences, but rather to construct the outposts of the Prospect Hill and Somerset Positions. By 1869, however, it was proposed to mount nine 10-inch guns on Moncrieff disappearing carriages at Ireland Island. Because of the expense

| H | G | F |

and delay in obtaining the Moncrieff carriages, Jervois suggested that the guns could be mounted *en barbette* immediately and this is the situation that prevailed.

Thus in the third quarter of the nineteenth century, the Keep was rearmed with Rifled Muzzle Loaders. With the exceptions of 'A' and 'E', all the bastions were rebuilt to house five 10-inch RMLs of eighteen tons (Fig. 7.60). In the curtains between some of the bastions were placed an additional seven 64-pounder RMLs. Two new magazines were constructed at the Keep near Bastions 'C' and 'G', with concreted shell-ways to the new RML emplacements. Another 10-inch RML was mounted in support of these at Bastion 'H' (Fig. 7.61), with eight 64-pounder RMLs at Bastion 'I' and the Land Front (see Fig. 6.47).[44]

FIGURE 7.61: *Looking north from Bastion 'I', Bastions 'H' on the North-west Rampart and 'G' and 'F' at the Keep of the Bermuda Dockyard mounted 10-inch RMLs in the 1880s (BMM: Ruberry Collection).*

• • •

MOBILE BATTERIES

While more evidence needs to be gathered, it seems that several works on the south shore of Bermuda underwent minor modifications as sites for mobile batteries in the RML period. These would have been 40-pounder Armstrong Rifled Breech Loaders on wooden siege carriages, such as the gun found in the 1980s at Bailey's Bay Battery (see Chap. 10).

Two sites are known to have been modified in the 1870s, namely, East and West Elbow Bay Forts (Fig. 7.62). At both places, expense magazines were built in concrete and covered to seaward by a sand bank.[45] The banks may have had embrasures for the guns, or the weapons may have been placed at one end or the other.

FIGURE 7.62: *An expense magazine for a mobile RML battery at the rear of West Elbow Bay Fort is examined by archaeologist Isabel Garcia Trócoli.*

[44] PRO CAB 11/11, Bermuda Defence Report, 1896.

[45] Fred G. Aldsworth, 'Excavations at West Elbow Bay Fort, Paget, Bermuda,' *BJAMH* 2 (1990).

• • •

C O N C L U S I O N S

In 1882, as the re-fortification and rearmament of the Bermuda works for the Rifled Muzzle Loader era was drawing to a close, a new type of steel was invented for use in the production of artillery. At a stroke, it rendered the wrought-iron RMLs and their attendant works of defence obsolete. The new steel made it possible to return to the use of breech loading guns, since it had the requisite strength to withstand the impact of firing. The great RMLs, reaching a weight of 100 tons in the case of guns for Malta and Gibraltar, were a reaction to the inability of wrought iron breech loaders to withstand the forces of firing guns in larger calibres. While the first Mark of the new 'rifle' came out of the foundry in 1882, it was not until the turn of the century that the perfected Mark VII began to be emplaced at Bermuda. In the interval, from around 1880, the following guns (excluding smooth-bore cannon for ditch defences) held the forts at this remote Atlantic outpost of the Victorian empire.

Fort/Gun	64 pdr	9" RML	10" RML	11" RML	12.5" RML	Totals
George	2	–	–	2	–	4
Victoria	8	–	–	3	–	11
Albert	–	–	4	–	–	4
Catherine	3	–	5	–	–	8
Alexandra	–	5	–	–	–	5
Cunningham	–	2	5	–	2	9
Hamilton	7	–	–	–	–	7
Prospect	6	–	–	–	–	6
Langton	4	–	3	–	–	7
Whale Bay	–	3	–	–	–	3
Scaur Hill	2	–	–	–	–	2
Dockyard	15	–	6	–	–	21
Totals	47	10	23	5	2	87

By the turn of the century, when the RMLs began to be replaced by the steel Breech Loaders, the number of guns at Bermuda had been halved. At the end of the smooth bore era in the late 1850s, the total stood at two hundred and sixteen pieces. The march of technology, which ushered in the rifled gun of the 1860s and saw the introduction of the projectile, increased not only the range of the weapons, but their size, weight and the calibre. By 1895, eighty-seven pieces did the work of a previous two hundred and sixteen. This progression caused by technological advances continued into the new steel Breech Loader period of the first decade of the twentieth century and as the guns increased in power, their numbers correspondingly continued to decline.

■ ■ ■

Men of the Bermuda Militia Artillery drill on gun 'B/2', a 6-inch Breech Loading rifle installed at St. David's Battery in the first decade of the twentieth century (Bermuda Library).

8

Imperial Fortress:
The Breech Loader Period

1 8 9 9 – 1 9 3 8

The Bermudas command no trade route, but they afford for His Majesty's Navy in time of war a secure harbour, refitting station, and convenient base for operations in the neighbouring seas, being about equidistant from Canada and the British West Indian possessions, with both of which direct cable communications exists. The adequate protection of this naval base, is therefore, of great importance, and the place has, for these reasons, been constituted one of the four Imperial fortresses.

—Defence Report 1904

AS QUEEN VICTORIA BEGAN THE LAST YEARS OF HER SIXTY-FOUR-YEAR REIGN, further changes were in train at the forts in outposts of her Empire: 'Bermuda as an Imperial fortress and naval base is being fortified on a scale which is considered sufficient to deter a considerable squadron, including one or two battleships, from engaging the coast defences.'[1] The Americans were still thought to be a force to be reckoned with and that 'all attacks on Bermuda would have as their definite objectives the destruction or capture of the Dockyard at Ireland Island, with coal-yard, stores, floating dock and workshops, or the severing of cable communications.'[2] Shipping and artillery technology had advanced much in the short period since Bermuda had been rearmed with Rifled Muzzle Loaders in the last quarter of the nineteenth century.

The Royal Engineers and Royal Artillery returned again to their task of re-fortifying Bermuda, starting as the century began and ending around 1910 with the construction of an entirely new work at St. David's Head. Four sites at the east end and two at the west were eventually drawn into this last major British cycle of the fortification of the Bermudas. In the east, Forts Cunningham and Victoria, Alexandra and St. David's Batteries were affected and at the other end of Bermuda, Whale Bay Battery and the defences of the Dockyard were modified (Fig. 8.1).

[1] PRO CAB 11/11, Bermuda Defence Report, 1904.

[2] Ibid.

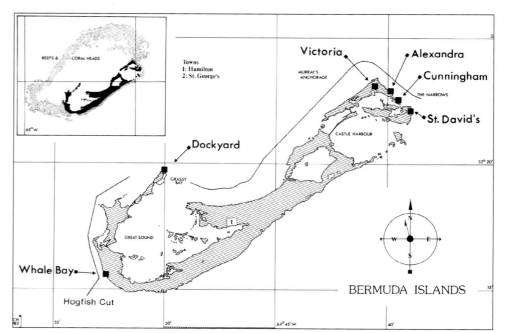

FIGURE 8.1: *St. David's Battery was the only new work to be erected at Bermuda when it was rearmed in the first decade of the twentieth century.*

FIGURE 8.2: *Two 9.2-inch Breech Loaders had been mounted on the northern perimeter of Fort Victoria by 1904.*

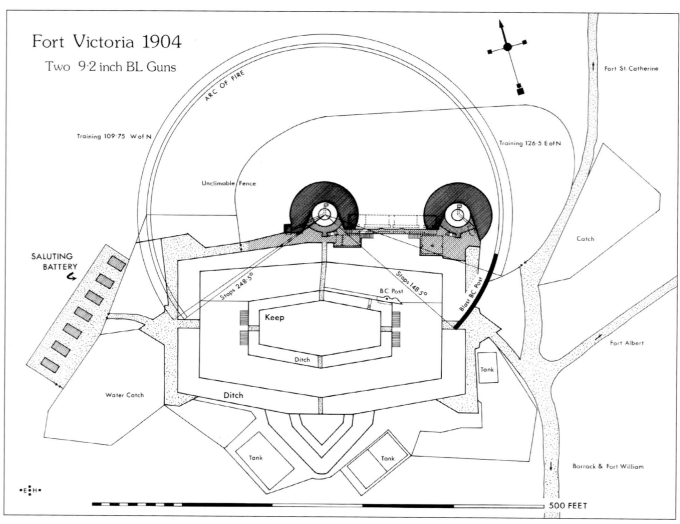

FIGURE 8.3: *An aerial view of Fort Victoria about 1944, by which time the eastern 9.2-inch BL gun had been removed: two U.S.A. 6-inch guns are on the far left (author's collection).*

FORT VICTORIA

On the northern side of Fort Victoria, the Ravelin Tower was buried under a 9.2-inch Breech Loader, one of a pair, the second being about twenty-five metres to the east of the Ravelin (Fig. 8.2). The range of the new guns made unnecessary any modifications to Fort George to the west and Forts St. Catherine and Albert to the east. Their fire would have crossed with that of Alexandra Battery to the south-east. It was at this period that the parapet of the Keep of Fort Victoria was reduced to the level of the terreplein (Fig. 8.3). A saluting battery may have been added at this time and was composed of 40-pounder Armstrong RBLs, three of which were still in place on decaying wooden field carriages in the early 1930s, when Roger Willock visited the site. The guns remained in use for several years and in 1907: 'At Fort Victoria fire was opened at a range of about 8,000 yards, position-finding case II, being employed. The four rounds were fired in 2 minutes 1 second, but no hits were obtained…The dust caused by the firing at Fort Victoria was excessive, and some means should be taken locally to correct this. It gives away the position completely, and obstructs the view of the target.'[3]

By 1910, one of the guns had been removed and may have been taken to St. David's Battery where a similar piece appeared that year in 'Mounted reserve.'[4] By 1935, the remaining gun, though emplaced, was not considered as part of the Bermuda armaments. The site was not reactivated in World War Two, but a position between it and Fort Albert was used for the American coastal batteries then in play.

• • •

ALEXANDRA BATTERY

To the south-east of Fort Victoria, the works of the 1870s at Alexandra Battery were about to be swept away, or buried under the modifications for two BL guns. An observation station and test room was not changed and may have remained in use (Fig. 8.4). At ground level (Fig. 8.5), new magazines for shell and cartridge storage were constructed with hoists for both to the guns above. The armament was two 6-inch BL rifles (Fig. 8.6) set in concrete emplace-

3 Royal Artillery Historic Trust, Dalton Papers, Report by Major-General J. C. Dalton, Inspector, Royal Garrison Artillery, on his Inspection of the Royal Garrison Artillery at Bermuda, March, 1907. I am indebted to Michael J. K. Turner for this reference.

4 PRO CAB 11/11, Bermuda Defence Report, 1910.

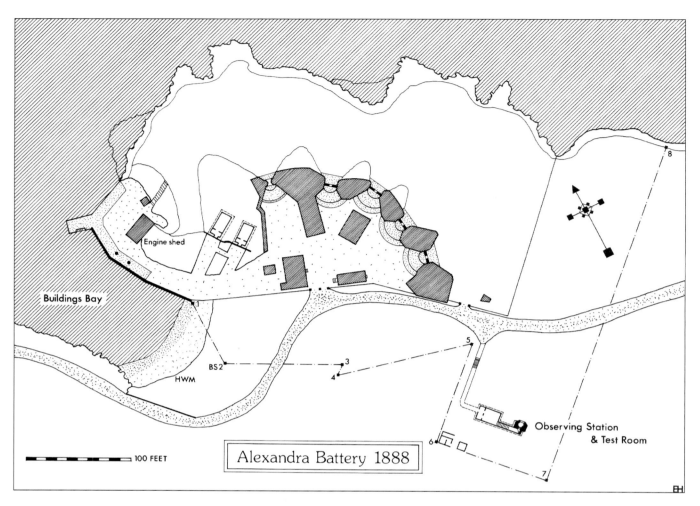

Engine shed

Buildings Bay

BS 2

HWM

3

4

5

6

7

8

Observing Station
& Test Room

100 FEET

Alexandra Battery 1888

FIGURE 8.4: Before its conversion to BL guns, Alexandra Battery had five RML positions and an Observing Station and Test Room, the latter probably reused in the BL era.

FIGURE 8.6: A man, possibly Lieut. Gerald Hughes, inspects the northern 6-inch Breech Loading gun at Alexandra Battery in 1902 (Bermuda Archives: Hughes Album).

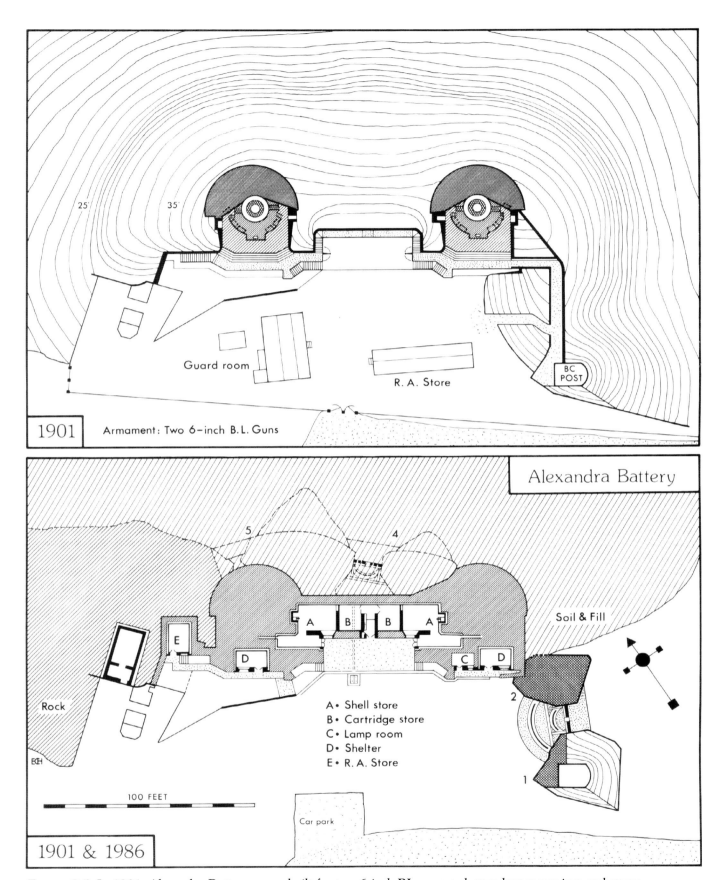

1901

Armament: Two 6-inch B.L. Guns

Guard room

R. A. Store

BC POST

25'   35'

Alexandra Battery

5   4

Soil & Fill

A   B   B   A

E

D   C   D

Rock

A• Shell store
B• Cartridge store
C• Lamp room
D• Shelter
E• R. A. Store

100 FEET

2

1

Car park

1901 & 1986

FIGURE 8.5: In 1901, Alexandra Battery was rebuilt for two 6-inch BL guns and attendant magazines and stores.

FIGURE 8.7: *At its conversion to a BL site around 1902, a glacis was added to the seaward of Alexandra Battery.*

ments in a new glacis extending down to the shoreline (Fig. 8.7). Constructed by 1899,[5] the guns appear to have been out of use before the First World War, as they do not appear in the Defence Report for 1913. The site was not used in the Second World War.

• • •

FORT CUNNINGHAM

At the January 1899 conference which considered the replacement of RML guns with BL and QF weapons, it was proposed to leave the two 12.5-inch RMLs at Fort Cunningham and to add two 6-inch BL rifles.[6] By that date, one of the 9-inch RMLs had already been removed and the second must have been taken away shortly thereafter.[7] It was subsequently decided to remove all of the RMLs and they were pushed into the northern ditch from the roof of the fort. The 9-inch guns were not found in the 1991 excavations of the site, but the remaining armament of five 10-inch and two 12.5-inch RMLs were discovered under part of the infilling of the ditch for the new glacis.

The ditch had already been partly filled up in the late 1880s, but that work was entirely covered by the soils of the glacis for the two 6-inch BL guns (Fig. 8.8), which had been placed on the roof of the fort. The glacis was brought right up to the concrete apron of the guns, the slope for the northern gun thus covering the old RMLs in the ditch adjacent to the new emplacement. The glacis was contoured to allow five of the RML gunports to be used as windows, for the old casemates were turned into barracks.

The southern gun had an Electric Light Directing Station built into the glacis in front of the emplacement. An Engine House for the generator for the two searchlight emplacements on the eastern shore of Paget Island was also added to the fort at this time.

The new guns were fired during the 1907 inspection, but 'No hits were

[5] PRO WO 32/6358, Defence Conference, January 20, 1899.

[6] Ibid.

[7] One of these guns may be that said to have come from Bermuda and mounted at Simons Town, South Africa, for the protection of that naval base.

FIGURE 8.8: Two 6-inch BL guns were placed on the roof of Fort Cunningham around 1906 and an extensive new glacis covered most of the front of the earlier structure.

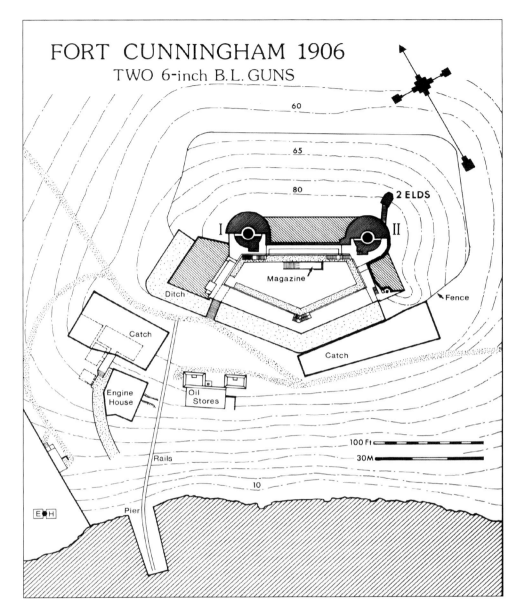

FIGURE 8.9: The ditch at the rear of Fort Cunningham was not filled up in 1906 when the front of the work was largely buried under a new glacis.

8 RAHT, Dalton, 1907.
9 PRO WO 33/580, Bermuda Defence Report, 1913.
10 PRO CAB 11/188.

obtained, every round falling to the right of the target …Mistakes were made in passing ranges on the "range indicators." As long as we have to use these antiquated appliances greater pains must be taken to train the men to use them without mistakes.'[8] The weapons do not appear as operational in the 1913 defence report[9] and were not included in a 1935 return (Fig. 8.9).[10]

• • •

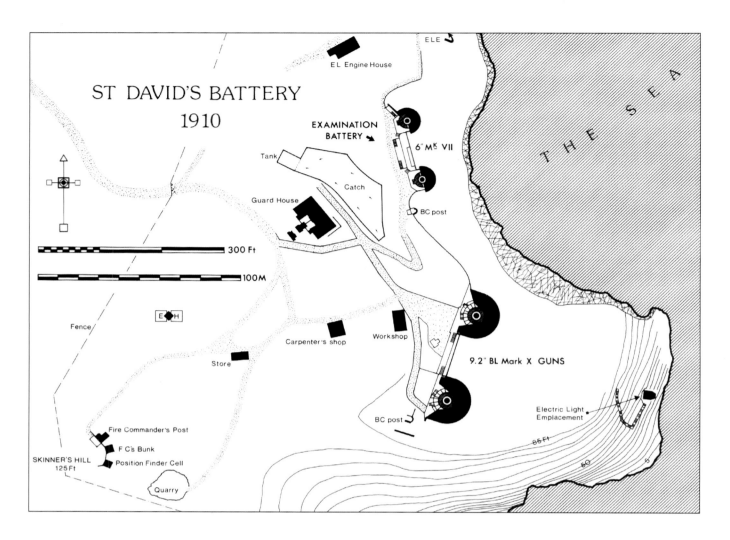

ST. DAVID'S BATTERY

The only entirely new work to be erected in the rearmament of Bermuda in the first decade of the twentieth century was the battery of four guns on St. David's Island (Fig. 8.10). The weapons were to be two 6-inch and two 9.2 inch BL guns and by 1907: 'The works at St. David's are now ready for their armament, and, I submit, should be armed before they deteriorate. The pedestals are ready in their places, and the works can be handed over at once.'[11]

Visiting General Dalton also recommended that the guns be acquired by taking one 6-inch from the Keep at Ireland Island, and another of the same calibre from Alexandra Battery ('now only used for drill'). This seems to have been done, for all of the gun, including its pedestal, at Bastion 'F' at the Keep was missing when the Bermuda Maritime Museum was established there in 1974. He also recommended that the 9.2-inch gun for St. David's in storage at the Ordnance Yard at Ireland Island be mounted forthwith (Fig. 8.11). Ammunition for the gun should be appropriated from the eastern gun at Fort Victoria. It is possible that that gun itself later went to St. David's Battery,[12] for by 1913, there was only one 9.2-inch gun at Fort Victoria, presumably in the western emplacement where it was still to be seen in the 1990s.

FIGURE 8.10: *St. David's Battery was the only new 'fort' added to the defence works at Bermuda in the first decade of the twentieth century.*

11 RAHT, Dalton, 1907.

12 Ibid.

FIGURE 8.12: *Gun drill by the Bermuda Militia Artillery on the two 6-inch BL guns at St. David's Battery, probably in the 1930s (Bermuda Library).*

FIGURE 8.11: St. David's Battery had two 9.2-inch BL guns to the south (left) and two 6-inch rifles of the Examination Battery to the north (right).

By 1935, the two 9.2-inch guns at St. David's Battery were no longer mentioned in defence reports. The two 6-inch BLs were the only operational guns in Bermuda at that time and during the Second World War became the weapons of the 'Examination Battery' and the only British defence at the entrance to the Narrows Channel (Fig. 8.12).

• • •

WHALE BAY BATTERY & THE DOCKYARD

The western defences were also modified, but only at Whale Bay Battery and the Dockyard (Fig. 8.13). The three 9-inch RML emplacements at Whale Bay were built over to take three 4.7-inch Quick Firing pieces (Fig. 8.14). The original purpose of the battery—to protect the entrance to Hog Fish Cut channel—was unchanged, as it was through that rear entrance to the Dockyard that torpedo boats could have had access. By 1913 and the beginning of the First World War, Whale Bay Battery ceased to be an operational unit and was not used in the 1939–45 conflict.

At the Dockyard, most of the modifications took place at the Keep, which by 1906 mounted seven new guns (Fig. 8.15), only two 12-pounder QF guns being erected on the Land Front. At Bastions 'A' and 'B', facing south-east and 'G', facing west, three 4.7-inch QF guns were emplaced for close work against

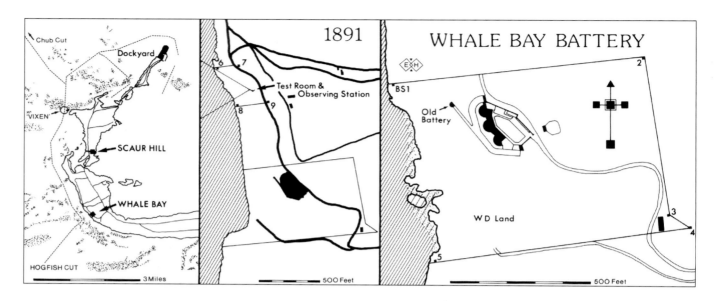

torpedo boats and light craft. Between these, Bastions 'C' through 'F' mounted 6-inch BL rifles, facing the channel to Grassy Bay from St. Catherine's Point and northward towards the reefs and the open sea. In 1913, one of the 6-inch guns was 'mounted in reserve without personnel,'[13] and three were operational: all were out of use by 1935.

FIGURE 8.13: *Whale Bay Battery was built in the 1870s to defend the entrance to Hog Fish Cut, the rear channel to the Dockyard and continued that function in the BL period.*

FIGURE 8.14: *Whale Bay Battery from the air in the 1980s shows the three emplacements of about 1905 for 4.7-inch Quick Firing guns.*

• • •

CONCLUSIONS

The rearmament of the Bermuda forts in the first decade of the twentieth century affected five earlier works and saw the construction of but a single new one. Around 1910, with all the works emplaced, only twenty-two guns now protected this Imperial Fortress, of the calibres listed below:

Fort/Gun	12 pdr QF	4.7" QF	6" BL	9.2" BL	Totals
Victoria	–	–	–	2	2
Alexandra	–	–	2	–	2
Cunningham	–	–	2	–	2
St. David's	–	–	2	2	4
Whale Bay	–	3	–	–	3
Dockyard	2	3	4	–	9
Totals	2	6	10	4	22

[13] PRO WO 33/580.

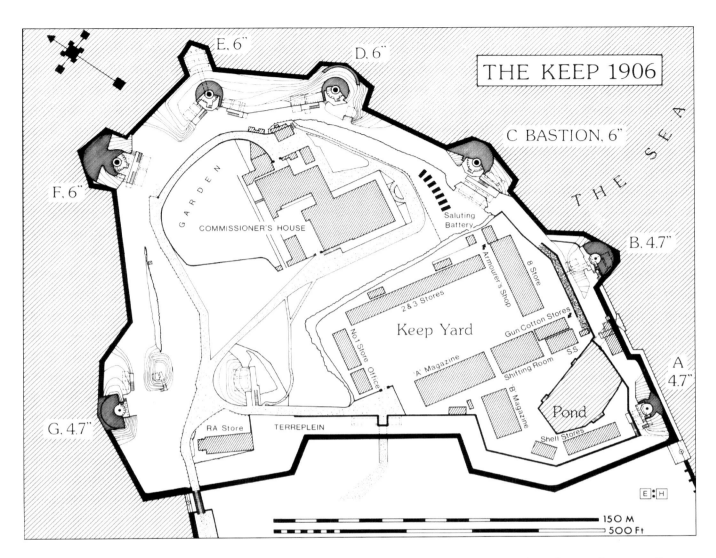

FIGURE 8.15: The Keep at the Dockyard was converted around 1903 for three 4.7-inch Quick Firing and four 6-inch Breech Loading guns.

By 1913, the total of twenty-two had been reduced to eight guns: four at St. David's Battery, one at Fort Victoria and three at the Dockyard. At the beginning of the war on September 3, 1939, between England and Germany, only the two 6-inch guns at St. David's Battery were in operation.

The final British work was constructed after the beginning of the Second World War at Warwick Camp, a work for two 6-inch BL guns, manufactured forty years before, but re-tubed for the new hostilities. Like the Prospect Hill Position before it, the purpose of the south shore emplacement was to keep the enemy, this time in ships, at a safe distance from the Dockyard to prevent its bombardment. In the end, as seen in the following chapter, it was the weaponry of the American foe of old which comprised the final period of the coastal defence of Bermuda and her Imperial Dockyard.

■ ■ ■

Men of the United States Army at some military works (possibly at Cooper's Island) at Bermuda during the Second World War.

9

Coastal Defence in the
Second World War & Later

1939 – 1957

*I trust that the evacuation which we recommended will be approved,
and that the strategic position of Bermuda will be fully recognised early
in this war. It is believed that Bermuda is of as great importance in the
Atlantic as Pearl Harbour is in the Pacific.*

—Captain Jules James, U.S.N., June 30, 1943

FROM THEIR EARLIEST SETTLEMENT, THE BERMUDAS WERE CONSIDERED TO be of strategic value in the advancement of colonisation in the Americas and were heavily defended in the seventeenth and eighteenth centuries. The independence of some of the continental American colonies and the cessation of war in 1783 underscored the strategic value of the Bermudas in a changing sea world. As the peace was concluded on the American continent, Royal Engineers were assessing the defences of Bermuda, in anticipation of future hostilities with the new American nation. This fear of an American threat to British dominion of the Western Atlantic gave rise in 1809 to a large dockyard and to successive rearmaments and works in the defence of Bermuda in the 1790s, 1820s and the 1870s, with a final round of armament begun in the last days of Queen Victoria's reign, as seen in the previous chapter.

By early 1939, the once numerous works had been inexorably reduced in size and number to two 6-inch guns at St. David's Battery. Attitudes changed more slowly, so that the 'Bermuda Defence Report 1935' could finally declare that 'attack by the United States of America need not be considered'![1] Captain Jules James, U. S. Navy, however, still met with considerable resistance from some of the British military at Bermuda, when he arrived to take up command of the new American naval base. Rising to the occasion, as noted in his Legion of Merit citation, 'he was equally successful in the establishment of a complete under-standing between the allied local armed forces and in his unique ability in gaining and maintaining the good will of the Colonial authorities' in Bermuda.[2]

[1] PRO CAB 11/188.

[2] Bermuda Maritime Museum, Tomasiewicz Collection.

253

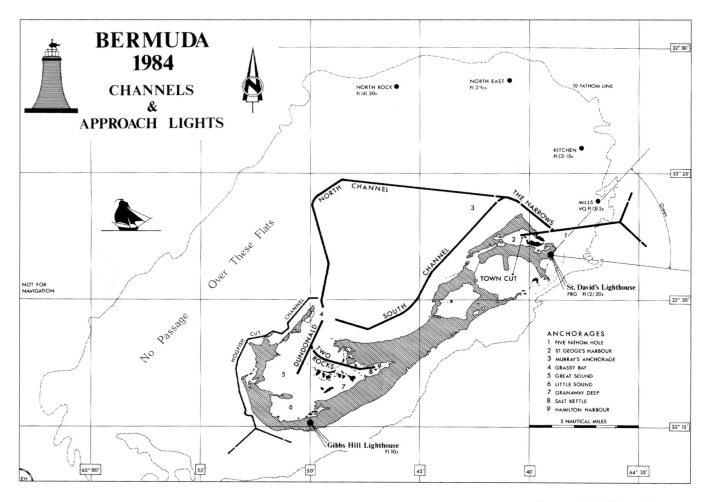

Before the die was cast on September 3, 1939, the value of Bermuda to a British and American war effort had been recognised, as was the inability of the Crown, over-extended in the defence of its empire, to assure the protection of Bermuda, and the mantle passed to the American Forces (Fig. 9.1). As such, the American works at Bermuda represent the last major phase in the history of its coastal defences, from 1612 to 1957. It is the purpose of this chapter to explain the nature of the American defence of British Bermuda during the Second World War, in line with the emphasis of this volume on the fortifications and armaments. It may be of interest to note the events surrounding the establishment of the American bases at Bermuda and their effect on the island, and to delineate the British role in the coastal defence plans of the war, including the building of their last 'fort' at Warwick Camp.

FIGURE 9.1: *The major Bermuda boat and ship channels: the United States Forces created the North Channel during the Second World War.*

ESTABLISHMENT OF AN AMERICAN BASE AT BERMUDA

The value of Bermuda in American military policy lay in the fact that it was 'the only base far enough off the central part of the Atlantic coastline of the United States to extend long-range patrolling by seaplanes into the Atlantic Ocean and to tie in coastal patrolling, both aerial and surface, with similar operations from Halifax and the West Indies...Under United States control, it

3 PRO WO 32/9590.

4 Ibid.

5 Sandy Tatem, 'U.S. Naval Station Bermuda: a history 1941–68' (1970), unpublished ms., 17 pp., kindly given to the author in 1990 by Capt. J. Phelan, USN, Commanding Officer, U.S. Naval Air Station, Bermuda. Morgan's Island belonged to Ruth Dill, then married to the American, John Seward Johnson. Her brother, Bayard Dill, had to obtain the papers secretly in person at her United States home, for 'with the Isolationist Party so strong in the United States now, it would be disastrous if word got out that we were trying to get a lease on behalf of the American Government from a country who might be going to war.' Sir Bayard Dill, *Reminiscences of an Islander* (1979), 7.

6 Stetson Conn and Byron Fairchild, *The Framework of Hemisphere Defense,* UNITED STATES ARMY IN WORLD WAR II (1960), 55.

7 Ibid., 58.

8 Tatem, Naval Station.

9 Corps of Engineers, U.S. Army, Historical Monograph. Bermuda: Fort Bell, Kindley Field and Auxiliary Installations (1945), Library of Congress, ms 49307, III-1.

10 Dolores G. Block, 'Kindley Air Force Base, Bermuda: the first twenty-five years' (1969), unpublished ms. 91 pp. Excerpts published in 1966 in *The Royal Gazette* and the U.S. NAS Bermuda newspaper, *The Skyliner*. See also David L. Woods, 'Bermuda, U.S. Naval Bases, 1918–19, 1941–', in Paolo E. Coletta (ed.), *United States Navy and Marine Corp Bases, Overseas* (1985), 30–9.

11 Corps of Engineers, Monograph, Appendix A-6.

provides a valuable location for a Naval Operating Base and for air operations against hostile air or surface forces in the Western Atlantic.'[3] At the same time, its fall to the enemy would turn these advantages around by using Bermuda as a forward station for an attack on the East Coast and its shipping. Because of the strength of the British and American Navies in the Western Atlantic, the 'local defensive forces in Bermuda need be only strong enough to protect against hostile raids by sea and air.'[4] In these statements of late 1941 lay the commencement of the three main aspects of American works at Bermuda, namely, the establishment of a Naval Operating Base, a land air base and the building of defence works for the protection of both.

The importance of Bermuda was heralded by an agreement for a seaplane base on Morgan's Island in the Great Sound that was signed on September 1, 1939, two days before Britain declared war on Germany. This was apparently a result of the work of the Hepburn Board, which was appointed in May 1938 to consider American defence requirements in the Western Atlantic and Caribbean. It also included some fast legwork by the Dills of Bermuda, who were given less than a week, prior to September 3, 1939, to go to the United States and obtain a lease for Morgan's Island, which was owned by a member of the family. Bayard (later, Sir) Dill managed to return to Bermuda on the evening of September 2 with the lease for Morgan's Island in hand; thus the United States avoided an infringement of its neutrality when Britain went to war with Germany the next day.[5] In early August 1940, Britain proposed a 'continuation' of this agreement as a part of the Destroyers-for-Bases proposal, but the establishment of major naval and air bases at Bermuda, along with others on a defensive line from Newfoundland south to British Guiana, was considered by President Roosevelt to be one of the major concessions he wanted from the British, to which Prime Minister Churchill agreed on the 15th.[6] Further negotiations on August 26 broke an impasse when the Americans suggested that Bermuda and Newfoundland bases 'be accepted from Britain as outright gifts, and that only the Caribbean base sites be specifically exchanged for the destroyers.'[7] On September 2, 1940, the United Kingdom Government informed the U.S. Secretary of State that it would 'secure the grant to the Government of the United States, freely and without consideration, of the [99-year] lease for immediate establishment and use of Naval and Air bases...on the East coast and on the Great Bay [Sound] of Bermuda.'[8] The next day, President Roosevelt told Congress that the 'right to bases in Newfoundland and Bermuda were gifts generously given and gladly received,'[9] and an American committee under Admiral John W. Greenslade immediately departed for Bermuda to choose the sites.[10]

The British had insisted that the siting of the bases be made by common agreement, which in the case of Bermuda was fortunate, for the original wording referred to a Warwick Parish site on 'the Great Bay,' which would have cut the main island in two. The airfield the Americans wanted to build on this site would have required a 'wide corridor from coast to coast dividing the Colony into two parts, and cutting railway and main road communications.'[11] In addition, about 1,500 people would be displaced and their resettlement would be an enormous problem. Recreational use of the Great Sound would have

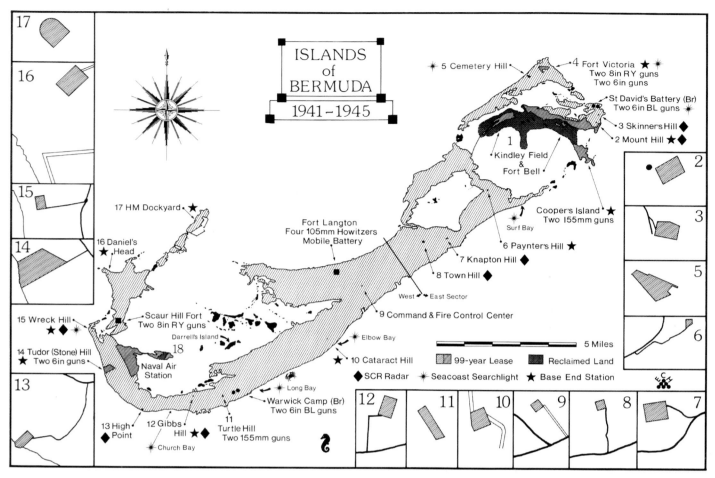

FIGURE 9.2: *The areas leased for 99 years to the United States of America (based on Plan No. B-1379, United States Engineer Office, St. George's, Bermuda, November 1942, with additions).*

been greatly interrupted, and the increase in shipping and the storage of munitions could have been extremely detrimental to the people of Bermuda. Strenuous objection was made by the Bermuda Government, and after a second meeting with the Greenslade Board on October 24, an alternative site for an airfield was chosen at the eastern end of Bermuda on Long Bird, St. David's and Cooper's Islands.[12]

Matters continued to move rapidly: on November 3, 1940, a American team under Major D. G. White arrived in the islands to survey, make land valuations on properties to be purchased, and amass engineering and construction data. The following month, the U.S. Survey Ship *Bowditch* began a hydrographic survey of the waters adjacent to the new bases. Representatives of the Surgeon General, the Office of the Chief of Engineers, the Army Signal Corps and others came and went with their recommendations.[13] In the final plans, Morgan's and Tucker's Islands and a part of the main island in Southampton were to become the Naval Air Station and Naval Operating Base; Long Bird Island ultimately became 'Kindley Field,' and St. David's and Cooper's Island, the army base, 'Fort Bell.' Additional parcels of land needed for base end stations and other facilities were added to the lease (Fig. 9.2).

[12] Ibid., III-2.
[13] Ibid., IV-1.

The 'Stars and Stripes' was officially raised at the Naval Operating Base on March 1, 1941.[14] So it was that the United States for the second time dramatically altered this small island nation: the first monumental changes—enacted in the building of the dockyard and its many associated fortifications in the 1820s—were entirely motivated by a need to defend Bermuda from an invasion from the mainland, for which American schemes and spies abounded in the 1840s.[15] If, however, the old foe was now seen as a friend, it was not without considerable misgivings that many Bermudians viewed the coming of the Americans in 1941.

• • •

BERMUDA IN THE FLUX OF WAR

In the Historical Monograph compiled in 1945 by the U.S. Corps of Engineers, there are several important sections on Bermudian reaction to the new bases. In 1939, the island had a population of 1,600 to the square mile, or about 32,000 inhabitants for a land mass of nineteen-and-a-half square miles, making it the most densely populated country in the world. It was largely self-governing, with a Parliament second only in age to Westminster and third eldest worldwide after London and Iceland. Voting was not universal, but based upon land holdings; still it could be claimed at that time that its people had 'lived quiet, orderly lives under an enlightened system of representative Government for over 300 years...The white and coloured races have lived side by side in a small area without serious difficulties arising and the racial problem has certainly been met in a manner not surpassed anywhere else in the world.'[16] A high standard of living was generally shared by the whole community and wages for unskilled labour ran at four times the Caribbean rate.

The final proposal for a Bermuda base far exceeded the original estimates and accounted for about eight per cent of the land, further limiting the living space for the local population. The arrival of some 5,000 Americans, and latterly their families, would increase the population by twenty per cent: 'It cannot be doubted that the establishment of a land air base of the magnitude visualised must destroy many of the attractions and amenities which have brought Canadian and American visitors to Bermuda.'[17] The bifurcation of the main island and the displacement of 1,500 Bermudians based on the Warwick Parish proposal was compared to the difficulties encountered in the 1920s when the Bermuda Development Company forced the resettlement of a small number of people living in the Tucker's Town area. Because of the disruption of communications between the western end of Bermuda and the rest of the island, and the resettlement problem, the Bermudians recommended the use of islands on the northern side of Castle Harbour for the land air base, some 150 souls being ultimately displaced from St. David's, Coopers and Long Bird Islands.

Appendix A in the Historical Monograph appears to be from a Bermudian pen and gives further insights into the fears held locally, noting that the 'Government has always pursued policies which have tended to preserve the

14 Tatem, Naval Station.

15 Edward Harris, 'American Spies at Bermuda's Forts, 1842–52,' *Post-Medieval Archaeology* 20 (1986), 311–331. Anthony Brescia, ' "Defences strong enough to defy the world," the visit of a U.S. State Department Special Agent to Bermuda in 1841,' *Bulletin of the Institute of Maritime History and Archaeology* 10 (1987).

16 Corps of Engineers, Historical Monograph, Appendix A-9.

17 Ibid., A-10.

peace, charm and amenities of the islands, not only for the purpose of attracting visitors...but because the preservation of such amenities is essential to the Bermuda way of life.'[18] One item then banned as a bane of modern life was the car and 'no responsible opinion would sponsor an attempt to reintroduce mechanical road transport,'[19] after a short fling with automobiles in the 1930s. The Government had refrained from introducing a land tax, on the grounds that the 'subdivision of large tracts of land would be detrimental and would impair the beauty of the islands.'[20]

Prior to 1920, the local economy was based on agriculture and the expenditures of the British garrison and dockyard. An American law destroyed the former trade in the 1920s; this sector was slowly filled by the tourist trade which had previously contributed little, but by 1940 yielded 85,000 visitors a year. Most local wealth was founded in real estate, and it was thought that the coming of the American bases would destroy its value, now largely funded by the tourist and foreign-resident trade. The collapse of land values would affect the franchise, which, in the eyes of the property holders, would result in serious political problems, since ordinary people of all races and classes might end up as voters.

The Appendix concludes by saying it was very difficult to over-estimate the importance of closer ties between America and Bermuda and that such co-operation was desirable and inevitable: 'Our people are intensely loyal to the Crown, have been happy and contented under British rule, and despite our admiration for the United States and its people, we dislike the prospect of any change in our present status. It is obvious that if the defence administration of Bermuda is to rest largely in American hands, for a period beyond the life span of any present Bermudian, succeeding generations will more and more come under American influence, and our British ties may similarly become imperceptibly weakened...We hesitate to appear to indicate that we do not welcome American co-operation in the defence of these islands...Nevertheless, it is the duty of the Bermuda Government to protect its people from economic chaos and financial bankruptcy. The war will end, but the lease continues in perpetuity [99 years] and it is essential that succeeding generations of Bermudians be given a fair opportunity to achieve a reasonable and decent standard of living, which might prove impossible if the present proposals become operative.'[21]

In the construction of Kindley Field and Fort Bell, Bermuda lost a unique piece of its social and topographical heritage. The island of St. David's was a world apart, having been isolated, except by water, from the main Bermudian society. Its inhabitants were an interesting amalgam of European, African, and American Indian descent and they maintained, especially in boating, many of the traditions being lost on mainland Bermuda. For the loss of some of their lands and the displacement of many St. David's Islanders, however, Bermuda gained its first and only airfield and an increase of some eight hundred acres of land by landfill operations in Castle Harbour.

Rather than diminishing the tourist trade, Kindley Field assumed the additional role of civilian airfield after the war; as a result tourism increased greatly. The American bases also injected a considerable amount of hard

[18] Ibid., A-7.
[19] Ibid.
[20] Ibid.
[21] Ibid., Appendix A-13.

currency into the local economy, and continued to do so until closed in September 1995. Historically speaking, the Americans were the last phase of a trend begun in 1783 in which military spending fuelled and sustained the local economy. It was a fortunate act of fate for Bermuda that the Americans were able to take over this background role in 1941 at the very time that the British Empire was heading for a decline from which it never recovered, necessitating the almost complete closure of its military facilities at Bermuda soon after the war.

The Americans were very conscious of the deleterious effect their bases might have had on Bermuda and the last half century reflects a sympathetic handing of the matter. If the Great Sound and inner harbours are less clean and idyllic than in 1941, it cannot be laid behind the propellers of American shipping. If the 'large tracts of land' are now much over-developed, it has not been the American Government which has pursued policies *contrary* to the preservation of the 'peace, charm and amenities' of this most northern of coral paradises. A tiny country, Bermuda will always be a pawn in the cut and thrust of international diplomacy and war. There is no doubt that its occupation by American forces during and after the war was made for American defence interests, but on principle, this was no different to British military concern with the island. Nonetheless, it is the Bermudians who have most benefitted from this use of their homeland, described in the 1980s as a 'land-based aircraft carrier.' They continue to reap more benefits than sorrows for being used as a part of the flux which was necessary in the welding of British and American military interests, which took shape at Bermuda in the spring of 1941.

• • •

THE NAVAL OPERATING BASE, KINDLEY FIELD & FORT BELL

[22] Jules James, Jules James Papers (1941–3), East Carolina Manuscript Collection, J. Y. Joyner Library, East Carolina University, Coll. no. 223.

[23] Ibid. Not perhaps an entirely anti-American happenstance for Jules recorded: 'On April 9th, in company with the Consul General, called on Major Dutton, the Colonial Secretary, who informed me that he was sorry there had been no one from the Bermuda Government to meet me. I told him that I, too, was sorry, but that I got along alright. He smilingly replied, "Well, so did I." '

[24] Ibid.

[25] Ibid.

[26] Ibid.

Captain (later Rear Admiral) Jules James was on duty at the Navy Department, Washington, D.C., when he received orders to proceed immediately to Bermuda as the Commandant, Naval Operating Base. Several conferences, including one with the President, stressed the 'delicate situation at Bermuda, as this Naval Operating Base was the first ever to be established on British territory.'[22] James arrived in Bermuda on April 7, 1941: 'There was no one present from the Bermuda Government or even the office of the U.S. Consul General. The reception was distinctly cold.'[23] Alone in an official sense, he took the train to Southampton upon misinformation about boating conditions. At 7 p.m. on the mainland, he read his orders commissioning the Naval Operating Base by raising the pennant of the Senior Officer Present. Meanwhile, local reporters coming by boat waited in vain for the ceremony to take place on the nearby Tucker's Island![24] Admitting his troubles were many, he found a sympathetic ear in the British Vice Admiral Kennedy-Purvis and 'discussed all questions with him with the same frankness I would have used with an American Admiral.'[25] Having completed his tenure in 1943, James thought that it was 'one of the toughest ever assigned in modern times, [but I] will leave Bermuda with real regret.'[26]

The Naval Operating Base encompassed two hundred and twenty-one

FIGURE 9.3: *The U. S. Naval Operating Base in Southampton shortly after completion in the 1940s* (BMM 77:151).

acres on Morgan's Island, Tucker's Island and King's Point on the mainland (Fig. 9.3). A further thirty-six acres was added by reclamation between the two islands and a causeway connected them to King's Point (Fig. 9.2, no. 18). Construction proceeded apace, but it was not until June 1942 that the Commandant's Office was located within the leased area, having been temporarily housed in the City of Hamilton. In July 1941, a part of the Base became the Naval Air Station with facilities eventually built for PB Y and PB M flying boats, which helped in the Atlantic patrols particularly against submarines. For an interim period, the planes worked out of the nearby Darrell's Island, which was the civilian air terminal, also used as the Royal Air Force base during the war.

It was a mission from the new Naval Air Station on June 30, 1942 that 'sank the third U-boat to fall victim to an American plane.'[27] This action was recorded in James' war diary.

> Obtained bearings on enemy submarine from British Y Station and plotted fix, placing submarine within four miles of actual position. 74 P-1 [a PB M of Squadron VP-74] was in that vicinity returning to the Base. Ordered her to return and attack. On approaching through the clouds, plane's radar picked up the submarine and an immediate attack was made. The submarine was enormously large, was full[y] surfaced, and the crew was on deck. One depth charge exploded under the stern, the other one landed on deck. The machine gun jammed after a few rounds fired at the submarine. The plane circled to make another attack as the submarine dived. Just before her stern disappeared, the depth charge which had landed on deck, just abaft the conning tower, exploded. There was plenty of debris, a very large amount of oil, and a very large air bubble. The plane took a picture of it. Sent two destroyers, one from the harbour and one which was at sea.[28]

Two weeks after James' arrival, the U.S. Army appeared on the scene and set up temporary headquarters at the Castle Harbour Hotel for offices and billeting, as it was conveniently situated on the water opposite the new works for the Army base and airfield. A private telephone line was installed between

[27] Stetson Conn, Rose C. Engelman and Byron Fairchild, *Guarding the United States and its Outposts,* UNITED STATES ARMY IN WORLD WAR II (1964), 549.

[28] James, Papers, War Diary, U.S. Naval Operating Base, Bermuda. 0000–2400 June 30, 1942. THE COMMANDANT'S NOTES. This action is often quoted as an example of the efficacy of high-frequency direction-finders, which picked up U-boat radio transmissions. In this instance, a message was intercepted and gave a fix one hundred and thirty miles W.S.W. of Bermuda for U-158, which was sunk with all hands aboard, as noted in Samuel Eliot Morison, *The Battle of the Atlantic* (1961), 227–8.

the James' office and that of the Army Commander, which was 'used almost daily since its installation.'[29]

The Army base and airfield were to be built on the northern side of Castle Harbour on the islands of Long Bird, St. David's, and other smaller isles and rocks, all to be joined by landfill. In late November 1940, the news broke that these islands were to be leased to the American forces and much sympathy was shown by the rest of Bermuda, particularly for the fate of the people on the most populous island, St. David's, half of which was to become part of the army base, Fort Bell.[30] While there was much sorrow at the displacement,

FIGURE 9.4: *Kindley Field after the completion of the long runway which extended into the area of Fort Bell (background right). The patch of ground (middle left) is the remnant of Long Bird Island (BMM 77:151).*

29 James, Papers.

30 Block, Kindley Air Force Base, 6. The base was named for Major General George Bell, Jr, an American officer who distinguished himself in command of the 33rd Division, AEF, in France in World War One and was decorated by the United Kingdom. The name was not used after 1946, when the entire base was called Kindley Field.

31 Ibid., 7.

32 *The Royal Gazette*, July 2, 1941, cited in Block. The nearby historic 'Carter House' was not demolished and was a small museum on the base until its closure in September 1995.

there appears to have been little dissent at the cost, which Churchill acknowledged the following spring: 'I take this opportunity of telling the House of Assembly, and through them the people of the Colony, how much we appreciate the magnificent way in which they have responded to this call upon their patriotism and understanding. I realise the sacrifices entailed, which are so much greater in Bermuda than in the other Colonies concerned, I know too how cheerfully they were accepted. To the people of Bermuda has fallen the honour and privilege of making a notable contribution to the cause of justice and freedom for which our Empire stands. Their act will not be forgotten.'[31] The local authority to establish the bases came under the terms of the 'Agreement for the Use and Operation of the U.S. Bases' on March 27, 1941.

Work soon began on the new bases, but the U.S. Army gave 'Mr Howard Smith at St. David's Island an opportunity to reap his lily crop, so that it was possible to unearth from a burial plot on the property the remains of five members of the Carter family, descendants of Christopher Carter, one of the three [*sic*, two] men left behind by Sir George Somers [in 1610] when he went away from the islands after being shipwrecked,' in the *Sea Venture* in 1609 on the way to James Fort, Virginia.[32]

An essential factor on both bases was the dredging of Castle Harbour to provide rock and sand for a landfilling operation, which eventually joined Kindley Field and Fort Bell into a single entity (Fig. 9.2, no. 1). The first dredge, *Norfolk*, arrived in March 1941 and was followed by the *Gulfstream* and the *Welatka*: all returned to the U.S. in June 1943. To assist ships going to the Naval Operating Base in the Great Sound, two other dredges, the *Wm. T. Rossell* and the *W. L. Marshall* were employed in 1941–42 in the Narrows and Dundonald Channels. Some thirty-five million cubic yards of material was dredged from the bottom of Castle Harbour, which added around eight hundred acres to the original area of four hundred and fourteen acres on the appropriated islands. Construction of buildings began in 1941 and by the end of 1943, when Kindley Field and Fort Bell were largely completed, the cost had reached a little over $40 million.

'Kindley Field,' so called in War Department Orders on June 25, 1941, was a facility of the U.S. Army Air Force, whereas Fort Bell was the province of the U.S. Army ground forces (Fig. 9.4). The American flag was raised on Kindley Field on July 4; by August 8 the first runway had been laid and on November 29, 1941, the landing field was declared open for traffic. The first plane to arrive was an F2A3 from the carrier, *Long Island*, on December 15, while the first land-based plane was an RAF B-24 Liberator from Montreal five days later. Anti-submarine patrols by planes of the U.S. Air Force staged out of Kindley Field began in April 1942 and ended in February 1944. Although pre-war plans called for a composite group of eleven Army bombers and twenty-five pursuit planes to be stationed at Kindley Field, subsequent events made this move unnecessary. Thus by December 1943, at a meeting in Bermuda, Col. Lawrence G. Fritze declared that the mission of the base, now that war activity had lessened in the area, would be to 'service transient aircraft between the base at the Azores and the U.S., to handle passengers, cargo and mail, and furnish air sea rescue when necessary,' which remained a part of its aims for the next twenty-five years.[33]

Col. Alden G. Strong had arrived in Bermuda in April 1941 to establish the Bermuda Base Command over Kindley Field and Fort Bell, then under construction; he was elevated to Brigadier General in September 1941. He remained in this position until July 4, 1944, receiving the Legion of Merit and the Order of the British Empire for his important work in setting up the bases, which included responsibility for the coastal defences of Bermuda. The local defences of Bermuda were particularly weak, comprising only four British guns.[34] The President considered its protection of the highest priority and admonished the War Department to 'get planes there as soon as any place can be prepared,'[35] which meant in practical terms three patrol bombers, which operated from Darrell's Island during the construction of the Naval Operating Base.

The American land force under Col. Strong on the *American Legion* had docked in Hamilton on April 20, 1941 with eight hundred and sixty men of Company G, 11th Infantry, Battery F, 52nd Coast Artillery, and Battery B, 57th Coast Artillery, with four 8-inch railway guns and four 155 mm GPF Guns. A week earlier, Brig. Gen. Francis B. Wilby, Chief of Staff, First Army and Lt. Col. Harold F. Loomis, War Plans Division, had come to choose sites

33 Block, Kindley Air Force Base, 26–7. The air base was named for Captain Field E. Kindley, an American World War One flying ace, credited with twelve enemy planes and decorated with a DFC by King George V in 1918.

34 James, Papers, Letter to Admiral Stark, April 9, 1941.

35 Conn, *Guarding the United States*, 388.

for coastal defence positions and awaited Strong's arrival. Within hours of disembarking, Col. Strong had drawn up a joint plan with Capt. Jules James for the defence of Bermuda. The railway guns were to be placed at the extreme ends of the chain of islands, one battery on Somerset Island, the other at St. George's. The 155 mm guns covered the ground between, with a battery at Cooper's Island and another in Southampton Parish. A mobile reserve would operate from the Castle Harbour Hotel.[36] Before considering these positions, the British defences should be discussed.

• • •

BRITISH COASTAL BATTERIES AT BERMUDA, 1939–45

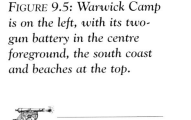

FIGURE 9.5: Warwick Camp is on the left, with its two-gun battery in the centre foreground, the south coast and beaches at the top.

[36] Ibid., 390.

[37] James, Papers.

[38] While plans existed for a British two-gun 6-inch battery at Turtle Hill from 1900, it was not until the late 1930s that it was built a short distance away to the east on the edge of Warwick Camp. On the acquisition of land for Warwick Camp Battery see: William S. Zuill, 'The Gibraltar of the West: a history of Admiralty and War Department Lands,' *Bermuda Historical Quarterly* 10 (1953), 84–106, and 'The Acquisition of Land (Warwick) Act, 1952,' whereby the Bermuda Government retroactively acquired the ground for the gun site.

[39] An inventory of guns at Bermuda was commissioned by the Bermuda Maritime Museum in 1985 and was carried out by the British historic artillery scholars, A. Collin and Jenny Carpenter.

[40] Conn, *Guarding the United States*, 357.

[41] Jennifer M. Ingham, *Defence not Defiance, A History of the Bermuda Volunteer Rifle Corps* (1992).

Writing to Admiral H. R. Stark, Chief of Naval Operations, on April 9, 1941, James noted that 'Bermuda is defended from the sea by only four six-inch guns. There is defence against landing parties at such vital places as the oil dock, the cable head and the radio station. There are also mobile units which provide striking forces, and furnish guards for protecting the dock-yard against sabotage. There are no anti-aircraft guns on the island, or even machine guns except a few 30-calibre machine guns carried by the infantry.'[37] The four guns referred to were mounted at Warwick Camp and St. David's Battery (Fig. 9.2, by name). The latter position was the sole surviving position of the British rearmament of 1898–1910, while the Warwick battery was built at the beginning of war in 1939 (Fig. 9.5).[38]

An examination in the 1980s of the pieces at Warwick Camp revealed that the barrels had been retubed, the eastern in July 1940 and the western in June 1939, the latter also marked 'overhauled 5/35' (Fig. 9.6).[39] A spare 6-inch barrel from St. David's Battery was retubed at the Royal Gun Factory, Woolwich, in 1941; the markings on the other barrels at St. David's have corroded away. It is probably the case, therefore, that there were three operational guns at Bermuda on September 3, 1939, with the fourth at Warwick Camp coming into operation after July 1940. In August 1940, these two batteries represented the full strength of the coastal defences of Bermuda, while the entire island was weakly manned 'by one British infantry company and two artillery batteries composed of militia,'[40] the latter being the Bermuda Militia Artillery, and the Bermuda Volunteer Rifle Corps,[41] augmented by the Bermuda Militia Infantry and the Bermuda Volunteer Engineers.

Designed in the late 1890s, the 6-inch and 9.2-inch guns were very successful models of breech-loading rifles and were removed from service only

FIGURE 9.6: An emplacement for two 6-inch Breech Loading guns was built at Warwick Camp, as war started for the British in 1939.

with the demise of British coastal defence in 1956. By the 1940s, they were outclassed by the big guns of many warships, which could have reduced much of Bermuda to rubble from a safe distance at sea. The guns at St. David's Battery were used during the war as the authority of an Examination Battery for ships impounded or under search in Five Fathom Hole, less than two miles offshore. The value the American weapons introduced by way of the *American Legion* in 1941 was in their range and their availability, for the British were hard pressed for munitions. The British 6-inch had a range of 11,000 yards, which did not compare well with that of the 155 mm piece at 17,400 yards, the 8-inch railway at 23,900 yards and the fixed 6-inch at 27,000 yards (Fig. 9.7).

An acceptance of the American defence of British Bermuda did not come easily with the Governor,[42] Lt. Gen. Sir Denis Bernard, who cabled the War Office on March 25, 1941: 'Now that base agreement has been signed I consider it most important personnel appointed to discuss future defences of islands...I would stress strongly importance of British (?retaining) responsibility for the siting and armament of main defence[s]...I know that your views were same.'[43] Three days later, the War Office replied with a broadside: 'You will have seen provisions...of draft agreement...These grant America very full powers including constructing bases, and installing defences...Agreement terms of which were insisted on by Americans does not (repeat not) give us right to order where American defences are to be placed.'[44] Three weeks later, the Americans landed and were pressing the Governor, but the message of March 28 from the War Office seems not to have been understood, and he claimed in a cable of April 14 that 'my present position here is most unsatisfactory owing to the fact that no decision has yet been communicated to me regarding joint [defence] board...and American representatives are insisting on immediate occupation of gun sites.'[45] Sir Denis then requested two 9.2-inch guns for Fort Victoria, a matter he returned to on July 2 in a further telegram to the War Office, because 'American Army representatives are asking permission to commence work on permanent 6-inch gun sites. This involves ceding crown lands St. George's area [Fort Victoria] and precludes all possibility of using this area as site 9.2 inch gun as recommended in Committee of Imperial Defence memorandum para 34 (J.D.C. 195).'[46] This last foray seems to have ended the matter, for the War Office replied firmly that 'no objection should be raised to the Americans using St. George's site for installation of defences.

[42] It appears that the Governor was not favourably inclined towards the Americans and James recorded that 'from the time of my arrival the Governor on many occasions mildly complained of my haste to get things done here and took the strange point of view that while his nation was standing on the edge of the cliff England would be better off if America did not enter the war but continued on as a supply center for England.'

[43] PRO WO 193/310, 50A.

[44] Ibid., 51A.

[45] Ibid., 52A.

[46] Ibid., 53A.

FIGURE 9.7: *The disposition of artillery at Bermuda in early 1943. The areas of the Fire Control chart are: 1, Wreck Hill/Dockyard; 2 and 3, Wreck/Gibbs Hills; 4, Gibbs/Cataract Hills; 5 and 9, Paynter's/Mount Hills; 6 and 10, Paynter's Hill/Fort Victoria; 7, Fort Victoria/Soldiers Point (Cooper's Island) and 8, Fort Victoria/Mount Hill. (Based on maps in 'Bermuda Base Command, U.S. Army, December 1, 1942', with additions).*

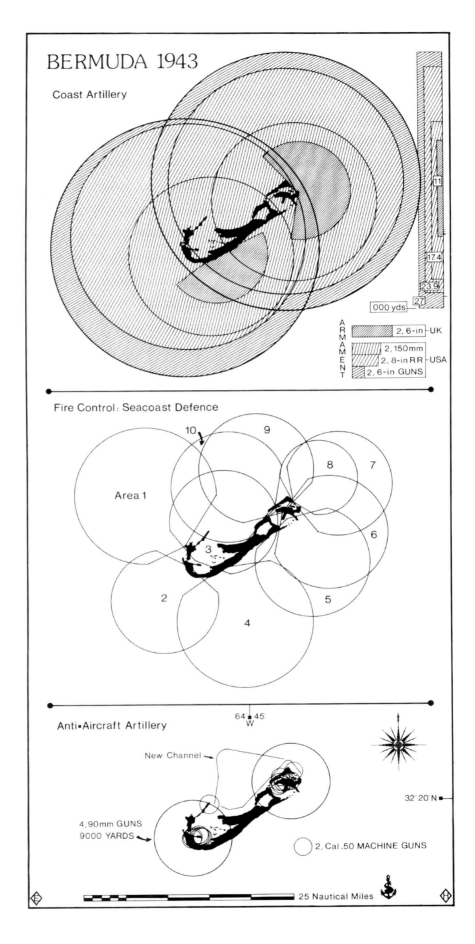

Prospect of implementing recommendations contained in Imperial Defence Memorandum, para 34 (J.D.C. 195) still remote...Colonial Office have been consulted and agree.'[47]

• • •

U.S. COASTAL DEFENCE WORKS AT BERMUDA

During the first phase of American coastal defence works at Bermuda, eight guns were put into position shortly after being off-loaded from the *American Legion* (Figs. 9.8 and 9.9). The railway guns were probably taken by water to the most convenient unloading spot near Scaur Hill Fort and Fort Victoria (Fig. 9.10). The 155 mm pieces were taken by tractor to Tucker's Town (and later by water to Cooper's Island) and Turtle Hill in Southampton. Other munitions may have been moved by rail.

FIGURE 9.8 (far left): A barrel for an 8-inch railway gun is off loaded from the American Legion at Hamilton, Bermuda, in April 1941 (BMM, Tomasiewicz Collection).

FIGURE 9.9: Ammunition for the American guns being loaded onto a barge (BMM, Tomasiewicz Collection).

Scaur Hill Fort had been built on the highest point of Somerset Island in the 1870s, its purpose being to defend the landward approach to the dockyard. Its two 64-pounder Rifled Muzzle Loaders were never upgraded and the fort was obsolete by the turn of the century. To the north-west of its entrance stood a sloping water catch above which was placed one 8-inch railway gun (Fig. 9.11). The second gun of this battery was probably on an adjacent hillock to the north-east. No trace exists of this battery, which was in position by May 1941.

Two pages from an unknown source of reports on the harbour defences of New Jersey and Bermuda in the author's possession make it possible to state that the guns at Scaur Hill were taken from Fort Hancock, Sandy Hook, N.J., where

[47] Ibid., 56A.

Figure 9.10: The barrel for an 8-inch railway gun from the American Legion being loaded on the Bermudian barge, Cristobal Colon, bound for Fort Victoria or Scaur Hill Fort (BMM, Beaudry Collection).

FIGURE 9.11: This American 8-inch railway gun was located just beyond the western edge of the water catchment (foreground) at Scaur Hill Fort (BMM, Tomasiewicz Collection).

they had been since at least 1931. Both guns were Model 1888 M.II, serial numbers 9 and 44, their carriages being Model 1918 MI, numbers 38 and 12.

Fort Victoria was on St. George's Island and to its east lay Fort Albert. On the slope between the two, facing the Narrows Channel, the two U.S. railway guns were cut into the hillside. The position of these guns was rediscovered on an aerial photograph during the 1989 visit of the Coast Defence Study Group (Fig. 9.12).[48] They were located between the U.S. fixed 6-inch guns and Fort Albert: the sun at the time of photography created a shadow in the cutting of the northern gun, which outlined its barrel, for otherwise they were well camouflaged. Based upon one of the unreferenced documents noted above, these two guns are the same model and carriage as those at Scaur Hill Fort, but they were serial numbers 20 and 40 (barrels) and 8 and 37 (carriages). In an interview with Edward Tomasiewicz, John Stewart Morton, Jr. (Battery A, 214th FA Bn) noted that the guns were 'left over from WWI...Sections of track, possibly fifty feet or so had been laid at the site of each piece. The flat car had then been assembled on the track, and then the weapon had been mounted on the flat car. Following that, the flat cars were jacked up off the track by means of out-riggers.'

The 8-inch railway guns were complemented by a two-gun 155 mm GPF battery at Turtle Hill (Figs. 9.13-15), and another on the eastern Cooper's

48 BMM, Tomasiewicz Collection.

FIGURE 9.12: *Just above Fort Albert are two American 8-inch railway guns: the barrel of the gun on the right casts a shadow against the limestone cutting (U. S. Navy Photograph 80-G-239753: April 2, 1944).*

Island. The 155 mm guns had been placed on Panama Mounts by the end of October 1941: they had come from Camp Pendleton, Virginia. One of the Panama Mounts survived at Turtle Hill (Fig. 9.16) in the 1980s, just to the east of the Southampton Princess Hotel. At Cooper's Island, the position on Well Bay Hill was buried in the building of the NASA tracking station in the 1960s. A visit to the site in 1989 with Col. Charles Beaudry, who as Lieutenant, had established the position in 1941, but had not seen it for about forty-five years, confirmed that the underground magazines (one for projectiles and one for propellant) still existed, as did the command, communications and plotting board bunker between them (Figs. 9. 17–19).

In April 1942, a second phase of American defence works commenced with the

FIGURE 9.13: *Men of the 155 mm GPF gun battery at Turtle Hill, Southampton, about 1942 (BMM, Beaudry Collection).*

FIGURE 9.14: *Lunch time at the mess at Turtle Hill with men of Battery B, 57th Coast Artillery: Philip J. Ceconi, left front, is identifiable (BMM, Tomasiewicz Collection).*

FIGURE 9.15: *One of the two 155 mm GPF guns at Turtle Hill prior to its emplacement in a Panama Mount (BMM, Tomasiewicz Collection).*

FIGURE 9.16: *One of the Panama Mounts for an 155 mm GPF gun seen at Turtle Hill in the 1980s.*

construction of concrete emplacements for two 6-inch guns (of Second World War design) and an intervening magazine at Tudor Hill (or Stone Hill) on the west coast (Fig. 9.20), a few miles south of Scaur Hill Fort (Fig. 9.2, no. 14). This was Battery Construction No. 284 and it was

FIGURE 9.17: *Towing an 155 mm GPF gun to Cooper's Island at the southern end of Point Finger Road (BMM, Tomasiewicz Collection).*

FIGURE 9.18: *The two 155 mm GPF guns in a grove of cedars at Cooper's Island before they were emplaced in Panama Mounts (BMM, Beaudry Collection).*

completed in May 1943; the guns were installed by August 15. The guns were model M1903A2, serial numbers 49 and 50 on carriages model BC MI, numbers 48 and 49). At Tudor Hill, the eastern emplacement and magazine had survived in the 1980s (Fig. 9.21). The western emplacement appears to have been destroyed or buried in the development of the site by the U.S. Navy for sonar testing facilities.

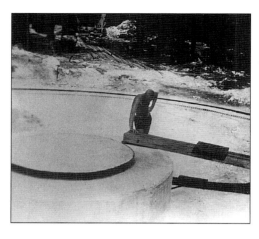

FIGURE 9.19: *Charles Beaudry examines his handiwork on the construction of a Panama Mount at Cooper's Island in 1941 (BMM, Beaudry Collection).*

Covering the eastern end of Bermuda and its seaward approaches, Battery Construction No. 283 was a two-gun work of fixed 6-inch guns located at Fort Victoria. These emplacements were begun on February 20, 1942 and completed on May 1, 1943 (Figs. 9.22-24). As at Tudor Hill, the ordnance itself was in

FIGURE 9.20: *The two 6-inch guns at Tudor Hill in Southampton in the late 1940s (right foreground), with the Naval Operating Base in the background (BMM 77:151).*

FIGURE 9.21: *Tudor Hill in 1988 with the surviving eastern emplacement for a 6-inch gun on the left; radio masts are on the top of the ammunition bunker.*

FIGURE 9.22: *Men of the U. S. Army installing the northern 6-inch gun at Fort Victoria; to the right of the shield can be seen the north-west corner of Fort Albert (U. S. Navy Photograph SC 231618: 14 May 1943).*

place by the middle of August 1943; all the 6-inch guns were on Barbette carriages. In the 1960s, the property which includes Forts Victoria and Albert was leased to an hotel chain, and new works in 1984 led to the destruction of the southern emplacement: it is not known whether the northern emplacement survives under a road.[49] The guns at this site were model M1903A2, serial numbers 41 and 43, on carriages model BC MI, numbers 11 and 12.

[49] Information on these batteries comes from unreferenced American papers, copies of which are in the author's possession entitled 'Report of completed works—Seacoast Fortifications (Batteries).' Some twenty of this type of 2-gun battery were constructed outside the continental United States during the Second World War: see Emanuel Raymond Lewis, *Seacoast Fortifications of the United States: An Introductory History* (1970), Fig. 60.

[50] BMM, Tomasiewicz Collection. DEFENSE PROJECT, Bermuda Base Command, U.S. Army, December 1, 1942.

As organised in the 'Defence Project for 1 December 1942,'[50] the personnel for the seacoast defence were the 27th Coast Artillery Battalion (HD) (Comp), augmented by the men of the two British batteries. It was under the charge of the Commanding Officer of the 27th CA Bn, headquartered at Burrow's Hill at Fort Bell, and was divided into an East Group and West Group. At the end of 1942, the former would have comprised the six guns at Fort Victoria, Cooper's Island and St. David's Battery, while the latter started with the British at Warwick Camp, followed by Turtle Hill and Scaur Hill Fort, again with six guns. In late 1943, the four 6-inch guns would have come into operation, giving a grand total of sixteen pieces of coast artillery under the Bermuda Base Command, evenly divided between the British 6-inch BL, and the American 155 mm GPFs, 8-inch railway and fixed 6-inch guns. After the modern 6-inch guns were installed and manned, the railway guns were sent away.

The fire control system for the 8-inch railway and 155 mm GPF batteries consisted of a series of 'Base End Observation Stations.' The fire control system was based on the principle of triangulation wherein pairs of observation stations formed the ends of imaginary base lines, typically three or four miles long. As the two stations at the ends of a base line tracked a ship, the direction to the target from each telescope was plotted, at fixed intervals, on a chart in the battery's central plotting room. The target thereby occupied the apex of a triangle, and the range and direction from the guns to the target—or to the point the target would occupy when the shells arrived—could be precisely measured.

FIGURE 9.23: *The southern 6-inch American gun at Fort Victoria awaits its shield (BMM, Tomasiewicz Collection).*

Thirteen Base End stations were erected, but not all of these could be located in the 1980s. Ten sites have been identified (Fig. 9.2), two of which—Gibbs and Mount Hills—apparently had two stations each, but no topographical clues support that assumption. A station on 'Beek Hill' in Southampton is not known, nor does a leased property for it appear in the documents.

FIGURE 9.24: *The 6-inch American guns were installed between Forts Albert and Victoria in 1943 (aerial view of the 1960s, BMM Archives).*

Working from east to west, the Base End Stations were: Fort Victoria (Fig. 9.2, no. 4); Mount Hill (Fig. 9.2, no. 2); Cooper's Island; Paynter's Hill (Fig. 9.2, no. 6); Cataract Hill (Fig. 9.2, no. 10); Gibbs Hill (Fig. 9.2, no. 12); Tudor Hill (Fig. 9.2, no. 14); Wreck Hill (Fig. 9.2, no. 15); Daniel's Head (Fig. 9.2, no. 16); and HM Dockyard (Fig. 9.2, no. 17). Daniel's Head, Gibbs Hill, Paynter's Hill, and Mount Hill are still standing, if in a decaying condition, due to the rusting of the reinforcing bars in

FIGURE 9.25: *The Base End Station at Daniel's Head in the 1990s, then a part of the Canadian Forces Base.*

their concrete structure. The best preserved are at Daniel's Head (Fig. 9.25) and Mount Hill, next to St. David's Lighthouse (Fig. 9.26), which is used as a lookout for the finish line of ocean yacht races to Bermuda.

A Fire Control Chart for the Base End Stations is given in Figure 9.7. Two of the stations had Surface Craft Detectors (Radar, type SCR-296, range 50,000 yards), namely, High Point (Fig. 9.2, no. 13) and Skinners Hill (Fig. 9.2, no. 3), while Gibbs and Mount Hills had General Surveillance Detectors (SCR-582). Searchlight emplacements for the coast artillery were located at Cemetery Hill (1), Fort Victoria (2 and 3), St. David's Battery (3, 4 and 5, British), Surf Bay (6 and 7), Elbow Bay (9), Warwick Long Bay (9 and 10), Church Bay (11 and 12), and Wreck Hill (13 and 14).

• • •

ANTI-AIRCRAFT ARTILLERY

The American bases were defended against attack from the air by the installation of anti-aircraft artillery, the range and cover of which is indicated in Figure 9.7. This artillery respectively covered the Naval Operating Base in Southampton in the west, and Kindley Field in the east and was in place by November 1942. The Kindley Field area was defended by four 90 mm guns manned by Battery B of the 423rd CA Bn (AA) at Burrow's Hill. The battery also manned four Cal .50 machine guns for local defence. Other groups of the 423rd CA Bn (AA) were at Whalebone Bay at the western end of St. George's Island (with a 40 mm AA gun and two Cal .50 MGs), and at the Oil Docks, next to Cemetery Hill (Fig. 9.2). They also controlled other guns at the airfield and Mount Hill. This eastern sector had about twenty pieces, probably four 90 mm, eight 40 mm AA and eight Cal .50 MGs.

A similar situation obtained in the western end of Bermuda where the Naval Operating Base was defended by four 90 mm guns at the Glebe in Southampton, with four Cal .50 MGs for local defence (Battery C, 423rd). Battery E comprised a dozen Cal .50 AA Machine Guns, which were positioned at the dockyard (but it was conceded that little protection was afforded to the dockyard itself) and around King's Point (NOB).

At least ten anti-aircraft artillery searchlight sections from Battery A, 423rd CA Bn (Comp) (AA) (SM) were sited around the island. The five at the east end were located at Whalebone Bay, St. David's, Surf Bay (Tucker's Town), Knapton Hill and Elbow Beach. The remaining five at the west end were to be found at Spanish Point, Turtle Hill, Tudor Hill, Scott's Hill (just north of Scaur Hill) and HM Dockyard, above Moresby Plain. All sectors had .50 Cal AA type machine guns dug-in or sandbagged. The anti-aircraft SCR 268 radars were located at Whalebone Bay, and Turtle and Tudor Hills. Each was specifically sited to provide early warning information to an Operations Center, known as the 'Central Training School,' which was located near the Middle Road at Prospect Barracks (Fig. 9.2, no. 9). The target information, if an aircraft, was provided in azimuth, angular height and range to the appropriate AA Gun Batteries and searchlight sections by telephone or radio. Where the SCR 268 radar was connected by cable to a searchlight, that information was provided by a servo motor transmitter/receiver component. Thus, the searchlight, which was positioned by the radar in azimuth and elevation, automatically illuminated the target for the gun batteries to engage. Subsequent improvements in radar and fire control directors were provided for the 90 mm guns with SCR 584 Radar and the M-9 Director. Joined by power and data cables, a 90 mm gun battery could track a target and position the weapons to engage it by remote control: the need for AA searchlights was eliminated.[51]

Longer range radar coverage for Bermuda was tackled by a series of stations for the Air Warning Service, under the control of the 693rd Signal Aircraft Warning Company, which arrived in the islands on June 7, 1942 (along with Battery A, 214th FA Bn). Two weeks later detectors SCR-516-C were in place at Mount and Knapton Hills, with long range detectors of the type SCR-271 installed in late June at Town Hill and in early October 1942 at Cove Point, St. David's.[52]

• • •

LAND & OTHER DEFENCE MEASURES

Another sector of the American defence of Bermuda covered the land aspects. It was admitted that the Bermuda terrain was not favourable for defence, as there were few obstacles to the movement of land forces and no topographical features which warranted permanent defensive positions. Landing places, by air or sea, were small and dispersed. A mobile force was thus considered to provide the best defence against a landing force and a Land Defence Task Group was organised in several sectors of the island to provide troops to that end. This Group consisted of U.S. Marines, and from the British Army, a Canadian Regiment detachment, the Pictou Highlanders, the Bermuda Militia Infantry and the Bermuda Volunteer Rifle Corps. The Harrington Sound Sector was thought vital to the defence of Kindley Field, in order that air operations could continue, and was assigned to the General Reserve, the second part of the land forces.

The General Reserve (Mobile) comprised the 3rd Battalion 89th Infantry and Battery A, 214th Field Artillery Battalion. The former group would be assembled near Harrington Sound in an emergency and was supported by Battery A, 214th FA Battalion, from its station at Fort Langton in the central parish of Devonshire. Battery A commanded four 105 mm howitzers on towed carriages and were positioned at Langton to give assistance to both the General Reserve and the Land Defence Task Group. This battery occupied Fort Langton from June 1942 until April 1943. Among their more peaceful

51 Information kindly provided in 1991 by Col. Arthur Jemmott, U.S.A. (ret.), who was the Executive Officer of Battery A, 423rd CA Bn (Comp) (AA) (SM), at its Bermuda Dockyard position.

52 BMM, Tomasiewicz Collection.

FIGURE 9.27: *Ordnance Island in St. George's Harbour was a small U.S. Navy Submarine Station during the Second World War (BMM 89:03).*

FIGURE 9.28: *One of the U.S. Navy patrol and torpedo boats, later sold to Bermudians for tourist cruise vessels (BMM 89:03).*

FIGURE 9.29: *Firing practice at the "Southlands" anti-aircraft school on the south shore in Warwick Parish (BMM 89:03).*

pursuits was unearthing in the moat the three 10-inch Rifled Muzzle Loaders, which comprised the seaward emplacements of the fort in the 1880s.

Had an enemy landed on the beaches at Bermuda, Battery A, 214th FA Bn, as a part of the Infantry Battalion Combat Team, would have furnished direct support for the infantry by 'fire and maneuver.' This was accomplished by the Field Artillery's ability to 'Shoot, move and communicate.' The Coast Artillery, with its long range weapons and stationary gun emplacements, would have been of little help once a landing had been effected. The 105 mm howitzers of Battery A could move into one position, shoot, and move to another position as required: it was the only mobile artillery in Bermuda at the time and was vital to its land defence. The howitzers could fire a 33-pound projectile up to 12,400 yards, with high explosive, armour piercing, incendiary and smoke, with point detonating fuse and time fuse. The high trajectories of the howitzer was of course one of its main advantages over coast artillery for local defence.

Battery A, 214th FA Bn was mustered into Federal Service at the home armoury at Pikeville, Maryland in late summer 1941. They sailed to Bermuda with the 693rd Signal Aircraft Warning

Company on Friday, June 5, 1942, on the USS *Joseph T. Dickman*, from the Norfolk Navy Yard in the company of two destroyer escorts. When they returned to the mainland the following year, several took their Bermudian brides home, while Frederick W. Clipper, executive officer of Battery A, stayed in Bermuda with his—taking to pleasant extremes a decision (recorded in personal reminiscences of John Stewart Morton, Jr.) 'that 'A' Battery was going to be liked by the Bermudians and that we were going to do everything possible to accomplish that [end].' This assertion was in response to a belief that Bermudians did not like the incoming American personnel.

In addition to the artillery and air defence of Bermuda, there were several other military facilities of note. The Naval Air Station at Southampton was home to a fleet of long- and short-range flying boats, which patrolled the sea lanes. There was a submarine base established at Ordnance Island in St. George's Harbour, from which patrols covered the Bermuda area (Fig. 9.27). Several torpedo boats (Fig. 9.28) were added to the range of weaponry (one of these was purchased in 1945 by J. Clyde G. Leseur, a Bermudian hotelier, who renamed her 'Priscilla' and began the local cruise boat trade for tourists, later a popular pastime). At Fort St. Catherine, there was a magnetic loop control station for the detection of submarines. At "Southlands" on the south coast of Warwick Parish (Fig. 9.29), a major Anti-aircraft Training Center (AATC) was established for the practise firing of 40 mm Twin Bofors and smaller 20 mm and 3-inch AA guns, as well as machine guns. The tracer fire at night provided a source of entertainment for the nearby residents. Other United States Army support or service troops, such as Medical, Military Police, Quartermaster, Engineers and Ordnance, also contributed to the defence of Bermuda, but their role and histories are beyond the scope of this book.

• • •

MISSION & GENERAL COMMAND

The Bermuda bases were acquired for the operation of air and naval forces for the protection of air and sea approaches to the United States in the Western Atlantic, and to provide defences to prevent the establishment of an enemy force in these islands. The mission given to the Combined Local Defence Forces, Bermuda—the Bermuda Base Command being its major part—by CINCLANT was to 'give warning of the approach of hostile forces by full use of such equipment as may be provided, including twenty-four hour operation of aircraft warning equipment. These forces will maintain and operate such facilities as may be needed and available for the destruction of Axis forces, for the defence of Bermuda, and for vessels operating from this Base and in this vicinity. These forces will provide a system of scouting and patrol to give timely warning of attack.'[53]

To achieve this mission, it was organised into the Combined Army Local Defence Forces (which was all U.S. and British army units, except Defence Security personnel); the Combined Naval Local Defence Forces (all naval forces in Bermuda, with the exception of the headquarters of the Admiral, America and West Indies Station, Royal Navy), and the Royal Air Force Local Defence

[53] Ibid.

FIGURE 9.30: The Royal Air Force flying boat base on Darrell's Island during the Second World War (BMM Archives).

FIGURE 9.31: Standing guard at Darrell's Island during the War (BMM Archives).

Forces. In the first instance, the headquarters was at the Bermuda Base Command, under which the air, coastal, land defence, and general reserve was placed. The naval force had its headquarters at the U.S. Naval Operating Base and covered defensive activities at HM Dockyard, submarine, aircraft patrol, offshore ship patrol, harbour and inshore patrols, mine sweepers and underwater defence. The Royal Air Force division had to defend its base on Darrell's Island and provide for other RAF requirements (Figs. 9.30–31). The exception to all this was the Defence Security Officer, British Army, who was responsible for sabotage and subversive activities outside U.S.-leased land, and for the examination of all shipping and aircraft, both people and goods, calling at the island. He was not under CINCLANT command, but responsible directly to the Governor of Bermuda.

• • •

SUMMARY

Looking back over the half-century since the raising of the American Flag on March 1, 1941, it is easy to see that this mission was carried out with considerable success. Yet while the United States, and the wider free world, benefitted from this major intrusion into a very small island, Bermuda itself has had many blessings to count from this historic turn of events brought about by the invasion of Poland by Hitler (Fig. 9.32). The end of the war ushered in a new age of airborne tourism: Kindley Field—entirely at the expense of the United

States—provided the only means by which Bermuda could take advantage of this evolution in worldwide travel. By the same token, the making of the new North Channel from the Narrows to Grassy Bay for the American forces in the Second World War allows the entry of large cruise ships, which otherwise would bypass the island. When the United States forces left Bermuda in 1995, they left behind a precious legacy in the form of eight hundred acres of ground which did not exist in 1941. Now it may be said that the support of the fragile tourist economy is the only defence Bermuda's American allies might now provide: given the

FIGURE 9.32: All's well: Sgt. Michael Q. Wagner, U.S.A.A.F. (formerly Battery B, 53rd Coast Artillery), marries Bermudian Miss Rita Alves during the Second World War (BMM Archives).

modern precision bombing seen in the 1991 Persian Gulf War, the idea of coastal defence for Bermuda is as much a thing of the past as the relics of World War Two which this chapter set out to describe.

In 1910, the British coastal artillery guns at Bermuda numbered twenty-two; at the beginning of the Second World War, these had been reduced to only two. During the War, two more were installed by the British and the Americans brought in twelve pieces. The calibre and placement of these weapons is listed in the table below:

Fort/Gun	6" British	155 mm GPF	6" USA	8" Railway	Totals
Victoria	–	–	2	2	4
St. David's	2				2
Cooper's Island	–	2	–	–	2
Warwick Camp	2	–	–	–	2
Turtle Hill	–	2	–	–	2
Tudor Hill	–	–	2	–	2
Scaur Hill	–	–	–	2	2
Totals	4	4	4	4	16

The American railway guns were removed as early as 1944 and the remainder of their weapons were taken away shortly after the war, ending any effective coastal defence of Bermuda after three hundred and thirty-three years.

During the War, the British military had recommended four 9.2-inch guns, two to be placed at Scaur Hill Fort, one at Ireland Island and one in St.

George's.[54] In December 1942, three 5.25-inch CA/AA guns were approved for St. David's and these were retained as approved, along with one 6-inch gun at Warwick Camp in July 1946, after the end of the War.[55] The death knell of coastal defence was already at hand, however, in the form of the German missiles:

FIGURE 9.33: Men of the Duke of Cornwall's Light Infantry leaving the City of Hamilton in 1957 on the Chauncey M. Depew, when the British Garrison was withdrawn from Bermuda after 256 years (author's collection).

In May, 1945, the Chiefs of Staff considered a report by the Defence of Bases Committee in which scales of coast artillery, based on the types of weapons approved by the Chiefs of Staff, were proposed for the future defence of ports and bases at Home and Abroad. Some of the weapons recommended have yet to be designed and it is now improbable that they will materialise for several years, if indeed, they ever do, for they may in the meantime be superseded by unorthodox weapons as a result of research at present in progress.[56]

In 1956, coastal defence was declared obsolete throughout most of the British possessions, including Bermuda. When the detachment of the Duke of Cornwall's Light Infantry embarked at Hamilton in the early summer of the following year (Fig. 9.33), the departure of the garrison signalled the end of a military purpose for the remnants of Bermuda's guns and fortifications. With the closure of the Royal Naval Base, HMS *Malabar*, on March 31, 1995, Bermuda's direct connection with a British military presence in the islands ceased, ending an association that began with the posting of a small garrison in 1701 and had endured nigh on 300 years.

■ ■ ■

54 War Cabinet, Review of Fixed Coast Defences at Defended Ports at Home and Abroad, June 1, 1942. I thank Cdr. Charles Robbins, U.S.N. (ret.) for copies of these papers.

55 Minister of Defence, Review of Fixed Coast Artillery Defences at Defended Ports at Home and Abroad, July 1, 1946.

56 Minister of Defence, Interim Scales of Coast Artillery Defence at Ports and Bases at Home and Abroad, December 2, 1946.

Schoolchildren examining the 12.5-inch RMLs at Fort Cunningham in 1992.

10

Camps, Magazines & Historic Artillery

1 8 4 0 – 1 9 9 7

The islands which make up Bermuda have one of the most outstanding and varied collections of historic artillery, which would be hard to find in such quantity in any other location. They range from forged wrought-iron guns of the sixteenth century through to the twentieth century, with examples of Armstrong's first successful breech-loading gun of the early 1860s. Very well represented are the Rifled Muzzle-Loading guns of Armstrong construction depicted by Armstrong's original Mark I of 7-inch of seven tons and the 9-inch of twelve tons. Until it can be proved otherwise, Bermuda holds the only remaining components in the world of the Mark II Moncrieff Disappearing Carriage of the 1860/70s.

—A. Collin Carpenter, 1995

THE BERMUDA CAMPS

WHILE BERMUDA HAD HAD A SMALL GARRISON FROM 1701 ONWARDS, IT was only during the nineteenth century that permanent accommodation was established at St. George's, at Prospect in Devonshire Parish and at Boaz Island in Sandys Parish. Two other sites, St. David's and Warwick Camp were used for occasional exercises.

The St. George's site was acquired from the late 1820s, when work began on four forts, which were eventually surrounded by the military lands (Fig. 10.1). The St. George's garrison occupied most of the land to the east of the Town of St. George and remained in the possession of the British forces until the early 1950s. The camp had all the necessaries, such as a recreation ground, a hospital, cottages for the married officers, a church and barracks (Fig. 10.2). It incorporated the original Royal Naval yard at Convict Bay, which was used by the Royal Engineers. The lands passed to the Bermuda Government in the early 1950s, following which many of the buildings went into a decline or were demolished.

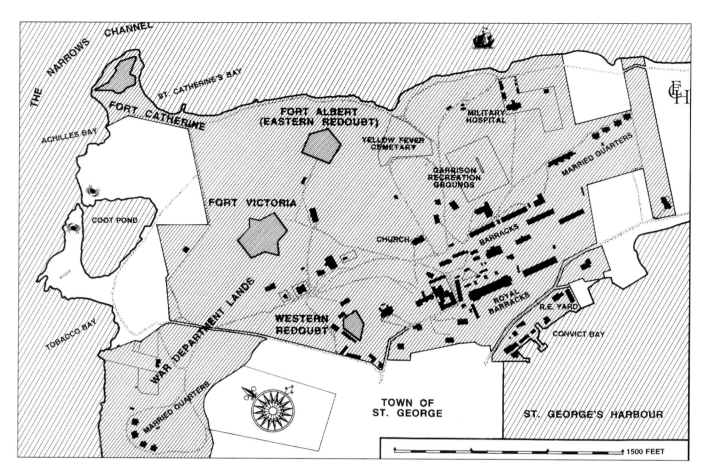

FIGURE 10.1: *The St. George's Camp and military lands occupied most of the eastern part of St. George's Island.*

FIGURE 10.2: *Drill on the parade ground in front of the Royal Barracks at St. George's Camp in the late nineteenth century (author's collection).*

After the establishment of St. David's Battery in the first decade of the twentieth century, it became a training camp for artillery drills on the two 6-inch BL guns (Fig. 10.3). After 1913, these appear to have been the only operational guns at Bermuda, so the site was of some importance as the only place where the local militias could gain gunnery experience (Fig. 10.4).

FIGURE 10.3: *A tent camp of the Bermuda Volunteer Engineers at St. David's Battery, possibly in the 1920s (Bermuda Archives, P. Acc. 82).*

FIGURE 10.4: *The Bermuda Militia Artillery training on the northern 6-inch BL gun at St. David's Battery, probably in the 1930s (Bermuda Library).*

In the central parishes starting in the 1840s, the military purchased several hundred acres of land to provide for the building of Forts Hamilton, Prospect and Langton and for a camp (Fig. 10.5). Prospect Camp eventually became the largest in Bermuda and the headquarters of the garrison (Fig. 10.6). The first barracks were built in the 1870s and appear to have been replaced some twenty years later (Fig. 10.7). As at St. George's, there were many ancillary buildings and the cricket ground was often seconded for drills (Fig. 10.8). Falling to the possession of the Bermuda Government in the 1950s, many of the buildings have since been demolished.

On the south shore in Warwick Parish, a training camp was established in the later nineteenth century, with stone barracks probably being built between the World Wars (Figs. 10.9–10). In the nineteenth century, there were several permanent buildings, but camping was in tents (Figs. 10.11–13). The beaches

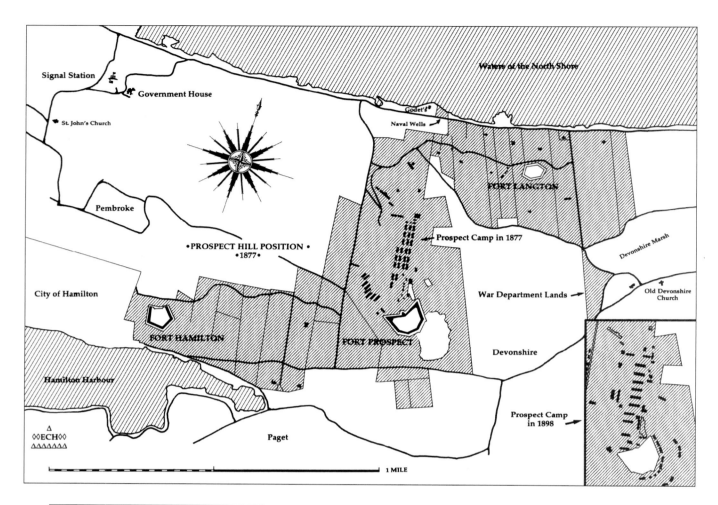

Signal Station

Government House

St. John's Church

Pembroke

•PROSPECT HILL POSITION •
•1877•

City of Hamilton

FORT HAMILTON

Hamilton Harbour

△
◇◇ECH◇◇
△△△△△△△

Paget

Waters of the North Shore

Godet'

Naval Wells

FORT LANGTON

Prospect Camp in 1877

War Department Lands

FORT PROSPECT

Devonshire

Devonshire Marsh

Old Devonshire Church

Prospect Camp in 1898

1 MILE

FIGURE 10.5: Prospect Camp and the forts of the Prospect Position separated the parishes of Pembroke and Devonshire in the later nineteenth century.

FIGURE 10.6: The Officer's Quarters at "Park Lane" at Prospect Camp, Lieut. Stewart Cleeve, R.E., with 'Sibyl' and 'Dot' in the 1870s (National Army Museum, 7511-26).

FIGURE 10.7 (inset): Two storey barracks with cast iron verandas were constructed at Prospect Camp in the late nineteenth century (Bermuda Archives, P. Acc. 64).

FIGURE 10.8: *The cricket ground at Prospect Camp in use as a drill parade in the later nineteenth century (National Army Museum, 7511-26).*

FIGURE 10.9: *Warwick Camp as it would have appeared on the ground in the 1940s, with masonry bases for tents.*

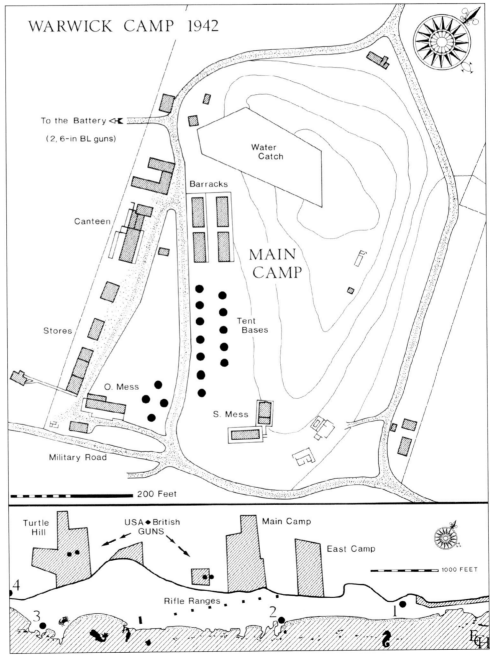

and sand dunes of the coast adjacent to Warwick Camp made an ideal training ground for military exercises and rifle practice. In 1965, Warwick Camp became the head-quarters of the newly-formed Bermuda Regiment.

There was also a camp on Boaz Island to the south of the Dockyard (Fig. 10.14): a fuller history of all the camps, however, must await the results of another study.

FIGURE 10.10: *Warwick Camp from the air in the early 1990s: barrack buildings have replaced the tent platforms of earlier decades.*

FIGURE 10.11: *The South Road as it passed Warwick Camp in the 1870s, the Officers' Mess is on the right (National Army Museum, 7511-26).*

FIGURE 10.12: *The Officers' Mess and tents at Warwick Camp in the late spring of 1910 (Bedfordshire Record Office, X550/1/80).*

FIGURE 10.13: *The main buildings and tent area at Warwick Camp in May 1910 (Bedfordshire Record Office, X550/1/80).*

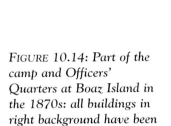

FIGURE 10.13: *The main buildings and tent area at Warwick Camp in May 1910 (Bedfordshire Record Office, X550/1/80).*

FIGURE 10.14: *Part of the camp and Officers' Quarters at Boaz Island in the 1870s: all buildings in right background have been demolished (National Army Museum, 7511-26).*

• • •

MAGAZINES & HISTORIC ARTILLERY

All of the fortifications had their own magazines and the Dockyard also had an ordnance yard, primarily for the Sea Service. In the first decade of the nineteenth century, two small outcrops in St. George's Harbour were joined together by land-filling and became 'Ordnance Island' (Fig. 10.15). This man-made island, just south of the Town Square, became a major depot for ordnance in the nineteenth century (Fig. 10.16).

FIGURE 10.15: *Ordnance Island from the air, looking north-east, in the 1980s, with the Town of St. George behind it.*

Two other independent magazines were built in the nineteenth century. The one on Agar's Island (Fig. 10.17) was the largest magazine ever constructed in Bermuda for the weapons of the Rifled Muzzle Loader period (1865–95). It consisted of ten ammunition bays, under a brick and concrete bomb-proof roof (Fig. 10.18). The other magazine was built at the end of the period on Boaz Island (Fig. 10.19): both were in reasonable condition in the 1980s.

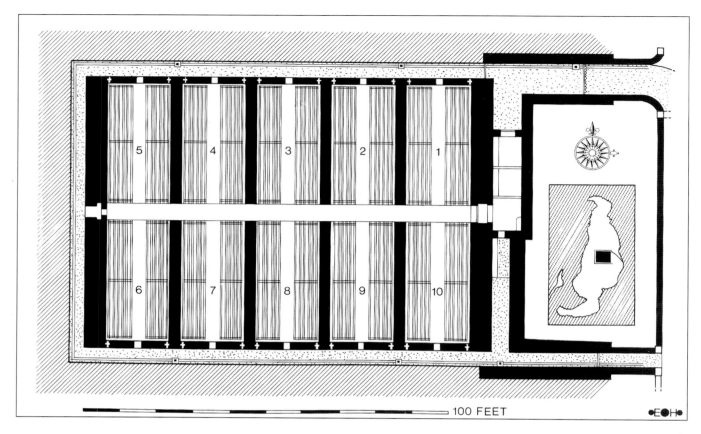

FIGURE 10.17: *The plan of Bermuda's largest Rifled Muzzle Loader magazine at Agar's Island, Pembroke Parish (redrawn from a record plan, courtesy of Donald Cox).*

FIGURE 10.16: *Ordnance Island in the later nineteenth century: RML projectiles are stacked to the left, with mortar shells to the right (Bermuda Archives).*

Of all the cannon used at Bermuda from 1612–1957, some one hundred and forty-odd pieces are still in the island. Many are used as bollards or as the pivots for later gun slides and carriages. In his classic work on cannon, Austin Collin Carpenter devoted a chapter to historical weapons at Bermuda, based on two research visits in the 1980s (Fig. 10.20).[1] The purpose of this chapter is to note briefly the nature of the guns which are located at forts which can

[1] Austin C. Carpenter, *Cannon: the Conservation, Reconstruction and Presentation of Historic Artillery* (1993). I am much indebted to Collin and Jenny Carpenter for their interest and inspiration on all matters to do with the historic artillery of Bermuda.

FIGURE 10.18: *A view of the RML magazine at Agar's Island under construction in the 1880s (courtesy of* The Bermudian*).*

FIGURE 10.19 (right): *The Rifled Muzzle Loader magazine built at Boaz Island in the late 1880s and its wharf, from the air in the 1940s (author's collection).*

FIGURE 10.20 (far right): *Collin and Jenny Carpenter, recorders and restorers of Bermuda's historic artillery with one of their English restorations.*

be readily seen by the public.[2] The reader is referred to Mr. Carpenter's excellent treatise for the development of artillery and the evolutionary history of certain types of guns, such as the Rifled Muzzle Loader.

• • •

FIGURE 10.21: *The 11-inch Rifled Muzzle Loader of 25 tons at Fort George is still on its original carriage and slide.*

[2] Most of the details on the guns were taken from the 1985 survey by Collin and Jenny Carpenter, commissioned by the Bermuda Maritime Museum.

FORT GEORGE

This site has the only RMLs still mounted in the 1990s in their original position on their original carriages and slides (Fig. 10.21).

RML	11-inch	25 tons	**RGF No. 12 II 1871**
RML	11-inch	25 tons	**RGF No. 14 II 1871**

• • •

ORDNANCE ISLAND

FIGURE 10.22: A converted 64-pounder Rifled Muzzle Loader was last used as a bollard at Penno's Wharf in St. George's.

FIGURE 10.23: The detail of the left trunnion of the Penno's Wharf RML reads: Sir W. G. Armstrong Co [maker] No 687 [serial number] I [mark] 1871 [date].

There are several guns of note on this site and at the Town Square nearby. Several converted RMLs and 40-pounder Armstrong RBLs are to be found as bollards at Penno's Wharf on the western end of the Town of St. George; one was dug up in the 1990s (Figs. 10.22–23)

Cannon	24-pdr	George III	**W Co.** 230
RML Converted	64-pdr	**No 687 I 1871**	**Sir W.G. Armstrong Co**
RML Converted	64-pdr	Victoria	**RGF No. 79? 18??**
RML	7-inch	6.5 tons	**RGF No. 144 I 1866**
RML	9-inch	12 tons	**RGF No. 142 I 1867**

• • •

FORT VICTORIA

Figure 10.24: The 9.2-inch Breech Loading gun photographed at Fort Victoria in 1934 (Bermuda Archives, Roger Willock Collection).

Figure 10.25: The 9.2-inch Breech Loading gun at Fort Victoria in the 1980s, looking eastwards.

Aside from those cannon used as pivots, the only piece at this fort is the well preserved 9.2-inch Breech Loader from about 1904 (Fig. 10.24–25).

BL	9.2-inch	**X No 272**	**V. S. & M. 1902**

• • •

FORT ST. CATHERINE

Four of the guns at this site were brought from Fort Albert in the 1960s; the original five were pushed into the sea, where they were in the 1990s. The single 9-inch RML may have come from Alexandra Battery or Fort Cunningham. The additional 10-inch RML barrel may have been a spare. The 9-pounder RBL stood for many years outside the Western Redoubt (Fig. 10.26) and the RBL 40-pounder probably came from the saluting battery at Fort Victoria, seen by Roger Willock in 1934 (Figs. 10.27–29).

FIGURE 10.26: A 9-pounder RML of 6 cwt on a wrought iron carriage outside the Western Redoubt in the 1980s, later moved to Fort St. Catherine.

FIGURE 10.27: A 10-inch RML at Fort St. Catherine on an original carriage and slide, brought there from Fort Albert in the 1960s.

RBL	9-pdr	6 cwt	**RGF No. 403 II 1875**
RBL	40-pdr	35 cwt	**RGF No. 236-G I 1863**
RML (in the sea)	10-inch	18 tons	Details corroded.
RML (on the rocks)	10-inch	18 tons	Details corroded.
RML (on the beach)	10-inch	18 tons	Details corroded.
RML (on the beach)	10-inch	18 tons	Details corroded.
RML (on the beach)	10-inch	18 tons	Details corroded.
RML (?Alexandra)	9-inch	12 tons	**RGF No. 148 I 1867**
RML (?Spare)	10-inch	18 tons	**RGF No. 156 II 1871**
RML (?Albert)	10-inch	18 tons	**RGF No. 180 II 1871**
RML (?Albert)	10-inch	18 tons	**? No. 195 ? ?**
RML (?Albert)	10-inch	18 tons	**RGF No. 221 II 1872**
RML (?Albert)	10-inch	18 tons	**RGF No. 224 II 1872**
RML (Victoria)	11-inch	25 tons	**RGF No. 1?? II 1871**
BL	6-inch	Retubed 7/40	**V.S.&M. 1901 No. 1368**

FIGURE 10.28 (right):
Awaiting rescue: one of the
original 10-inch RMLs
from Fort St. Catherine lies
on the beach below the fort.

FIGURE 10.29 (far right):
This position for a 64-
pounder RML was modified
to take the 6-inch BL gun
as a part of the exhibition of
Fort St. Catherine in the
1960s.

• • •

ALEXANDRA BATTERY

FIGURE 10.30: The 9-inch
RML at the restored
'Gibraltar Shield' at
Alexandra Battery is missing
its traversing slide.

FIGURE 10.31: The restored
'Gibraltar Shield' at
Alexandra Battery from
seaward with the muzzle of
the 9-inch RML.

The five RMLs from this site were missing in the 1980s, at which time a gun
of the right type and calibre was placed on display, on loan from the Bermuda
Maritime Museum (Figs. 10.30-31).

RML	9-inch	12 tons	**RGF No. 272 III 1868**

• • •

TOWN CUT BATTERY

These two guns have been at the site for many years, but in the 1980s they were mounted on cast iron garrison standing carriages, replicated under the supervision of A. C. Carpenter.

Cannon	24-pdr	George III	**W Co. ?89**
Cannon	24-pdr	George III	**W Co. 54**

• • •

FORT CUNNINGHAM

FIGURE 10.32: Seven RMLs were pushed into the ditch from the roof of Fort Cunningham in the early twentieth century.

FIGURE 10.33 (far left): Details of the 10-inch RML, No. 338, Royal Gun Factory, Mark II of 1878: the edge of the trunnion was crushed when the gun struck another when it was pushed into the ditch at Fort Cunningham.

FIGURE 10.34 (left): Six 12.5-inch RML shells with bronze studs to engage the rifling in the gun barrel, thus imparting a spin to the projectile, each weighing 800 lbs.

Seven of the original nine Rifled Muzzle Loaders emplaced at this site after 1878 were pushed into the northern run of the ditch about twenty years later. They were covered by a new glacis for the BL guns and were discovered in archaeological excavations in 1991 (Figs. 10.32–34).

RML	10-inch	18 tons	**RGF No. 338 II 1878**
RML	10-inch	18 tons	**RGF No. 340 II 1878**
RML	10-inch	18 tons	**RGF No. 342 II 1878**
RML	10-inch	18 tons	**RGF No. 356 II 1878**
RML	10-inch	18 tons	**RGF No. 357 II 1878**
RML	12.5-inch	38 tons	**RGF No. 87 I 1878**
RML	12.5-inch	38 tons	**RGF No. 95 I 1878**

• • •

ST. DAVID'S BATTERY

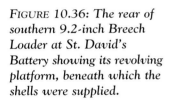

FIGURE 10.35: *The southern 9.2-inch Breech Loader at St. David's Battery after sandblasting and painting in the 1990s.*

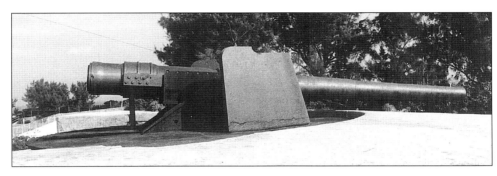

FIGURE 10.36: *The rear of southern 9.2-inch Breech Loader at St. David's Battery showing its revolving platform, beneath which the shells were supplied.*

The guns at this site were installed towards the end of the first decade of the twentieth century and were still in place in the 1980s (Fig. 10.35–36).

BL	6-inch	North gun.	Details corroded.
BL	6-inch	South gun.	Details corroded.
BL	9.2-inch	North gun.	**E.O.C. 1901 No-. 193**
BL	9.2-inch	South gun.	**E.O.C. 1902 No-. 205**

• • •

FORT HAMILTON

FIGURE 10.37: *Two of the three 10-inch RMLs from Fort Langton that were mounted in the pits for the 64-pounder RMLs on disappearing carriages at Fort Hamilton.*

The three guns at Fort Hamilton were taken there from the ditch at Fort Langton in the 1960s (Fig. 10.37). Details on the trunnions are partly buried in concrete, so it was not possible in the 1980s to ascertain all of their serial numbers and dates of manufacture. The original guns at this site were converted 64-pounder RMLs on disappearing carriages, all now lost.

RML	10-inch	18 tons	**RGF No. 194** ? ?
RML	10-inch	18 tons	**RGF** ? ? ? ?
RML	10-inch	18 tons	**RGF** ? ? ? ?

• • •

GOVERNMENT HOUSE

From the time of its establishment on its present site in the later nineteenth century, it appears that there were three carronades at Government House, perhaps for signalling. They appear in a watercolour by a relative of Governor J. Henry Lefroy in the 1870s (Fig. 10.38). The guns are mounted in front of the present Government House on their original cast iron carriages (Fig. 10.39–40).

FIGURE 10.38: *A water-colour of the 1870s looking west from the then Government House at Langton Hill, with two carronades (courtesy of Hugh Davidson).*

FIGURE 10.39 (right):
Three 24-pounder
carronades at Government
House on original cast iron
carriages, probably two of
those shown in Figure
10.38.

FIGURE 10.40 (far right):
A detail of the markings on
the underside of the cascabel
patch of one of the
24-pounder carronades
at Government House.

Carronade	24-pdr	George III	**24PDR 1783 No 39926**
Carronade	24-pdr	George III	**24PDR 1783 No 39930**
Carronade	24-pdr	George III	**24PDR 1783 No 39960**

• • •

WARWICK CAMP

FIGURE 10.41: The barrel
for a 6-inch BL gun being
moved from the City of
Hamilton docks around the
beginning of war in 1939,
possibly bound for Warwick
Camp (Bermuda Library).

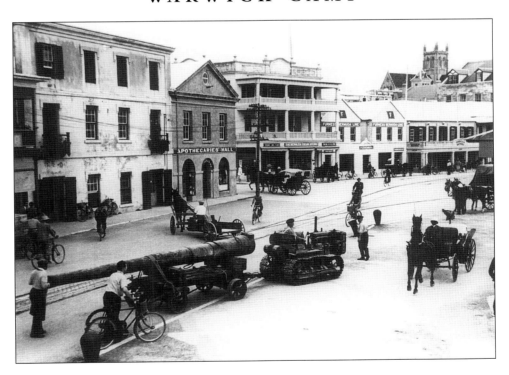

The two Breech Loading guns at this site were brought there in 1939 and
1940 and remain intact (Figs. 10.41–43).

FIGURE 10.42 (far left): The eastern 6-inch BL gun at Warwick Camp with the barrel resting on the tampion and the gun encased in a shrapnel shield.

FIGURE 10.43 (left): The eastern 6-inch BL gun at Warwick Camp from the rear, showing its concrete emplacement of 1939, but typical of works in 1905.

| BL, east gun | 6-inch | Corroded. | **RGF 1900 No. L/1376** |
| BL, west gun | 6-inch | **Retubed 7/40.** | **RGF 1900 No. L/1467** |

• • •

SCAUR HILL FORT

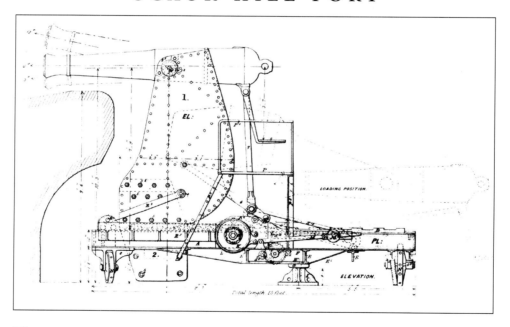

FIGURE 10.44: An 1875 drawing of the 64-pounder converted RML on a Moncrieff disappearing carriage, Mark II, of which some parts survive at Bermuda (Royal Artillery Institution, Woolwich).

There were two 64-pounder RMLs at this fort, converted from 32-pounder smooth-bore guns by the insertion of a rifled liner. They were installed on Moncrieff disappearing carriages (Fig. 10.44), of which a few pieces have survived and were on display at the site in the 1990s (Figs. 10.45-47). Two barrels were at the Bermuda Maritime Museum in the 1980s, at which time one was sent to Scaur Hill.

| RML Converted | 64-pdr | 59 cwt | **RGF No. 774 I 1877** |

FIGURE 10.45 (right): The gun pit at Scaur Hill Fort in the late 1980s with its 64-pounder converted RML and racer and pivot for a disappearing carriage.

FIGURE 10.46 (far right): Michael Lohan, left, of Stevedoring Services, Ltd, donated a counterweight for a Moncrieff disappearing carriage, Mark II, for display at Scaur Hill Fort (Robin Sturdy on right).

FIGURE 10.47: Two cheeks for a Moncrieff disappearing carriage, Mark II, for a 64-pounder converted RML at Scaur Hill Fort.

• • •

THE DOCKYARD KEEP

FIGURE 10.48: A 32-pounder smooth-bore cannon on a replica cast iron garrison standing carriage at the Bermuda Maritime Museum.

The Bermuda Maritime Museum, which occupies the Keep of the old Royal Naval Dockyard, has been collecting cannon since its inception in 1974. The following list is not complete, but relates to guns on display in the 1980s. The collection of the Museum comprises some fifty pieces, a number of which are used as pivots in the emplacements of the Keep. Others, including important sixteenth-century pieces, have come from shipwrecks and were not used on the Bermuda forts, but represent the types of weapons which could have been employed had the island been settled in earlier times (Figs. 10.48–60).

FIGURE 10.49 (far left): A canister of grape shot was found in the barrel of one of the 32-pounder cannon from Fort Langton by the late Douglas Little of the Bermuda Maritime Museum.

FIGURE 10.50 (left): Two 40-pounder Rifled Breech Loaders on siege carriages of the 1860s, photographed at Fort Victoria in 1934 (Bermuda Archives, Roger Willock Collection).

FIGURE 10.51: A 68-pounder smooth-bore cannon on a replica cast iron traversing carriage and slide at the Bermuda Maritime Museum (designed by A. C. Carpenter).

FIGURE 10.52: Capt. Adrian Caruana firing the 68-pounder smooth-bore gun at the Bermuda Maritime Museum in 1993.

FIGURE 10.53 (right): A 40-pounder Rifled Breech Loader was found at Bailey's Bay Battery in the 1980s and donated to the Bermuda Maritime Museum by Richard and Helen Fraser.

FIGURE 10.54 (far right): Dennis Correia donated his services to recover three 9-inch RMLs, Mark I, from the wreck of HMS Irresistible.

FIGURE 10.55: The late Major W. H. ('Bubbles') Burnard, Bermuda Regiment, and Collin Carpenter fire the 40-pounder Rifled Breech Loader from Bailey's Bay Battery from the ramparts of the Dockyard Keep in 1990.

FIGURE 10.56: A reproduction carriage for the 9-pounder RML of 8 cwt at the Bermuda Maritime Museum, designed by Collin Carpenter and donated by Charles and Maud Rheault.

FIGURE 10.57: The ramparts of the Dockyard Keep were under restoration by the Bermuda Maritime Museum in the 1990s: the gun is a 10-inch RML.

FIGURE 10.58: Earlston Cann and Dennis Butterfield of the Bermuda Maritime Museum and other workmen discuss the two 10-inch RMLs found at the Dockyard Keep in the late 1980s.

FIGURE 10.59: Two 6-inch BL barrels, a Mark II and possibly a Mark IV of the 1880s have been mounted at Bastion 'E' on the ramparts of the Dockyard Keep.

FIGURE 10.60: A spare 6-inch BL barrel was moved by the U. S. Navy in the late 1980s from St. David's Battery for display on an existing carriage at Bastion 'D' of the Dockyard Keep.

Dockyard Keep armaments

Cannon	9-pdr	Tudor Rose	?
Cannon, Bronze	6-pdr	George II	**W. BOWEN FECIT 1756**
Cannon	18-pdr	George II	**B**
Cannon	18-pdr	George III	**B SOLID**
Cannon	24-pdr	George III	**B SOLID**
Cannon	24-pdr	George III	**Z SOLID 601**
Cannon	24-pdr	George III	**Z 107**
Cannon (Langton)	32-pdr	George III	**70680 CARRON 1807**
Cannon	32-pdr	George III	**70696 CARRON 1807**
Cannon (Langton)	32-pdr	George III	**70721 CARRON 1807**
Cannon	32-pdr	George III	**71362 CARRON 1807**
Cannon (Langton)	32-pdr	George III	**W Co 15**
Cannon (Admiralty)	68-pdr	Victoria	**W Co 693 1858**
RBL	9-pdr	8 cwt	**RGF No. 1180 II 187?**
RBL (Bailey's Bay)	40-pdr	35 cwt	**RGF No. 263-G I 1864**
RML (Scaur Hill)	64-pdr	59 cwt	**RGF No. 801 I 1878**
RML	9-inch	12 tons	**RGF No. 182 I 1867**
RML	9-inch	12 tons	**RGF No. 195 I 1867**
RML	9-inch	12 tons	[RGF No. ?] **I** [18??]
RML (Keep)	10-inch	18 tons	**RGF No. 183 II 1871**
RML (Keep)	10-inch	18 tons	**RGF No. 344 II 1878**
BL	6-inch	**80 CWT.**	**RGF II 1882**
BL	6-inch		Possibly Mark IV.
BL (St. David's)	6-inch	**Retubed 1941**	**RGF 1899 No. L/1029**
BL (Warwick Camp)	6-inch		? ? ?

• • •

SUMMARY

The forts and surviving artillery at Bermuda represent almost the entire span of artillery fortifications. This is certainly the case with regard to the coastal defence of the British Empire outside Europe. While it does not have any of the large bastioned works of the eighteenth century, there is little to compare with the early Bermuda works of the seventeenth century. The collection of RML guns is perhaps the largest in the world and there is every suggestion that none of these guns left Bermuda, so that there are more to be discovered in the fullness of time. Taken as a whole, Bermuda would have few competitors for the breadth and quality of its artillery fortifications, sites and guns, all contained within a mere twenty square miles, if properly conserved, reconstructed and professionally presented to the public.

■ ■ ■

Regiments Stationed at Bermuda

1 7 0 1 – 1 9 5 7

With the return of the detachment from Bermuda in May or June, our association with the colony will probably end...Except for a short period in 1953–4, a British Garrison has been stationed at Bermuda continuously from 1701 and was restored in 1954 at the instigation of Sir Winston Churchill 'to help maintain the British position in the Western Atlantic.'

—Journal of the Duke of Cornwall's Light Infantry, May 1957

1701–1764	The Independent Company
1764–1768	Detachment IXth Regiment
1779–1783	Royal Garrison Battalion
1783	47th Regiment
1804	The Royal Fusiliers
1806	99th Regiment
1808	1st Somersetshire Regiment
1814	85th King's Light Infantry
1815	Detachment 3rd Battalion, 27th (Inniskilling) Regiment
1815	1st Battalion, 27th (Inniskilling) Regiment
1816	100th Regiment
1819	62nd Regiment

1819–1821	Right Wing, 15th Regiment
1821	Left Wing, 2nd Battalion, 60th Regiment
1825–1826	96th Regiment
1828–1830	74th Regiment
1829–1831	81st Regiment (Royal Lincoln Volunteers)
1830–1832	37th Foot
1831–1834	71st Regiment
1833	8th Regiment
1835–1840	30th Regiment
1838	11th Regiment
1840–1841	76th (Hindoostan) Regiment of Foot
1841–1847	1st and Reserve Battalions, 20th Regiment
1847–1851	1st and 2nd Battalions, 42nd Regiment
1851–1853	56th Regiment
1854–1859	26th Foot
1859	39th Regiment
1866–1870	61st Foot
1866	2nd Battalion, 2nd Queens Regiment
1868–1870	1st Battalion, 15th Regiment
1870–1875	53rd (Shropshire) Regiment
1870–1873	69th Regiment
1873–1876	1st Battalion, 20th Regiment
1875–1877	97th Regiment
1876–1879	46th Regiment of Foot
1877	87th Regiment
1877–1880	1st Battalion, 19th Regiment
1877–1878	87th Royal Irish Fusiliers
1880–1881	99th (Duke of Edinburgh's) Regiment
1880–1881	86th Regiment of Foot
1881–1883	2nd Battalion, Royal Irish Rifles

1883–1886	2nd Battalion, The York and Lancaster Regiment
1886–1888	2nd Battalion, The Duke of Wellington's Regiment
1888–1891	1st Battalion, The Leicestershire Regiment
1890–1891	2nd Battalion, The Grenadier Guards
1891–1893	1st Battalion, The King's Regiment (Liverpool)
1893–1895	1st Battalion, The Royal Berkshire Regiment
1897	2nd Battalion, The Leicestershire Regiment
1897–1899	2nd Battalion, The Worcestershire Regiment
1901	1st West India Regiment
1902–1904	3rd Battalion, The Royal Warwickshire Regiment
1903	4th Battalion, The Worcestershire Regiment
1903–1905	3rd Battalion, The Royal Fusiliers
1904–1905	3rd Battalion, The King's Royal Rifle Corps
1905–1907	2nd Battalion, The Hampshire Regiment
1907–1910	2nd Battalion, Duke of Cornwall's Light Infantry
1910–1912	2nd Battalion, The Bedfordshire Regiment
1912–1914	2nd Battalion, The Queen's Regiment
1914	2nd Battalion, The Lincolnshire Regiment
1914–1916	Royal Canadian Regiment, 38th Ottawa Battalion 77th French Canadian Regiment
1916–1919	2nd/4th Battalion, The East Yorkshire Regiment
1919–1921	Wing, 2nd Battalion, The Royal Sussex Regiment
1921–1923	Wing, 1st Battalion, The East Lancashire Regiment
1923–1925	Wing, 1st Battalion, The Royal Norfolk Regiment
1925–1927	2nd Battalion, The Green Howards
1927–1929	2nd Battalion, Argyll & Sutherland Highlanders
1929–1931	Wing, 1st Battalion, The West Yorkshire Regiment
1931–1934	Wing, 1st Battalion, The Northumberland Fusiliers
1934–1938	Wing, 1st Battalion, The Manchester Regiment
1938–1939	Wing, The Sherwood Foresters

1939–1940	Wing, 2nd Battalion, (85th) The King's Shropshire Light Infantry
1940	The Winnipeg Grenadiers
1942	Detachment, 4th Battalion, The Queen's Own Cameron Highlanders
1942	The Pictou Highlanders of Canada
1946–1947	Detachment, 8th Battalion, The Suffolk Regiment
1947–1948	Detachment, 2nd Battalion, The Gloucestershire Regiment
1948–1949	Detachment, 1st Battalion, The Gloucestershire Regiment
1949	Detachment, The Highland Brigade
1949–1953	Detachment, The Highland Brigade
1953	The Garrison temporarily withdrawn
1954	'A' Company, 1st Battalion, Duke of Cornwall's Light Infantry
1957	The Garrison withdrawn

Compiled from honour boards at Prospect Camp in the 1980s and from information supplied by Lance Furburt II, Curator, Fort St. Catherine, 1996.

■ ■ ■

The 2nd Battalion, the Bedfordshire Regiment at the unveiling of the Memorial Monument to Sir George Somers, St. George's, Bermuda, February 15, 1911.

Colour Plates

PLATE 1: *At what is now Guayanilla Bay, Puerto Rico, Sir Richard Grenville built the first English fort in the northern New World in 1585 (courtesy the Trustees of the British Museum).*

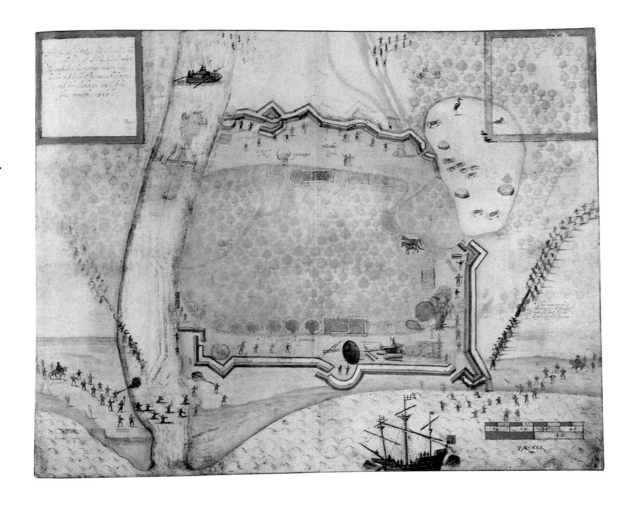

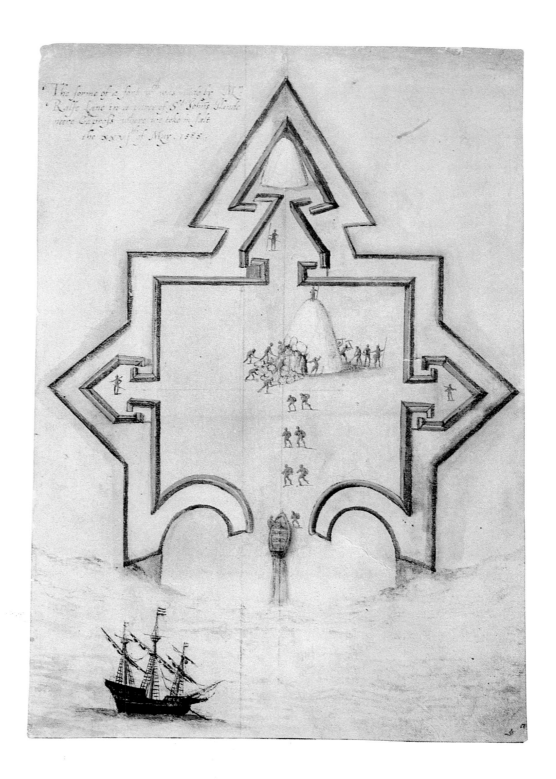

The forme of a fort w[hi]ch was made by M[aste]r Raife Lane in a place of St. Johns Ilande neere Capros where we tooke in Salt the xxvj of May 1585.

PLATE 2: *The second English fort in the northern Americas was erected near Cape Rojo, the south-western point of Puerto Rico in 1585 (courtesy the Trustees of the British Museum).*

PLATE 3: *A geological map of Bermuda shows that the older limestone, or 'hard-stone' only appears (orange) on the surface in a few places, the largest deposits which could be quarried being at the site of the Dockyard (courtesy of Mark Rowe).*

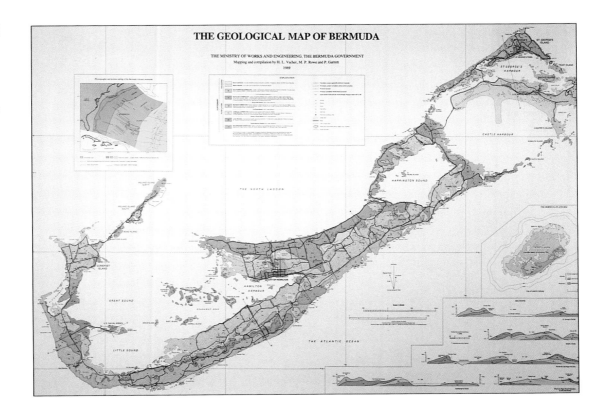

PLATE 4 : *Richard Norwood's third and last survey of Bermuda was made in 1662-3 and this copy survives in the Blathwayt Atlas (courtesy of The John Carter Brown Library).*

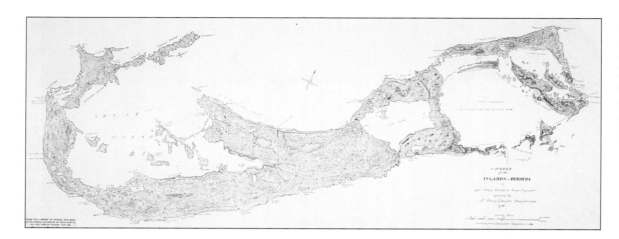

PLATE 5: Capt. Andrew Durnford, R.E., undertook the first ordnance survey of Bermuda in the early 1790s (courtesy of the Vaughan Library, Acadia University).

PLATE 6: Bermuda in an aerial photograph from the west; the Dockyard is in the left background (most of the aerial views are from the late 1980s and early 1990s).

PLATE 7: *Bermuda in an aerial view from the east; St. George's Island on the right.*

PLATE 8: *The eastern end of Bermuda with the airfield constructed by the American Forces in the Second World War in the centre.*

PLATE 9: Paget and St. George's Islands from the air, looking west (St. George's Island in right foreground).

PLATE 10: Castle Roads Channel with Charles and Castle Islands to the left and Southampton Island in right background.

PLATE 11: Castle Island and its three forts from the air, looking north-west.

PLATE 12: The Lower Battery of the King's Castle from the air.

PLATE 13: *The Captain's House and defensive ditch to the rear of the King's Castle in 1994.*

PLATE 14: *The tower and parapet (right) at Devonshire Redoubt date to 1621.*

PLATE 15: The Great Battery in the foreground at Devonshire Redoubt was built by Andrew Durnford in the 1790s.

PLATE 16: Castle Island from the south with the Landward Fort in the foreground.

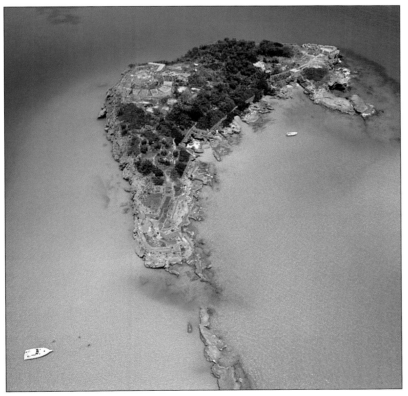

PLATE 17: *The Landward Fort on Castle Island was built before the 1680s.*

PLATE 18: *Southampton Island from the south with Southampton Fort standing almost as built in 1621.*

PLATE 19:
*Southampton Fort
from the north showing
the crenellated
landward defences.*

PLATE 20: *Fort Popple
in the right foreground
was excavated into the
bedrock at Little
Head, St. David's
Island.*

PLATE 21: *The magazine at Fort Bruere was cut into the bedrock and protected by an over-hang of rock.*

PLATE 22: *The position of Bailey's Bay Battery is preserved by two replica cannon in front of a home on the south shore.*

PLATE 23: *Hungry Bay Fort was a small half-moon battery defending the entrance to a small south shore inlet.*

PLATE 24: *The channel at Daniel's Island was partly blocked in the 1890s by the sinking of the obsolete HMS Vixen.*

PLATE 25: Daniel's Island Fort, a half-moon battery, was examined by archaeologists in the early 1990s.

PLATE 26: Burnt Point Fort on St. George's Island protected the Ferry Reach channel on the western side of Castle Harbour.

PLATE 27: *Ferry Island Fort occupies the summit of a small island on the northern side of the Ferry Reach channel.*

PLATE 28: *By the late 1820s, the channel at Ferry Reach was protected by a Martello Tower and a magazine was built to its rear (left centre).*

PLATE 29: *The Martello Tower at Ferry Point was placed within a ditch and entered by a drawbridge.*

PLATE 30: *The causeway from the mainland to Coney Island with the Martello Tower on the left and Fort George on the far right. (Plates 30 to 46 are reproduced from The Fay and Geoffrey Elliott Collection—held at the Bermuda Archives—courtesy of Mr. & Mrs. G. Elliott. Gaspard Le Marchant Tupper, the artist of these water-colours, was stationed in Bermuda with the Royal Regiment of Artillery from 1856 until 1858, to which years these views may be dated.)*

PLATE 31: *Ferry Reach passage with the bridge to Ferry Island and its fort on the left; on the opposite shore is the Ferry House on Coney Island.*

PLATE 32: *Looking east towards St. George's Harbour with St. David's Island in the right background and St. George's Island and Fort George at left.*

PLATE 33: *Looking west towards Ferry Reach with Fort George and its natural eastern escarpment.*

PLATE 34: *St. George's Harbour with Fort George on the left and the Town in the centre background.*

PLATE 35: *The eastern entrance to the Keep at Fort George; the cannon is mounted on a cast iron carriage and traversing slide.*

PLATE 36: *Looking south-east towards St. George's Harbour with Fort Victoria and the Western Redoubt on the left.*

PLATE 37: *The Royal Artillery Mess House at the St. George's Camp to the east of the Town of St. George.*

PLATE 38: *Looking east at Fort Albert from Fort Victoria; a cannon is mounted on a cast iron carriage and traversing slide.*

PLATE 39: Fort St. Catherine from the Narrows Channel with Fort Victoria on the hill with Fort Albert to its left.

PLATE 40: Looking towards Fort St. Catherine and the Narrows Channel from the south.

PLATE 41: The Bermuda Dockyard from the east.

PLATE 42: *The Dockyard from the south with the Land Front glacis and in the foreground is the small magazine on Cross Island.*

PLATE 43: *The Dockyard from the south-east; the Land Front is to the left and the Keep with the Commissioner's House on the far right.*

PLATE 44: *The Ravelin Tower and South Orillon of the Land Front of the Dockyard are to the left of the convict hulks, Dromedary and Royal Oak.*

PLATE 45: *The Dockyard from the Commissioner's House; some of the guns of the Keep are on the left and those of Bastion 'H' are on the far right.*

PLATE 46: *The Dockyard from the north-west with the Keep on the left and the Land Front to the right.*

PLATE 47: *Fort George was armed with two 11-inch Rifled Muzzle Loaders in the 1870s, which are still in position.*

PLATE 48: *The Western Redoubt was roofed over in the 1890s but its epaulment remained intact.*

PLATE 49: The cavalier barracks and ditch at Fort Victoria were slighted in the 1960s by the insertion of a swimming pool.

PLATE 50: Fort Albert was modified in the 1870s to emplace four 10-inch Rifled Muzzle Loaders.

PLATE 51: *Fort St. Catherine occupies a strategic peninsula fronting the Narrows Channel at the eastern end of St. George's Island.*

PLATE 52: *Fort St. Catherine had several major phases in the nineteenth century culminating with its rearming with RMLs in the 1870s.*

PLATE 53: Alexandra Battery was remodelled in 1900 to take two 6-inch Breech Loading Rifles.

PLATE 54: Four 9-inch RMLs fired through wrought iron gunports during the first phase of Alexandra Battery in the 1870–90s.

PLATE 55: Fort
Cunningham occupies
the summit of Paget
Island and covered the
beginning of the
Narrows Channel.

PLATE 56: Fort
Cunningham was
built in masonry in the
1820s, altered with
iron fronts in the
1870s and modified in
the 1890s for two
6-inch BL guns.

PLATE 57: *In the 1870s, the main facade of Fort Cunningham was a continuous wrought iron front with five gunports and camouflaged.*

PLATE 58: *A second facade of Fort Cunningham was a continuous wrought iron front for two guns.*

PLATE 59: *Prospect Camp and Fort Prospect occupied the central ground of the Prospect Position in Devonshire Parish.*

PLATE 60: *Fort Hamilton was built in the 1870s as a pentagonal work for seven 64-pounder RMLs on Moncrieff disappearing carriages.*

PLATE 61: Whale Bay Battery was rearmed in the late 1890s with three 4.7-inch BL guns for the protection of Hog Fish Cut channel.

PLATE 62: Looking east over Wreck Hill towards the southern end of Somerset Island where Scaur Hill Fort was built in the 1870s.

PLATE 63: Scaur Hill Fort was placed in the centre of a ditch which cut Somerset Island in two from the Great Sound to Ely's Harbour.

PLATE 64: The Royal Naval Dockyard was established in the 1820s at the tip of Sandys Parish (looking west).

PLATE 65: The Dockyard was expanded to include a second breakwater and additional wharves in the 1910s (looking north).

PLATE 66: The Keep was the citadel of the defences of the Royal Naval Dockyard and has housed the Bermuda Maritime Museum since 1975.

PLATE 67: *St. David's Battery was constructed in the 1910s for two 9-inch and two 6-inch Breech Loading rifles for the protection of the Narrows Channel.*

PLATE 68: *Next to St. David's Lighthouse the American Forces built one of their base-end stations for gunnery control, plotting the movement of shipping for gunners.*

PLATE 69:
Government House,
Bermuda, has been
home to three
24-pounder carronades
on cast-iron carriages
from the late nineteenth
century.

PLATE 70: Replica
cast iron garrison
standing carriages
have been produced
for the re-mounting
of historic cannon
at Bermuda.

PLATE 71: A 68-
pounder cannon was
mounted on a replica
cast iron carriage and
slide on the western
rampart of the Keep
of the Dockyard in
the early 1990s.

PLATE 72: The remnants
of a 40-pounder Rifled
Breech Loader were
found at Bailey's Bay
Battery in the 1980s.

PLATE 73: *The 40-pounder RBL from Bailey's Bay Battery was restored for display at the Bermuda Maritime Museum in the early 1990s.*

PLATE 74: *Three Mark I 9-inch RMLs were recovered from the wreck of HMS Irresistible in the 1980s.*

PLATE 75: *Two 10-inch RMLs were discovered on the grounds of the Keep at the Dockyard in the late 1980s.*

PLATE 76: *In 1991, two 12.5-inch, 38-ton, and five 10-inch, 18-ton RMLs were found in the ditch at Fort Cunningham.*

PLATE 77: Several early (1882 and 1889) models of BL guns have been reclaimed for exhibition at the Bermuda Maritime Museum.

PLATE 78: A spare BL barrel from Warwick Camp will be emplaced on an existing mount from 1900 at the Dockyard Keep.

Index

Casemate Barracks   170, 190-1

Castle Harbour   60, 62

Castle Island   57, 62, 86-7, 89, 126, 132

Castle Roads   62-3, 73, 144

Cavendish Fort   78, 86

Cedar, Bermuda   42

Centre Bay Fort   103

Charles Fort   57, 59, 61, 77, 79, 85

Charles Island   61, 88, 132, 134

Church Bay East Fort   87, 110

Church Bay West Fort   111

Churchill, Sir Winston   255, 261

City of Hamilton   38

Clarke, Thomas   85

Clipper, Frederick W.   276

Columbus, Christopher   29, 37

Commissioner's House   151, 183, 192, 195

Common Land Battery   131

Coney Island   132, 138, 143

Coney Island Fort   144

Convicts   186

Cooper's Island   60

Couvre Porte   184, 186

Crow Lane Battery   103

Crow Lane Fort   102

Cunningham, Capt. Thomas   51, 66, 89, 107, 125, 136, 156, 179, 183, 213, 215

Daniel's Island Fort   116

Danvers, Sir John   78

Darrell's Island   260, 262

Davers Fort   78, 86, 122

Deal Castle, Kent   81

Delafield, Maj. Richard   151

De La Ware, Lord   35, 45-6

Deliverance   45

Devonshire Bay Fort   86, 99

Devonshire Redoubt   58-9, 63, 70, 78-9, 86, 131, 133, 140, 144, 178

Dickinson, Capt. Francis   111

Dickinson, James   102

Dill, Col. Thomas Melville   228

Dill, Sir Bayard   255

Dockyard Keep   192

Driver, Thomas   73

Duke of Cornwall's Light Infantry   279

Duke of Richmond   131-2, 136, 140

Duke of Wellington   157, 160, 171, 184, 195

Durnford, Maj. Andrew   54, 56, 70, 90, 108, 123, 129-131, 133, 140, 144, 157, 174, 178

East Elbow Bay Fort   103, 238

Eastside Fort   122

Elizabeth   53, 63

Evans, Capt. Andrew   139, 182

Experiment   115

FA Battalion (214th, Battery A)   274-5

Fair American   115

Fanshawe, Col. Edward   157, 184

Ferry Island Fort   143-4

Ferry Point Battery   120

Fitz, Albert   149, 160, 166, 171

Flying boats   260

Fort Albert   171, 173, 185, 205, 213, 243, 267, 271, 292

Fort Algernon, Virginia   34

Fort Bell   256, 258-259, 262, 271

Fort Bruere   89, 124-125

Fort Clinton   122

Fort Cunningham   51, 124, 136, 149, 173, 182, 186, 199-200, 213, 215, 219, 236, 241, 246, 292, 294

Fort George   54, 122, 141, 149, 157, 159, 173, 185, 201, 213, 243, 290

Fort Hamilton   221-2, 283, 296

Fort Langton   221, 223, 227, 283

Fort Newbold   112

Fort Paget   134

Fort Popple   124, 126, 132, 137, 144

Fort Prospect   221, 224, 283

Fort Raleigh   30

Fort Roanoke   81

Fort Southampton   134

Select Bibliography

Philip L. Barbour, *The Complete Works of Captain John Smith (1580–1631)*, 1986.

W. M. Bisset, *Fort Wynyard (Cape Colony)*, 1981.

H. L. Blackmore, *The Armouries of the Tower of London: the Ordnance*, 1982.

Robert L. Bradley, *The Forts of Maine, 1607–1945*, 1981.

Jeffrey P. Brain, *Fort St. George: Archaeological Investigations of the 1607–1608 Popham Colony on the Kennebec River in Maine*, 1995.

Martin H. Brice, *Stronghold: A History of Military Architecture*, 1984.

Alexander Brown, *The Genesis of the United States*, 1964.

David Buisseret, *The Fortifications of Kingston, Jamaica*, 1971.

Courtland Canby, *A History of Weaponry*, 1962.

Austin C. Carpenter, *The Cannon of Dartmouth Castle, Devon*, 1984.

Austin C. Carpenter, *The Cannon of Pendennis and St. Mawes Castles, Cornwall*, 1984.

Austin C. Carpenter, *Cannon: the Conservation, Reconstruction and Presentation of Historic Artillery*, 1993.

Adrian Caruana, *The History of English Sea Ordnance 1523–1875*, 1994.

Andre Charbonneau, Yvon Desloges and Marc Lafrance, *Quebec: the Fortified City from the 17th to the 19th Century*, 1982.

George Sydenham Clark, *Fortification: its past achievements, recent development and future progress*, 1907.

David A. Clary, *Fortress America*, 1990.

Jonathan G. Coad, *Historic Architecture of the Royal Navy*, 1983.

Comisión de Estudios Históricos de Obras Pœblicas y Urbanismo, *Puertos y Fortificaciones en América y Filipinas*, 1985.

Stetson Conn and Byron Fairchild, *The Framework of Hemisphere Defense*, UNITED STATES ARMY IN WORLD WAR II, 1960.

Stetson Conn, Rose C. Engelman and Byron Fairchild, *Guarding the United States and its Outposts*, UNITED STATES ARMY IN WORLD WAR II, 1964.

Wesley Frank Craven, *An Introduction to the History of Bermuda*, 1990.

Richard Delafield, *The Art of War in Europe in 1854, 1855, and 1856*, 1860.

Sir Bayard Dill, *Reminiscences of an Islander*, 1979.

Christopher Duffy, *Fire and Stone: the Science of Fortress Warfare, 1660–1860*, 1975.

Christopher Duffy, *Siege Warfare: the Fortress in the Early Modern World 1494–1660*, 1985.

Christopher Duffy, *The Fortress in the Age of Vauban and Frederick the Great 1660–1789*, 1985.

Howard Douglas, *A Treatise on Naval Gunnery*, 1855.

Dale E Floyd, *United States Coast Defense 1775–1950: A Bibliography*, 1985.

Terry Gander, *Military Archaeology*, 1979.

H. Garbett, *Naval Gunnery*, 1897.

S. James Gooding, *An Introduction to British Artillery in North America*, 1965.

Edward C. Harris, *Great Guns of Bermuda*, 1987.

Marguerita Z. Herman, *Ramparts: Fortification from the Renaissance to West Point*, 1992.

Ian V. Hogg, *A History of Artillery*, 1974.

Ian V. Hogg, *Coast Defences of England and Wales 1856–1956*, 1974.

Oliver F. G. Hogg, *English Artillery 1326–1716*, 1963.

Quentin Hughes, *Military Architecture*, 1974.

Quentin Hughes and Athanassios Migos, *Strong as the Rock of Gibraltar*, 1995.

Paul Hulton, *America 1585: the Complete Drawings of John White*, 1984.

Lieut.-Colonel I. H. Humfrey, *An Essay on the Modern System of Fortification adopted for the Defence of the Rhine Frontier*, 1838.

Jennifer M. Ingham, *Defence not Defiance, A History of the Bermuda Volunteer Rifle Corps*, 1992.

A. J. B. Jackson, *Defending Halifax: Ordnance 1825–1906*, 1981.

Journals of the Bermuda Maritime Museum.

Journals of the Fortress Study Group.

Journals of the Ordnance Society.

Journals of the Society for Post-Medieval Archaeology.

A. P. Kaestlin, *Museum of Artillery*, 1963.

A. N. Kennard, *Gunfounding and Gunfounders*, 1986.

Jean Kennedy, *Isle of Devils: Bermuda under the Somers Island Company 1609–1685*, 1971.

Wilfred Brenton Kerr, *Bermuda and the American Revolution: 1760–1783*, 1995.

Paul M. Kerrigan, *Castles and Fortifications in Ireland 1485–1945*, 1995.

G. H. King, *Brimstone Hill: The Gibraltar of the West Indies*, 1965.

John Laffin, *Battlefield Archaeology*, 1987.

Brian Lavery, *The Arming and Fitting of English Ships of War 1600–1815*, 1987.

Major-General J. H. Lefroy, *Historye of the Bermudaes or Summer Islands*, 1882.

Major-General J. H. Lefroy, *Memorials of the Discovery and Early Settlement of the Bermudas or Somers Islands 1515–1685*, 1981.

Emanuel Raymond Lewis, *Seacoast Fortifications of the United States: An Introductory History*, 1970.

William Livingston, *A Million Years on Mount Bermuda*, 1947.

Colonel K. W. Maurice-Jones, *The History of Coast Artillery in the British Army*, 1959.

Alfred Mordecai, *Military Commission to Europe in 1855 and 1856*, 1860.

Samuel Eliot Morison, *The European Discovery of America: the Northern Voyages A.D. 500–1600*, 1971.

John Muller, *Elements of Fortifications*, 1746.

Richard Norwood, *Fortification or Architecture Military*, 1639.

Cyril Outerbridge Packwood, *Chained on the Rock: Slavery in Bermuda*, 1975.

Colin Partridge and Trevor Davenport, *The Fortifications of Alderney*, 1993.

A. Temple Patterson, *"Palmerston's Folly": The Portsdown and Spithead Forts*, 1970.

Simon Pepper and Nicholas Adams, *Firearms and Fortifications: Military Architecture and Siege Warfare in 16th Century Siena*, 1986.

Charles W. Porter III, *Fort Raleigh and the First English Settlements in the New World*, 1985.

David Beers Quinn, *The Roanoke Voyages 1584–1590*, 1955.

David Beers Quinn, *England and the Discovery of America 1481–1620*, 1974.

Williard B. Robinson, *American Forts: Architectural Form and Function*, 1977.

H. C. B. Rogers, *A History of Artillery*, 1975.

Denis Rollo, *The Guns and Gunners of Hong Kong*, 1991.

Mark P. Rowe, *An Explanation of The Geology of Bermuda*, 1990.

R. F. Sarty, *Coast Artillery, 1815–1914*, 1988.

Andrew Saunders, *Fortress Britain*, 1989.

Singapore Artillery, *The Singapore Artillery, 100th Anniversary, 1888–1988*, 1988.

Louisa Hutchings Smith, *Bermuda's "Oldest Inhabitants"*, 1969.

Ian Stranack, *The Andrew and the Onions, the Story of the Royal Navy in Bermuda, 1795–1975*, 1978.

Sheila Sutcliffe, *Martello Towers*, 1972.

Sidney Toy, *A History of Fortification*, 1955.

Terry Tucker, *Bermuda, Today and Yesterday 1503–1973*, 1975.

Henry C. Wilkinson, *The Adventurers of Bermuda*, 1938.

Henry C. Wilkinson, *Bermuda in the Old Empire*, 1950.

Henry C. Wilkinson, *Bermuda from Sail to Steam*, 1973.

Cornélis De Witt Willcox, *A French-English Military Technical Dictionary*, 1917.

Roger Willock, *Bulwark of Empire, Bermuda's Fortified Naval Base 1860–1920*, 1988.

D. A. Wood, *An Illustrated Guide to Victorian Forts and Equipment*, 1989.

F. W. Woodward, *Citadel: History of the Royal Citadel, Plymouth*, 1987.

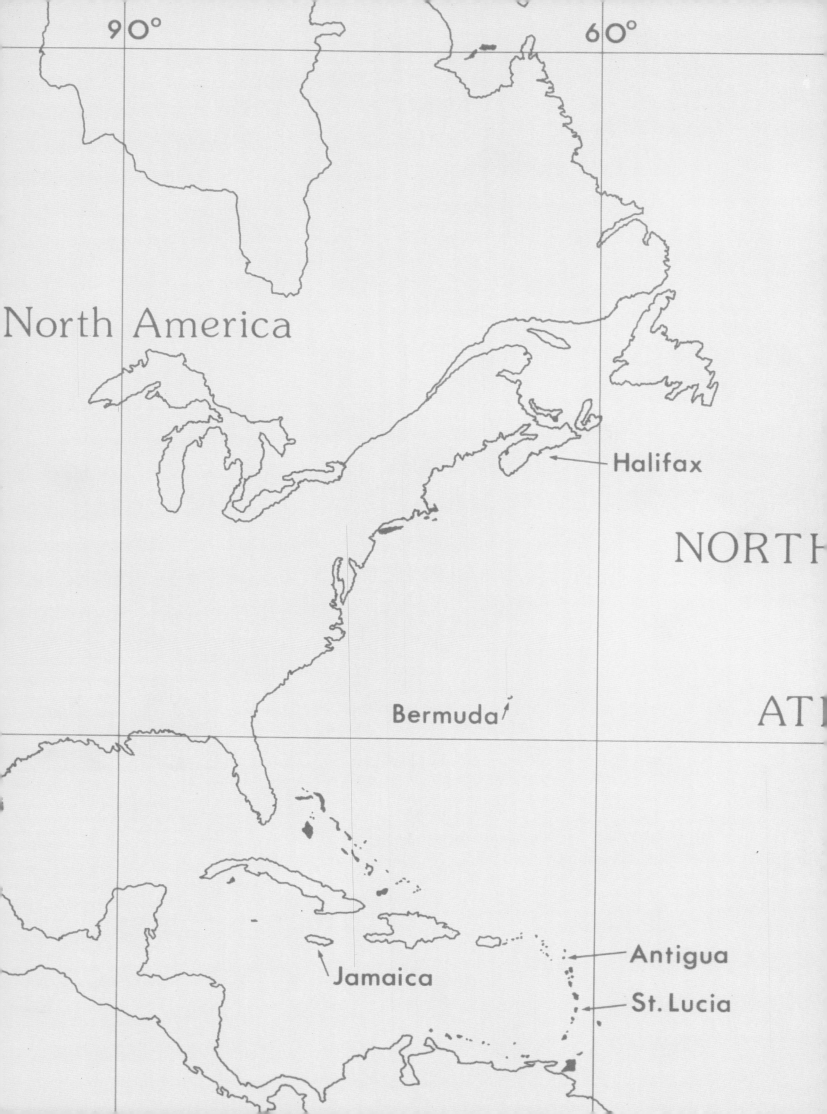

90°

60°

North America

Halifax

NORTH

Bermuda

AT

Jamaica

Antigua

St. Lucia